HARVARD HISTORICAL STUDIES • 140

Published under the auspices
of the Department of History
from the income of the
Paul Revere Frothingham Bequest
Robert Louis Stroock Fund
Henry Warren Torrey Fund

James Livesey

Making Democracy in the French Revolution

HARVARD UNIVERSITY PRESS

Cambridge, Massachusetts, and London, England   2001

For Joanna and Avriel

Scholars increase the peace of the world

Library of Congress Cataloging-in-Publication Data

Livesey, James.
    Making democracy in the French Revolution / James Livesey.
       p. cm. — (Harvard historical studies ; v. 140)
    Includes bibliographical references and index.
    ISBN 0-674-00624-0
    1. France—History—Revolution, 1789–1799.   2. Democracy—France—History—
18th century.   3. Republicanism—France—History—18th century.   4. France—Politics
and government—1789–1799.   I. Title.   II. Series.
JN2468 .L58 2001
944.04—dc21   2001024226

Contents

Acknowledgments

This book comes weighed down by my many debts. My first is to Joanna Stephens, who recognized the book I was writing even when I did not. Any worthwhile insights and ideas in the book were generated in discussions with friends. Thinking and writing about democracy and France would have been less fun without Patrice Higonnet, Stuart Murray, Orla Smyth, Rebecca Spang, Frank Trentmann, and Richard Whatmore. Avriel Butovsky cannot know how much he helped in every way. My siblings continue to teach me lessons in the nature of fraternity. In recent years the Directory has become a vibrant field, and I have learned enormous amounts from Howard Brown, Steve Clay, Judith Miller, and Isser Woloch. I hope this book will contribute to a continuing conversation.

My colleagues at Trinity College, Dublin, especially John Horne and David Dickson, have been encouraging and supportive throughout. I am also grateful to Trinity for generous research leave and for funding from the Dean of Arts and Social Sciences Benefaction Fund and the Provost's Academic Development Fund. The O'Mahony Bursary and an exchange fellowship from the Royal Irish Academy both helped support my research at vital stages. Research funding from the Hagley Library allowed me to consult the Dupont de Nemours papers. Much of the writing was done in the stimulating environment of the Minda de Gunzburg Center for European Studies at Harvard University, where I benefited greatly from the company of Paul Rosenberg and Steve Hanson.

Making Democracy in the French Revolution

Introduction

The French Revolution no longer inspires. In the nineteenth century it was a living memory, a promise of a world of liberty, incarnated in the Parisian revolutionary tradition. That moment ended with the *mur des fédérés*, but the reputation of the Revolution survived the end of the direct tradition and moved from memory to history. Throughout the twentieth century the Revolution was the obsession of historians, political scientists, and political activists who sought to understand the nature and possibilities of modern politics through its study. Debates on the relative virtues of Robespierre and Danton, on the utility of the Terror or the economic effects of the Revolution, had direct relevance to contemporary political debate in Europe. Many of these debates were complicated by their treble nature. The Bolshevik revolution and the subsequent fortunes of the Soviet Union became the third point of reference, along with revolutionary France and the moving horizon of the present, in this increasingly entangled series of issues. For obvious reasons the contemporary political imagination does not include the Soviet Union as a realistic model for a modern political order, and with the collapse of one leg of the triad the whole structure of debate has become unbalanced and much less compelling.

The evolution of ideas about the present has had its usual effect on the past. The fascination of the Revolution had been that it seemed to prefigure and embody both the utopian possibilities of the modern world and its brutalities. It was an urgent problem to understand why the Jacobin of 1792, filled with public spirit, the Declaration of the Rights of Man in his hand, and the love of humanity in his heart, should have become the Terrorist of 1794. Was there a fundamental incoherence in the set of formal rights and liberties through which the revolutionaries had sought to act? Was there an incompatibility between the ideas of liberty and equality inscribed in revolutionary

1

legislation and political structures and the class nature of modern society? These were important questions in a world where the project of Enlightenment was understood to be the extension of precisely those rights and liberties enunciated by the Revolution. In the new consensus, associated with the school around François Furet, the Revolution does not have this paradigmatic nature. The audacious claim advanced by Furet is that the liberals, radicals, socialists, and communists who tussled over the ownership of the French Revolution for two hundred years were simply mistaken. Their assumption that the Revolution revealed the possibilities for modern political communities was a projection of Jacobin rhetoric in which these communities participated, not a meaningful observation about the nature of politics.

Scholars currently argue that the French Revolution did not significantly contribute to the development of modern political values; they also no longer hold that the study of the Revolution offers any particular insight into the dynamics of historical change. The Revolution has ceased to pose vital problems of explanation for the human sciences. The study of the Revolution had been a cornerstone of the claim that the human sciences were incomplete without a strongly historical dimension. In the absence of any strong program of historical explanation, such as those offered by the *Annales* school or Marxism, it has become difficult to defend the intellectual centrality of historical knowledge. As historians have abandoned explanation of historical process in favor of interpretation of conjunctures, they have abandoned the field to more formal strategies of interpretation, such as game theory. The devaluation of the study of the French Revolution has contributed enormously to the general devaluation of historical study. It is precisely those periods in which the very categories of social and political life are in flux that are the privileged locus for the historian's awareness of contingency and agency.[1] If people did not make their own history in the Revolution, if their willed action did not have genuine historical effect, then the close-grained empirical work of the historian is of antiquarian rather than scientific use. If agency was not important in the French Revolution, then where might it be?

This book seeks to reassert the importance of the French Revolution to an understanding of the nature of modern European politics and social life. It argues that the European model of democracy was created in the Revolution, a model with specific commitments that differentiate it from Anglo-American liberal democracy.[2] The most fundamental argument in the book is that these democratic values were created by identifiable actors seeking to answer political, economic, and social problems between 1792 and 1799. The book traces the development of this democratic idea within the structures of the French Republic and the manner in which the democratic aspiration moved beyond formal politics to become embedded in institutions of economic and cultural life. The goal of the analysis is to describe how a profound innovation became a fact, a concrete value toward which groups and individuals would orient their action in the aftermath of the Revolution.

Using an explanatory strategy centered on agency, I seek to rescue the Revolution from the dead hand of nineteenth-century philosophies of history. As the categories of nineteenth-century political theory were designed to control and manage the consequences of the Revolution, it is unsurprising that they distort it. Michel Foucault observed of this period of the birth of the social sciences, "probably because we are still caught inside it, it is largely beyond our comprehension."[3] This book is animated by the idea that since we no longer are so located, we are not so limited. To confront the Revolution anew and make the centrality of its questions visible demands a different kind of argument, a kind of explanation that is not a structuralism. Marxists and revisionists share a positivist epistemology; their claims coincide even though they disagree about evaluation. Furet completely accepted the epistemological demands of the Marxist historians for an explanatory strategy based on the reduction of complex behavior to a mechanism grounded in transhistorical categories. He rejected class as such a category but effectively replaced it with discourse. Any structuralism, by definition, reduces agency to structure, and so refocusing the history of the Revolution on agency demands nonreductive explanations.[4] In recapturing the historical relevance of the Revolution we face the additional challenge of recovering our confidence in the explanatory power of historical scholarship.[5] The Revolution, as ever, refuses to end and continues to make demands of us, epistemological as much as political.

Revolutionary Scholarship, Class, and Democratization

Revisionism sought neither to undermine the importance of the Revolution nor to rob history of its importance to the human sciences. Those effects were the unforeseen result of some brilliant scholarship. The perception that the Revolution dramatized the nature of historical change in a direct way inspired two centuries of work on the phenomenon. The plausibility of the social interpretation of the Revolution was based on the mechanism it developed to explain the popular mobilization of 1789. Any useful interpretation has to be able to explain the near universal involvement of the French people in the Revolution and their enthusiasm for its forms and institutions, from festivals to elections. What other cause had the universality of class interest? The key class in this explanation of the Revolution was the bourgeoisie. With an optimism and a creativity motivated by its increasing power, it was ready to generalize its self-understanding, in terms of formal rights and property ownership, as the universally valid criteria of political legitimacy. The vision from the economic base served to explain the dominant position of the bourgeoisie in the Revolution. It also explained the involvement of peasants trying to protect their communal forms of property, artisans seeking a "just price" for staples, and aristocrats trying to get compensation for suppressed feudal privileges. The political forms of the Revolution expressed both the real alliances of interests that underpinned its rationality and the illusions that concealed the dominance of the bourgeoisie within that revolutionary alliance. Georges Lefebvre drew an analogy between politics and another opium of the people: "the calling of the Estates-General assumed in the eyes of the people an almost mythical character . . . It is in this aspect that the Revolution, at its beginning, can be compared to many religious movements in their early stages, in which poor men see a return to the early paradise."[6] The Terror, the central problem of the Revolution, was explicable as the action of interests after the incense of the original political illusion lost its savor. Historians understood that by investigating the French Revolution through this optic they were rescuing the real course of history, without illusion, and so making available to humanity a true understanding of the relations of humans to one another and to the nature of things.[7]

The search for a bourgeoisie that could anchor this vision of the French Revolution has proven fruitless.[8] There is some predictive power to membership in estate groupings, especially in the early years of the Revolution, but class is not explanatory in the manner that is demanded by the Marxist interpretation.[9] Furet did not hesitate to draw the logical inference from this development. If the Revolution was not the moment that revealed the real history of the coming to power of the bourgeoisie behind the illusion of politics, then attention must be redirected to what had seemed most illusory, the politics of 1789–1794. Moreover, he argued, the Revolution did not dramatize the universal triumph of capitalism in the form of the bourgeoisie; rather, it was the particular French instance of the democratization of the state, a process that was far from universal but that had parallels in Britain and the United States.[10] He reminded his readers that the historical cycle opened by the Revolution ended not in the proletarian revolution but in the Third Republic. The question raised by the Revolution was not that of the possibilities of universal history, but that of explaining the pathologies of French politics and of pointing out their nefarious consequences. The real problem of the Revolution became the Terror: "it was not until the twentieth century, with the injection of bolshevism and the development of a communist extreme left, that a cult of the Terror, associated with that of Robespierre, was established on the grounds of revolutionary necessity, where for half a century it flourished in the shadow of the Soviet example."[11] Furet's argument was that the only deep illusion was that of contemporary Jacobin historians, and a terribly dangerous illusion it was.

Furet subsequently developed the hypothesis, one that has inspired twenty years of scholarly work on the Revolution, that the driving force of the Revolution was not the class interests of the bourgeoisie but the premises of political culture. For Furet the Revolution was occasioned by the collapse of the Old Regime. The appointment of Necker and the calling of the Estates General were acts of capitulation by the monarchy that created a power vacuum and a crisis of legitimacy. This power vacuum touched off a struggle between all groups for power and advantage: "here was the opening through which the ideology of pure democracy surged in, even though it did not gain full control until the spring of 1789."[12] This idea, of a moment in 1788 where the normal constraints of politics collapsed allowing the premises of a political culture to become determinant, is the keystone of Furet's interpretation of the Revolution. He portrays 1788–89 as a fundamental break during which history was "set adrift," whereas up to that moment the political forms and structures of the Old Regime were still meaningful. Thereafter the social content "drops out" of politics, and completely new modes of political communication, aimed at the "people" rather than the educated public, are invented; these modes then condition the unfolding of the Revolution. In later essays and in the *Critical Dictionary of the French Revolution*, edited by Furet and Mona Ozouf, historians inspired by this approach argued that revolutionary democratic ideology had been incubated in the institutions of the late Enlightenment, inspired by Rousseau's distaste for the commercial and moderate spirit of modern life, and mobilized, in the first instance, as antiseigneurialism.[13] In Furet's view the tendency of revolutionary ideology to define itself against perceived enemies rather than in terms of particular rights was one of its most salient features.

Mona Ozouf's idea of a *discours révolutionnaire* gave flesh to the bones of

Furet's hypothesis and provided a methodological viewpoint from which to extend it as a research program. In *Les festivals de la Révolution française* she gave an early, and classic, analysis of one aspect of revolutionary culture's logic of regeneration that sought to institute a reign of virtue. Furet's "ideology of pure democracy" became in subsequent works an entire array of cultural practices whose totalizing premises led inexorably to the Terror. The new consensus is that the Revolution was not a paradigm of modern politics but a parable of its possible pathologies. The school of historical scholarship inspired by Furet and Ozouf argues that the real meaning of the Revolution was the Terror, which was inscribed into the very premises of revolutionary political culture: "this ideology, present in the Revolution of 1789, predated the circumstances and enjoyed an independent existence."[14] Revolutionary culture was "obsessed with the need to create a collective spirit so powerful that it could hope to subjugate the individual spirit completely."[15] It rejected rights in favor of the popular will, sought to create an impossibly transparent community in which the interests of all would coincide in a prescriptive moral order.

The Terror was important for Furet because he argued it revealed the effects of the logic of unmediated democracy.[16] While the interpretation and explanation of the Revolution in this light has moved far beyond the early formulations of Furet in *Penser la Révolution française,* it has not, and cannot, go beyond his conceptualization. Furet's argument, and that of all historians of this ilk, is primarily formal. His approach identifies the regimes of representation, languages of politics, and cultural practices that were current in late-eighteenth-century France and argues that the superimposition of the logic of democratization upon them was the essential moment of the Revolution. The power of the interpretation rests on its explanation of the radical nature of the Revolution. This radicalness is understood in two ways: through the constitutional novelty of the claims of the Third Estate in 1789 and through mass participation, or near mass participation, in political life. The anterior Marxist interpretation of the Revolution had a strong interpretation of the first of these elements and a weak view on the second. The entire thrust of the Marxist theory was to account for the historical novelty of bourgeois society. The strength of the approach lay in the manner in which there was a tight fit, theoretically at least, between the novel language of liberty, equality, and fraternity and the mode of life of the bourgeoisie who promoted it. However, having committed themselves to a mechanism in which politics reflected social novelty, the Marxists were at a loss to under-

stand and to explain why subaltern elements of society that did not represent any kind of social innovation should have become involved in the Revolution. One might find economic reasons for popular mobilization, but
there could not be an economic explanation for the co-optation of novel
languages of social and political identity by the popular classes. The Marxist
interpretation of the Revolution was weakest when attempting to explain its
universality. The strength of the cultural interpretation of the Revolution is
that it seems to be able to fill this gap.

Cultural historians have constructed a different account of the relationship between politics and society in the revolutionary era. Using the concept
of discourse as their master category, cultural historians offer us a new view
on that relationship by revealing the cultural construction of social habits.
Whether we consider Keith Baker's description of the construction of interests around the new formal language of publicity just before the Revolution,
or Pierre Rosanvallon's account of the promotion of a new model of autonomy through the acquisition of the suffrage, this body of work has stressed
that no social formation could fix the meaning of political categories and
that political categories were themselves creating new social formations.[17]
Nor has this work been confined to the broad canvas. Gail Bossenga, for one,
has shown that the political crisis of the late monarchy created a social crisis
in "French home towns," as debt eventually undermined the privileges of
office holding. Sarah Maza has demonstrated at the microcosmic level how
the political crisis put the most intimate categories of value and individual
worth in doubt.[18] From this perspective there is no problem of integration of
social and political categories of interpretation; the subaltern classes of Paris
become just one more element of a society dislocated by the collapse of the
state and ready to reconstruct social life through politics. The project of regeneration, the call to self-creation in a democratized state, was bequeathed
to French society by an evidently failing French monarchy and was absolutely general.[19]

Thus we come to the Revolution of the historians, which can be found
within the pages of one book, *Qu'est-ce que le Tiers Etat?* There is found the
mixture of democratic will, centralizing impetus, and sovereign claim of
which Keith Baker writes, "the logic of *Qu'est-ce que le Tiers Etat?* threatened
the entire standing order of international relations no less radically than
it subverted the institutional order of the French monarchy. Once it was
adopted, the history of humanity could be nothing but the story of national
self-determination inflicted everywhere upon it in the two centuries since

the French Revolution."[20] The formalism of the interpretation of the Revolution threatens to generalize itself until it becomes the only content possible for history. This manner of writing the French Revolution narrates the drama from 1789 to 1794 as universally applicable parable, not as particular history.

The fall of the French Revolution from privileged location to forerunner of totalitarianism has been swift and heavy, but the intellectual foundations of the Furet-Ozouf interpretation of the Revolution are not secure. The hypothesis of a "revolutionary discourse," derived from a structuralist model of culture, is signally inappropriate as a tool for the analysis of symbolic communication in the revolutionary situation. Kaja Silverman neatly defines "discourse as the agency whereby the subject is produced, and the existing cultural order sustained."[21] The notion of a revolutionary discourse is spectacularly unhelpful as a tool to analyze an obvious rupture of cultural continuity. We need a far more dynamic category to comprehend the phenomenon of the political culture of the Revolution. Roger Chartier has criticized the revisionists for their assumptions "first, that it is possible to deduce the practices from the discourses that serve as their foundation and justification; second, that it is possible to translate the latent meanings of social operations into the terms of an explicit ideology."[22] A credible account of cultural change in the Revolution has to be more subtle and more empirically sensitive than the discourse studies we have relied on.

Moreover, the model of politics that infuses revisionist scholarship is radically impoverished. The rupture between the mundanities of social life and the concerns of legitimation, which underlies Furet's thesis, so simplifies the nature of the revolutionary problematic that it makes opaque just what it should illuminate. Charles Taylor has persuasively argued that one of the most important developments of the century was the rise to moral dignity of the features of everyday life, such as the family and the world of production and exchange, a genuine process of the democratization of experience.[23] It is difficult to imagine how the onset of political democracy could have made these concerns recede from public dignity. As the Revolution wore on and the institutions through which the French people conducted their collective life and understood themselves, especially the monarchy, failed, the problem of getting the carriages to run on time and of finding the ground of political legitimacy became entangled with each other. The idea of pure democracy did not "rush in"; it was created in response to political and social crisis. To understand the high theory of the Revolution we must have the mundane realities it referred to in view. The constant references to Rousseau's model of popular sovereignty are no substitute for an examination of the actual evolution of the idea of democracy and its practices.

The distortions generated by our current understanding of the political culture of the Revolution are obvious if we look at work that studies later stages in the history of the development of democracy. Philip Nord's study of the networks that incubated republican ideas under the Second Empire barely mentions the inspiration of the Revolution.[24] He thus avoids the problem of explaining how the difficult memory of the Revolution was overcome but makes the normative horizon that attracted the various civil society entities he analyzes obscure. Sudhir Hazareesingh adverts to the flexibility and dynamism of the republican tradition and its contribution to the evolution of democracy in France. To rescue the republican tradition, though, he has to divorce it almost entirely from the Revolution. He asserts that "even a cursory survey of the condition of France in the early nineteenth century, after a decade of republican rule, would raise the question of how subsequent generations could have derived any inspiration at all from such a legacy."[25] The central claim of the multivolume *French Revolution and the Creation of Modern Political Culture* is that modern democracy evolved in Europe despite, rather than because of, the revolutionary experience. A research program whose original intent was to "rediscover the analysis of the political as such" has ended up as a systematic denial of the possibilities of politics.[26] The inability to find categories of analysis that would allow the ambiguities and possibilities of revolutionary politics to represent themselves has driven the cultural interpretation of the Revolution to a simplistic moralism. Take, for example, Keith Baker's analysis of the foundational understandings implicit in the Constituent Assembly's refusal to grant a veto to the monarch in the Constitution of 1791:

> To the extent that their acceptance of the suspensive veto implied a repudiation of Sieyès's arguments for a theory of representation based on the division of labor, the assembly was setting aside a discourse of the social, grounded on the differential distribution of reason, functions and interests in civil society, in favor of a discourse of the political, grounded on the theory of a unitary general will. In the most general terms, it was opting for the language of the political will, rather than of social reason; of unity, rather

than of difference; of civic virtue, rather than of commerce; of absolute sovereignty, rather than of government limited by the rights of man—which is to say that, in the long run, it was opting for the Terror.[27]

The polarities that characterize this quotation illustrate the limits of this research agenda. How could one begin to understand how the possibility of democracy was created in the Revolution when the political "as such" is systematically aligned with the Terror? We may well suspect that the absolute nature of the choice offered to the French revolutionaries, between representing social interests or unleashing violent utopian fantasies, exists more in the minds of historians than it did in the historical reality of the French Revolution.

Revisionists are driven by their commitment to an uncontextualized understanding of democracy to argue that the Revolution is the context for itself, that there was no context that explains it, that the "social content" as it is phrased, "dropped out" of politics.[28] This strategy of explanation depends on a conflation of the idea of democracy with that of sovereignty. It ignores the local and specific mechanisms of democratization, understood as the capacity of groups and individuals to represent themselves in public life, be it at the state or substate level, in favor of a grand narrative of the transfer of sovereignty from an absolute monarch to an absolute nation.[29] This account does tremendous work in explaining how states developed their doctrine of legitimacy, but none at all in explaining the mobilization or public life of a population. We need to reexamine the commonplace that the transference of sovereignty in the Revolution was the central feature in the creation of modern political culture, and at least supplement it with an understanding of how principles other than sovereignty, such as those of rights, institutionalized themselves in political life.[30] Our current research agenda boils down to a philosophy of history in the worst sense, one in which philosophy, a claim about the necessary relationships between concepts, replaces history, the reading of those concepts in context. We have been so fascinated by the drama of sovereignty and its part in the development of the state that we have ignored the conditions of legitimacy that were created *de novo* by the actions of the French revolutionaries.

There is a body of work that has already begun to rescue a more complex and diverse account of revolutionary political culture. Patrice Higonnet, for one, has established the enormous gap between the High Jacobinism of theory and the Jacobins of provincial France.[31] In his account it is precisely the mundane features of democratization, of providing for the welfare of the population, that most concerned the Jacobins, not the themes of political theology. This argument points up what is a general problem with accounts of the fabric of revolutionary political life: they are enormously thin. One of the most obvious problems with what one might call the Furet thesis is that while it is a theory about the concepts with which French people organized, or more accurately failed to organize, their experience in the late eighteenth century, it has nothing to say about the practice which supplied the vast majority of French men and women with their language for interpreting that experience: religion, especially Catholicism. Suzanne Desan and David Bell have both established that the space between the languages of politics and religion was a fertile area for alternative models of revolutionary democracy.[32] Even this limited amount of work on religion serves to undermine any faith in the credibility of an explanation of the Revolution that relies so heavily on a single logic of development. The elucidation of the religious content and context of revolutionary politics is but one element of the reimposition of context. The Anglo-Scottish group of John Hardman, Muhro Price, and Julian Swann has reopened debate on the high politics of the late eighteenth century and has reminded us that revolutionary politics were not entirely improvised by political neophytes.[33] French public life under the late monarchy had more registers than the search for public opinion. It also taught the languages of factional advantage to the prospective elites of the new France.

The plausibility of the more bleak view of the French road to democracy through the Revolution derives much of its power from an implicit, and in some cases explicit, comparison with the less tortured trajectories taken by the other Atlantic societies: America and Britain. The affection of the French revolutionaries for the ideal of the Rousseauian society of the General Will is contrasted with the more thoroughgoing defense of individual rights built into American constitutionalism and British parliamentarianism. This seemingly clear contrast disappears, however, once it becomes more closely investigated. If anything, the French Revolution was more thoroughly and coherently animated by the language of rights than was the American.[34] As Higonnet has remarked, one of the paradoxes of the Franco-American comparison is that in America the practice of rights could become institutionalized because of sustaining communitarian practices, while the problem of fixing rights became intractable as the social and cultural context for those rights collapsed in France. Some commentators have even gone so far as to dismiss eighteenth-century American individualism as a "myth," an obfuscation of the Protestant communitarianism that animated the revolutionaries.[35] In contrast, the majority, Catholic religious tradition in France could not be articulated to the new ideal of rights, and so the republic could not rely on deep religious assumptions to animate the more formal ideas. The French revolutionaries could not rely on cultural context to give meaning to rights language. Instead, they had to specify the meaning of rights. The revolutionaries were not just failing to be Anglo-American liberals, they were informed by a different vision of a free society, one that the historian must work to represent in its coherence and power. A major problem with our approach to the Revolution is our lack of a sympathetic understanding of the vision of liberty that animated it.

The work of articulating a new understanding of democratic rights, as well as the culture that would sustain them and the state that would institutionalize them, was carried on after the Terror, especially under the Directory. Isser Woloch has long argued that we underestimate the importance of the period, and even his first work pointed to the continuities in democratic politics from the early days of the French Republic.[36] He and Suzanne Desan have both argued that civil society played an increasing role in revolutionary politics after the fall of Robespierre.[37] Pierre Rosanvallon has also pointed out how many long-term changes in state structure began then.[38] A period long seen as a backwater in revolutionary history is attracting attention for its institutional innovations. Michael Walzer has perhaps best expressed the point of the new interest in the period between the Convention and the Consulate. He argues that interest in the political intrigue of 1794 and the rejection of the period after as one of reaction and stagnation are misplaced: "What made the intrigue possible was the defection of revolutionary forces from the Jacobin dictatorship and the widespread sense of alternatives short of a restoration of the *ancien régime*. Thermidor is not a counter-revolution, . . . it is rather the self assertion of the revolutionary class against the politics of the vanguard."[39] Thermidor and the Directory opened up new possibilities rather than closing them down. As I will argue at length in the following chapters, the Directory was the period that was most fertile in efforts to institutionalize the new terms of political life. However, the eventual failure of the Directory has discouraged serious attention to the work and innovations that occurred under it. The parallel of Robespierre to Napoleon, the Jacobin in knee breeches and the Jacobin on horse-back, has made a compelling narrative, so much so that the five-year period between them has simply been occluded. There has been serious work on the era, but it has rarely asserted the importance of the years 1794–1799 to the meaning of the Revolution and its legacy. The Directory struggled with the problems of creating a democracy; not until the Third Republic would any European country have so wide a suffrage and such commitment to modern republican values. My argument is that despite the institutional fail-ure of the Directory, it was during those five years that a democratic culture was created, that the norm of democracy found a content. The deficiencies of that culture made the regime vulnerable, but those deficiencies were not Jacobin intolerance. They were more systematic, more common among democratic regimes generally. The great theme of the Revolution was the ef-fort to find a principle of legitimacy and a form of citizenship; the Directory's democratic republicanism was the most innovative, and in many ways most historically significant, of the models that were generated.

The creation of the ideal of democracy as the acme of political value, re-mains a mystery. The history of this value, like many others, remains largely unwritten. As Niklas Luhmann notes laconically, "the basic semantic terms used to describe either society or time underwent a radical change during the second half of the eighteenth century . . . Historians, however, have not explained the reasons for this transformation, but have merely confirmed that it did occur."[40] Approaches that have revealed the mechanisms promot-ing change in values in the prerevolutionary period, such as David Bien's ac-count of the constituency for rights language in eighteenth-century France, help us to specify exactly what it was the Revolution changed, but they can-not stand in for an account of the Revolution itself.[41] While we await a com-pelling account of the reasons for the great value transformation of the late eighteenth century it would be worthwhile to abjure those that make it more rather than less obscure. In particular we need a far more nuanced un-derstanding of the idea of democracy. The deficiencies of the Furet thesis de-rive from the purely formal model of democracy he inherits from Tocque-ville. A reevaluation of the political culture of the Revolution must be grounded in a more sophisticated and historically sensitive understanding of this idea. To understand the historical contribution of the Revolution, and especially the Directory, we must rescue the idea of democracy from its taken-for-granted nature and restore the historical specificity and political power of the original idea.

Democracy and Revolutions

There is no obvious research strategy through which one writes the history of a norm, especially one as embedded as democracy. To recapture the historical meaning of the term is a task proper to the history of ideas, but the history of ideas alone cannot explain the currency, power, and use of the idea. Some other research agendas do offer a point of departure. The problem of institutionalizing democracy, of democratization, is an old one, and we can gain valuable insights from the efforts of political scientists and historical sociologists to understand this process in comparative perspective. Two main research traditions try to explain the historical evolution of democracy in modern political communities. One, inspired by Barrington Moore's *Social Origins of Dictatorship and Democracy*, has sought to identify the class alliances and oppositions that predispose a democratic resolution to the transformations of modern political life.[42] The second tradition has emphasized the qualities of citizenship, that is the behaviors and attitudes necessary in a population to sustain democratic institutions. Gabriel Almond and Sidney Verba's *Civic Culture* is the core text for this approach.[43] While neither research tradition offers us a sufficient ground for understanding the evolution of democratic norms through the French Revolution, we can glean valuable insights from both, which can help us overcome the deficiencies in the cultural history of the Revolution.

The French Revolution is of more obvious relevance to Moore's work since his theme is the creation of democratic regimes. His argument turns on the dynamics of class fractions and coalitions; where "weak" capitalist and market-oriented groups allied with the "labor-repressive" landed upper classes, centralized and oppressive state authority continued to keep the lower orders at work and politically repressed. When that alliance broke, as in France or Russia, the agrarian bureaucratic regimes were overthrown. This argument has been subject to intense critique. Theda Skocpol, in a friendly revision, has established the importance of state institutions and of the nature of the projects offered to a population by competing elites to understanding the outcomes of political change.[44] Dietrich Rueschmeyer, Evelyne Huber Stephens, and John Stephens have argued that the fundamental axis of class relations that determines political outcomes is not that between a bourgeoisie and a land-owning elite, but that between the urban working class and the labor-dependent landowners.[45] And another critique of Moore cites his absolute rejection of culture or ideas having any role, which left the problem of legitimation hanging.[46] This lacuna limits the utility of Moore's approach for the French Revolution, since our problem is how and why democracy became a norm, not primarily which class alliances were most likely to make the norm operative. Moreover, the class-alliance explanation has had little success in accounting for the outcomes of the Revolution. However, Moore's basic point, that a democratic order needed a social base, remains cogent, and in this regard what the historian of the French Revolution takes away from this body of work is a renewed attention to the peasantry. No political theorist makes a strong argument for the agency of the peasantry in the process of political change, yet all agree that political struggle turned on control of rural surplus and rural populations.[47] Relations in the countryside were the final determinant of political outcomes.[48] Moore argues, for instance, that the peculiar trajectory of England in the early modern period was due to the steady rise of market-oriented agriculture and landlords from the sixteenth century onward.[49] Agency might be elite or urban, but the transition to a new political order depended on capturing the peasantry.

The approach to democratic political orders through their "civic culture" parallels more closely the view of contemporary French historians. Almond and Verba argue that there is a difference between the systemic logic of democratic institutions, based on individualism and the principle of consent, and the working principles of the democratic polity. In their view the latter are more important to the long-term health of a democratic order but also more problematic. While political structures can have clear principles, "the ways in which political elites make decisions, their norms and attitudes, as well as the norms and attitudes of the ordinary citizen, his relation to government and his fellow citizens—are subtler cultural components."[50] In other words, according to Almond and Verba, that the extrapolitical associational life of a society determines its capacity for democratic self-governance. Taking Britain and the United States as their paradigm for democratic orders, they argue "that people can so easily co-operate with each other in political activities" because "despite political differences, they are tied to their fellow citizens by a set of interpersonal values, and these values overarch the political and non-political aspects of the system."[51] This insight has been of the first importance to a series of sociological and historical studies. Robert Putnam's analysis of local government reform in Italy and Thomas Ertman's explanation of the evolution of state forms in early modern Europe both argue that preexisting informal structures of cooperation determined the capacities of communities for formal self-governance.[52] Democratic political structures depend on the social capital of the civil society they govern. As Putnam writes, "social capital here refers to the features of social organization, such as trust, norms, and networks, that can improve the efficiency of society by facilitating coordinated actions."[53]

This notion of the relationship of social capital to democratic self-governance gives us precisely the kind of alternative model of democratization that we need to overcome the deficiencies of the formal model. It has even been endorsed by thinkers who had been committed to more institutional accounts of the possibilities of democracy.[54] This new model is particularly useful because it coheres with the concerns and practices of the revolutionaries themselves. As I will show, the central debate on the possibilities of democracy in the French Revolution centered on social capital rather than institutions, or even constitutional frameworks. The priority given to republican *moeurs* reflected the realities of political practice where citizenship was understood to be an active commitment to political agency. Recent scholarship on voting underlines the way in which institutions were co-opted to reflect these assumptions on the part of the population. Low voting numbers did not mean low turnout or indifference on the part of the electorate. The numbers merely reflected a form of political practice that held the informal networks of debate in civil society to be more important than the formal process of opinion formation through voting. Bernard Gainot's work on the elections of the late Directory shows how the formal franchise was understood to be a proxy to speak for the community and describes how little the forms of speaking and voting resembled the prescribed formalities.[55] In fact, one of the great problems of the French Revolution was defending formal structures against the normative power of networks of social relation.

The literature of civic culture has deficiencies that have to be overcome if its insights are to be useful for the study of the Revolution. The problem is not that it derives political structure from political culture; Almond's defense against this charge is entirely compelling.[56] The real problem is its assumption that political culture is a product of long-run cultural processes. The most successful study inspired by this approach, Putnam's book on Italy, argues that democratic institutions of local governance in Italy are the beneficiaries of dispositions generated by the medieval communes.[57] Almond and Verba have similarly argued that Britain was the paradigm of democracy because of its political continuity: "we have concentrated on British experience because the whole story of the emergence of civic culture is told in British history."[58] But this notion of British history as a continuous evolution of an inspired community of free men and women is a Whig myth. Moreover, the contention that Britain was the touchstone of political democracy for the nineteenth and twentieth centuries is historically inaccurate. The commitment to long-term evolution of consensual cultural forms drives this research tradition to underplay the role of political action in the creation of the sorts of social capital it is interested in. As Putnam remarks, "historical turning points can have extremely long-lived consequences"; unfortunately, the research strategies to which he is committed cannot explain to us how and why this is so.[59] The problem of democracy in the French Revolution is to understand how the idea could come to have so much meaning invested in it, how the social and intellectual capital around the notion of democracy was created rather than how it was exploited.

Understandably historians and political scientists who deal with democratic transformations have already run up against this limitation. They have not identified a mechanism for the creation of democratic culture, but they have noticed some characteristic features of it. Joe Foweraker, in his study of the evolution of democratic norms in southern Spain, has strongly argued for the importance of networks of actors in civil society inspired by ideas of status equality.[60] He argues that labor activists in the Jerez region developed their desire for democratic structures through action in support of social and economic rights. The idea of equality was learned and then generalized as a political principle. Tom Garvin's account of the democratization of the nascent Irish state observes a different phenomenon. He notices that the ingredients for an antidemocratic form of romantic, irredentist nationalism were present in Irish political culture. Nevertheless, the state continued to respect democratic norms even when the victors in the civil war of 1921–1923 had to hand over power to their opponents after elections ten years later.[61] Garvin argues that the most important reason for a democratic outcome to that political crisis was the commitment to democratic values by the elite. In the 1920s "a determination to create an Irish democracy existed not only in the minds of many senior Sinn Féiners but also in the minds of senior civil servants, businessmen, labour leaders and churchmen."[62] Although Foweraker looks at the social base and Garvin the elite structures, both argue that democratic transformation depended on a contingency, a network of actors committed to the idea. Neither deny the necessity for structural antecedents, but both argue that relative economic equality, relative prosperity, and the other features famously identified by Seymour Martin Lipset were necessary but insufficient conditions for democratic outcomes.[63] Democratic culture depends on a political contingency, it is highly caught up with the fortunes of the democrats, and it is they who tap the structural possibility for democratic political transformations.

The historian committed to unearthing a more historically sensitive account of the evolution of the meaning of democracy in the French Revolution carries a series of insights away from this literature but no model. Some of the relevant dynamics, such as the capacity of political life to create social capital, have no explanatory model in the literature in any case. This literature points us to the conjunction of a social base, a network of politically committed activists, and an animating ideal. From that conjunction we would expect to find a series of institutions in which the social capital generated in the Revolution was invested. Our first task then is to identify the roots of the democratic ideal. Democracy, in the research tradition organized around civic culture, is a norm before it is a set of practices; it is an idea with a history of its own. In France that history has a specific trajectory: the democratic idea grew out of the republic.[64] We can reconstruct the creation of social and intellectual capital around the idea of democracy through a study of the adherence to and co-optation of the idea of the republic by actors in French eighteenth-century politics. The studies of democratic transformation also give us a vital clue. We have to pay attention to the political strategies of republicans, their successes and failures at building alliances around particular policies and ideas. Democratic transformation is not a slow and general process. Rather, it is a project highly influenced by the contingencies of politics.

With the history of republicanism and republicans as our point of departure we can then fulfill the demands of the literature for an account of the evolution of the democratic principle. First, we must specify the development of the idea of the republic as it existed in the eighteenth century and its evolution into the democratic ideal. This intellectual history should give us the historically current concept whose circulation and adoption during the Revolution can then be traced. Second, we need to understand how the notion of the democratic republic was expressed through institutional forms that could be sites of political learning for elements of the population and how it created a social basis for itself, especially among the peasantry. Finally, we need to understand how the republicanism that was institutionalized and circulated in this way expressed its universalism. The republic became the political aspiration for populations far removed from the circuits of intellectual debate. To understand how this might be we must identify the institutions that incubated a democratic understanding of the world.

This is a modest and highly empirical research agenda, but its goals are ambitious. The last twenty years of research on the Revolution have been animated by the hypothesis that its lasting importance was the transformation it promoted in the conditions of sovereignty. The vision from the principle of sovereignty certainly reveals one axis of the Revolution. The Rights of Man are rights that must be acknowledged by the sovereign state if it is to exist in a state of legality. The ambiguities of the doctrine of popular sovereignty, and the consequent difficulties of generating a theory of representation, clearly played a role in mobilizing the sans-culottes. However, the principle of sovereignty was invented and substantially elaborated by the absolute monarchy, not the Revolution, and so by viewing the Revolution through the optic of sovereignty we blind ourselves to its originality. The Revolution created and elaborated the idea of legitimacy—the balancing norm to that of legality—and the ideal of democracy, which forms the creative tension with the notion of sovereignty that informs the functioning of modern democratic liberal states. This was the truly original contribution of the Revolution to modern political culture. My analysis of the actions and ideas of republicans will be conducted through a humble methodology, but the aim is to account for one of the most important events in European history, the invention of democracy.

The theme of this book is the construction of the idea of democracy as the dominant political ideal for modern societies. Its structure takes us from the world of political theory through that of practice and on to innovations and critiques. These three stages are represented in three distinct sections. The first two chapters establish the richness and complexity of democratic republican thought in the late 1790s and provide us with the categories through which we can understand the political practice of the era. The second two chapters investigate the relationship between the new understandings of citizenship created by republicans and the practice of the majority of French citizens, the peasantry and other rural dwellers. This section concerns itself with the totality of the life of the citizen, from farming to voting, and traces the interaction of new ideas and new practices in economic and political life. The final section moves us back to the cultural institutions of the late republic: education, religion, and the arts. Here again the theme is the interaction of practice and reflection and the innovations of the republicans in the creation of new institutions. Democratic republicanism, as it evolved in the late 1790s, was not a closed system but a dynamic set of ideas and practices, which were to have profound relevance to the following two centuries.

CHAPTER 1

Modern Republicanism
and Revolution

Though in everything else he was the universal man of the Enlightenment, Denis Diderot did not share the taste of his century for travel. Nevertheless, in early 1773, he found himself on a coach bound for Saint Petersburg, via Amsterdam, on a genuinely philosophical voyage.[1] He had been invited to Russia by Catherine the Great to consult on the creation of a new fundamental law for the empire, creating an irresistible temptation to play out the role of philosopher king or at least philosopher counselor. Reflecting as he traveled on the nature of constitutions, he came to the startling conclusion that his own country lacked one.[2] This was a radical position to take in 1773 and one that few of his countrymen would share before the 1790s.[3] Diderot argued that a French constitution had once existed and reflected exactly what Montesquieu described as a limited monarchy mediated by intermediary institutions, namely, the Parlements. "We could have enregistration or bayonets, no middle ground," he wrote. Either the Parlements had a right to control the promulgation of royal legislation, or the monarchy was unlimited, and therefore despotic.[4] Though the monarchy might have claimed absolute authority, any unbiased observer had to acknowledge the competing principles that had been represented by the Parlements. The tussles over control of the clergy, the expulsion of the Jesuits, and the continuing wrangles over the fiscal system of the country were all features of the competition between monarch and sovereign courts, most markedly after the 1750s. Thus before 1770, France had a constitution, complete with loyal opposition, almost without knowing it.[5] That constitution had been destroyed by the actions of Chancellor René de Maupeou, who by closing the fourteen sovereign courts and creating new institutions to replace them had revealed to the French that they lived not in a limited monarchy but under a potential despotism. The French, according to Diderot, had been returned to some-

20

thing approaching a state of nature. They had before them the task of reconstructing the polity from first principles, of finding the fundamental axioms of government under which basic freedoms, however interpreted, might be made secure, and the actions of the state legitimate.[6] As he explained, the French nation was about to act out the greatest experiment in political innovation in Europe. It remained to be seen under what conditions and with what model in mind.[7]

Like many other commentators on this topic, Diderot was heavily influenced by events across the Atlantic. The *Histoire des institutions des européens dans les deux-Indes,* which he coauthored with the abbé Raynal, evolved and expanded with the fortunes of the American revolutionaries. The efforts by the inhabitants of the newly independent United States of America to create an entirely new polity had obvious implications for political reformers in France. Were not the principles of sociability, rights, and legitimacy everywhere the same, and so might not the American experiment prove a model for Europe? This question was given even greater urgency by the Americans' choice of the most antique and theoretically outdated form for their new polity, the republic.

For us republicanism is a variant of nationalism; it stands for a sovereign people representing itself through the forms of a constitution. It thus seems to derive directly from Italian civic humanism, the theory of the functioning of a free, that is to say independent, popular state.[8] Republicanism has been traced as a coherent doctrine from its Italian roots through its development in the English republic of the 1650s to its definitive expression in the writings of James Harrington, Algernon Sidney, and the other anti-absolutist Whigs in the Restoration.[9] This body of writing has understood republicanism to have offered a historical alternative to liberalism for the creation of modern polities. J. G. A. Pocock has argued that republicanism enshrined a call to civic commitment from the citizen, and that this preference for public duty over private interest was based on the claim that individual excellence was attained through the practice of virtue rather than the protection of rights.[10] In creating a republic, the Americans, from this point of view, were choosing the historical and philosophical alternative to the legal or moderate monarchies. These monarchies were committed in their most sophisticated form to embodying the principles of natural law and of rights. To choose the republic was to choose the theoretical and historical alternative to liberalism.

There is considerable ground for skepticism about this account of the political options open to societies in the eighteenth century, since by then this classical republicanism was neither a robust nor a compelling theory of politics.[11] Civic humanism had failed so spectacularly in the seventeenth century, even in the Netherlands and England, that it was not a credible theory of civil order.[12] Of the European republican states the Netherlands was the most powerful and the most admired in the eighteenth century, but there was no development of a specifically republican theory of liberty in that state.[13] Even in England, which developed a strong and self-conscious republican movement during the Civil War, after the settlement of 1689 republicanism settled down into the diffuse sentiment in which a safe opposition might be articulated.[14] The common assumption of early-eighteenth-century political writers was that republicanism fomented factionalism and civil discord. Poland was the best known example of, as Dupont de Nemours put it after his return from that country, "a republic without a public interest, where everything is abandoned to pillage."[15] Civic humanist rhetoric survived in odd places, such as the Bolingbroke circle and among American colonists or Presbyterian conservatives in Scotland battling against moderate reformers. Outside these fringes the European political imagination in 1750 was dominated by monarchies and animated by the concerns of natural jurisprudence, not issues of representation and citizenship.[16] Republicanism survived as a language of moral excellence and of moral rebuke, much in the manner that the jeremiad functioned in colonial America.[17] The ideal of the ancient citizen was used by moralists as a form of appeal to their countrymen to pursue virtuous ends, not as a viable option for the creation of political institutions.

The figure of Phocion, the Athenian who refused to collaborate with invading Macedonians, was a favorite vehicle for this kind of moral discourse. Phocion was entirely ineffective, but that did not matter; he was still a model of virtue. Gabriel Bonnot de Mably even made his ineffectiveness a kind of virtue in itself. He has Phocion advise his student Nicodes, "the Republic may perish, but the consolation of a good citizen, as he is buried under the ruins, is to have done everything in the effort to save it."[18] Mably's real point was the superiority of principled behavior over pragmatic compromise. Mably recommended the republic not for the traditional reason that a flourishing state would provide the theater for the glorious self-assertion of the republican hero, but because "the happiness of every individual is the peace of his soul, and that peace comes from the knowledge that he has followed the rules of justice."[19] Phocion's virtues were paradoxically private; François de Neufchâteau used him as an exemplar of morality precisely because he was a good man rather than a good citizen: "I have not taken him in the law courts or at the head of the armies of Greece. I have taken from his private life one incident best suited to display the moral beauty of his character."[20] This strain of classic republicanism diffused political duty into an undifferentiated call to act well.

Communities and individuals still genuinely understanding themselves through classic civic humanist rhetoric, or variants of it, were marginal and vulnerable. The Genevan republic had been torn apart as the privileged citizens of the city sought to resist the claims to political participation by the *natifs*.[21] It effectively lost any political independence it had enjoyed after the French crushed the revolution of 1782.[22] Communities that had been burdened with a civic humanist self-understanding were forced to abandon it to adapt to modern conditions. The most dramatic example was the Scottish vote to end independence and to unite with England, which required abandoning the entire Scottish civic tradition founded on enmity toward England.[23] Richard Sher has argued that the Scottish Enlightenment was fundamentally an effort by reform-minded ministers to extend the logic of the union and rescue the Church of Scotland from debilitating antiquarianism and the association of "country" ideology with Jacobitism.[24] It is an irony of history that John Witherspoon, whose attachment to the older politics of Scottish Presbyterianism was such that he emigrated to found a new academy in the wilds of North America, should have found himself delivering "The Dominion of Providence" to possibly the last sizable group of Anglophones who still thought in terms of virtue, liberty, and the rights of freeborn Englishmen.[25] Even then most Americans were only too aware of the limitations of classical republicanism; as Alexander Hamilton pointed out to his countrymen in 1782, "we may preach till we are tired of the theme, the necessity of disinterestedness in republics, without making a single proselyte. The virtuous declaimer will neither persuade himself nor any other person to be content with a double mess of porridge, instead of a reasonable stipend for his services."[26] Up to the publication of *Common Sense*, the term "republican" was almost always, in even American discourse, a term of opprobrium.[27] Everywhere in the North Atlantic world even the rhetoric of the ancient constitution was by now legal or social rather than political.[28] Modern people were understood to be the creatures of their interests and so incapable of acting like antique republicans, committed to the public good and exercising virtue in its pursuit.

The creation of a new, extensive republic in the New World reopened what had seemed to be a closed issue in the old. Understanding this new phenomenon posed many difficult problems precisely because classic republicanism had been discredited. Was the new republic to be understood as a passing phenomenon, to be abandoned as the necessities of the age made themselves felt, or a revelation of a new possibility? Moreover, if the republic did prosper, how was it to be understood, as a variety of modern or antique liberty, through Venice or Sparta? The most enthusiastic interpreter of the new United States through the optic of classical republicanism was also the enthusiast for Phocion, the abbé Mably. Mably's republicanism was specific and idiosyncratic; as Kent Wright has shown, he rejected the military imperialism of the Roman example as well as the commercial decadence of Athens.[29] His imagined United States was therefore a resurrection of the free cities of Greece, and its ideal element was the newly founded state of Georgia, comprising 14,000 citizens entirely devoted to yeoman agriculture, because this most closely approximated to Sparta.[30] He recognized that Georgia was a special case, and the bulk of his text sought to show how the principles of the Greek city-states in the republican period were guides for the creation of modern states.

Mably's genuine commitment to "antique prudence" drove him to some eccentric recommendations for the young republic. For instance, he praised the institution of slavery. The constitutions of the new states, he noted, respected the rights of the people "and have even taken under their protection those persons who are not members of the Republic because they do not pay taxes and sell the labor of their hands to masters. These men, under the name of slaves, which was disgraceful among the ancients, and who in contemporary Europe enjoy the name of free men, while languishing in a real slavery, have been yoked to the interests of the republic by you by granting them a means of escaping their status by acquiring the dignity of citizenship through work and acquiring property."[31] He understood the term *peuple* to comprise the "citizens" in the classical meaning of the term, the property-owning heads of households. From this perspective workers and servants were equivalent to the slaves of antiquity. Using this model of citizenship he criticized the constitution of Pennsylvania because it was too democratic. By extending the suffrage widely and uniting all classes in one representative chamber, Pennsylvanians would recreate the dynamic of social competition between patricians and plebeians that had destroyed the Roman republic.[32] He thought the bicameral constitution of Massachusetts more closely approximated the subordination of Helots to Lacedemonians that had guaranteed the social peace of Sparta and so recommended it to the other states. In conclusion he argued that across the United States sumptuary laws and a civil religion ought to be instituted to protect the virtue of the citizenry from corruption. Under these conditions the several states of the union, united in an amphictyonic council, the Congress, would present to Europe the same example of a flourishing free state as the Swiss.[33] Mably saw the success of the United States in its war with Britain as a confirmation that France should have embraced antique republicanism and abandoned commercial politics to be successful in its own wars with the modern Carthage.

Every commentator in the European debate rejected Mably's interpretation of the meaning of the American Revolution.[34] The hypothesis that the American Revolution was the self-assertive gesture of frugal, anticommercial farmers whose strength could be maintained only in relation to their poverty seemed absurd to Turgot. From the first months of the revolution he argued that it was commercial by definition.[35] The revolution had been caused by the inability of the British monarchy to acknowledge and represent the developing commercial interests of the Americans within their constitution. In his later correspondence with Richard Price, he expressed his greatest criticism of the new constitutions that the Americans had given themselves: they did not recognize the origins of their own freedom and enshrine the principle of free trade.[36] Etienne Clavière, the Genevan financier and later revolutionary, even argued that the British were likely to profit in the long term from their political defeat. They would no longer be distracted by imperial concerns from their true commercial interests in America. France, by contrast, might have only the glory of her victory over her old enemy as her reward.[37] The new American republic was not evidence for a revival of antique prudence but a product of the new possibilities of a commercialized world.

Other writers understood the American citizen, who Mably idealized as a Spartan returned to modern life, differently. The idea of citizenship as a privilege, and of different legal statuses for different grades of republican, was identified by Brissot as an entirely false representation of the American notion of citizenship.[38] Filippo Mazzei devoted a preamble to his four-volume discussion of the errors of French writers on the American Revolution to pointing out that when he used the terms *peuple, citoyens,* or *habitants* of the United States, he took them for synonyms.[39] The central theme of his refutation of Mably's ideas on the new republic, which took up the entire second volume of his book, was the difference between the American and the Greek republics.[40] The most important feature of American citizenship was equality of rights, not participation in virtue. Thus the greatest threat to the new American republic, it was argued, was the possibility that social processes might undermine that equality. Sébastien-Roch-Nicolas Chamfort, writing at the behest of Mirabeau, condemned the foundation of the order of the Cincinnati, an association of veteran officers of the Continental Army. The order threatened to create a dynamic of social difference; "being created outside the Constitution and the law, the law has no power to restrain it, and it will have a huge influence on the Constitution of which it is not part; until finally by means of both open and covert attack, it will become constitutive of the constitution, or after undermining it, finally destroy it."[41]

The defense of political participation by Condorcet, Turgot, and Price was pragmatic and instrumental. They believed the republic, which allowed the greatest possible number of citizens to participate in public life, was not a good in itself, but rather was the most rational and efficient system through which the inherent rationality of law could express itself. These defenders of the republic as a principle emphasized the limited character of modern legislation and political life. Whereas classical republicanism understood participation in the creation of law as the most important feature of the life of the citizen, French partisans of the American republic saw lawmaking as a residual function of civic life. As Condorcet put it, laws were necessary only when citizens could not spontaneously order their interactions through their reason and will and had instead to resort to an explicit common rule.[42] Even when laws were necessary, he argued, in most cases the necessary measure could be found rationally, from evidence, without reference to competing wills and ideals.[43]

Condorcet followed Turgot in arguing that the best constitution would be one in which property, rather than individuals, would be represented.[44] Even Richard Price, a radical in English politics, stressed that his enthusiastic support for the American revolutionaries should not be understood as an endorsement of republics. Republics, and especially democracy, were only relevant in special circumstances: "I must admit, that by what is here said I do not mean to express a general preference for a republican constitution of government. There is a degree of political degeneracy which unfits for such a constitution. Britain, in particular, consists too much of the high and the low (of scum and dregs) to admit of it. Nor will it suit America, should it ever become equally corrupt."[45] In the French debate on the United States the consensus was that the democratic elements of the new country were accidental, and that the real lesson to be learned there was a historically relevant possibility of enjoying equal rights. The hope was that a regime of equal rights would create a general similarity of condition that would, in turn, render political conflict irrelevant and unnecessary. If economic developments in Europe could foster a commercial equality there, analogous to that enjoyed by Americans due to the abundance of land, then eventually Europeans would be able to enjoy the same rights as Americans. Price even foresaw an eventual "withering away of the state" as universal rights eliminated war and thus the need for taxation.[46] Citizens of the new republic would enjoy the liberty of having their rights respected, not of representing themselves in the definition of those rights.

American participants in the European debate on the meaning of their new republic were nowhere near as ready to reject the relevance of the principle of political representation to the possibility of liberty. John Adams, who was hardly a committed democrat by American standards, commented, "Democracy, simple democracy, never had a patron among men of letters. Democratical mixtures in government have lost almost all the advocates they ever had out of England and America."[47] William Vans Murray argued that the Europeans were misled by their monarchical experience and classical learning and did not understand that the American republic was democratic by nature and essence.[48] Mazzei agreed in principle, arguing that the suffrage restrictions that Mably celebrated were nothing less than failures of nerve on the parts of the state conventions that had written their constitutions. Where Mably saw a principled decision to restrict the quality of "citizen" to a particular section of the population, Mazzei saw nothing more than the retention of old habits and injustices.[49]

Authors such as Mazzei and Adams could not, however, completely rid themselves of a fundamental ambiguity in the meaning of the republic. They vacillated between seeing it as a series of fundamentally democratic institutions and seeing it as any state managed for the public good.[50] In his reply to Turgot, Adams claimed that "a simple monarchy, if it could be in reality what it pretends to be—a government of laws, might be justly denominated a republic. A limited monarchy, therefore, especially when limited by two independent branches, an aristocratical and a democratical power in the constitution, may with strict propriety be called by that name."[51] This view was indistinguishable from Turgot's own position that he was in the last analysis indifferent to the form of government as long as it guaranteed the rights of the citizenry. But later in the reply Adams took up a different line, arguing that "the name republic is given to things in their nature as different and contradictory as light and darkness, truth and falsehood, virtue and vice, happiness and misery. There are free republics, and republics as tyrannical as an oriental despotism. A free republic is the best of governments, and the greatest blessing which mortals can aspire to . . . An empire of laws is a characteristic of free republics only, and should never be applied to republics in general."[52]

Where European commentators, locked in the conflict between rights and virtue, could understand the republic only through the classical ideal, Americans had developed a new notion of a republic, one compatible with commercial manners, even if they found difficulty in defining this new object. They argued that a genuinely new possibility had been revealed by the American Revolution—that of a commercial, democratic republic, one in which rigorous adherence to legality, economic expansion, and the widest possible participation in public life reinforced one another. The incoherence in Adams's text reflected the novelty of the idea of a commercial republic and the confusions possible between it and the more familiar notion of the regime of laws. As Murray put it, "It hath been urged, that Democratic forms required a tone of manners unattainable and unpreservable in a society where commerce, luxury and the arts, have disposed the public mind to the gratifications of refinement. This proposition is difficultly opposed. To dislodge it, it will be necessary to take a new ground and a new scene of detail, for the antiquity of the idea hath given it a prescription superior to every thing but arguments drawn from a novel series of political events."[53] The French Revolution would provide just such "a new ground and a new scene of detail" and eventually shatter the organizing assumptions that had limited the possibilities of the republic.

As the revolutionary crisis developed, French republicans would be driven to confront the specificity of the modern republic. The consensus that the modern republic respected rights in much the manner of a moderate monarchy would collapse, and a sharper understanding of the nature of citizenship in modern conditions would differentiate the two political forms. Republicans, who proposed a novel political structure, exploited novel political understandings to do so. In America the tradition of republicanism was transformed; in France it would be abandoned and a new one invented. French republicans were to become the first exponents of praxis as they sought to create a new regime.

The New Republicanism of the Eighteenth Century

If we follow the strict meaning of republicanism, a commitment to the widest democratic participation in the institutions of the republic as a condition for liberty, then one of the common problems of historical analysis does not afflict the historian of French republicanism before the French Revolution. There is no great problem of scale. The republic, understood in this way, was not generally considered an appropriate answer to the institutional problems of the French state and society. Of course, republican themes in the more general sense were more ubiquitous than actual republicans. The thinker who most clearly articulated the ideals of the Revolution in its early phase, the abbé Sieyès, was utterly indebted to the ideas of a legal state developed by figures like Condorcet and Turgot.[54] Nevertheless, the point of Sieyes's arguments in favor of representative government was the inappropriateness of classical republican forms to modern social and economic conditions and the irrelevance of actual political participation for the majority of the population. For Sieyes the equality of all citizens before the law did not demand their equality in its production. Those who exerted "moral industry" were equipped, under the modern principle of the division of labor, to create the most reasonable laws.[55] This was a far cry from a consistent republicanism. Yet it took only three years for the unthinkable institutional solution to occur, for France to become a republic. The republic did not have deep cultural roots in France; it had not been the object through which a community developed its political ideals.[56] It was, therefore, a genuinely revolutionary ideal, an institutional form the content and meaning of which was radically open. It was also a difficult political regime to manage.

Certainly France had not been entirely devoid of consistent republicans. Most prominent were the Genevan revolutionaries of 1782, such as François d'Ivernois, Etienne Dumont, and, most important, Etienne Clavière.[57] These men were republicans in the most obvious sense; they had led the people in a struggle to overturn the oligarchy of Geneva. The revolution had ended in invasion from France. Paradoxically France was to end up the home of many of the men consequently exiled, and in Clavière would acquire the most advanced theorist of republican economics in Europe.

Mirabeau was the first person to capitalize on the intellectual resource represented by these figures and turned them into his ghost writers. The Genevans were the most concentrated knot of republicans in late-eighteenth-century France, but not all republicans were Francophone rather than French. The tradition of Jansenist republicanism, which shared the debt of Genevan republicanism to the monarchomach writers of the late sixteenth century, was alive though flickering.[58] David Bell has analyzed the way in which the understanding of liberty enshrined in this tradition transformed itself into a rhetoric of the defense of the public interest in the law courts after 1771.[59] The potential radicalism of Jansenism was to be ignited by its conjunction with the French co-optation of rights language.

The peculiar reception of rights theory in France made it a latent reservoir of republicanism. The major interpreter of natural rights theory in France was Jean Barbeyrac.[60] He developed his rights doctrine from Locke's *Two Treatises of Government,* which encompassed the most radical, and neorepublican, doctrine of rights in the seventeenth century.[61] Locke's derivation of rights from the nature of men as property-owning creatures was a standard argumentative strategy of natural jurisprudence and was perfectly compatible with the monopolization of political power by a landed gentry class.[62] However, embedded within Locke's property doctrine was a labor theory of right: "whatsoever then he removes out of the state that nature hath provided, and left it in, he hath mixed his labour with, and joyned to it something that is his own, and thereby makes it his property."[63] A reading of Locke's rights theory in France, without the Glorious Revolution to frame the meaning of the text, could unearth its roots in the radical Leveler theories of the English Revolution.[64] Barbeyrac's transmission made such a reading even more logical by amalgamating Locke's rights doctrine with Hobbes's doctrine of sovereignty.[65] The notion of a democratic sovereign, which would have made no sense in the Anglophone tradition, was perfectly sensible in the French understanding of the relationship between rights and sovereignty. First exploited by Simon Linguet, though his particular understanding that the democratic principle was monopolized by the sovereign was not shared, the notion inspired some judicial reformers in the 1780s.[66] Democratic sovereignty would require a transformation in the nature of the sovereign to become an effective ideal.

The French variant of new republicanism derived from of a conjunction of Genevan political practice, French political theory, and Anglo-American experience. The conjunction occurred in the persons of Brissot and Clavière.[67]

They began their partnership after the failure of the Genevan revolution. Their first collaboration, *Le Philadelphien à Genève,* attacked the aristocratic despotism they believed had been imposed on Geneva by France, and defended the republican principles equally represented for them by the American and Genevan revolutionaries.[68] Of the two, Clavière's republicanism is the easier to understand and was closest to classic themes. The experience of defeat turned a patriot and lukewarm republican into a thoroughgoing republican, a critic of the French monarchy and the values it enshrined, and made a democrat of a constitutionalist. The republic was Clavière's faith; people, like the French, unfortunate enough to be born under monarchies understood force not law, and so were "more miserable, more ignorant and more ill behaved" than any people in the world.[69] Nor did he ever really abandon his polarity of good republicans and decadent monarchists. Dupont de Nemours had to rehearse French contributions to commercial civilization for Clavière in 1787 in refutation of his condemnation of French values.[70] The French were not the only people Clavière found insufficiently patriotic. In 1788 he berated Mirabeau for not chastising the Dutch, who had failed to die on their borders rather than be invaded by the Prussians.[71] Clavière's development of republicanism was novel, but its motivation was unquestionably old-fashioned.

Brissot's republican commitment was more complicated and more revealing. Robert Darnton has dismissed Brissot's efforts in the early 1780s as hackwork, but Brissot was more than a pen for hire for Clavière. He was a genuine ideological ally.[72] Brissot's *Traité des lois criminelles* had attracted the praise of the Genevan group even before their revolution, and d'Ivernois had offered to print any future work he might produce.[73] The *Traité,* along with its author, was attractive to the Genevans because it exploited the radical reading of Lockian rights theory that was a latent possibility in the French tradition and so could provide a justification for their revolution on a more comprehensive basis than the Genevan constitutional tradition. Having trained as a lawyer, Brissot continued to be identified with a universalistic rights doctrine. Dupaty of Bordeaux, the jurist and friend of Voltaire's, told Brissot that his work on law was a pump to bail out any sort of vessel, while Dupaty's own was good only for those in good order.[74] This radicalism could reach beyond Locke at times; Brissot and Mirabeau corresponded on the roots of American liberty, not in Locke, but in the Levelers.[75] From universal rights to political equality was not a large step, but one needed a spur to make it.

The existence of slavery provided such a spur. Slavery presented the problem of rights in the most marked way, and the codification of slave-owning practices in the Code Noir created a particular tension within French jurisprudence.[76] The very effort within that code to grant particular protections to slaves merely underlined the peculiarity of the institution. Brissot's *Examen critique des voyages dans l'Amérique septentrionale de M. le marquis de Châtelleux*, published in July 1786, argued that commercial manners entailed opposition to slavery and to the oppression of nonwhite races. He went on to develop the view that slavery was not an accident but the result of the failure to defend political rights along with property rights.[77] The issue of principle was sharpened by France's dependence on slavery for its commercial expansion in the 1770s and 1780s. The enormously profitable plantations of Saint Domingue had developed owing to a massive importation of slaves in that period.[78] As Leonore Loft has shown, the extension and development of Atlantic slavery persuaded Brissot of the essential decadence of his civilization.[79] As a result, Brissot became a founding member, along with Clavière, of the Société des Amis des Noirs in May 1788.[80] The loose equation of a regime of rights with any sort of modern commercial development was not a temptation to anyone who recognized the importance of slavery to French prosperity. The absurd coexistence of slavery and modern economic forms drove Brissot to argue in favor of fundamental and universal political rights. Brissot therefore imagined the republic as the antithesis of slavery.

Paradoxically, Brissot's conceptualization of slavery as a particular instance of a general problem of the denial of political rights probably retarded the movement to free the slaves by distracting attention from the central grievance.[81] France did not abolish slavery until 1794, largely as a response by the Convention to the efforts of the slaves themselves.[82] But the rejection of slavery gave content and meaning to Brissot's embrace of the idea of political rights. In Brissot's comments on the provincial assemblies projected by Dupont de Nemours's mentor Turgot, he revealed the depth of his commitment to political rights. Brissot admitted Turgot's praiseworthy goal of enshrining the rights of the people but criticized him for not acknowledging the lesson of British and American history, that there can be no safe enjoyment of rights where an absolute legislator is left in place.[83] Turgot's mistake was to underestimate the importance of political representation. Without the right to contest the will of the sovereign his new assemblies were worse than even the old estates, "because in the power given to them in the Estates the people were free, the people had a defense against absolute power. Now in the plan of M. Turgot . . . there is neither defense nor liberty. The people are therefore slaves, though in a different way."[84] Clavière and Brissot were united by their commitment to the idea that liberty was inherently political and had to be exercised to be secure, but they also acknowledged the centrality of rights to any modern conception of liberty. Finally, they argued for a progressive idea of the republic. The republic guaranteed not only that citizens had protected rights and were free to pursue their interests, but also that they were free to explore the norms they thought best, their particular conception of the good life. As Brissot expressed the idea: "The dignity of man consists in his liberty, in his legal equality, in his independence, in his capacity to recognize only those laws to which he has consented, in his control over those to whom he delegates his authority. The dignity of man also consists in the perfect development of his moral and intellectual faculties, in the efforts he makes to discover truth and have it reign. In a word it consists in great ideas, in a strong and constant will."[85] Such a political ideal was a far cry from the defense of virtue and the small republican state.

Clearly, the notion of the republic that exercised Clavière and Brissot had nothing to do with the antiquarianism of "real Whiggery." Nevertheless, the question remains, what did they understand as republicanism? These "new republicans" came close to the American understanding of the idea of the republic, but in the absence of the practical context it is difficult to discern the exact meaning of their endorsement of citizenship. If it was not the largely discredited idea of civic humanism, then what kind of civic commitment did republicans intend? The *vivere politico* had had few triumphs over the art of the state after the early fifteenth century, and the very language of rights had been developed from the political tradition opposed to the civic commitment.[86] Was their writing inspired by nothing more serious than a nostalgia for an impossible regime, Genevan if not Spartan? Their engagement with commerce and political economy was clear, but did it allow them to just collapse republicanism into a diffuse liberalism? To understand how these men could stake out such confident positions in the politics of the 1780s we have to understand the changes in political science that made a new republicanism compelling, as well as the movements in political life that made it attractive. Why did they think they were right?

The Intellectual Origins of the New Republicanism

As I have noted, the American example opened the way for a reconsideration of the terms of political and social life, but the political experience of the

Americans could not be reproduced. Rather different resources had to be mobilized to make their political creativity negotiable in the French context. Judith Shklar has termed the set of ideas that achieved this connection the "new republicanism," which radically differed from "country" ideology.[87] The new republicanism held that liberty could be assured only by the full participation of the populace in the institutions of a democratic society. Republicanism transformed itself from a claim for the priority of political equality to one for the priority of social equality. Rights theorists might have identified the conditions under which the state respected and protected the autonomy of the citizens; republican theorists sought to identify the social and economic institutions that would provide the texture of a free society, or in more contemporary terms, a civil society.[88] The new republicanism argued that the exercise of virtue might not be necessary to the maintenance of political liberty but was central to the development of a free society.

The most obvious change in the political and social world for eighteenth-century people was the emergence of commercial societies, societies in which increasing numbers of people were engaged in market relations.[89] The new republicanism directly addressed this reality. It redirected the question of what structures would generate civic commitment among the population away from the state and toward society, itself a new object for political theory in the period. The new republicanism was a theory about how society works and how it should be represented, not a theory about the structures of a virtuous republic. It sought to discover the means by which the population could acquire self-command, which it understood to be good mores or, to use the French phrase that retains the force of the original idea, *bonnes moeurs. Moeurs,* or mores, is a term that has dropped out of the English-language lexicon of political thought. It refers to the habits and customs of a people, as well as their beliefs about those habits and customs. It is, in effect, the idea of social capital, which contemporary political theorists argue is central to the possibility of a civic order.[90] Eighteenth-century republicanism was a theory of the best kind of political culture for a modern commercial nation. It was a body of thought that sought to extend and develop the new thinking on the nature of modern commercial civilization, rather than resist commercialization.

Montesquieu's *Spirit of the Laws (De l'esprit de la loi)* was the breviary of the theorists of commercial civilization. He was not the first figure to capitalize on the realization that a language of politics that contrasted monarchies, aristocracies, and republics—the available ways of understanding political life—simply did not represent the features of the political world he saw around him. David Hume, in his essays of 1742, had come to the same idea. Hume perceived that a world of paper money, extensive long-distance trade, mingled genders, rising consumption, and large unitary states could not respond to the oppositions of virtue to luxury, honor to liberty, or subordination to equality. Practice had far outstripped theory. "I must observe," noted Hume in an optimistic mood, "that all kinds of government, free and absolute, seem to have undergone, in modern times, a great change for the better."[91] The reason was the spread of luxury, for "the ages of refinement are both the happiest and the most virtuous."[92] However, for all his insight, Hume did not, or could not, escape the fascination of the ancient virtues. While in practice he celebrated commercial civilization, his moral categories remained fixed. Even in his later *Enquiry concerning the Principles of Morals* he was still deferring to "the ancients, the heroes in philosophy, as well as those in war and patriotism, [who] have a grandeur and force of sentiment, which astonishes our narrow souls, and is rashly rejected as extravagant and supernatural."[93] Hume thought the ancient virtues were inapplicable to modern social life, but he could not identify a set of virtues proper to modern people. Where Montesquieu outstripped Hume was in identifying a new way of understanding the value of modern social life without becoming trapped in an impossible nostalgia for the old, uncorrupted, world.

Montesquieu turned the assumptions of political theory on their head. The Aristotelian assumption that the character of a people is determined by the form of the political constitution under which they live had never been seriously challenged. *The Spirit of the Laws,* in a brilliant *reductio,* showed that social structure created the conditions for political constitution, that society was prior. This was a revolutionary idea, for it raised the prospect that the principles of political legitimacy might be as various as the forms of social life that humans could create.[94] Montesquieu was not content to operate a revolution in the cognitive basis of political science. He also proposed a normative revision of the basis of the understanding of liberty. Where the ancients understood liberty to be the power to participate directly in the making and the application of the law, the moderns understood it as the representation of their interests allied to the freedom to develop the private sphere of intimacy. Liberty was the duty "to do what one should want to do . . . in no way being constrained to do what one should not want to do."[95] Montesquieu concentrated on identifying the *moeurs* necessary to sustain the curious complexity of such a system of modern liberty. Every form of government has its principle, which gives it life and makes it legitimate. For pure, that is ancient, democracies, it was virtue; for aristocracies, honor; and for modern commercial monarchies, the principle of moderation. The best example he found of the last was England, and from it he derived much of what is commonly known of his theory of politics, such as the division of powers.[96] Montesquieu described England effectively as a representative republic under monarchical forms, a state of liberty, but not one in which the citizen was consumed by his political role.

Although Montesquieu gave new ground to political theory and opened the way to a new understanding of republicanism, he was no republican himself. His direct legacy is liberalism in its many guises, not modern republicanism.[97] Rousseau did the work of generating a specifically republican understanding of the new conditions of the eighteenth century. He took this new insight—that modern social life demanded a specific set of *bonnes moeurs*—and gave those *moeurs* a name, autonomy. Furthermore, he generated an argument for the institutional context necessary for autonomy or, to use a term more familiar to eighteenth-century thinkers working from the vocabulary of neostoicism, self-command.[98] Rousseau argued that if the moral capacity of every person in modern society, the very ground of their liberty, was not institutionally protected, that capacity would be erased by the plasticity and dynamism of modern social relations.[99] The institutional context identified by Rousseau as the necessary guarantor of modern liberty was democracy, embedded in popular sovereignty. By participating in the formation of the General Will, individuals retained their participation in sovereignty, their freedom. The democratic sovereign would guarantee that every individual would retain his or her moral autonomy. The General Will was necessary to give moral guidance to individuals. Only a legitimate General Will could discern what was morally necessary in a complex and confusing modern world: "either the will is general or it does not exist, it is that of the body of the people, or of a faction."[100] The claim that only democracies were legitimate was to become the most contested ground of modern politics. Rousseau was the first thinker who specifically argued that republican democracy was the definitive political form for modern life.

If Montesquieu turned the assumptions of political theory on their head, Rousseau in turn inverted the assumptions about social theory. He exploited a line of weakness in the fundamental understanding of the nature of modern life promoted by Montesquieu. Montesquieu had assumed that the categorical difference between political life and social life would automatically be sustained under any regime committed to law. Thus he was indifferent to the actual governing structures, though he thought monarchies more easily sustained. As long as the difference was retained, no great threat to liberty could arise from the political system. In fact, at times he portrayed the sphere of politics as one of frustration and inertia, almost entirely without meaning: "As each individual, always independent, would largely follow his own caprices and fantasies, he would often change parties; he would abandon one and leave all his friends in order to bind himself to another in which he would find all his enemies; and often, in this nation, he would forget both the laws of friendship and those of hatred."[101]

Rousseau argued that though the categories of public and private life were logically separate, the institutions of public and private life were mutually interdependent. He asserted that the space between public institutions and private life, where values were forged (an area, following Jürgen Habermas, that we have come to term the public sphere), was the most important element in the constitution of a society. Individuals constructed their core identities in the public sphere; "laws act on the exterior and merely guide behavior, only *moeurs* penetrate the mind and guide the will."[102] Hence a civil religion was necessary to attach the sentiments of the population to the law: "it is of the first importance to the state that every citizen have a religion that directs him to love his duty."[103] The political capriciousness that Montesquieu saw as a sign that the real interests of moderns were ultimately expressed elsewhere than in the political sphere was understood by Rousseau to be the greatest danger to the ability of modern people to be free.[104] In his novels, occasional writings, and developed philosophical writings he argued that self-command could be guaranteed only by a perfect equality. Thus, paradoxically, working from rigorously individualist premises, Rousseau was driven to denounce every concrete feature of modern social life, especially the social equality of the sexes, in defense of the principle of individual autonomy.

Chapter 19 of *The Spirit of the Laws* praised the modern delight in fashion as a necessary device to enhance sociability and social cohesion. Rousseau, who was a far more reflexive thinker than Montesquieu, argued that the inauthenticity of the world of fashion, to take just one target of his wrath, would eventually rob modern individuals of the sense of their individuality, of their knowledge of themselves as moral agents. The closing pages of his *Social Contract* portrayed the mechanisms that would impel all commercial societies to barbarism. In his projection of the course of civilization the very idea of law and right had collapsed into force and power: "from the extreme inequality of condition and fortune, from the diversity of passions and talents, from the useless arts, from the pernicious arts, from the frivolous sciences are generated prejudices, equally opposed to reason, happiness, and virtue."[105] This was the reason for his famous assertion that only poor, small, agrarian states could be virtuous. People could act well only if they knew how to act, and they could not know the good in the pernicious hubbub of modern life. Modern individuals could be saved only if they abandoned all the distinctive features of their modern lives.

It might seem strange to us that Rousseau's apocalyptic vision of modern life could have been so attractive to the beneficiaries of the commercial world of the mid-eighteenth century. It is tempting to attribute the attraction of Rousseau to a nostalgic yearning for an imagined cohesive golden age of simplicity and morality. A strong tradition sees Rousseau's model of democracy as inherently totalitarian and threatening to the complexity and diversity generated by the forms of individuality it sought to comprehend.[106] In fact, eighteenth-century readers were far more sophisticated in their appreciation of Rousseau's texts than we might think. While they were not blind to the problems in his work, they recognized the acuity of the question he had posed; what were the structural tendencies in modern life that either promoted or destroyed the capacity for self-command, for independent moral action? Adam Smith, in 1756, acknowledged that this was the central problem of the "science of man," and that on the face of it Rousseau's description of the debilitating effects of societies without virtue was only too accurate:

> It belongs not to my subject to show, how from such a disposition arises so much real indifference for good and evil, with so many fine discourses of morality; how everything being reduced to appearances, everything becomes factitious and acted; honour, friendship, virtue, and often even vice itself, of which we have at last found out the secret of being vain; how in one word always demanding of others what we are, and never daring to ask ourselves the question, in the midst of so much philosophy, so much humanity, so much politeness, and so many sublime maxims we have nothing but a deceitful and frivolous exterior; honour without virtue, reason without wisdom, and pleasure without happiness.[107]

Rousseau's antidote to the corruptions of modern life was unpalatable, but his diagnosis of the disease was impeccable. Political theory after Rousseau had at its heart the fundamentally republican question of the autonomy of the citizen.

There were many responses to Rousseau's question. Smith's own idea that the market might create disciplining structures that would inculcate civility and self-control is well known. Less appreciated is Diderot's exploration of the aesthetic as a realm that might offer grounded values to modern commercial society, though the later development of this idea by Schiller has been enormously influential. The most interesting, and most republican, response to Rousseau was Adam Ferguson's development of the idea of civil society. Ferguson was in some sense overdetermined as the figure to rescue civic values in a commercial age. A son of the manse, he was born at Logariat, in Perthshire, Scotland, right on the highland line. He straddled the modernizing, polite culture of the lowlands and the martial world of the north. He fought, if an army chaplain fights, at the battle of Fontenoy, with a highland regiment and was afterward professor of moral philosophy at Edinburgh University.[108] His *Essay on the History of Civil Society,* first published in 1767, gave a name to the particularly modern context in which the independence and vigor of the highlander might be replicated, without the poverty and incessant warfare that bred his distinctive virtues. His effort to unite his own experience was also the most perceptive account of where and how self-command, the distinctive feature of the republican citizen, might be fostered and upheld.

Ferguson's coinage of civil society has attracted much attention of late, and the idea is modish, but the contemporary discussion does not accurately represent the eighteenth-century version. There is no one, dominant, idea of civil society; liberals such as Ernest Gellner defend it as a completely apolitical space of association, a counterweight to politics, while radicals such as Michael Walzer develop the notion of the interdependence of a democratic political order and the existence of those associational networks.[109] However, as Jean Cohen and Andrew Arato have pointed out, the contemporary discussion is relatively impoverished by comparison with the eighteenth-century development of the concept, and in particular the complexity of Ferguson's position still escapes it.[110] He was not celebrating private life, nor pointing out the necessity for countervailing institutions to the state. Rather, he was looking for the loyalties and connections that might tempt modern people out of self-interest and into commitment. Ferguson's challenge to liberal life was fundamental because he recognized a tendency toward isolation within it. Isolation of individuals could undermine such a civilization

because as individuals sought their private ends there was no individual reason to defend the collective commitment to individualism. Ferguson needed
a countervailing principle to individualism that would mobilize individuals
to enter public life. He found this principle in associations and, most important, in the competition and enmity among the associations characteristic of
modern social life. Ferguson asserted that the greatest threat to individuality
in modern conditions was concord and peace. In totally peaceful conditions
men would consult only their private interest and the individual utility of
their actions. As long as there was contestation in the public sphere, individuals could be motivated to unself-regarding action. Ferguson then devoted
much of his attention to understanding the conditions of limited competition and enmity in modern life. Ferguson ended up arguing that you could
reconcile modern commerce with liberty only if they were united with the
widest and most democratic participation in political life. He was under no
illusions that a commercial society characterized by a large array of particular associations would be a pretty sight:

> In states where property, distinction and pleasure are thrown out as baits to
> the imagination, and incentives to passion, the public seems to rely for the
> preservation of its political life, on the degree of emulation and jealousy
> with which parties mutually oppose and restrain each other. The desires of
> preferment and profit in the breast of the citizen, are the motives from
> which he is excited to enter in public affairs, and are the considerations
> which direct his political conduct. The suppression therefore, of ambition,
> of party-animosity, and of public envy, is probably, in every such case, not a
> reformation, but a symptom of weakness, and a prelude to more sordid pur-
> suits and ruinous amusements.[111]

For Ferguson, civil society was not a system but a space where modern urban dwellers might generate the same beneficial effects of independence
and public-spiritedness as highlanders created by raiding cattle. A social democracy of intense competition was the essential basis of liberty, but Ferguson was silent on the actual political institutions that would represent such a
tumultuous entity. His ideas were demotic rather than democratic; political
practice would make the democratic potential actual. Ferguson accepted
the insight of Montesquieu and Rousseau that the conditions of modern liberty were set by the *moeurs* of the people and identified a new institutional
context for the creation of political culture. The new republicanism was a
theory of how a modern society could assure liberty to its citizens by the

mutual interaction of political and social equality embedded in the institutions of civil society.

One of the best examples of the practical consequences of this set of ideas was Clavière's plan for a life insurance company, which he circulated in 1787.[112] Life insurance would rescue the poor from the paradox that robbed them of control of their own lives. Without a scheme through which the poor could invest the little they had, there was no incentive for them to work hard. "Is it at all surprising that since they cannot fruitfully save for the long term, they barely save at all, especially if food is cheap and they can make the amount necessary for two days bread in one day's work?" Clavière asked.[113] The scheme he proposed would make nobody rich but would make it rational for the poor to save. It would in fact make *bonnes moeurs* rational for individual working men, whose "savings [were] created through what is often a punishing labor." The rich, the investors in the scheme, would acquire the obligation to meet the needs of widows, orphans, and the old. Interaction in this institution would simultaneously foster autonomy and fellow feeling, the self-definition of the individual and the bonds of society. Clavière would later argue in favor of the assignat in precisely the same way. He conceived of the assignat as a share held by the population in general in the fortune of the country.[114] This financial instrument would animate the citizens and drive them to protect their individual well-being through oversight of the government in tandem with their fellow citizens. Rational investors could, ideally, exhibit civic commitment equivalent to the warlike spirit of ancient Gauls or Scottish highlanders if economy, society, and politics were properly aligned.

At its most ambitious, the republican imagination of the late eighteenth century grappled with the idea of the interdependence of the democratic political order and the competing institutions of a healthy civil society. Yet these transformations at the apex of political theory might well have had no effect whatsoever on political practice were it not for the crises that racked every North Atlantic state in the late eighteenth century.[115] Nobody, outside marginal figures such as Clavière and Brissot, considered an actual republic the solution to the problems of France in 1789. Within three years, however, the new republicanism, which sought to articulate the fact of civil society, the desire for individualism, and the need for collective representations and politics, became the central ideological resource for societies in crisis. Even countries that staved off systemic collapse, such as England, developed a new republicanism. Where William Godwin understood politics in a way that would have made sense to the participants in the Putney debates, John Thelwall spoke a language that was completely novel.[116] Still, it is vitally important to recognize that the new republicanism did not drive the revolutionary process. Rather, it offered tools to master it, new concepts and collective understandings that could generate stable institutions for societies and states in crisis.

Jacobinism and the New Republicanism

Despite the sophistication and insight of new republican political theory, and the successful example of the Americans, the new republicans failed to understand and lead the French Revolution. Their failure was of the first importance for the development of the republic. Harold Parker has long argued that by discrediting the modern version of the republic, the commercial republic, the Girondins left the Revolution no model other than that of antique republicanism.[117] The test for the modern republicans came in the summer of 1792. Although the war declared in April of that year did not develop in the way Brissot and his friends had anticipated, it did have the result they hoped for, discrediting the king. As the French armies gave way before Austrian and German troops, and as evidence of the monarch's ambivalence toward what was technically his cause mounted, it became clear that the monarchy would fall. The republicans were therefore in the unfortunate position of getting what they wanted. Moreover, the circumstances under which they achieved their republic made the kind of moderate, slowly evolving, lightly governed state they envisaged difficult to establish. The republic might have been the work of time and the slow evolution of society, but it was more proximately the work of the sections and the *fédérés*.

The frailty of new republicanism was startling, especially since much of the groundwork for a commercial republic had been laid. The republic declared in September 1792 inherited an impressive set of political reforms from the Constituent and Legislative Assemblies that had already created much of the institutional basis for such a regime. The formal equality of all French citizens before the law had been established, and the idea of rights firmly implanted in the new jurisprudence.[118] The power and authority of the landed elite had been undermined leaving no possibility of a capture of the state by a conservative alliance to impose an authoritarian solution to political crisis.[119] The state itself had been reformed; administrative rationality had replaced the patchwork of venal office holding that characterized the late monarchy; and the transition to the new local government system of departments had been smooth.[120] All of these transformations of the formal political system needed only a civic culture, generated from the society, to give life to the new polity. The new republicanism seemed finely calibrated to do exactly that, and yet it was a weak force in the crisis years of 1793 and 1794.

It is tempting to identify political culture as the reason for the eclipse of commercial republicanism in the Convention. The trial of Louis XVI, effectively the first business of the Convention, defined the core issue of revolutionary politics as that of sovereignty. Worse still, the roll-call votes on the fate of the monarch created factional interests around differing ideas of sovereignty.[121] The fate of the king's body, the site of monarchical sovereignty, and that of the nation became fatally entangled with each other. The first appearance of a living liberty, a young woman personifying the attribute, was at the Festival of Reason on 10 November 1793. Lynn Hunt argues that this innovation was motivated by a desire for transparent representation, free of all idealization, for a simple model of national sovereignty.[122] After the execution of the king, the practices of sovereign power were driven by just such a simple model, a metaphor of the body politic, one whose sublime resonance evacuated the abstractions of civil society, legality, and the other objects of political theory.[123] As Marie-Hélène Huet points out, Saint-Just's last entries in his *Fragments d'institutions républicaines,* "I do not like new words, I like only the just and the unjust; these words are understood by all consciences," reflected the imperative for political ideas to be simple and unitary.[124] Dorinda Outram has explored the wellsprings of Saint-Just's (by that stage) suicidal commitment to a unitary ideal of sovereignty.[125] Suicide was the ultimate use of the body. By destroying the body, one displayed one's fitness to wield authority in a moral fashion on the part of the nation. If kings could die well, then republicans had to, and not only Montagnards emulated the royal sacrifice.[126] The Girondins found the unity of purpose, and indeed the collective identity they had lacked when directing the republic, by dying together.[127] Even infatuation could be raised to the height of tragedy; Adam Lux demanded the death penalty for himself, when tried for placarding in support of Charlotte Corday, in order to assert his republican seriousness.[128] In a political world driven by such a somatic metaphor modern republicanism could find no purchase.

However tempting it may be to identify the defining moment of the Revolution as the conjunction of an event, the trial, with a hegemonic metaphor, that of the body politic, it is ultimately facile. The power of the somatic metaphor across the range of the Revolution is undeniable, but its compelling power was not endogenous. French political actors regressed to older languages of politics when republicanism failed to find representations for the social movements that emerged from the very civil society celebrated by republicanism. The inability of the modern or commercial republicans to create a political repertoire through which Jacobins and sans-culottes could express their identity and aspirations drove both Jacobins and sans-culottes to explore other, older, political registers. While Brissot and Clavière may have embraced the idea of civil society, they were unprepared for the kinds of social movements that actually emerged from it in the Revolution.

It is important to recognize that the sovereign body was not an innovation in political culture. As Sarah Hanley has pointed out the idea was invented and elaborated as a projection and rationalization of Bourbon power.[129] Nor was it unusual for actors other than the monarch to use their body as the appropriate site for the expression of politics. The Chevalier d'Eon had manipulated his body precisely to manage his relationship to politics, becoming a woman in the 1760s in response to the military failures of France, failures for which he or she felt responsible.[130] Moreover, the metaphor had become entirely banal by the late eighteenth century. Far from being the site of a sacral authority, the body of the king, and especially that of the queen, was made vulnerable to desacralization through political pornography.[131] The idea of the sovereign body had been so degraded that the state had abandoned, in the 1750s, a politics of metaphor in favor of "a more immediate and more obvious imaginary of power."[132] The Revolution led to a resacralization of the body. Tellingly, it was precisely as the Revolution entered a crisis that political pornography went out of favor.[133] A reinvestment in an older repertoire of political images demanded a reevaluation of the presentation of the political body in public. Modern republicanism was not overpowered by the dominating power of the imagery of the body politic; rather, the image of the body politic was revived as modern republicanism failed to organize the political life of the country.

Sans-culottes and Jacobins were republicans by 1793, but they were not commercial or new republicans. Why did new republicans such as Brissot and Clavière fail to relate their ideas to Jacobinism and sans-culotterie? Brissot and Clavière described the manner in which *moeurs,* the interests of actors in civil society, and the rights enjoyed by the individual and recognized by the state were dynamically interrelated. But they failed to capitalize on this insight, and their actual political strategies were formal and institutional. They developed no model for the democratic citizen, no suggested basis for political participation.[134] They appealed to the rights of the people against those of the executive, but they did not attempt to build and maintain a popular base of support. In effect their appeal to popular authority was revealed to be a rhetoric rather than a promise.[135] Alphonse Aulard thought the distance between Brissot and the popular movement was created by his distaste for plebeian culture, but though Brissot may have been a snob, his real problem was his failure to devise a conceptual machinery through which to represent democratic citizenship.[136] From his observations of the United States of America Brissot drew the conclusion that in conditions of modern liberty the actions of the state would become increasingly irrelevant, that politics as such would become merely a residual compensation for the minor failures of the social system.[137] The insight that prosperity and liberty could develop together was the basis of the idea of the commercial republic, but this form of the idea did not account for the competitive conflict-ridden nature of the politics of civil society, as Ferguson had understood it. Brissot conflated popular sovereignty with the rule of law, and he was to be rudely shocked by a populace that took popular sovereignty at face value. In particular he underestimated initially how important antiseigneurial feeling was to the mobilization of the French population and later how important the idea of equality was to become.[138] Commercial republicans like Brissot did not understand and could not channel the desire of significant portions of the population to use the institutions of the state to reform society.

Circumstances made modern republicanism an irrelevance in 1793, but inherent weaknesses in its conceptualization made it less effective than it might have been. Another profound reason for the lack of support in the country was the new republicans' inability to manage the relationship between religious ideas and political action.[139] This particularly affected their relationship to Jacobinism. The new republicanism, like any political theory, was as much a discipline as an inspiration. Its central claim was that a free state could be created out of the interaction of a commercial economy, an emulatory civil society, and democratic political institutions. Behind this eminently rational political ideology lurked a fear of the deployment of religious authority in public. The lack of a coherent response to the presence of claims to religious authority in the public sphere severely hampered the attractiveness of the new republicanism to the mass of Jacobins. In Patrice

Higonnet's phrase, the Jacobins sought goodness beyond virtue, a politics after and beyond politics. Jacobin universalism was so unconstrained that it could not confine itself to the sphere of politics and found its most distinctive expression as a religious commitment, seen most obviously in institutions such as the cult of the Supreme Being. In the absence of a political ideology that could unite such aspirations and more mundane interests Jacobinism fell into a dynamic of fundamentalism. As Jacobins made greater claims to represent the sovereign people, they cut themselves off from their roots in social life.[140] Crane Brinton was surely right in this respect when he argued that the later stages of Jacobinism were best understood as a religious phenomenon.[141] This is not to say that Jacobins were not concerned with the mundane realities of poverty, education, local government, and so on, but to assert that the intellectual and cultural milieu within which they pursued these concerns was, in the last analysis, not that of eighteenth-century republicanism.

Ideological coherence was not the most important characteristic of the revolutionary government. The vast improvisation aligned Parisian popular radicals with technocratic army engineers—via libertine aristocrats such as Hérault de Séchelles and the ranks of provincial Jacobins—and was heterogeneous by definition.[142] The consequences of the period for the development of republicanism were immense nonetheless. The very fact of a sans-culotte movement transformed the nature of politics and any claim to represent "the people."[143] While the innocence of Albert Soboul's acceptance of sans-culotte claims to speak for the ordinary wage earners of Paris is behind us, the novelty and significance of sans-culotte politics remains intact.[144] Even if the base of political mobilization was the rather traditional *quartier,* the idealization of the working man as the model of the citizen, the claim to new kinds of social rights, and the promotion of equality as a fundamental characteristic of citizenship irretrievably radicalized republicanism.[145] An old repertoire of great and small councils, larger and smaller states, and ancient constitutions was swept away. The republic became a promise of a new kind of freedom and equality rather than a memory of an old. To be a citizen, for Brissot, was not to be a slave; to be free for the sans-culottes was to be the equal of any other citizen. Republicanism after 1794 was driven into the sans-culotte trajectory, even as it sought to distance itself from the sans-culottes.

It would be a mistake to see Thermidor as a return to the conditions of debate and analysis of 1789 or 1792. The politicization of the bulk of the

French population, on whatever terms, was now a fact. Latent tensions between the ideas of law, representation, politics, and administration were now explicit and had to be confronted. Moreover, the republic as an institution had to be defended. The great problem facing the country was finding some terms under which the republic and modern society might coexist. This was not simply, or at all, a problem of legitimating difference, of limiting the clams of public life. It was also, and more centrally, a problem of representing and accepting the aspirations and ideals of the subaltern elements of the population. What model of citizenship was extensive enough to comprise all the elements of French society? What terms could articulate the specific local nature of the many lives of the people with the universal, formal idea of rights? Jacobinism and sans-culotterie had not created specific ways for the people to imagine themselves and through which they might live their lives, but could anyone else do any better?

CHAPTER 2

Happiness Universal?
Commercial Republicanism
and Revolution

The Terror destroyed Jacobinism as a mass movement, and Germinal and Prairial ended the popular movement as an organized phenomenon, but political culture retained its democratic aspirations.[1] The neo-Jacobin movement remained an important placeholder for those aspirations after 1795.[2] With the *Journal des hommes libres* as a rallying point and the Constitution of 1793 as an ideal, the neo-Jacobins continuously articulated a radical republican vision for the republic. Nor were they a purely intellectual faction. As Isser Woloch argues, the neo-Jacobins were the only popular base on which the Directory could count and so, especially in moments of crisis, concessions had to be made by the regime toward the radicals.[3] By 1799 sixty-five deputies were identified with this tendency, and they formed the left end of an identifiable republican party in the Council of Five Hundred.[4] This political force retained continuity with the mobilization of 1793 and kept the central problem of citizenship before the supporters of the regime. Where was a model for the citizen to be found that was capacious enough to include the popular classes but high-minded enough to preclude popular violence? The modern republic was to articulate social and political life, the problem at hand was to find the representation of the modern republican who could do so.

The Citizen in the Directory

The work of defining the egalitarian citizen of the modern republic was taken on by a heterogeneous collection of persons, institutions, and publications. Although earlier groups—such as the figures in the Lycée Républicain, the Cercle Social, and the group around Mirabeau who wrote for the *Courrier de Provence*—had attempted to express the experience of the Revolution and its meaning in a new key, it was not until 1795, with the publication of Condorcet's *Esquisse d'un tableau historique du progrès de l'esprit humain,* that a revolutionary theory of modern politics emerged.[5] That theory focused on the nature of the modern citizen; his, and in many cases her, cultural makeup, which was expressed as the problem of *moeurs;* and the context necessary to promote those *moeurs,* the problem of institutions.[6] It was debated in the second class of the Institut National, in the pages of intellectual journals, such as Pierre-Louis Roederer's *Journal d'économie publique, de morale, et de politique* and the *Décade philosophique,* and in extensive pamphlet literature. It would be no exaggeration to say that the debate on the constitution of the modern citizen was the dominant debate in France in the late 1790s.

Searching for an authoritative model of the modern citizen drove political thinkers toward psychology, which, in France, meant the sensationalist psychology inspired by Condillac.[7] Sensationalist psychology was contested ground, and the republican idea of the citizen had to engage with powerful traditions of interpretation, which were inimical to the republican commitment to political democracy. Condillac's *Essai sur l'origine des connaissances humaines* was the common source for all writers on this topic. His theory of signs offered a technology, a means of both understanding and manipulating contemporary ideals, through which republican and antirepublican writers could imagine a solution to the political problem they faced.[8] Condillac's theory, which asserted that the moral constitution of a human being was created through his or her interaction with the social and natural environment, opened up a plethora of strategies of interpretation. One strategy, which has attracted a lot of attention from historians, was the creation of a positive science of politics. This science took the deterministic elements of Condillac's thought and developed them to offer a vision of virtuous politics produced through the determined actions of a population, rather than the free action of a nation.[9] This view, developed from Helvétius's ideas, depended on a fundamentally passive psychology, one that stressed memory and reason rather than the imagination or the will, and was best represented in the period by the work of Charles François de Saint-Lambert. Saint-Lambert explicitly placed himself into a genealogy of moral determinists, arguing that Helvétius and Condillac should be read together to understand the real meaning of Locke.[10] He developed this view in arguing that the moral development of an individual was entirely determined by his or her experience and so could be strategically managed by an enlightened elite.[11] He remained consistent in his argument by holding that politics, by definition the area of meaningful willed action, was an illusion and was in reality the determined effect of humans' struggle to satisfy their material needs. Saint-Lambert's moral philosophy was perfectly compatible with what Martin Staum has termed the therapeutic approach to politics favored by the Ideologues, and in particular by Georges Cabanis.[12] The modern republic, understood in this fashion, could only be a regime managed in such a way as to eliminate the necessity for politics, as classically understood.

The intellectual and political consequences of Saint-Lambert's ideas were revealed by his critic Louis-Claude de Saint-Martin. Saint-Martin pointed out that there was a massive inconsistency built into any materialist account of politics; it could not explain the special nature of the legislator, who alone seemed to be exempt from the determination of consciousness by physical need and so could be relied on to run the state. In the face of this paradox Saint-Martin argued that materialist political theory was entirely self-interested. Just as priests preached virtue and practiced vice, so materialists preached the common good in pursuit of their own material advantage.[13] Moving away from a critique of materialist accounts of politics while remaining within modern moral theory was not easy. Saint-Martin retained a sensationalist epistemology but hypothesized a spiritual area of experience as the ground of human freedom, of politics. This allowed him to create a different, though equally deterministic, account of politics.[14] Saint-Martin constructed a version of human psychology that shared Helvétius's explanatory strategy but rejected his categories. Materialism could not account for liberty, or for the legislator, so Saint-Martin argued that liberty was the grace of God and the legislator the agent of God in history.[15] The difficulties with this position deformed it into something far from what was generally understood as republicanism. Saint-Martin's simple notion of the common good, and his highly theological understanding of the concept of sovereignty, drove him to define the republic as a theocratic dictatorship. He understood sovereignty as he understood property, as functions performed under the will of God. Property and sovereignty could be exercised only in pursuit of the common good, and in the political sphere that meant the creation of the institutions that would give expression to the preexisting natural law.[16] The effort to save the republic replaced the doctor with the priest, and neither could find the citizen.[17]

Happily the political agents of Thermidor and the Directory were not faced with a choice between accepting the authority of either the doctor or the priest to anchor the behavior of the citizen. Some writers were aware of the problems of the derivation of politics from such readings of Condillac, and sought to fashion a specifically republican psychology that would save the modern subject for citizenship. The most important term in the creation of a republican psychology was "sentiment." Moral sentiment, in eighteenth-century social science, referred specifically to the moral sensations experienced by every human. Sentiment was an active perception of moral value, which was a natural attribute of a human body, analogous to a sense. The language of sentiment was the ground on which the limited utilitarianism of the philosophes could be contested.[18] Indeed, Helvétius's characterization of the development of consciousness as entirely passive had been challenged in this manner from the first. Rousseau had pointed out that Helvétius's reading of Condillac had ignored the active principles of passion and sentiment, and Mably had gone on to claim, in his argument against the Economistes, that such an impoverished psychology made the language of natural law into a mockery. The new republicanism was committed to an active psychology of sentiment from its first formulations.[19]

The value and scope of these observations were limited by the particular French history of the development of the idea of sentiment. While in Scotland, and to a lesser extent in Germany, there was an extensive philosophical literature on the idea of sentiment. In France the notion was largely elaborated through the novel.[20] In French public culture, dominated by the tussles between Jansenist and Jesuit, and later philosophe and Jansenist, the older psychology of reason and the passions remained dominant.[21] The struggle between religious and materialist accounts of moral experience deformed more nuanced explanations of the possibility of moral agency. Julien Offroy de La Mettrie's *L'homme machine,* for instance, collapsed Albrecht von Haller's distinction between sensibility and irritability to make sensationalism more purely materialist.[22] Even Condillac suppressed Locke's stress on the importance of ideas of reflection as a form of experience to close down any possibility of an appeal to transcendental authority in moral matters.[23] By 1795, however, the gap in the conceptual vocabulary of the French had been filled, and the less than helpful dichotomy of Aristotelian and neo-Baconian psychologies rejected. The science of man, as it was termed, was able to differentiate itself from the natural sciences.

The study of language was an important ground on which the psychology of sentiment intruded into moral discourse: as Destutt de Tracy emphasized in his prolegomena to the human sciences, society was self-created, not natural, and the use of language in particular, which generated consciousness, separated humans from nature and demanded that the study of man have methods and approaches particular to itself.[24] The evidence for this evolution in assumptions reaches even into parody; Leclerc's satirical *Treatise on the Moral Diseases Affecting the French Nation in Past Centuries,* termed *logomanie* the disease of confusing the moral and natural sciences, a disease the French had caught in the twelfth century.[25] Théophile Giraudet, more seriously, introducing his work on the constitution of the family, was less than convinced that "analysis, the method of modern science," could usefully be applied to the study of society. And Perreau, in a work entitled *Physiological Considerations on Human Nature,* flatly stated that the use of the natural sciences as a model for the moral had to be abandoned.[26] The psychology of sentiment provided a basis for a political science that was not modeled on the natural sciences.

Moral sentiment did not have to become the foundation for the development of a republican moral psychology. There was some interest in Kant's ideas on the autonomy of the individual being founded on the autonomy of the will. François de Neufchâteau, the minister of the interior, published translations of Kant's work on civic religion in his compilation of philosophically interesting pieces in 1801, and we can see traces of his reading of Kant in his speeches to graduating classes of polytechnic and veterinary schools in Year VII.[27] He invoked the idea of individuality as rational self-mastery for the polytechnic graduates, analogizing their mastery of nature to the rational man's moral mastery of self.[28] The veterinarians, by contrast, were invited to consider themselves cosmopolitans, agents of the moral world of the French Republic, which had revealed the rights not just of men but even of animals.[29] Though there are scattered references to Kant's work in various republican moral and political theorists, the possibility of basing a republican ideal of citizenship on Kant was rendered difficult by the interpretation of Kant promoted by Adrien de Lezay-Marnesia. Lezay-Marnesia argued that the republic envisaged by Kant could not be democratic and had to be characterized by a rigid division of powers based on the social division of labor.[30] Lezay-Marnesia captured Kant for the physiocrats, and so for the constitutional monarchists. His strategy was only too successful: thus it was to Italians, Scots, and the English that the republicans looked.

The idea of moral sentiment was itself contested. The most authoritative account was Smith's *Theory of Moral Sentiments,* the seventh edition of which appeared in 1792. Smith, writing from the Scottish tradition, did not supply a mechanism for the generation of moral sentiment. Instead, following Francis Hutcheson, he took moral sentiment as a sense in itself. French authors seeking to capture the authority of Smith for their own positions sought to supplement him by appending an account "to show how [moral sentiment] is generated in every sensitive being capable of reflection."[31] The debate over Smith turned on whether the idea of moral sentiment was a critical norm or an explanatory mechanism. Liberals, such as Cabanis, defended the position that moral sentiment was a mechanism which explained moral expression. Moral judgment was a particular instance of the general phenomenon through which repeated experience produced "comparison, then judgment, and finally choice."[32] The consequence of this argument was the corollary that the positive virtues were conventional and prudential, "generated from our desire to have the good-will of others."[33] This position was easily reconciled with Smith's own view that the virtues were grounded in admiration and emulation of the great rather than in utility: "upon this disposition of mankind, to go along with all the passions of the rich and the powerful, is founded the distinction of ranks, and the order of society. Our obsequiousness to our superiors more frequently arises from our admiration for the advantages of their situation, than from any private expectations of benefit from their good-will."[34] The alliance of sentiment with prudence made a mockery of the republican ideal of equality. If emulation, the ground of moral learning, depended on a society of ranks, then republican equality undermined morality.

Sophie de Grouchy criticized Smith on this very point. The notion that a population was mesmerized into moral consciousness by the grandeur of its social superiors was "an offense to natural equality."[35] She argued that moral experience was grounded not in admiration and envy but in compassion, the imagined participation in the pain of another. We respond profoundly to tragedy and melodrama, she explained, because they satisfy our need to express our moral faculties while developing and educating them.[36] Those who were shielded from the "school of sadness and pain, . . . the rich and powerful, guarded from even the idea of poverty and misfortune by the almost insurmountable barrier of wealth, egoism, and the habit of rule," were not the paradigmatic emblems of moral rectitude, but dubious characters whose compassion may never have been stirred and who might lack moral insight.[37] This notion of a developing capacity for moral reflection helped Grouchy to depart from the mechanism of Smith and his *Ideologue* interpreters. Compassion might be the basis of moral experience, but reflection took the natural reaction and raised it to the status of reason. Compassion merely creates the potential for a moral person; reflection gives it a content.[38] The interaction of compassion and reflection generated moral rules that were critical norms rather than prudential reflections of locally approved behaviors.

To generate a series of moral rules Grouchy set up an alternative social drama to that employed by Smith. Smith's static society was contrasted to Grouchy's notion of society as a dynamic space. As society becomes more complex, she argued, human subjects extend their identification beyond those they actually share their lives with to those with whom they might interact and those who have already created the tastes and habits they have inherited.[39] From this psychic development emerges the notion of humanity as the ultimate community to which the moral agent ought to orient his or her behavior. The abstraction and generality of the human community demands a correspondingly universal norm, that we act to promote in others the pleasures approved by reason.[40] This is preferable to the utilitarian maxim that we act to promote the greatest happiness of the greatest number, Grouchy believed, because it would be impossible to know what would produce the greatest happiness, whereas it was possible to follow the best understanding of the rules of justice and equity.[41] This procedural idea, that the capacity for compassion is guided by the community's rational reflection on the imperatives of justice and equity, underlay her defense of equality:

> One of the primary goals of the laws ought to be to create and maintain an equality of wealth among the citizenry, from which should result, for each of them, without exception, a degree of comfort such that the preoccupation caused by the continual worry about the needs of life and the means to procure them does not render them incapable of the degree of reflection necessary for the perfection of all natural sentiments, and particularly that of humanity.[42]

If the egalitarian grounds of moral communication were not protected, then individuals would guide their actions not by universal reason but by prejudice, a real danger in complex, differentiated modern societies.[43] Grouchy's republican reading of Smith derived a normative content from the idea of moral sentiment. The consequence of her argument, which she explicitly aligned with Rousseau's ideas, was that the moral reason necessary for self-command was derived from the civic communication of a socially egalitarian society.[44] The republican idea of an active, equal citizenry, far from being a threat to the social order that generated moral action, was its condition.

Sophie de Grouchy's idealization of the communicating citizen was at the heart of a series of arguments developed in the late 1790s defending a republican social order. The theme was ubiquitous and emerged in writing across the range of the political and moral sciences. The primary characteristic of the republican subject as defined by Grouchy was his or her participation in the common work of society. Perreau, for one, argued that the Ideologues failed to understand Locke because they did not realize that his theory of cognition concerned itself with the activity of understanding, rather than the passive effects of intelligence.[45] The other salient characteristic of the modern subject was his or her capacity to communicate, to use language. Again, the republicans saw this not as a simple capacity to decipher signs but as a positive need to interact with others and to express oneself.[46] From the sociable, that is communicative, and active nature of humans, republican writers derived the notion of the self-creation of humans through their action in society. "Men," argued Benjamin Maublanc, "are made mostly by education," and that education is our interaction with all our social contexts, with the government under which we live and our upbringing.[47] For republican theorists the reflexive nature of this idea of individuality was both a powerful representation of the human individual and a somewhat troubling idea. For instance, the status of the idea of natural law was difficult to establish in this reading. B. E. Manuel pointed out the obvious corollary of defining human beings as reflexively self-creative when he argued that of all creation humans alone were not subject to natural law.[48] Human beings can discern natural law, but they are not constrained by it. There were a variety of responses to this problem. Louis-Marie de La Révellière-Lépeaux and André Thouin revealed their Jansenist education in arguing that the only way to create a context in which the natural law would become a social law was to institute a civil religion, contending that "without some external religious signs you will not be able to inculcate the principles of morality in the minds of the people or get them to practice morality."[49] They were not alone in asserting that modern republicans needed a religious sanction to their practice of virtue, Maublanc agreed that the worship of God was a duty for republicans, to keep the imperative of perfectibility and regeneration forever before them.[50] Such ideas, and La Révellière-Lépeaux's position as director, lay behind the Directory's support for theophilanthropy from the Year V.

However, the image of humans at liberty to create even the most fundamental categories of their moral being did not frighten all republican moralists. Figures such as Jean-Baptiste Say, Guillaume le Febure, and Jean-Bapiste Salaville sought to delineate the immanent principle of moral order in a self-creative being. They found such a principle in the idea of *industrie,* or creative labor. Say's *Olbie,* written for the Institut National's prize competition of the Year VI, was the most complete statement of the value of *industrie.*[51] Say's fundamental argument was that only dependence creates a taste for immorality, "by forcing people to prostitute their talents or their person."[52] The essential precondition for the moral education of humans is their capacity to earn a living. Moreover, the awareness of being socially useful is what sparks citizens to love virtue. Thus Say pictured his utopian Olbiens as carrying the name of their function or profession. "In this manner," he wrote, "the Olbiens learn to separate the value of the work itself from the profit they gain by it. The Olbiens know that that the love of profit is a vice almost as dangerous as laziness."[53] The work of the Olbiens contributes to their sense of social and self-worth rather than their self-interest, and in this fashion Say differentiated them from the commercial Venetians and Dutch, who were hard-working but had not developed a proper consciousness of the value of labor.[54] This particular ideal of *industrie* was not Say's alone, nor was its consideration restricted to the most rarified level of political theorizing. Bulard's republican catechism for the *écoles primaires* was constructed around this notion. Bulard differentiated between humans and animals on the grounds that animals worked and organized themselves through instinct, whereas people directed their *industrie* to exercise their perfectibility.[55] Work, for Bulard, was the safeguard of virtue and honor; "the man who occupies his body and mind is never assailed by unreasonable desires, never acquires bad habits, and lives honestly."[56] This articulation of *industrie* and perfectibility was also a feature of Maublanc's work, and he argued that working toward perfectibility was the central duty of a citizen.[57] In the absence of fixed immutable moral precepts delivered by some version of natural jurisprudence, or at least in the awareness that arguments skeptical of any version of such a theory were unanswerable, the more sophisticated republican moralists were willing to invest the ethical core of the republic in the process of moral self-creation.

The writer who developed this theory of the modern citizen with the greatest articulateness was Jean-Baptiste Salaville. Salaville wrote on the nature of a regenerated regime from the very start of the Revolution, as one of the editors of Mirabeau's *Lettres à mes commetants* along with Clavière and Say, and he continued to insist on the epochal significance of the Revolution, even after 1794.[58] In his *L'homme et la société* of Year VII he attempted to generate a theory of the necessary connection between humans' moral being, their social nature, and the republic.[59] Salaville's point of departure was his assertion that the condition of liberty was the indeterminacy of the moral will: "liberty consists in doing that which is required by the moral will; when that is found in conflict with the physical will, to give way to the latter is not to choose, it is to lack liberty."[60] If the real free self was the moral self, then the engagement of persons in society was not contractual but natural. This was because existence in society was itself the ground of possibility of moral development: "men and women are the only beings that can affect our moral sense, are the only objects whose presence makes us experience those sensations which are necessary to the development of that quality which constitutes our real being; if we have no communication with them, it does not develop in us, and that lack of development is equivalent to the privation or absolute negation of that being."[61] Salaville's emphasis on society, rather than politics, as the primary sphere of self-creation directly quoted the Scottish moral sense philosophers, Ferguson in particular. Salaville mirrored Ferguson's rejection of Helvétius's determinism and his suspicion of the state-of-nature hypothesis as a useful fiction for political theory.[62] Ferguson's derivation of a moral sense specific to humans could almost be cited as Salaville's: "he is formed not only to know, but likewise to admire and to contemn; and these proceedings of his mind have a principal reference to his own character, and to that of his fellow creatures, as being the subjects on which he is chiefly concerned to distinguish what is right from what is wrong."[63] The Scots provided Salaville with a theoretical vocabulary with which to express the nature of the modern citizen.[64]

Ferguson, rather than the more conservative Smith, reveals Salaville's true debt to Scottish moral sentiment theory because of his doctrine of property. Smith held property to be the keystone of society, providing, as it did, a visible mark of station. "Nature has wisely judged," he wrote, "that the distinction of ranks, the peace and order of society, would rest more securely upon the palpable difference of birth and fortune, than upon the invisible and often uncertain difference of wisdom and virtue. The undistinguishing eyes of the great mob of mankind can well enough perceive the former: it is with difficulty that the nice discernment of the wise and the virtuous can sometimes discern the latter."[65] Ferguson denied that society was based on a hierarchy determined by property, rooting it instead in a universal disposition to social interaction: "men are so far from valuing society on account of its mere external convenience, that they are commonly most attached where those conveniences are least frequent."[66] Salaville agreed entirely, asking, "if, as you contend, it were true that the propertyless multitude was the natural enemy of society, do you believe that the civil society could continue, despite all the means of repression and compression that can be employed by the rich and propertied?" He went on to assert, "property is in the city, not the city in property."[67] Since moral consciousness was a natural quality of all people, expressed through their participation in social interaction, social existence was necessarily democratic.

Exalting the modern republic as a social and democratic structure allowed Salaville to transcend the republican eulogy of the poor, small state. Salaville's republican citizen was not the self-abnegating stoic of Rousseauian theory but an exemplar of self-love. "The secret of their moral perfection," Salaville explained of his citizens, "is not to seek to detach them from their self-interest as it so pleases people to repeat, but to teach them to love that being to which, as much as they are accused of egoism, they are almost all indifferent; the mysteries and inward pleasures of that love must be shown, so they can be touched and seduced by them."[68] The keystone of Salaville's argument was his contention that the reading of ancient history that identified the care of the body with luxury and corruption was a mistake. There was no need to suppress pleasure, the goal of physical being, in order to follow duty, that of moral being. What the ancients and their modern followers had failed to realize was that society, the distinctively modern form of community, created an economy of interactions between both sides of human nature that reconciled one side with the other and promoted both together. According to Salaville, "there is no longer any contradiction between the two systems; opulence and liberty, happiness and pleasure, are combined in the social economy by the same artifice that combines the desires and liberty in the human economy."[69] The idea of *économie* denoted both the interior and exterior worlds of the modern citizen: the modern republic would perforce be commercial. In Salaville's work the core meaning of *industrie* becomes apparent: the work done by the citizen in society through which he or she creates a self.

The dependence of republicans on this idea of active moral self-creation in society becomes obvious once we attend to the debate on social institutions. The republicans, in a curious inversion, became suspicious of the power of the government; Bulard, in his history of republics, argued that liberty was more often lost than expressed through the machinations of "the agents of the government."[70] The redirection of the democratic ideal of the republic from government to society allowed for a reimagination of various elements of republicanism as well. In his moral catechism for the schools, Bulard identified the dignity of the republican not in his participation in the making of the law, or in his right to bear arms in the defense of the *patrie,* but in "the legitimate right one has acquired to the esteem of others and the self."[71] In other words, the essential equality of the citizenry was social, and so the duty of the republican was not to vote but to work. "Every man enjoying the advantages of society is obliged to contribute to it by his work," Bulard stated.[72] While the Ideologues, such as Destutt de Tracy, who did not subscribe to the republican interpretation of the psychology of sentiment retained their faith in the capacity of laws to shape behavior through the appeal to self-interest, modern republicans asked whether moral agency could be fostered in the population through the imposition of law. In Manual's words, "do they not endlessly wreck and destroy their own work? Force has only ever made tyrants, tyrants can only make slaves, and slaves, even slaves of the law, are far from being citizens."[73] Even republicans of a Rousseauian stamp who were suspicious of modern commerce expressed a fear of corruption of *moeurs,* not laws: "the moral sentiment of self-love, which cannot flourish under corrupted *moeurs,* cannot be felt under the pomp of riches and the vanity of decorations."[74] The government press made the neatest conjunction of the dependence of a modern republican regime on a model of civil society when the *Bulletin décadaire* declared "that it is no longer necessary today to make the effort to prove how much the dignity of man is reinforced by the representative regime and how much it is abased by despotism; it is a demonstrated truth, a truth of sentiment."[75] Truths of sentiment were exactly those on which the republic had to be built.

The duality of sentiment and *industrie,* the first denoting the affective and social nature of citizenship and the second its universal nature, gave content to what had been an empty category. While Brissot and Clavière derived their idea of good *moeurs* directly from their observation of commercial relations, the republicans of the Directory developed a more sophisticated and articulated ideal of the actions of the citizen. Communication and labor were inherently rather than consequentially social, and so overcame the utilitarian bias in the earlier ideals. Finally, the idea of sentiment, which idealized human communicative relations, was open to translation into a variety of religious idioms. As I shall explain, one of the most important republican movements of the late 1790s was theophilanthropy, which would make a religion of this set of ideas. It was a small step from the notion of the active creation of the moral self in society to that of the worship of society as a sacral object. This new republicanism was far more calibrated to the registers of actual public expression—political, moral, legal, and religious—while encapsulating a critical ideal. Republicanism claimed to represent the moral nature of human beings in a manner compatible with their commercial behavior but not reducible to it. The continuity with earlier versions of republicanism lay in the commitment to the specifically political duty of the citizen, but the understanding of that duty was transformed. The elaboration of a language of democracy was provoked by the pressures generated by the Revolution itself. The unique circumstances drove political actors to forms of innovation and creativity in the effort to articulate for themselves and others the goals they sought to attain. The sets of associations described here did not exist in a vacuum, however; republican understandings of the nature of modern life and its demands were contested by conservatives, and by liberals. While the republicans tried to occupy the ground of society to support their claim to understand the nature of things, they had to contend with strong conservative accounts of the nature of state authority and with liberal analyses of the demands of a modern economy. Republicans could not abandon political economy even as they recognized its insufficiency as a basis for a republican theory of politics. Republicans had to explain not only how to do good but how to do well.

Political Economy and the Modern Republic

Political economy was the most prestigious social science of the late eighteenth century, hailed by Dupont de Nemours as the "new science."[76] Paradoxically physiocracy, Dupont's own variety of political economy, was unsuccessful among the reading public in France.[77] The professionalization it promoted made political economy into a specialization after 1760 and removed it from general public discussion. It was the Scots, such as James Steuart, Hume, and especially Smith, who were to reestablish political economy as the master discipline for an understanding of modern life and be the inspiration for the economic thinking of many of the revolutionaries. Jean-Claude Perrot has mapped the evolution in Condorcet's thinking in 1788–89 in terms of his education away from physiocracy and toward Smithean economics.[78] Sieyès was similarly in debt to Smith, and Clavière's ideas on public debt were inspired, at least in part, by his reading of Steuart.[79] This period in the history of French political economy is therefore one of appropriation of the new perspectives of the Scots and their integration into other social and political commitments. The new political economy found a place as a central element in a republican science of politics.

Between 1795 and 1799 there was a flowering of political economy along these lines in France.[80] Republican political economists sought to delimit the ties among modern commerce, society, and the republic.[81] Capturing political economy for a democratic understanding of a modern republic was not as simple as appropriating moral sentiment theory. The latter had inherently democratic elements, but the reception of political economy in France had tended to exaggerate its hierarchical elements. The most prominent commentator on Smith, Germain Garnier, went so far as to criticize him for not recognizing the central role that large landowners had to play in the economy, and thus the privileged role they should ideally play in the polity.[82] Even Sieyès, a sophisticated reader of Smith, reserved a key role for landowners in the notes he made on the organization of *industrie morale* in Year V.[83] Thus when we look at the appropriation of political economy by the personnel of the Directory, we are really looking at their capture of a social science from the opposition.

Liberals and constitutional monarchists had developed an argument for the incompatibility of a democratic republic with modern economic forms. This interpretation of the Revolution turned on fiscal matters, the most obvious sphere through which the state interacted with the economy, and had as its direct inspiration the writings of François d'Ivernois.[84] D'Ivernois had been one of the republican revolutionaries in Geneva in 1782; proscribed after the French intervention, he, along with the other Genevan refugees such as Etienne Dumont and Clavière, became an enthusiast for the new political economy of Adam Smith.[85] While Clavière developed a belief that a republic might be possible in a large state, d'Ivernois's intellectual maturation took the form of a systemic distrust of politics. Clavière became a theorist of republican economics; d'Ivernois one of the most cogent critics of the republic. The core of d'Ivernois's argument was that republican forms, especially in a large country like France, were completely incompatible with modern political economy. The assignats, in particular, he saw as the antithesis of proper commercial relations; they were, he argued, nothing more than fiat money imposed on a society.

D'Ivernois developed his critique of the political economy of the French Republic from within the premises of the new republicanism. He shared the belief of Rousseau that civil and political liberty mutually defined each other; he departed from Rousseau by arguing that civil liberty was the most fundamental form of liberty. As Pierre-Louis Roederer, an intellectual ally of d'Ivernois, put it, modern people did not desire to display virtue but sought to achieve happiness, and for this they had no need "for any qualities other than those that are necessary for a successful business enterprise."[86] Since modern people were self-regarding and self-interested, a republic, based on the idea of the common interest, could only be fantastical. A modern republic could be nothing other than a chimera under the guise of which elements of the political class competed to further their own self-interest.[87] From this perspective it was worthless to investigate the actions of the revolutionaries in the light of the values they claimed for themselves—liberty, equality, and fraternity. Instead, the revolutionaries' actions had to be seen as a kind of perverse commercial politics, denying the reality of commercial competition even as that competition motivated everything. From this perspective came the clarity of d'Ivernois's analysis of the relationship between paper money and the Terror: "for this purpose the system of terror was adopted in its fullest extent, merely as a measure of finance, in which view Robespierre undoubtedly considered it; and such was the success of his horrible proscriptions, that in some instances the very same estates have actually been three times confiscated and sold again. The assignats issued were but a sort of bills of exchange, drawn on the Revolutionary Tribunal, and paid by the Guillotine, which Robespierre is said to have called *an engine for making money.*"[88] François-Dominique de Reynaud, comte de Montlosier, a constitutional monarchist and a political ally of d'Ivernois, did not hesitate to draw out the political consequences of this insight. The republic, he argued, was nothing more than a political contingency, "its goal nothing other than the plundering of the upper classes and confiscations of every variety."[89] In his view all that stood between France and its natural political state, monarchy, was the impolitic demand by the nobility that it be reinstated with all its privileges.

D'Ivernois's argument, that the laws of political economy drove the Revolution on even as the revolutionaries themselves denied this, was a powerful heuristic through which to understand the entire Revolution. Barnave had warned in 1793 that the republican state might become militarized. D'Ivernois could, on the face of it, show exactly how and why such an eventuality had come to pass.[90] Since the republic was antithetical to commercial life, which was the real interest of the moderns, it could not base itself on the support of public opinion, which had to turn against it. Thus it had to rely on the army. D'Ivernois argued that the economics of supporting the army would inevitably destroy even republican forms. Faced with the reality of the depreciating assignat, the republicans would be forced into bankruptcy and a repudiation of their debts, or some "desperate coup through which they could procure the resources necessary to continue for a little while longer the precarious existence of the republic."[91] The outcome could only be a dictatorship.

An anonymous émigré writing to Lord Auckland in 1793 extended the point. The awful strength of the "French Democracy" threatened to overturn all of Europe, and the only hope of the powers was to act in concert to restrain it until economic weakness could undermine political strength.[92] Mallet du Pan took the same contrast between the political and economic structures of the republic to argue that the predatory logic of a modern republic would drive it to become a universal dictatorship.[93] This analysis seemed to reveal the reason for the coup of 18 Fructidor, Year V (4 September 1797), and the subsequent rupture in peace talks with the British emissary Lord Malmesbury. Notwithstanding the Directory's desire to act as intermediary between the neo-Jacobin and royalist representatives in the legislative body, it could not do so under republican forms.[94] Its need for resources to sustain its power base in the army drove it to an alliance with the neo-Jacobin minority against the royalist, propertied majority. This alliance could be effected only at the cost of destroying the constitutional basis of their own power and so opening the door to a Bonaparte or a Hoche.

This battle for possession of the new science of political economy had a logic of its own, which turned on the compatibility of the republic with modern forms of commercial life. But its general importance derived from the greater issue of the relationship of the Enlightenment, and its more extensive idea of liberty, to the republic and specifically to republican democracy. The defining quality of the modern polity was liberty, and modern peoples had been taught to recognize oppression and love liberty by the *lumières*. In 1790 Raynal could confidently assert that the Revolution would be the "peaceful action of *philosophie*," that *philosophie* would unproblematically lead the French people to liberty through revolution.[95] By 1797, while the connection between the teachings of the philosophes and liberty was still secure, the connection between that teaching, the Revolution, and especially the republic was under threat. The men of letters who were so numerous among the personnel of the Directory were denied the mantle of the philosophes that they affected; "in general the men of letters, or at least those who affect the title, have dishonored themselves in the Revolution by their servility and lowliness."[96]

Royalists, and opportunists, denied the connection between the Directory and the philosophes. Roederer imagined the relationship between the *lumières* and the republic through the figure of Voltaire. He argued that Voltaire's constitutional politics were ambiguous, though his commitment to liberty was not: "He was a royalist leaving for Berlin, he was a republican on his return. While retired he was skeptical of all positions. He was changeable in his love for liberty . . . one can change political opinions, but one cannot arbitrarily overturn moral affections."[97] Bernard-François-Anne, chevalier de Fonvielle, asserted that the republicans just did not understand Rousseau.[98] The opposition attempted to take away one of the central legitimizing claims of the Revolution, that of its being the culmination of the Enlightenment.

More than rhetorical jousting for its own sake was at stake here. *Philosophie* provided the post-Thermidorian republican political elite with its integrating identity. Their relationship to the figures of the Enlightenment was not ornamental but functional. The institutions that defined the republic after Robespierre, notably the Institut National, and the personnel of the regime understood themselves as the expression of *philosophie*. The personnel of the central institutions of the republic often used the language of a persecuted philosophical remnant to describe themselves. There developed a martyrology of philosophers dead or persecuted in the quest for liberty. The lists served to denote a community of the living who had a project to fulfill, as in the abbé Grégoire's identification of the surviving philosophes with the dead who had created the project in the first place.[99] The martyrology of the Revolution became an evocation of the tradition of sacrifice for republicans to admire, rather than a stain on the Revolution itself: "Ah! Without a doubt we should remember and grieve for so many illustrious and unhappy victims of the Revolution, Bailly, Vergniaud, Lavoisier, and the rest. But how can we honor their memories today? By loving and serving the public good, as they loved and served it."[100] The attack on the legitimacy of the Directorial republicans' claim that they were within the apostolic succession of *philosophie* struck at the heart of the ability of that political community to organize itself and coordinate its action.

The declared opposition of some surviving philosophes to the republic lent enormous credibility to this attack. Jean-François Marmontel's allegorical *Le peuple et le sénat traités comme ils le méritent* depicted the Directory as the late Roman republic, steadily sliding to anarchy.[101] André Morellet wrote in favor of an amnesty for émigrés, a royalist cause of Years IV and V, and developed his criticism of the Directory in correspondence with Roederer.[102] Raynal had excoriated the revolutionaries for their incompetence and denied any connection between his *Histoire des deux-Indes* and their actions as early as May 1791.[103] The critics of the Directory made good use of the distance opened between the republic and the philosophes. Marmontel was depicted as the epitome of virtue, the true model of the philosophe, in contrast to the factious *gens de lettres* who composed the Directory.[104] Mably, Rousseau, and Voltaire were variously invoked in support of Catholicism and royalty.[105] Defenders of the regime were maddened by this effort to harness *philosophie* and liberty to the Catholic throne: "They preach intolerance, they demand a dominant religion, they reawaken fanaticism and superstition, they revive the most shameful prejudices; and cowardly apostates of *philosophie*, they call on the religion of their fathers after having shouted with Voltaire and Diderot: *Ecrasez l'infame!*"[106] The danger, from the perspective of the Directory, in the counterrevolutionary devil citing philosophical scripture for his own purposes was that the forces of light and the forces of darkness could become confused.

The defenders of the Directory's right to the mantle of the philosophes were forced onto the defensive. They could not credibly stand over the Revolution in its entirety. Their strategy was to assert that 1795 was heir to 1789 but that all that lay between was aberration: "*Philosophie* began the work of the Revolution, the clamor of arms and the revolutionary storms interrupted it; it has reappeared now to take up its work again."[107] The Directory was to be the privileged moment when the unfulfilled potential of *philosophie* could be brought to bear on the task of the regeneration of France. Rather than rhetoricians, real philosophers, "those rare and extraordinary men, who have created, discovered, or developed some fertile ideas in public administration, and some constitutive principles of the social art or of public happiness," would have control of the regime.[108] The strategy stood or fell on its capacity to tell true from false *philosophie*, on the identification of the damning mistake that had set the Revolution adrift. They found their analysis of the mistake in Condorcet's nuancing of the dichotomy between virtue and luxury: "That philosophy which hopes to raise itself above nature, and that which only wishes to submit to it; that morality which knows no other good but virtue, and that which finds happiness in dissipation, lead to the same practical consequences, while following such contrary principles, and using such contrasting language.[109]

Condorcet moved from a concern with Rousseauian virtue to an appreciation of the uses of the more earthly philosophy of Epicurianism, itself a source for the Diderotan ideal of sagacity. Diderot was intimately linked to this strategy of differentiating true from false *philosophie*. His works were published by Jacques-André Naigeon, with a subsidy from the Directory, in 1795. Reviews of the edition identified Diderot's ideal of sagacity, and his praise of Seneca for embodying it, as a mode of thought uniquely suited to the needs of the revolutionary moment.

> God grant that only philosophers like Diderot would have created the Revolution. Then the Revolution would not have been soiled which, while not undermining its principles in the eyes of those who reflect, has created so many enemies for it. Diderot understood how difficult it is to make free a people that long habit has fashioned for slaves; he expressed this with the profundity and originality that characterized his work in the *Life of Seneca,* which we are going to talk about.[110]

Concern with this complex of ideas was widespread among the intellectual classes, not confined to some isolated philosophes. Even a figure like Maine de Biran, later to be an influential monarchist, moved to this position between 1793 and 1795. In language that directly quotes that of Diderot in the *Essai sur les règnes de Claude et Néron* he asked if when faced with the misery and ignorance of man "rather than rail against it, would their genius not be better employed finding the means to lead them, to make them address themselves to the happiness of society?"[111] The philosophes of the republic "take all their happiness from the good they do for people."[112] The redirection of the inheritance of the Enlightenment from virtue to utility while keeping it within the context of the republic could not be carried off quite so easily, though. The critics of the Directory posed difficult questions for the "rare men" who claimed the insight necessary to create the republic. Crucially, what if the republic itself was *l'infame?*

The debate over political economy was not a technical or narrow matter, therefore, but one on which central issues of legitimation turned. The republican state needed an understanding of how its structures promoted happiness and utility as well as liberty. The attraction of political economy was its claim to be the social art that could establish how the principles of modern life could be reconciled. Republicans had to articulate an understanding of political economy that defended labor, or *industrie,* and sentiment—the fundamental characteristics of the modern citizen. The newly founded regime was well aware of the deficits in its understanding of political economy. The first organized effort to define a new sort of republican economics, Alexander Vandermonde's lectures and classes at the Ecole Normale of the Year III, illustrated their problem. The lectures were not particularly interesting, being largely a commentary on Steuart, but the classes with the students focused on exactly the issue of principle.[113] Vandermonde's students resisted his idea that *besoins factices,* or individual preferences, could be compatible with liberty; one even argued for sumptuary laws to restrict luxurious consumption.[114] In response, Vandermonde robustly denied the relevance of the idea of luxury to modern conditions, arguing that wealth was the basis on which any country had to defend its liberty and that general wealth was generated from the activity of individuals in pursuit of their individual preferences.[115] But he failed to explain how a market economy automatically created equality. His subsequent clarification that he meant equality of opportunity rather than of outcomes was rejected by his class. The students developed a crude theory of alienation as a critique of his consumption ideal: "the more needs a people has the greater its dependency . . . if all the capacities of the soul are taken up in the pursuit of individual preferences, what resistance can be mounted to the seductions of pleasure, and what attraction will be left in that austere liberty that so often demands such terrible sacrifices?"[116] Consumption and citizenship were difficult to align.

The republican state continued to work on this problem. At the beginning of Year IV the new minister of the interior, Pierre Benezech, organized the Office of Political Economy under the control of the director general of public instruction, Pierre-Louis Guinguené, whom he ordered to acquire the necessary texts, principally Herrenschwand's *De l'économie politique moderne: Discours fondamental sur la population.*[117] This was an ambiguous text for use as a textbook in republican political economy. Herrenschwand's thesis was that political institutions were determined by the mode of organization of their economy and left little scope for willed action, either social or political, by the population.[118] His work on population was closer to Malthus than to the progressive Scots. Nevertheless, Herrenschwand's praise for industry, and his argument that a modern nation had to have a large manufacturing sector, were major contributions to the development of republican political economy. Herrenschwand's redirection of the discussion of political economy from consumption to production rescued republican theorists from an insoluble paradox. In his review of the book Roederer, by this time a constitutional monarchist and so committed to the proposition that a democratic republic could not work, was at pains to argue that such a reliance on manufacturing would be inherently unstable.[119] But Herrenschwand's book was a contribution, not a solution: its concentration on *subsistences* inherently made the text useful for administrators rather than educational for citizens. This deficiency was noted and attended to in the further efforts of the bureau, which asked for funds to acquire texts that would reveal the inherent principles of the modern British economy.[120]

By Year VI the Ministry of the Interior had overcome these initial difficulties and felt confident enough to distribute, as prizes for the students of the *écoles centrales,* writings from its canon of republican political economists.[121] Topping the list of Charles-Louis-François-Honoré Letourner, the minister of the interior, were Gaetano Filangieri and Cesare Beccaria, and their names more than anything testify to the increasing sophistication of the regime's engagement with political economy. Filangieri was from the school of Neapolitan social thinkers that had produced the abbé Ferdinando. Galiani, a figure he cited as his inspiration, and his *Science de la législation* exhibited an even more radical approach to political economy.[122] Filangieri's compendium of the political science of the eighteenth century was written from a confessedly republican point of view. In his introduction Filangieri explained his goal, to establish that a modern society could be rich and virtuous at once, precisely the position of the republican moralists.[123] The conclusion of the first book, a philosophical history of political institutions, recalled the republican city-states of early modern Italy and argued that the new American republic would emulate them, not through force of arms but through commerce.[124] This endorsement of the republican form as the most modern and the most likely to encourage economic development exactly chimed with the goals of the Directory and was asserted in the strongest terms by Filangieri in his sections on economics: "Today the richest nations are those where men are most hard-working and most free. We have no reason to fear wealth, on the contrary we should desire it; and the first object of the laws should be to create it, because it is the only source of the happiness of peoples, of civil liberty within and political liberty without."[125] This explicit alignment of hard work and liberty was the ground from which an entire new republican political economy would grow. The selection of Filangieri as the paradigmatic republican political writer, and the demotion of

Smith to one among many others, reveals that in three years the regime had made political economy its own. What allowed this change was the existence of a republican social science into which political economy could be integrated.[126]

Filangieri's articulation of happiness with liberty was a constituent idea of commercial republicanism. Commercial republicans imagined political economy as the investigation of the civil action of the man of sentiment. The stress on labor was the characteristic element of republican political economy. Critics of the republic, such as d'Ivernois, argued from Smith's defense of property and exchange but were less aware of his views on labor. The standard reading of Smith in France, that of Germain Garnier, criticized Smith for not realizing that all wealth was ultimately the product of the soil and so was created by landowners.[127] Garnier's reading of Smith's work revealed its physiocratic basis, and many of the arguments against political democracy were based on this element of their political economy. Garnier, for instance, while endorsing free trade argued that it would depress wage levels to subsistence.[128] Roederer went even further and argued that since wealth had to be so unequally distributed in a modern economy, a modern polity in turn had to be based on the imperial Chinese model.[129] This was a natural result of Turgot's iron law of wages, yet that law was based on precisely the assumptions about value that Smith had exploded. Turgot's model of a market price assumed low growth and further assumed that the maximization of wealth as capital demanded that salaries be kept as low as possible.[130] Smith argued for precisely the opposite position, holding that high wages were a function of increases in the wealth of the nation not a tax upon it: "the demand for those who live by wages, therefore, necessarily increases with the increase of the revenue and stock of every country, and cannot possibly increase without it. The increase of revenue and stock is the increase of national wealth. The demand for those who live by wages, therefore, naturally increases with the increase of national wealth, and cannot possibly increase without it."[131] The liberal monarchist articulation of political economy and politics was based on the presumption that though modern commercial relations would materially benefit everyone, the differential effects were such that only a small proportion of the population could accede to political rights. This position was undermined by looking at the modern economy as a dynamic system, rather than at the structure of property ownership as a stable structure.

Republican political economy claimed that a modern market economy worked most efficiently—that is, maximized wages—under conditions of political democracy, under a republic. D'Ivernois and political economists of his ilk were unable to conceive of a political economy organized around the concept of growth because they held that the possibilities for growth in a country were limited by the productive capacity of the soil. Republican political economists, with their emphasis on labor, conceived of the economic possibilities of modern states differently. They synthesized the ambition of older thinkers, such as Vincent de Gournay, to find an egalitarian form of modern economic life with the new techniques of political economy.[132] Property was the defining element of modern commerce for the liberals; labor, or *industrie,* was such for the republicans. The idea that society could be based on property ownership seemed absurd to republican political theorists. "If," asked Jean-Baptiste Salaville, "it was true, as you argue, that the unpropertied masses are the natural enemies of society, do you really believe that the social state could survive, despite any number of repressive measures that the rich property-owners might employ?"[133] While property ownership was a fundamental element of civil liberty, labor, the common capacity for work, was the fundamental element that allowed participation in the economy and in society.[134] Early versions of this view, particularly Clavière's, overstated the role of labor and reduced capital to merely an incentive for labor to produce. In encouraging the printing of assignats, Clavière foresaw no problems of inflation and even argued that putting 400 million livres into the money supply would actually lower interest rates.[135] Joseph-Antoine-Joachim Cérutti went so far as to claim that *industrie* was the only factor of production: "real wealth derives from *industrie,* which alone occupies idle hands, invents the useful arts, exchanges surplus, stimulates production by creating demand, increases wealth without overturning society." [136] This one-sided view, based on a confusion about the nature of the paper currency, contributed to the eventual failure of it. But the republican political economy that inspired the assignat was to survive its failure.

The facility of the republican use of political economy can be illustrated with the debate on the fiscal system in Year VII (1799). This was a privileged moment in the history of the French Republic. In the aftermath of the treaty of Campo Formio and before the outbreak of the War of the Second Coalition it looked as if the revolutionary wars had ended. Though the negotiations with Britain at Lille had been inconclusive and the Rastatt conference with the Holy Roman Empire was dragging on, exhaustion and political unrest at home seemed to warrant confidence on the part of the French that their antagonists would not reengage in hostilities. In the interim the republic, its extraordinary expenses lessened, sought to regularize its finances. Effectively this was a mopping up operation, as the real decision—who would suffer from the debt crisis of the state—had been taken in September 1797, directly after the coup of Fructidor, when the bankrupt state effectively defaulted on two-thirds of its debts.[137] Ideological impediments to the use of particular financial instruments, such as indirect taxes, had been lifted throughout the years V and VI, so the legislative body had a range of possibilities to debate. As one might imagine, every possible means of financing the state, from the confiscation of émigrés' parents' property to the institution of an income tax, was entertained.

What is interesting from our perspective is not the schemes that were floated but the terms under which they were discussed. Camille Saint-Aubin, speaking against the proposal to confiscate émigré estates, did not argue from natural justice or even from legal equality, but from economic rationality. The measure would be self-defeating, he predicted, because confiscating some property would make the tenure on all property insecure. The subsequent loss of value in property would mean the sums raised for the state through their sale would be negligible.[138] The physiocratic obsession with land as a basis for value came through in plans to recreate the currency through a land bank. Both Jules Gautier and Gérome, who argued for two different versions of a land bank, held that the tax system could not be addressed until the repayment of the state's remaining debts was guaranteed. Both plans sought to create independent central banks, which would manage the debt, and cited the Bank of England as their example.[139]

Jean Barthélemy Lecoulteaux, taking the republican ideal of labor as his lodestar, responded to all these plans on their own terms, capturing their insights to create a scheme that he felt would protect republican equality while maintaining economical efficiency. His immediate problem was Jean-Baptiste Treilhard's proposal for an income tax.[140] This, on the face of it, was the most obviously egalitarian form of tax and, as Lecoulteaux admitted, did indeed bear less heavily on the poor than indirect taxation.[141] Yet Lecoulteaux argued that the formal egalitarianism of the income tax proposal was illusory. The goal of a republican political economy, he contended, should be "the general well-being," which demanded work for all. Personal taxes were massively inefficient in this regard since they created an incentive for citizens to hide their wealth, rather than make it evident by investing it. "It is not so much the quantity of personal taxation that is the problem," he explained, "as the effects that the fear of its extension has on investment."[142] He strengthened his argument in favor of indirect taxation with the observation that even though it would have to be levied on necessities, necessities changed as societies progressed. As labor created wealth, so the perceived needs of a population grew. It was no injustice, he argued, to tax the population to encourage the growth from which it directly benefited.[143] The capstone of his argument was his contention that the legislators had the wrong end of the fiscal stick in hand in any case. Since growth was the ideal, they should be more attentive to credit than taxes. They should seek to emulate the English budget in which, he asserted, six-sevenths of income went on debt servicing yet new issues were well supported. Taxation, he claimed, was only an element of the economic system of the republic, which should be directed at general happiness and wealth.

The very fact of debate between left and right positions using a shared vocabulary is in itself interesting; for the most part debate between revolutionaries and counterrevolutionaries was nonexistent. While the revolutionaries deployed languages of exclusion, such as that of aristocracy, the counterrevolutionaries defined all revolution as either the political instantiation of the sin of the reformation, in the de Maistrian form, or the wholesale assault on civilization through Burke and LaHarpe.[144] Parties to political debate tended to deem the issues between them irreconcilable differences of world-historical import. Yet the counterrevolutionary Montlosier, the disillusioned constitutionalist Roederer, and the ultra-Jacobin Saint-Just all shared the same term for the highest good of the polity: the happiness of its inhabitants, as expressed in their utility. Saint-Just famously termed the happiness of the people "the great discovery of the eighteenth century," which might seem something of an exaggeration of the importance of what to us seems a banality.[145] But this shift in the terms of legitimation of the polity is of the first importance if we are to understand the evolution of modern politics and society. The emergence of a shared vocabulary of political economy between left and right, themselves terms generated from the revolutionary experience, organized around differing rationalizations of the utility of the community, understood as the aggregate of the happiness of the individuals that composed the community, denoted a revolution in political culture. "Utility" was an abstract concept through which differing conceptions of the common good could be articulated and compete. This shift was prefigured throughout the eighteenth century: Hutcheson had already coined the term "the greatest good of the greatest number" as the ultimate arbiter of political right in the 1720s. And Rousseau, though clearly of republican sympathies, had avoided the civic humanist definition of the good life in order to replace it with the more open-ended idea of perfectibility. We do not actually see the institutionalization of the abstract language of utility, which allowed particular goods to be expressed as some shared notion of value, until the Revolution. Time and again in the pamphlet literature of the late 1790s it was asserted that only through political economy could the republic be secured. What that meant was that only through the understanding of the complexities of modern life granted by political economy, and through the languages for representing that complexity, could a rational politics of interest be constructed.

As William Scott has pointed out in a recent article, one of the central claims of the revisionist historians was that the revolutionaries could not derive abstract languages of politics through which interests could be articulated.[146] Inspired by this view, recent research agendas in cultural and intellectual history have been dominated by the search for the concrete commitments demanded for inclusion in the nation. The central bequest of the revolutionary era to political modernity is now seen as the institutionalization of national identity as the primary, and in some cases the only, real form of collective identity. Linda Colley's fine book on the Britons is a good example of an account of the legitimation of the nation-state through the creation of an integrating selfhood.[147] This stress on consensual integration has led to a neglect of the institutions and features of modern societies that allowed them to function not through the imaginative suppression of difference but through its articulation in political and social terms. Languages of political faction and class were not necessarily destructive of the polity once they could be articulated in the public sphere. As political culture has come to be studied as a self-referential entity, we have lost sight of how social and political identities were intertwined. This seems to impoverish nineteenth-century political debate of much of its content.[148] Although it would be fruitless, and inaccurate, to deny the legacy of the era of the French Revolution to nationalism understood as a specifically political phenomenon, these other, more abstract languages that could negotiate rather than obviate social difference were just as important a legacy. Moreover, if we allow ourselves the hypothesis that these disenchanted languages of interest became institutionalized in the public sphere in the course of the Revolution, we have some means of explaining why it was that the revolutionary ideals that seemed to have been crushed in the defeat of France in 1815 revived themselves so effectively by 1830.[149]

The evolution of commercial republicanism as a central feature of a new

kind of democratic political culture was not an exclusively French phenomenon. Just as the Revolution reflected the dynamics of political change
across Europe, so it fostered the new style of abstract, ideological politics
outside France.[150] As I have noted, the debate on the new republicanism before the Revolution was international in scope; the questions raised for radical political theorists by the Revolution had the same paradigmatic nature.
The problem of understanding the Revolution especially affected England,
with its vibrant radical culture. The study of the articulation of political and
economic arguments in Britain has been bedeviled by a misunderstanding of
E. P. Thompson's idea of the moral economy.[151] As Thompson himself has
complained, critics and friends alike have extrapolated from a limited argument about political communication during eighteenth-century food riots to
a more general argument that the new political economy was resisted in the
name of older ideals of social cohesion. Thompson did not intend to polarize
"economy" and "morality" in that way, and his reply to his critics betrays a
certain frustration that the debate ran out in that fashion.[152]

As we would expect, therefore, ideas of political economy were to be
found in the 1790s among political radicals as well as defenders of the status
quo such as Burke, Arthur Young, and John Sinclair. The *locus classicus* of
British radical economic ideas was, of course, Paine's fifth chapter in the second part of *The Rights of Man*. Here again we can see the radical language of
virtue, associated with civic humanism, being displaced in favor of the new
language of utility, asserting that "whatever the form or constitution of government may be, it ought to have no other object than the *general* happiness."[153] Paine was no Smithean however, and his radical political economy
relied on the Montesquieuan opposition of *doux commerce* with the terrible
economic effects of wars.[154] This old style of radicalism, which owed a tremendous amount to the radical Whigs of the seventeenth century, could be
ambivalent about the effects of commercial life all told. The suspicion of luxury lurked beneath the embrace of interest as a necessary curb on the passions. William Godwin, for instance, seems to champion the language of
utility. The opening essay of his *Enquirer* borrowed the new language, placing happiness as the goal of political science.[155] He also echoes Smith in his
abandonment of the Stoic maxim that riches were of no benefit to virtue
and poverty no vice: "if this maxim were true, particularly the latter member, in its utmost extent, the chief argument in favour of political reform and
amendment would be shown to be utterly false."[156] But Godwin's definition
of poverty: the lack of property—"in a country where wealth and luxury

have already gained a secure establishment"—was testament to his evolving romanticism and anticommercialism. He retreated into pure pastoralism in his condemnation of the circulation of money and his flat denial that industry and virtue might be allied. No one could take on a trade or profession with a good heart, since "the trader or merchant is a man the grand effort of whose life is directed to the pursuit of gain. This is true to a certain degree of the lawyer, the soldier and the divine, of every man who proposes by some species of industry to acquire for himself a pecuniary income."[157]

The older English radical tradition, fashioned out of ideas of natural rights and civic humanism, did not necessarily end up as nostalgia and antimodernism, though. Paine opened a bridge between the two in his 1797 pamphlet *Agrarian Justice*.[158] Paine was still in the natural justice tradition and flatly stated that his ideas turned on natural rights rather than the common welfare.[159] In trying to save a concept of natural rights, however, he used much of the vocabulary of political economy. He did not point, as Godwin did, to the common property in land held by the species in a state of nature. Rather, his argument for a land tax for the benefit of the community was based on the inequity of the monopoly in land held by landowners. The criterion for judging this scheme, just as it was for assessing Lecoulteaux's tax proposals, was the general happiness. "The first principle of civilisation ought to have been, and ought still to be," he avowed, "that the condition of every person born in the world, after a state of civilisation commences, ought not to be worse than if he had been born before that period."[160]

At the other side of the bridge from the old radical tradition to new radical political economy were the English Jacobins, John Thelwall in particular, and the English agrarians, inspired by Thomas Spence.[161] Spence and Thelwall, like Paine, were particularly exercised by the problem of property. This issue, in the England of the eighteenth century, was both a theoretical problem and a pressing practical one. Enclosure acts had, in Thelwall's words, threatened to create a class of "territorial monopolist, who thus grinds and tramples underfoot on the laborious cultivator, without whose toil his vaunted estate would be a barren wilderness, alters the very nature of his tenure and turns his property into usurpation and plunder."[162] In no way were Spence and Thelwall against property or commerce in principle. Rather, their argument, as did Paine's, turned on the inefficiency, and consequent injustice, of monopoly.[163] In the manner of the French radicals Thelwall argued that the modern economy operated most efficiently when it maximized the amount of industry generated in it rather than the amount of profit. "Property" therefore, was not a right in itself but "the fruit of useful industry, and the means of being usefully industrious are the common right of all."[164] The core of Thelwall's argument was that the feudal government of Britain distorted and perverted the salutary effects of the development of civilization, turning benefits to mankind into scourges: "machines would be invented and improvements made, not indeed, with the benevolent view of diminishing the toil of the labourer, but to further a cheaper substitute for manual industry, and thus increase, at once, the dependence of the cultivator and the wasteful enjoyments of the landowner."[165] Monopoly was decried as an impediment to the exchange that could benefit the community and as a moral evil that degenerated human beings. Under conditions of monopoly in land even acts of benevolence could become oppressive: Thelwall decried charity under the Poor Laws as it was instituted "not for the purpose of *removing* the *distress*, but of *increasing* the *dependence* of the lower orders of the people."[166] Poor Laws were but one instance of the great evil whereby government denatured property by loading it with privilege.[167] "Monopoly" was the term that denoted the unnatural and despotic intermingling of political and economic power: "their rotten borough system of corruption, peculation, and monopoly," was the great enemy of happiness.[168]

The problem with this line of argument was that it had a tendency to relegate politics in favor of economics. The rights of free-born Englishmen to welfare could leave parliamentary reform untouched and reinforce paternalism. Thelwall avoided this tendency by defining exactly what kind of well-being one had a right to. The fundamental right was not to food, to work, or to property, but to act as "a moral agent; and that therefore it is his duty to enquire into the manner in which that agency is to be employed."[169] Thelwall filled in the idea of utility, of welfare, with the qualities of citizenship in order to create a critique of the British system of government that saved modern commerce while retaining the primacy of politics. Thelwall's strategy was to ground politics in his assertion of the right of democratic participation in society. Thelwall's catalog of rights amounted to a charter for the pursuit of happiness:

> you have still a right to employ your faculties for your advantage; and in the reciprocations of society, to receive as much from the toil and faculties of others, as your own toil and faculties throw into the common stock. You have a right to the gratification of the common appetites of Man; and to the

enjoyment of your rational faculties. The intercourse of sexes, and the en-
dearments of relative connection, are your right inalienable. They are the
bases of existence; and nothing in existence—no, not even your own direct
assent, can, justly, take them away.[170]

Commercial society democratized the conditions of moral agency, and the
capacity to be a moral being in turn generated political rights among the
population. Thelwall could even see a species of cunning of history in operation whereby the effort to deny political rights would merely accelerate their
acquisition by the bulk of the population.

> The fact is that monopoly and the hideous accumulation of capital in a few
> hands, like all diseases not absolutely mortal, carry, in their enormity, the
> seeds of cure. Man is, by his very nature, social and communicative, proud
> to display the little knowledge he possesses, and eager as opportunity pre-
> sents, to encrease his store. Whatever presses men together, therefore,
> though it may generate some vices, is favorable to the diffusion of knowl-
> edge and ultimately promotive of human liberty. Hence every large work-
> shop and manufactory is a sort of political society, which no act of parlia-
> ment can silence, and no magistrate disperse.[171]

Commercial society, for Thelwall, produced citizens, and the logic of commercial society would provoke them to reclaim their political rights.

What was wrong in Britain was not its modernity but the feudal laws that
overlay that modernity, particularly primogeniture, which reinforced monopoly in land. The most obvious instance of this contradiction, for Thelwall, was the continuation of the war with France. The war, he argued, was
a conspiracy to maintain high food prices and impoverish the working poor.
In conditions of free trade there would be no want, and therefore prices
would be low. "Let us consider, he suggested, "that while the ports of nations are open, scarcity can never exist to any alarming degree. Every country, if not prevented by political impediments, will send its surplus productions to the best market. The best market is always the country which is
most in want."[172] War reinforced the monopoly in land that was the most
damning feature of British political economy and also provided the pretext
for the national debt, which Thelwall argued was nothing more than a tax
on the poor for the benefit of the rich. "It is upon the shoulders of the industrious poor that the enormous weight of this burden is laid. For it is they
who must produce those articles which are given in exchange for that specie

which defrays, not only the interest of the debt, but the whole expenses of the government."[173]

Thelwall's specific criticisms of the conduct of the war were shared by elements of British society that would not have shared his enthusiasm for political democracy. Vicesimus Knox, Thomas Bigge, and the other Friends of Peace used almost exactly the same words to describe Pitt's war policy in their publication *Oeconomist*, founded in 1798.[174] Even Malthus, who was to become a fervent critic of the French Revolution and its egalitarian hopes, wrote, in 1796, in the antiwar idiom of the common good.[175] This was a new style of argument in favor of democracy, which it guarded against monopoly, rather than an argument against politics. It took the more daring imagination of Spence to argue that political democracy could be assured only through structural changes in the economy itself, but even Spence's arguments in favor of land nationalization, which long predated the Revolution, were couched in terms of the achievement of happiness by the population through the exercise of its political rights.[176] Although Thelwall's Jacobinism was to be a historical dead letter, his ideas implicated themselves across the political spectrum.

In both Britain and France, then, we can see that, despite appearances to the contrary, radicals and conservatives shared a common vocabulary of the common good, one that could allow them to express their own interests and argue rationally for their positions in terms of general utility. Further, I have argued that Smithean political economy was the backbone of this language and that it found its home in the public sphere in both France and Britain in the era of the French Revolution. One might, however, credibly question the extent to which the evolution of a new ideal of the common good as the aggregate happiness of the population was a genuine innovation in the terms of political discourse. In particular one might question the use of such languages outside the core metropolitan countries, France and Britain. Could the language of political democracy and that of modern commercial relationships remain linked in a radical discourse in any other context, especially one in which the fundamental premises of inclusion of the community, let alone of political representation, were far from settled?

Ireland in the 1790s offers a test of this question. While Theobald Wolfe Tone had celebrated the French Revolution's debunking of the terms under which Catholics were excluded from political agency, the fact remained that in Ireland colonial relationships and religious history distorted the possibilities of radical politics. Ireland turned many of the terms of British politics on their head: the 1793 Catholic Relief Act, for instance, was pushed through an Irish Parliament that thought of itself as patriotic by the enemies of revolution, Pitt and Dundas. Moreover, Thomas Bartlett has cogently argued for the inutility of any notion of a moral economy in Ireland.[177] Irish economic relations, especially around land, soured early and were the occasion of mortal conflict rather than the resolution of interests. This would seem unlikely ground for the emergence of shared political concepts. Yet the environmental impediments did not necessarily preclude the new radicalism from finding a following. Irish radicals saw themselves as part of a more general movement and were avid consumers of its literature, as David Dickson has shown in his study of the publishing history of Paine in Ireland.[178] Iain McCalman has established the existence of key radicals, like Thomas Evans, in both London and Ireland.[179] However, local evidence of the introduction of a language of modern democracy is thin, and historians who have looked at the ideas of the United Irishmen have stressed the continuity of a Hutchesonian amalgam of civic humanism with moral sentiment rather than any radical innovation.[180] Was, therefore, the Irish experience of revolution uninformed by the transforming effects of the creation of new ideologies of politics? Should it be understood as the eruption of violence into a vacuum unpopulated by civil society or public sphere?

Arthur O'Connor certainly did not think so.[181] O'Connor's *State of Ireland* of 1798 was not the only text written in Ireland to approach the Revolution through the optic of political economy, but his text was the most sophisticated and most like those of the French and British commercial republicans.[182] The goal of O'Connor's argument was to justify a total break with Britain, parliamentary reform, and an enfranchisement of the Catholics of Ireland, ends to which he mustered new arguments. O'Connor imagined a nation as a society, an emulative system that generated liberty and happiness. The mainspring of the system was the "liberal reward [that] invigorates industry."[183] A republican politics promoted industry—socially useful work—to create the appetite for liberty. Industry could be promoted only through high wages, which in turn produced more property. O'Connor cast his vision within a metaphor of the liberty tree: "Industry is the scion of liberty: she can spring but from her root; she can exist but under her shelter. Industry lives but by the sacred fund which rewards her exertions. It is liberty which rears and protects this sacred fund, it is by despotism, corruption and treason it is squandered."[184] The core of O'Connor's argument for an Irish republic was his thesis that the colonial connection with Britain destroyed emulation and so vitiated the energies of the nation. O'Connor asserted that the costs of empire borne by the colony were nothing other than deductions from the "national fund." The costs of church, police, justice, and education were added to by the imposition of bounties that distorted the Irish economy in favor of the British. The consequent depression of manufactures produced by "the robbery of your national capital" was the reason for "the low rate of wages by which your national industry is so miserably paid."[185] Ireland could not reach a "mutual and just state, [in which] the improvement of the mind and the exertion of talents are called forth, from their being the only means by which men can gratify their natural wants and desires," without political reform.[186] In the hands of O'Connor the language of commercial republicanism could take on a distinctively anticolonial hue. To imagine that Britain could prosper from the profits of commercial despotism "would be to suppose that distributive justice was banished from the earth, and to set at naught the moral principles which govern the world."[187] O'Connor united an anticolonial nationalism with a will to "inculcate those maxims of economy and liberty, without which no nation can be grand or respectable," and so revealed another layer of possibility within commercial republicanism.[188]

Radical political economy was the catalyst for the transvaluation of the terms of political life, and in particular of the meaning of political democracy, in France, Britain, and Ireland. The confluence of the French Republic and radical political economy even inspired American radicals, such as William Manning.[189] The new terms of politics, such as "happiness," "utility," "sentiment," and *industrie* created a new lexicon for political life even in countries that resisted the Revolution. But the development of these abstract and universalizing languages of politics did not occur in similar ways in these different contexts. The failure of the 1798 rebellion in Ireland brought experiments in new modes of politics to a shuddering halt. The embryo of a genuinely novel language of politics was aborted in favor of far simpler projects of identity; sectarian and national models of integration became the models for the politics of the nineteenth century in Ireland.[190] In Britain the contest with Napoleon allowed conservatives to resist the radical challenge and reassert a traditional understanding of the nation. The major radical movement of the early nineteenth century, Chartism, would express itself within the older idioms of the English political tradition, avoiding the universalizing languages of the French Revolution.[191] Only in France did republican institutions emerge. Only there could this lexicon find a concrete meaning through use. Only there could the practice and principles of a republic become an object of study and reflection rather than speculation. Commercial republicanism was a near universal intellectual phenomenon of the 1790s, but the exploration of its concrete commitments and its democratic potential could happen only in France.

The Tragedy of Citizenship

The complexity of the terms of political communication in the late 1790s were such as to frustrate the best efforts at systematization. The very creativity of the political culture—the novelty of its elaboration of the ideas of labor, rights, interests, property, and autonomy—posed intractable practical and theoretical problems. Modern political and moral argument had an inherent tendency to generate plural value orientations, which had to be coordinated for political life to be possible. The evaluative terms of political debate, such as happiness, might be shared among different political groups motivated by different interests, and the very abstraction of these terms meant that different contents might be proposed for them, creating a plural political debate. Yet the ambiguity and complexity that allowed for political communication were destructive of the civic commitment of any citizen who was not *parti pris*. The form of republican virtue was sustained in commercial republicanism, but the content was evacuated. The force of the republican argument derived from its protection of the moral autonomy of the citizen. The democratic institutions of the republic stabilized the beneficent effects of commercial society. But the civic commitment that had this salutary effect was formal; the commercial republic protected the moral nature of the citizen but abandoned the traditional republican goal of identifying the good life for the citizenry. Commercial republicanism celebrated the morally enabling aspects of life in a modern society. It did not describe the political duties of the citizenry clearly. Representing the plural values of the citizenry was a necessity for the political health of the republic, but finding the ultimate commitments of a citizen was a necessity for some citizens if they were to maintain their integrity.

This understanding of the problematic nature of the modern republic was clearest to Benjamin Constant. He committed himself to the idea of the republic precisely because it incarnated a free political culture: "Republican forms conserve a sort of tradition of liberty, which return it to its roots, even after intermissions of tyranny; despotic forms, on the contrary, conserve slavery, in such a way that the servile spirit becomes accustomed to its servitude, so that at the fall of a master no fiber of the spirit of the slave resonates with independence."[192] This commitment to republican forms was no substitute for political principle, though. In his first engagements with the dynamics of real politics Constant was liable to be blown about by the force of events. The most pressing issue at the foundation of the Directory was the rectitude of the law guaranteeing that two-thirds of the seats in the new Councils of Five Hundred and Ancients would be reserved for Conventionnels. Constant at first argued against limiting the choices open to voters; justice was a powerful enough force to consolidate the new regime, and the anti-Robespierrist party would emerge from true elections stronger for their acquisition of democratic legitimacy.[193] He rejected out of hand the suggestion that an abrupt transition to normal politics was impossible because political France was polarized between Terrorists and Royalists.[194] By September of that same year his confidence that anti-Robespierrism could hold together the political class around a constitutional consensus was shattered. On the second of the month he wrote in favor of the two-thirds law.[195] The Vendémiaire uprising showed that the appeal to political violence had become part of the repertoire of political action of all factions and was not restricted to the sans-culottes. The change in Constant's position on the issue of representation was highly pragmatic and reasonable, but it was not principled.

One consequence of Constant's capacity to see the attraction of all the value orientations of modern society was a collapse into relativism. Not that this could not have its own uses; his *De l'esprit de conquête et de l'usurpation* of 1813 effectively contrasted the impossibility of a military dictatorship in modern conditions with the solidity of a dynastic monarchy.[196] The effectiveness of this work was in no way compromised by Constant's view that a hereditary monarchy offered no resolution to the political crises of modern peoples.[197] Another consequence was a kind of shallow eclecticism, as his engagement with Bentham's utilitarianism revealed. Constant recognized the principle of utility as a useful idea capturing the modern orientation to enjoyment, but he rejected utilitarianism as a description of human agency, much less as a normative value and moral principle.[198] Constant was rescued from these dead ends by Germaine de Staël's sharper appreciation of the connection between moral plurality and the health of a modern republic, and of the need to defend moral plurality and republic in principle, rather than pragmatically: "there is nothing as monarchical as the heads of certain moral and political metaphysicians. They wish to derive everything from a single principle, while moral nature is moved by many principles."[199] Her imperative for the republic to recognize and amalgamate the moral principles of "law, interest, power, and reason" is at the root of Constant's efforts to understand the nature of the citizen who could do just that.[200] What drove Constant's exploration of the specific nature of political commitment to depths unplumbed by Staël was his experience of the psychological consequences of a world without compelling public faiths. Constant saw the most obvious effects of public indifference in the morale of the citizenry: "there is always something dull and insipid, in those who care only for themselves."[201] He described his civilization as anomic in this fashion: "we no longer know how to love, nor to believe, nor to will. Everyone doubts what he says, and smiles at the vehemence with which he says it . . . as a result the heavens offer no hope, earth no dignity, the heart no haven."[202] As he established in his novel *Adolphe,* modern freedom might be oriented toward the value of happiness, the fulfillment of the individual, but it would not make the moderns happy.[203] A different principle that would save them from total privatization would have to be found to describe the paradoxical nature of the public commitment of the moderns.

The double problem that faced Constant, of defending the private nature of modern people while at the same time overcoming that nature to find a ground for civic commitment, was central to his most developed piece of writing on politics, the *Principes de politique.*[204] Constant developed his famous parallel of the liberty of the ancients and the moderns in this book precisely to explore this theme. The core of his argument was that the participatory liberty of the ancients was impossible in modern conditions of large states and complex societies, and that in any case the liberty of the moderns was preferable since it did not rely on slavery. Modern liberty was egalitarian; everyone could be independent even if they were not materially equal. But hidden in this contrast was a set of more nuanced, almost paradoxical judgments. On the one hand, moderns could not live like ancient republicans because their psychic economy was differently ordered. Imagination inspired ancient citizens, whereas "the moderns have lost the ability to believe without proof. Doubt dogs their steps."[205] Because of the skepticism of modern people a legislator could not create a series of social institutions in a modern society to foster a spirit of liberty.[206] The capacity to believe that would animate such an institution among the ancients was absent among the moderns. On the other hand, modern people were more dependent on one another in social life: "social ramifications are greater than before. Even the classes that seem to be enemies are connected to one another by imperceptible but indissoluble ties."[207] The complex web of social relations tempered modern rationalism with habit, but these social habits were impervious to political manipulation. Constant's characterization of the modern social system as a mutually beneficial network, but one for which no one was responsible and which was impervious to willed political action in any case, accentuated his problem of collective action enormously. Nor did his problems end there; as Constant explored his comparison, the initial clarity of the opposition between the happiness of modern people and the virtue of ancients lost its sharpness. Ancients were self-abnegating, moderns sought only peace, tranquillity, and domestic happiness, but "more sacrifices have to be made to that peace than the sacrifices made by the ancients."[208] Since domestic happiness could be guaranteed only by citizens performing their political duty and "political liberty offers fewer pleasures than before," the protection of domestic happiness demanded its abandonment. But who would act to protect the pleasures and domestic joys of everyone else?

Buffeted by paradox, Constant was driven to analyze the condition of modern politics as tragedy. His most well known description of the tragic nature of modern political action is given in his 1819 speech *De la liberté des modernes comparée à celle des anciens*.[209] In its concluding paragraphs he again laid out the fundamental paradox of modern liberty: "the danger of modern liberty is that, absorbed as we are in the pleasures of our private independence, and in the pursuit of our particular interests, we too easily give up our share in political power."[210] The experience that tempted private individuals into the public sphere was the tragic sense of sublimity. The renunciation of private pleasures had its own reward in the creation of a new, sublime, individual. The modern political world had its equivalents of the fates and furies that had driven the characters of antique drama, but they were now internal to the psychology of individuals. "I will attest to this better part of our nature," Constant wrote, "that noble restlessness which pursues us and torments us, that ardor to extend our insight and develop our abilities."[211] He configured the political life of the moderns as a Promethean drama, which, ideally, would transfigure the entire population: "political liberty drives all citizens, without exception, to examine their most sacred interests, to widen their spirit, ennoble their thoughts, and establishes amongst them all a sort of intellectual equality, which is the glory and the power of a people."[212] The condition of a modern citizen might be tragic, bereft of a compelling public faith, but tragedy held its own rewards.

Constant's idea of the strange attraction of tragedy was derived from Burke's thoughts on the patterns of interaction of sublimity and beauty in society. Burke expressed the attraction of political tragedy over any sort of private experience even more vividly than did Constant:

Chuse a day on which to represent the most sublime and affecting tragedy we have; appoint the most favourite actors; spare no costs upon the scenes and decorations; unite the greatest efforts of poetry, painting and music; and when you have collected your audience, just at the moment when their minds are erect with expectation, let it be reported that a state criminal of high rank is on the point of being executed in the adjoining square; in a moment the emptiness of the theatre would demonstrate the comparative weakness of the imitative arts.[213]

Constant's sense of the real nature of the tragedy of modern politics did not respect Burke's adherence to classical aesthetic norms. While contemplating the actual and proximate experience of modern politics, the Revolution, Constant could not conform to the idea of the sublimely tragic public actor. Instead, Constant portrayed public life in the Revolution as tragicomedy.

The lack of faith characteristic of the modern condition was present, "even in the explosion of the most well planned outbreak."[214] The crowd, in Constant's description, "seems not to believe in its own ideas." Even as members of the crowd shouted encouragement to its leaders, the former mocked the latter in asides. The sublime pose of the leadership was undermined by the knowledge of the crowd: "you see them, as they follow their leaders, already looking forward to the moment when they will fall, and you notice in their counterfeit excitement a strange mixture of analysis and mockery."[215] Modern revolution was ironic, and the greatest irony was that the revolutionary crowds were aware of this, while those who thought they were leading the process were not. The sublimity was false, the fall of the revolutionary more a pratfall than an immolation in the fires of historical necessity. "The good sense of the human species understands that one does not do this for them," declared Constant.[216] The defense of liberty, which was the function of political life, was in most cases necessary but absurd; the only means to guarantee that the revolutionary did not become the victim of irony was to resort to violence, but the means would destroy the end, so there could be no guarantee of not being a historical fool.[217] The absurdity of public life in conditions of irony was almost bottomless; political cowardice "does not just call itself, prudence, reason, wisdom, understanding of how matters stand, it even sometimes names itself independence."[218] Constant was too clear-eyed about the actual conditions of political life he had seen genuinely to believe in the possibility of a general sublime political state. He conceived of politics as an experience of sublimity sodden in irony. However, after many pages describing the absurdities of modern politics he finished by reiterating the absolute necessity of political liberty: "to say that people can abandon liberty, is to hold that they resign themselves to being oppressed, incarcerated, separated from the things they love, stopped in their work, robbed of their goods, tormented for their opinions and their secret thoughts, dragged through dungeons and to the gallows."[219] The modern citizen, in his or her public role, was an ironist, but a passionate ironist and that passion was driven by fear.[220]

Constant's critical development of republicanism drew on the tension between the competing needs for a comprehensive political culture and a set of distinct political values. Sophie de Grouchy and Jean-Baptiste Salaville resolved this tension by focusing on sentimental dynamics played out in families, workshops, and markets. Benjamin Constant's drama was played out in the theater of the streets and revealed another possible outcome to the game of democratic politics. Constant's citizens were engaged in spectacle rather than work or communication and could be isolated and immobilized. Constant faced the possibility of anomic ironists constituting the citizenry of the republic. This critical perspective rescued modern republicanism from what could have been a debilitating dogmatism. Constant opened up an understanding of the limits of democracy from within the democratic camp.

The rich creativity of the republican political imagination was represented in the efforts of the Directory to create political, social, economic, and cultural institutions. As we follow the debates and institution building of the era, we see its themes enunciated repeatedly. The modern republic was democratic of necessity, committed to the defense of equality and the idea that the labor of every person qualified him or her for participation in political life. It embraced the forms of modern economic life as instrumentalities to foster moral independence among the citizens, which needed material independence to exist. It took an abstracted, universalist language—shared by the liberal, or constitutionalist, opposition—to express these explicit republican commitments. The interactions of republicans and liberals generated a novel landscape of political debate, an ecology within which differing values could be represented. The very abstraction of the key terms of republicanism allowed for varieties of interpretation and opposition. The greatest challenge for republican political culture was to align the universalism of its terms with the concrete commitments to the autonomy of the body of the citizenry. This challenge was met, and the meaning of modern republicanism was generated in the practical resolutions found in institution making. The practices of the republic fixed the meaning of its terms. Through participation in practical debates on such topics as the school system, the citizenry made meaning of these principles. Republicanism evolved from an ideology to a political culture that could represent the complexity of a modern society and sustain the life of a democracy.

CHAPTER 3

The Agricultural Republic as Rhetoric and Practice

Republican political thought was vibrant and creative in the later period of the Revolution. Writers like Salaville developed complex models of citizenship that acknowledged the criticisms of republican liberty put forward by liberals and conservatives. The contrasting answers to the problem of the constitution of the modern citizen created a robust and capacious understanding of the republic. Constant and Staël revealed how capacious modern democratic republicanism could be. Their rigorous interrogation of the logics of commitment and withdrawal that characterized modern individuals laid the basis for a republicanism without utopian illusions. To be effective, however, political language had to be as compelling as it was insightful. The speculations of Salaville, Say, or Constant were more normative than descriptive. They sought to persuade the citizens of the French republic to understand themselves as particular sorts of modern men and women and to guide their political actions appropriately. The categories and concepts they used to analyze the politics of the modern republic had to be given life and color in parliamentary debates, political assemblies, pamphlets, and journalism.

This junction of critical reflection and rhetorical performance had fascinated republican thinkers since antiquity. Political expression of this form was highly dependent on tropes. According to Quintilian, by use of "the right kind of metaphorical images, as well as by the figures of speech, the right reflections, and finally the right type of arrangement," the political actor should be able "to commend to our hearers what we are arguing, whether by winning approval for our conduct or prompting them to view the cause we are pleading in a favourable light."[1] As Quentin Skinner explains, classical rhetoricians, Quintilian in particular, understood that the power of metaphorical language lay in its ability to provoke the mind of the auditor to imagine vivid mental pictures encapsulating the vision of the speaker.[2] The commercial republicans would need such compelling images to persuade the population that their distinctive accommodation of the divergent tendencies in modern political life could provide the basis for a flourishing civic order and happy individual lives.

From Terror to the Fields

The rhetoric of modern republicanism crystallized in the general disillusionment with Jacobinism after Thermidor, Year II.[3] The perception that the understanding of citizenship promoted by the Montagne was antithetical to the nature of modern life, and particularly inimical to the arts and commerce, was generally shared. As discussed in the preceding chapter, republican writers were driven to provide an account of how the civic virtues and political commitment played a role in a modern commercial society. Their conception of a happy, industrious citizenry, uniting public good and private interest in an economy of pleasure had to be encapsulated in compelling tropes to be politically efficacious.

The abbé Grégoire created one of the most forceful and innovative images of the unity of the republic with modern commercial life in his coinage of the rhetoric of vandalism.[4] Grégoire argued that revolutionary violence was, in effect, antirevolutionary, that the destruction of the instruments and personnel of economic and cultural life was the result of the *ancien régime,* which had trained the people in infamy. The September massacres, he maintained, were "the fruit of a government without morality, and of the depravity of a court that had raised its scandalous monuments on the ruin of morality."[5] Grégoire created a polarity between the vandal, who stood for the degenerate subject of the *ancien régime,* and the republican, who understood how learning underpinned liberty.[6] The commercial life and learning of the republican were different from that of the citizen under the monarchy. Republican commercial life was based on the fulfillment of needs, not on the vagaries of fashion; it fostered virtue, rather than creating luxury; and it was generated from agricultural development rather than the unearned profits of long-distance trade. Grégoire used the image of the kitchen garden to describe the activity of the commercial republican:

> The precarious commerce in fashion, founded on the corruption and luxury of a destroyed court, will no doubt collapse, so much the better! Morality will be the gainer, and the improved mills of Durand will win us a more reliable profit than all the trash sold to the North every month. The Revolution

will destroy some English gardens: so much the better again! It is of greater consequence for us to have plentiful harvests than to build picturesque ruins, and the prospect of a good vegetable garden is fundamentally more pleasing than that of a cunningly designed formal garden.[7]

The false republican was the vandal, enemy of social life, and the true republican was the farmer. The field of the farmer became the defining image of the modern, commercial republic. The image was still in use in Year VI when J. M. Heurtault-Lamerville, proposing the creation of art schools, used it to distinguish his proposal from the academies of the Old Regime. Formal gardens were the epitome of the bad taste and bad morals of the monarchy: "architecture is reprehensible for having entered into the conspiracy against agriculture, . . . for having given itself to tastelessly overturning, for no good reason, our productive gardens, with no object but to amuse some bored men with a painstaking variety, with complex views, and with fictions whose only merit is the difficulties overcome to achieve it."[8] The citizen farmer became the central figure in the rhetoric of the modern republic, a rhetoric that sought to marry the civic commitment of the republican to the distinctive forms of modern social and economic life.

Grégoire gave a series of speeches on agricultural education through which he articulated a vision of a republican France regenerated through its commitment to improved agriculture. Training in agricultural science would make citizens of all Frenchmen, and their agricultural disposition would found an alternative political economy to one based on luxury goods.[9] The ruinous imports of colonial goods, which he alleged cost up to 300 million livres, could be replaced by French produce, if ingenuity and art were turned to the soil. Even money, that most corrupting of substances, could be cleansed by plowing it into the earth and, by creating work for the poor, helping to extirpate "the leprosy of poverty."[10] By instituting the first of the arts, agriculture, as the queen of the arts, modern commercial life could be integrated into the duties of republican citizenship. Agriculture was as virtuous as it was useful, and even profitable. Its satisfaction of personal needs would help to inculcate the habits of "questioning, experiment, and diligence."[11] It was the perfect activity for a modern republican, virtuous and commercial at a stroke.

Grégoire's reports were applauded in the *Décade philosophique*, which, while less convinced than he was that revolutionary vandalism could be totally distinguished from the Revolution, saw his ideas as a part of the reconstitution of republicanism.[12] His ideal of the reforming farmer as the proto-type of the republican was embraced with total enthusiasm, particularly by Joachim Le Breton, who wrote on rural economy for the paper.[13] Le Breton hammered home his message that the republican destiny of France could be achieved only through a commitment to reforming agriculture at every opportunity. He gave way to political lyricism in a piece on his hobbyhorse of swamp drainage: "When the laws have purified the moral atmosphere, and the industrious spirit of the French character has regained its luster, how beautiful the outcome of these projects will be . . . Agriculture and *moeurs* are the basis of the happiness that awaits us."[14] His most precise statement of the value of the ideal of the republican farmer was developed in his article on the report of Joseph Eschasseriaux to the Convention.[15] Two themes stand out of the approving account of the technical improvements that were to be encouraged in agriculture by the republican state: the idea of agriculture as the mainspring of a commercial society, and the defense of property. The first announced what was to be one of the recurring themes of the commercial republicans: "agriculture declines without commerce, and commerce is impossible without circulation"—therefore the state should promote the perfection of the transport system of the republic.[16] The idea of circulation and the policy of promoting the internal market was to be one of the most distinctive features of the Directory. The second, the defense of property, was more fundamental. Le Breton congratulated the committee for having declared "its respect for property, the incontrovertible basis of civil society."[17] This notion of the republican farmer as an element of civil society connected the rhetoric with the most important themes of commercial republicanism and broadened the basic figure of the virtuous farmer for a more developed rhetoric.

The conjunction of Eschasseriaux's report and the fall of Robespierre stimulated Joseph Borelly of Marseilles to attempt to develop his ideal of the republic as an agricultural regime in the summer of 1794. In his prospectus for the newspaper he founded, the *Journal d'agriculture et d'économie rurale*, he made exactly the same connection as Grégoire, accepting that virtue was necessary for the republic and that a commercial society might be corrupt, taking England for his example, but finally arguing that agriculture avoided this danger by promoting happiness "a new idea in Europe."[18] This idea of happiness was the central normative term of the commercial republicans, and Borelly extended his debt to their social thought by explaining how that happiness, which was the special virtue of a modern republic, was to be achieved. The action of improved farmers, left to their own devices, would generate social happiness through emulation: "Let us encourage the industrious citizens who apply themselves to the first of the arts, and thereby emulation, which we will generate amongst them, will spur them to make every effort to improve their produce and make it generally pleasing."[19] The idea of emulation, rather than competition, as the relationship between citizens as members of civil society was the basis for Borelly's argument that the proper economic commitment of the republic was to unrestricted circulation in internal and international free trade. "When internal commerce creates abundance, international trade generates itself, without any effort on the part of the government," he explained.[20] The logic of commercial society was to generate these happy results once that society was grounded in agriculture, "which conserves simplicity, innocence, and the purity of *moeurs*, and preserves them from the contagion of vice."[21]

The idea of agriculture opened up new ways to imagine a republican regime in 1794, but, other than Eschasseriaux, who commented on the means of improving the national herd, all these observers were interested in agriculture more as a principle of social organization than as an actual practice. Jean-Baptiste Dubois allowed himself the indulgence of a little irony, commenting that though everyone knew that the prosperity of the republic depended on agriculture, nobody seemed to know how to bring it about.[22] Dubois's thinking was both more reflexive and more concrete than that of other commentators. His knowledge of the state of agriculture was unsurpassed: he was editor of the *Feuille du cultivateur,* wrote on agricultural topics for the *Décade philosophique,* had been deputy commissioner to the Commission on Agriculture and the Arts, and was to be head of the fourth section of the Ministry of the Interior from the Year IV. Agriculture was for him a matter of direct concern rather than of philosophical speculation. He argued, though, that intensive agriculture, rotation of crops, new fodder crops, and other elements of the agricultural revolution inspired by English practice could be introduced only as a result of a change in values among farmers, despite their obvious technical superiority. Farmers might, ideally, be the backbone of the republic, but they would have to be transformed into communicating citizens before they could become productive exemplars: "It is only by operating all the levers of public opinion at the same time, by uniting theoretical and practical training, generating emulation and clarifying interests, rewarding hard work and compensating those unable to innovate, that we can assure the success of these measures."[23] Dubois cautioned that a system of emulation could not be forced into existence. There was a contradiction between working toward a nation of active, experimental farmers, who had "broken the chains of routine," and any kind of coercion.[24] He also pointed out to his readership the risks of change for any small farmer, who was likely undercapitalized. The debts incurred by changing farming methods might outweigh any profits earned. Lack of capital meant new lands could be underutilized. These risks meant that obvious educational methods, such as experimental farms, were unlikely to succeed, and explained why seemingly progressive developments, such as the clearing of waste ground, were in fact a disaster.[25] Dubois worked within the standard complex of republican ideas—of virtuous farmers, civil society, emulation, the democratic structures of the republic, and markets—but he did not indulge in the hope that one element of this system, be it farmers, markets, or the republican state, could order all the others. Instead, he foresaw a more complex pattern of alignment of these elements.

Dubois's point that an improvement in agricultural practice and a reorganization of the social and economic life of the republic were mutually interdependent was well taken. The reviewer in the *Décade philosophique* noted that according to Dubois's views, the real enemy of progress was not any particular agricultural practice but the tyranny of routine, and asserted that the only remedy for this was education widely conceived.[26] Dubois went on in subsequent writings to amplify the point, emphasizing that the success of agricultural reform in Britain and in Germany was due to the prestige given to agriculture in those countries. Even in the midst of a costly war the English had created a Board of Agriculture and put Arthur Young at its head.[27] France could go further by putting agriculture at the heart of a reformed educational system, and thereby integrate the nation through the creation of a common agricultural culture. Dubois imagined the classroom as a theater of the fields, creating a representation of the soil for the inhabitants of the towns who did not share in it directly: "The buildings that house the *écoles primaires* in the large towns should be adorned with exact representations, either painted or sculpted, of the productions of agriculture . . . this decoration should be designed in the form of the twelve months of the rural year, pointing out, for every month, the tasks to which the farmer should attend."[28] Universal agricultural education would foster liberty and commerce together by overcoming the prejudices and resistance to change that had characterized the degenerate peasantry of the *ancien régime*. Education in agriculture would be an education in the reality of the nation, the soil of the communes, and the skills needed to make that soil flourish. Agricultural education would thereby provide a new focus for fraternity. Armed with a positive knowledge of their country and its inhabitants, citizens should be encouraged to unite in societies to share and develop their useful knowledge—associations that would create a fraternity far removed from the political fantasies of the Jacobins.[29] Regenerated France would be a nation of fraternal, efficient, citizen farmers.

The convergence of so many authors on the idea of the citizen farmer as the antidote to the problems of the republic was obviously related to the political moment of the summer of 1794. Several concrete ideals to fill in the category of citizenship had been tested to destruction by the Revolution, from the ideal of loyalty to "nation, law, and king" to that of the sansculotte. The fall of Robespierre, and the subsequent discredit of the politics of the Montagnards, created another vacuum in revolutionary idealism that had to be filled. The diverse ways in which the notion of the citizen farmer could be explored and deployed, from Grégoire's simple use of it to establish categories of good and bad republican to Dubois's sophisticated development of the complex interactions of political and economic development, reveal its richness as an element of the political culture. The formal richness of the idea, its capacity to be developed as a metaphor for the nature of a modern republic, raises more questions than it answers. Did the rhetoric of the citizen farmer circulate in any effective way, or was it simply a placeholder for revolutionary idealism as it gave way before the emerging imperatives of class and social revolution?[30] Did it have scope to provide a ground from which the complexities of life in a large nation-state could be understood, or did it reduce to a moralism? Even more important, did this rhetoric speak across the bounds of politics, society, and economy the way it was designed to? Could the creative citizen farmer be found in France, or was he a fabrication derived from the premises of political economy? The notion of the citizen farmer was clearly close to the hearts of many republicans as they sought to redirect the regime in the summer of 1794. What remains to be seen is to what extent they could succeed in turning the sentiments of others toward the same object.

Ancient and Modern Farmers

The roots of the rhetoric of the citizen farmer were buried deep in European culture; the citizen farmer was one use of the ancient notion of the superior-

ity of the country to the city. The notion that the preeminently moral man is
the independent farmer, living amidst nature, was not revolutionary or even
Rousseauian in origin. The idea was classical, codified in the *Odes* and *Epistles*
of Horace and Virgil's *Georgics*. Horace's description of the joys of his Sabine
farm celebrated withdrawal from public life and was difficult to capture
for republican politics. His most obvious eighteenth-century legacy was the
praise of the art of living in Addison and Pope.[31] The georgic, by contrast,
was an intensely politicized form, especially in England. Anthony Low has
characterized the seventeenth century in England as a period of "georgic
revolution," a period in which the genre was the site of a reevaluation of
work as a social value.[32] As Low explains, the georgic configures labor as
heroism and turns the lowly peasant into the pillar of civilization. The flavor
of this English reception of Virgil is well transmitted in the verbs used by
Dryden in this section of his 1694 translation of the *Georgics:*

> Nor is the Profit small, the Peasant makes;
> Who smooths with Harrows, or who pounds with Rakes
> The crumbling Clods: Nor *Ceres* from on high
> Regards his Labours with a grudging eye;
> Nor his, who plows across the furrow'd Grounds,
> And on the Back of Earth inflicts new wounds.[33]

The smoothing, pounding, laboring, crumbling, and plowing going on here
idealized a much more dynamic relationship to nature and the self than the
alternative mode, the pastoral, which was associated with aristocratic *otium*.
The georgic sensibility held the farmer to be the basis of civilization and
the paradigm for every civilized art. Low argues that the georgic spirit contributed to and was promoted by the English Civil War, and "this georgic
revolution prepared the way for widespread acceptance of the modern agricultural revolution during the eighteenth century."[34] Andrew McRae even
argues that Low underestimates just how potentially revolutionary the
georgic could be and points to Gerrard Winstanley's primitive communism
as one terminus for the trajectory of the form in the seventeenth century.[35]
In the eighteenth century the georgic as a genre in England eventually went
from being a revolutionary assertion of the value of labor to being the dominant sensibility of the improving country gentleman, and thus lost much of
its critical edge.[36] Addison in particular was central to the reinterpretation of
the georgic as a form, with its more radical content suppressed: "the precepts
of husbandry are not to be delivered with the simplicity of a Plow-Man, but

with the address of a Poet."[37] French versions of the Addison georgic did exist but had limited social resonance.[38] Instead, the political idea of the value of agricultural labor was most strongly represented in the tradition inspired by Fénelon, which praised agriculture for incarnating a possible alternative to absolutist statecraft.[39] The georgic was still potentially a revolutionary genre in France, where the work of reorienting society toward the worldly and common virtues of labor and exchange was still to be done.

The newspaper *La feuille villageoise* was the most important agent that sought to align the early stages of the Revolution with an agricultural ideal.[40] First published in September 1790 under the editorship of Joseph-Antoine-Joachim Cérutti, the weekly newspaper was the most successful periodical of the early years of the Revolution, attaining a circulation of 15,000 at its peak in 1791.[41] Cérutti deliberately positioned the newspaper equidistant from all factions and explained that its function was to support the Revolution by explaining the new constitution and laws for rural dwellers. Its message, that the Revolution heralded a transformation of agricultural practice, was not politically neutral. Addressed as it was to "rich landowners, well-off farmers, patriotic curés, doctors and surgeons," the *Feuille villageoise* painted a picture of a socially immobile world.[42]

In Cérutti's ideal, inequality of station would be balanced by mutuality of respect, and the regime of liberty would not threaten rural elites. He drew this moderatism directly from Horace. His edition of translations of three of the Odes in 1789 was inspired, he wrote, by their applicability to the moment.[43] He contrasted Horatian harmony and moderation with the "military and popular anarchy" that had massacred Foulon de Doué and Bertier de Sauvigny.[44] Configuring himself as the peaceful moderate to Barnave's uncontrolled anarchist, he used Horace's voice to condemn Barnave's dismissal of the murders: "As cold as Scylla, some Frenchmen have tried to justify the executions by the populace by comparing them to the numberless murders committed in a battle . . . an entire army, wiped out its weapons in hand, is a greater calamity, but a less revolting crime than having a single man, without arms or defense, assassinated by a mob motivated by misery."[45] The alternative to Horatian harmony was social war. Cérutti exerted himself to paint the delights of rural harmony in a manner most compatible with the premises of the Revolution. He exercised his rhetorical skills to persuade his audience that the Revolution would not destabilize the society but strengthen, in the manner of the Swiss, "the love of the *pays* [locality], which never leaves them no matter where they are, which connects them, be they abroad or at home, to their wild mountains, to their rustic *moeurs,* and to their native laws."[46]

One of the favored pedagogical devices of the *Feuille villageoise* was the letter sequence between individuals from different social groups. In one sequence a fictive peasant and his landlord discussed the formal nature of equal rights and their fundamental inequalities of duty, position, and function. In another, written by Madame de Genlis, Félicie addressed Marianne, her one-time servant now married to a farmer. They explored how equality of recognition and respect did not entail social equality: "nothing other than vice is low, and we owe respect only to talent and virtue: soon good women will be the only *Grandes Dames.*"[47] But *grandes dames* there still would be, and as Félicie explained, this was providential, because "human society is founded on the need people have of one another . . . this is why God has placed poor and rich on earth, because God would not have distributed his blessings so unequally, were it not to have us all connected through charity and gratitude."[48] The frame for the Horatian politics of the *Feuille villageoise* was not the practice of agriculture but the prospect of landscape, which composed all the elements of the rural world into an ideal order. As Cérutti put it, in his poem on the gardens at Betz:

> The nourishing farm and the opulent castle
> Seem to acknowledge one another from afar
> One blesses its treasure, the other its master.[49]

In the context of the rural revolution the *Feuille villageoise* under the editorship of Cérutti was conservative in inspiration. It sought to buttress the social power of rural elites, whose position was under threat from the peasant mobilization first seen in the Great Fear and sustained in peasant refusal to acknowledge the difference between "feudal" and "real" property in the privileges abolished on 4 August 1789.[50] Most important, it had little or nothing to say about actual agriculture. It was concerned about the politics of the peasantry but vague on agricultural improvement, alternatives to the three-field system, or any other specifically agricultural question. Agriculture, for the *Feuille villageoise* until 1792, was a synonym for political revolution with social stability and only a gesture toward economic modernization. This bucolic vision could not survive the intense political competition of the Revolution.

When Cérutti died on 3 February 1792, the editorship quickly passed to Philippe-Antoine Grouvelle and, after his appointment as ambassador to

Denmark in 1793, to Pierre-Louis Ginguené.[51] After Cérutti's death the paper abandoned its apolitical stance and explicitly supported the Gironde; in so doing it lost its publisher, Jean Desenne, and became part of the Imprimerie du Cercle Social.[52] This political evolution was mirrored by a generic evolution as the newspaper's vision developed toward the georgic. The departure was most marked within the eulogy of Cérutti written by his friend François de Neufchâteau. While he praised Cérutti's moderation and hard work, he drew a distinction between the commitment of the man of letters, such as Cérutti, and himself. Whereas the peasantry were an object of contemplation arranged in a social order and a landscape for Cérutti, François de Neufchâteau "was born amongst them, live[d] amongst them and for them, and look[ed] forward to dying amongst them. I know intimately how they are worthy of the work put into enlightening them in order to rescue them from the barbarous old ways."[53] The peasant rather than the landowner was the focus of this way of conceiving of the rural world. The idea that the peasants were the readers of the paper also guided Ginguené's editorial redirection toward more practical farming advice. The georgic voice did not debar ethical speculation in favor of market reports; it merely demanded that political and ethical ideals be envisaged through the identity of the peasant rather than the man of letters.

Ginguené's most achieved version of this idea was the series he ran on "the rural Socrates" through Brumaire and Frimaire of Year III.[54] The rural Socrates was based on a French translation of the work of the same name by the Zurich agronomist Hans Hirzel, which had appeared in 1762.[55] In the version published by the *Feuille villageoise* Ginguené described the rural Socrates, named Kliyog, as the model peasant and as the vehicle of the idea of agricultural labor as the essence of the republican; "a free man would be hard pressed to find more satisfying work and a more agreeable way of life than that of the farmer . . . by generating activity in the soul and the love of work, it sows the seeds of the purest pleasures."[56] The series was characterized by the distinctive realism of the genre, giving specific instructions on such topics as stall-feeding cattle and the importance of fertilizer for the production of fodder crops. The realism was even brought up to date by the attention to debt. Kliyog's 94-*arpent* farm was inherited encumbered with a 12,500-livre debt, which demanded repayments of 500 livres every year, exactly 4 percent of the principal, at the traditional rate in the notarial, small-scale credit markets of rural France.[57] Ginguené defended debt and deplored consumption. Every profit should be reinvested to extend the farm; to do otherwise would be to instrumentalize the work that was its own reward: "it is only through dedicated and constant work that the earth gives up its treasures."[58] The expanded description of the peasant of the georgic made the limitations of its original version all too apparent. The eulogy of agricultural labor came at the expense of every other kind of activity. The children of the household were not allowed to eat at table until they could contribute work to the family economy, "and they learn in this way that the person who does not work, and gives no help to society, can only be considered an animal, who may have a right to his sustenance, but not to the honor of being treated as an equal and one of the family."[59] The economic behavior of the Kliyog family did not seek to maximize production and exchange, the circulation of a modern economy, but to accumulate land and assert autarchy. According to Ginguené, the family should be a tiny, Spartan republic, dedicated to work and absolute autonomy. All the offspring of the family should remain under patriarchal authority, sharing their goods in common: "one carefully avoids the tiniest appearance of personal profit, and thereby every form of immoderate love of money is banished from the house."[60] Even village festivals were spurned by Kliyog, for fear his children might acquire some influence from outside the family and a taste for any pleasure other than work. The georgic eulogy of labor, unmediated by any other principle, was unrecognizable as an account of a modern republicanism.

Despite its limitations, the georgic remained an attractive genre through which to attempt to rectify the problems of the Revolution. The preeminent translator of Virgil, Jacques Delille, whose version of the *Georgics* went through twenty editions in the eighteenth century, created his *L'homme des champs, ou les géorgiques françaises* of 1797 in the hope of bringing peace.[61] He drew a direct analogy between himself and Virgil, both writing in time of civil war, and idealized both the peace of the farmer, removed from public life, "cultivating, his gardens, the virtues, and the arts," and his contribution to the republic, gaining more victories than the armies by doubling the harvest.[62] Delille's real preoccupation was the politics of culture (rather than agriculture); his argument was that the Revolution had been undermined by the aesthetic preferences for tragedy and comedy and the absence of a taste for georgic moderation.[63] He aimed to narrow the gap between the overproduction of tragedy and the underproduction of georgic, whose thin genealogy he traced from Virgil and Lucretius, through Boileau, Pope, and Saint-Lambert.[64] Delille was criticized for this ambition. Pierre Jean-Baptiste Chaussard rejected georgic in favor of the preeminence of the traditional neoclassical hierarchy.[65] Despite its less than enthusiastic reception, the idea that the Revolution was best represented and stabilized through a "middle" aesthetic, adequate to the emotions and texture of common life, was a creative move in the cultural politics of the Revolution. It even still has resonance, but it was far removed from political economy and its relationship to republicanism.[66] The georgic voice was a necessary, but insufficient, ground for a rhetoric of an agricultural republic.

The "agrarian law" was the third classical referent, after pastoral and georgic, through which the revolutionaries imagined the relationship between agriculture and revolution. The idea of an agrarian law, of a general redistribution of either public lands or all land, was derived from Roman and Spartan history.[67] As R. B. Rose has shown, the agrarian law circulated as a speculative idea among publicists, especially those close to the Cercle Social, such as Fauchet and Bonneville, rather than as a real political demand of any group of peasants or the sans-culottes.[68] Yet despite being a phantom threat, the Convention, on 18 March 1793, acceded to Barère's demand that those promoting an agrarian law face the death penalty.[69] As Peter Jones has pointed out, the only real analogy to a demand for an agrarian law was the *partage* movement, aimed at breaking up common land.[70] Yet even though the agrarian law had no social constituency, and the proposal that it be outlawed was introduced only as a result of the incoherence of the Convention's response to rural agitation, the idea was important in the development of the rhetoric of the citizen farmer.[71] Babeuf's political development toward total egalitarianism, for instance, was grounded in his fascination with the idea.[72] More important, it made way for a specifically republican form of agricultural improvement, the small, mixed farm, by creating a ground from which to critique the English practice of enclosure and the political economy of the physiocrats. The fascination of the agrarian law was that the end it envisaged, a nation of property-owning smallholders, was shared, while the means, expropriation, was abhorred. The practical problem was to find another means of creating the citizen farmer.

The independent citizen smallholder was far removed from the economic and social forms promoted by the British agricultural revolutionaries. John Sinclair, the head of the British Board of Agriculture, had denounced independent smallholding as "republican farming" and proposed a community of tenant smallholders working under the inspiration of their landlord.[73] Arthur Young went so far as to argue that independent farmers were inherently tyrannical, putting large landowners "at the mercy of the many, who were so lately his inferiors," and would inevitably lead to the ubiquitous agrarian law.[74] The British commitment to the leadership of landlords in agricultural reform was mirrored by the same commitment among physiocrats. Mirabeau père had stressed the irrelevance of political principles to economic transformation: "There is only one production and consumption in the world. The only difference between one nation and another is that the first obeys a monarch, the second a Doge, the third a Senate, etc. But production and consumption, which only obey the universal social order, are not divided into states and provinces."[75] Young and Sinclair's defense of landlords was also a defense of their mode of improvement: large enclosures and high rents. What their defense made obvious was that this preference was political rather than primarily economic.

As Robert Allen and Cormac O'Gráda have argued, there was no evidence that large farms were more productive than small, and on the contrary the major improvements in agricultural productivity had been promoted by smallholders despite enclosure.[76] The enclosure movement in England emerged as the preferred strategy of agricultural reform because of the political decision to take no account of the property rights of smallholders. Thus the power of political institutions—and not the internal search for increased productivity within the rural economy—determined the outcomes.[77] The ground of the agrarian law made explicit the connection between economic logic and political interest and allowed the politics of the landowner to be met with a politics of the peasant. This political polarity became so embedded in the political culture of revolutionary France that it could be used as an analogy for other forms of illegitimate domination. In Year V, Louis-Pierre Couret-Villeneuve analogized those who lacked respect for teachers to "the rich *économiste* actively scorning the country dweller who works for the landowner for a modest wage, placing him among the men condemned to drudgery, forgetting the respect due to him and the fact that the harvest is gathered with the sweat of his brow."[78] The agrarian law was the site on which the georgic voice acquired its political color. The comparison with the politics of English methods of enclosure and improvement created the ground for a modern republican project for the creation and support of the small-scale citizen farmer. Just as English politics sustained its agricultural economy, so French politics could create a different agricultural world. What was needed to complete the foundations of a developed rhetoric was an insight into the manner in which French political institutions would generate a republican agriculture.

The political figure who best exploited the possibilities for explaining the interaction between republican politics and republican agriculture was

François de Neufchâteau. In his various writings on agronomy during the Revolution he had tried to work out how a series of institutions—such as public granaries, improved bureaucratic oversight of agricultural practice, or the foundation of new villages in waste lands—might contribute to the creation of a virtuous economy.[79] These ideas, especially public granaries, were criticized for being too dependent on the economic practice of the Italian republics and thus inappropriate for a large state like France.[80] His years spent (from 1795 to 1797) as a commissioner of the Executive Authority, the forerunner of the prefect, provoked him to a new consideration of the relationship of agriculture to the republic.[81] His ideas were generated from a further development of the critical comparison of France with England characteristic of commercial republican thought. English prosperity, he argued, was a result of enclosure, long leases, and a uniform tax on land; any progress in France would have to be based on English agricultural science and fiscal insight.[82] However, his praise for England was tempered by his realization that agricultural improvement there had operated solely to the benefit of large landowners: "I am far from sharing the enthusiastic preference of Arthur Young, Stewart, and the English in general for large holdings."[83]

France would need a land reform measure that reflected its republican constitution and would avoid promoting shameful private luxury, "which is the devouring ulcer of despotic states."[84] He stated that the means to this end was the application of democracy. The goal of republican land reform should be independent farmers on consolidated holdings; communes should have the right to vote to redistribute and consolidate their lands on the basis of a cadastral survey to be undertaken at the expense of the state.[85] The law enabling these changes should define the grades of land and the means of division, he said, but the act was to be at the will of the inhabitants of the commune. Since the measure would acquire democratic legitimacy, it could not offend particular interests, and therefore only a majority, rather than unanimity, was necessary to initiate it. It would be a signal example of the superiority of the republican over other forms of commercial society: "I do not wish to promote larger farms by the consolidation project that I am proposing . . . A few rich men do not make a nation. A great number of men, content, sober, hard-working, that is the basis of a free people."[86] Moreover, such a measure would come about as a result of the application of republican principles to the problems of commerce. The modern commercial small farmer would have to be republican, because only the republic had the means to create him and an interest in supporting him. While the particular legal instrument François de Neufchâteau desired was never passed into law, the strategy, of using the norms and institutions of the republican state to create the republican economy, was the economic policy of the latter years of the Directory. This was especially so after François de Neufchâteau became minister of the interior in 1797.

The rhetoric of the agricultural republic was grounded in deeply held ethical and political assumptions. The moral superiority of farming to other kinds of social participation was a trope shared by political cultures as different as that of the new American republic and the Jewish community of Metz.[87] By co-opting this idea as a means of illustrating their conception of the polity, the commercial republicans captured a powerful instrument for the legitimation of the regime. However, under the conditions of the Revolution mere alignment with a powerful tradition of moral and political expression was not a functional political strategy. The rhetoric of the agricultural republic would have to enable social and political action as well as legitimate social and political institutions. The agricultural republic had to be made, not simply administered, and had to be made in adverse conditions. Despite the acknowledged importance of agriculture to the country the revolutionary assemblies before 1795 had not succeeded in creating a coherent agricultural policy or even a coherent legal framework within which such a policy might evolve. The Code Rurale, hastily cobbled together as one of the last acts of the Constituent Assembly, asserted the rights of property without limiting the communal rights of pasturage and gleaning. It made no provision for the consolidation of scattered holdings, the first prerequisite for an improved agriculture.[88] A vague awareness that the long-term success of the Revolution required some transformation in landholding and agricultural practice was no substitute for a more considered approach to the tasks of consolidation, the encouragement of stock-holding, and the introduction of new fodder crops, to mention but three of the themes of the *agronomes.* The invention of the figure of the improving citizen farmer was a powerful strategy for constructing a modern republic. The original insight would have to be developed into a detailed representation of a commercial republic from which a series of policies and actions could be derived if the rhetoric was to have any political effect.[89]

Developing the Commercial Republic

The publicists who elaborated the idea of the commercial republic formed an identifiable network around the Ministry of the Interior and especially its most effective minister, François de Neufchâteau.[90] Two of the most important figures, Dubois and Ginguené, headed departments in the ministry and had been editors, respectively, of the *Feuille du cultivateur* and the *Décade philosophique,* the most important newspapers to this political tendency. The *Feuille du cultivateur* was so important to the goals of the ministry that it subsidized three thousand copies a week for circulation to the departments.[91] Other agrarian publicists, such as Jean-Baptiste Rougier la Bergerie and Henri-Alexandre Tessier, were appointed as supplementary members of the Agricultural Council.[92] The ministry was both the administrative and the intellectual heart of the effort to construct a commercial republic; "all the other elements of the government can progress without effect, if the interior falls behind or is even just neglected."[93] Political circumstances conspired to give the minister of the interior unwarranted freedom of maneuver. The section of the interior, the subcommittee of the Directory with oversight over the actions of the ministry, was headed by La Révellière-Lépeaux, who was unable to assert himself.[94] François de Neufchâteau could exploit this lassitude, since his appointment as minister was achieved through the good graces of Jean-François Reubell, the dominant figure on the Directory.[95] During his office, and that of his intellectual ally Letourneur, the ministry, understood in this wide sense, was the central motor for the development and the circulation of the commercial republican project. The importance of the ministry as the heart of the republic became widely recognized. Dominique-Joseph Garat, proposing the department's budget to the Council of Five Hundred in 1798, stated that "through the departments of justice, finance, war, and the navy, we further the most salient interests of the Republic; in the administration of the interior we govern the Republic itself."[96]

The notion of the commercial republic, as I have discussed, was inspired by the insight that modern politics and modern social life could, ideally, reinforce each other, that a prosperous country would be a free one. Conservatives and liberals contested this notion of the modern citizen as both political and social. Boissy d'Anglas, for one, separated work and citizenship in his comments on the regime: "to make France a country in continual assembly was to deprive agriculture of those men who should attend to it with assiduity, and to deprive the warehouse and the workshop of those who would better serve the country with their work than by useless speeches and superficial discussions."[97]

In the publications of the ministry, agriculture was used as a proxy image for a way of life, a set of *moeurs* that could unite work and citizenship: "Citizens, the task of a republican government that has triumphed over its enemies is to employ all our forces to consolidate the basis of liberty and its own power. All our ills derive from the oppression and demoralization of agriculture . . . It is by perfecting that fruitful art which promotes morality, enhances the population, creates and maintains liberty that we will induce a new vigor in our commerce."[98] The agricultural mission of the commercial republic was not merely economic, nor was it relevant only to farmers. Rather, it was a political representation of the republic that was offered to all citizens. As a letter from the ministry to the commissioners in the departments put it, "every French citizen must be aware of the importance of agriculture and assign it first place in the sources of national prosperity."[99] In his portrayal of the agricultural republic François de Neufchâteau reimagined many of the features of revolutionary political culture. In his explanation of the rather prosaic necessity to conserve the republic's forests he transformed the tree of liberty: "We have restricted ourselves, up to now, to a single liberty tree in every commune. A lone tree is a sad thing, what does one tree per commune amount to? Let us plant two before every house. Let us sow entire woods, vast forests; let us raise natural temples to liberty with portals of greenery, and may the Republic grow in strength with its trees."[100] His image took the already existing symbol of the republic, the tree of liberty, and turned it into a new symbol of a commercial republic. Liberty trees became commercial forests but retained their sacral aura. The plantation policy became the paradigm of the practice of the commercial republic: "happy the man who inspires this spirit in his countrymen, and who arouses in them the love of plantations."[101] The idea was to infuse commerce with the values of the republic and the republic with the values of commerce.

The notion of agricultural, or commercial, liberty was complex. It was understood as a structural possibility of modern life, but not as a spontaneous resolution of its many facets. Commercial liberty would have to be induced by government action inspired by agricultural science.[102] The government's role was to provide credit and education, as an aid to improvement, and to guarantee protection for the results of improvement through the principle of respect for property.[103] That the government had this role in creating the conditions for liberty was a result of the unfortunate history of the nation. The inheritance of monarchical rule meant that economic liberty, like political liberty, would have to be taught to the people. Agricultural policy was presented as a paradigm of a new politics of regeneration, more the education of the population than the excision of the counterrevolutionaries. It was also a kind of therapy: "as with those long illnesses which require a convalescence longer again, so oppression has produced a laziness, an inertia from which the farmer cannot be rescued except through the attention of the government."[104] The farmer encapsulated within himself the history of the nation. The Revolution had returned him to his liberty; it was now the task of the government to make him capable of exercising it.

The most pressing inertial effect that had to be overcome, if the ideal of the individual peasant family farm was to become a reality, was the three-field system. Joseph Eschasseriaux had argued as early as Year II that consolidation, enclosure, and improvement could happen only if this system was suppressed.[105] It was used as a symbol of everything that was wrong with French agriculture. The vast tracts of land left fallow could more profitably be sown with the new root crops to support a larger national herd; the introduction of fodder crops and the replacement of commons by meadows would promote a significant improvement in breeds.[106] As a result, agriculture would feed a larger population with the meat of liberty rather than the thin gruel of slavery.[107] The issue of the growing population became an important plank of the development of commercial republicanism. As Mathieu Depère pointed out, the very improvement in life fostered by the Revolution could be self-limiting, unless the republic created the conditions for increased productivity. "Better food and the sentiment of happiness will infallibly contribute to growth in population; if food supply commensurate with that growth can be found, the population will strengthen the republic; if not, then the most grave consequences will follow."[108] Small, improved farms would supply the growing population, without demanding the wholesale clearances of peasant proprietors, as happened in Scotland.[109] The three-field system was also a political symbol of considerable importance. Its continuation was a standing memorial to monarchical oppression. Its pattern of land use—with villagers living in nucleated villages rather than as free men on their own land—inscribed feudal relations into the landscape. François de Neufchâteau drew the political point: "superstition, in league with feudalism, seeing mankind as a herd under its control, would not allow its slaves to remove their cabins from the shadow of the castle or the sound of the bells . . . Finally, the land is freed, man emancipated."[110] As a rural manifestation of the routine and ignorance of the *ancien régime* it could legitimately be excoriated without denigrating the peasants who lived under it. The problem facing the development of a productive republic, in this discourse, was not peasants' resistance to the demands for increased agricultural production from the state, but their lack of education in rural science, and the fault for this lay with the monarchy.[111]

Considerable practical and legal obstacles complicated attempts to encourage individual peasant proprietors. Notwithstanding, the image of the individual peasant proprietor promoting commerce and exchange through the circulation of goods became the central image of the economy for commercial republican thinkers. Agriculture made modern commercial life safe for republics, and improved agriculture would stimulate increased manufacturing. "One may imagine manufactures as outlets offered by the arts to primary goods . . . one may further argue that extended commerce, increased domestic consumption, and an expanded exportation of manufactured goods will increase agricultural production by encouraging the farmer to raise from the earth the primary goods to exchange for manufactures."[112] The vision of the republican economy as an exchange of the goods of the city and the country allowed republican writers to imagine the city not as the site of degenerating luxury, but as the mainspring of a virtuous economy. The commerce and the arts of the city would respond to a flourishing agriculture.[113] Conversely, the prerequisite for agricultural improvement was the existence of towns like Paris, where the density of population meant that emulation drove innovation and efficiency forward.[114] France, writers argued, because of its geographical situation, was uniquely suited to reconcile city and country, virtue and pleasure, modern and ancient; the role of the government was simply to aid in the achievement of that destiny.[115]

The discourse of the agricultural republic provided a representation of the citizen as farmer and from that basis could function as a means of reconciling the features of a modern society with the demands of republican politics. The power of this language can be seen in its ability to reconcile the republic to two of the most troublesome features of modern commercial life, property and markets. This was already inherent in the ideas of republican political science discussed in the last chapter, but the discourse of the agricultural republic was able to put rhetorical meat on the formal bones. The fundamental argument was that property and markets were the conditions for trade, and trade created prosperity: "liberty of commerce incontestably creates abundance, abundance in turn encourages speculative activity, and these are always conducted where one enjoys the greatest liberty . . . the liberty to dispose of goods internally, or abroad, necessarily augments and multiplies the products of agriculture and the arts; the competition created by that liberty causes the works of industry to be perfected and improves the harvest."[116] Agriculturally oriented republicans stressed the contribution of free trade to the welfare of the country. A free grain trade, they argued, was essentially an egalitarian measure since it lowered the death rate of the urban poor.[117] Infringements on the rights of property, such as uprooting hedges, were effectively theft from the poor and so a crime against the republic.[118] Without the protection of property the engines of republican improvement—emulation and *industrie*—would lose their effect.

Such an argument in favor of modern commercial life was not necessarily an argument in favor of a modern democratic republic. The necessary nexus between politics and the economy needed a moral and political argument. This was established through the idea that free trade was the economic principle of modern republics and its restriction that of monarchies.[119] Monopoly, they argued, had evolved from the reactions of early modern monarchs to the successes of the free Italian states.[120] They developed this idea through an elaboration of the innovative reading of the British political economists, especially Smith, characteristic of the commercial republicans. When commenting on Smith they put forward their clearest statements of the superiority of a commercial society to any other social form. "In all large societies the progress of industry and commerce forms a common stock of riches, in which everyone has an unequal share, but from which no one is excluded. This is one of the admirable laws of the supreme legislator, who has created no privileges, and who wishes that all of humanity share in the discoveries of one people, or even one man."[121] Their great criticism of Britain was that it did not live up to Smith's vision.

Monarchical Britain was at war with republican France because "it feared to see the domination of the seas that it had usurped taken away from the English nation."[122] The idea of a Britain hamstrung by its own monarchical institutions was a significant nuancing of the rhetoric of the British Carthage that had inspired Robespierre.[123] The British ministry's perverse strategy to crush the emerging competitor was to establish "a universal monarchy of the seas," in alliance with the continental despots who would be allowed the "domination of the land."[124] The British could not fulfill the promise of economic liberty because they did not have full political liberty. Their revolution had not been profound enough, whereas "here, on the contrary, France has been shaken to its foundations and created a revolution so total and profound, that no other example of the type exists in the world."[125] The British instead were driven to continue the process of undermining the "Gothic Constitution" of Europe that had begun with the attempt at world domination by the Hapsburgs.[126] The task for the commercial republic of France was to separate the wheat from the chaff of English experience: "let us abjure their appalling politics, detest their corrupting government; but let us compete with their agriculture, and study the methods for improving that useful art."[127] In emulating, and so transcending, the British experience, the French nation would have its best possible revenge on Britain.[128]

The comparison with Britain was extended to develop an ideal of the regenerated international trading system that would be promoted by France once it was successful in its war with England. France, in the view of the commercial republicans, was only the latest in the line of agricultural free states that had struggled with Britain.[129] While Britain could see the war only as a struggle for control of the colonial trade, France, mindful of the crimes that had created and sustained that trade, wished to transform it.[130] One strategy for transformation was to do away with the necessity for slavery by replacing colonial products with home-grown commodities. A scheme for the production of sugar from honey promised that "no longer will we owe the sweetest of our foods to the tears and sweat of some thousands of slaves, but to free men, property-owning and happy."[131] Products that could not be grown in the metropole would be raised in new colonies of free citizens.[132] What could not be produced by France could be traded for in a new republican trading bloc, with the United States for partner. "Would it not be pleasant if this country was a second France, a piece of ourselves, a peaceful France, even when the other is warlike and victorious?" Constantin-François de Chasseboeuf de Volney asked La Révellière-Lépeaux.[133] Fighting for the freedom of the seas against English monopoly was even a cause that could unite all of Europe behind France.[134]

The model of a world order governed by a republican ideal of trade relations was the most comprehensive vision generated by the commercial republicans. It was also the ground on which the commercial republicans were driven to confront both the insights of the liberals and the exigencies of politics. How might such a republican trading block be constructed? Some figures around Reubell conceived of it as an imperial project for France, arguing for aggressive colonization in Louisiana.[135] Everyone with any knowledge of America thought this absurd. The United States would not allow itself to be brought into the orbit of any European power: "nobody wants either the English or the French for masters."[136] The only sensible political strategy for the French was to create as much good will as possible in the United States while quietly supporting the anti-Federalists.[137] Cultural diplomacy met with some success; Harvard College, for one, had expressed its warm thanks for the gifts of mineral samples and copies of the *Journal des mines* in 1795.[138] A Franco-American trade axis seemed to make sense.

For all the attractions of the American option, which was to resurface in the trade negotiations of 1801 after the election of Jefferson to the presidency, it was a chimera. The commercial republicans understood that the Federalists had no desire for a Franco-American axis, and suspected them of the worst possible intentions: La Révellière-Lépeaux thought John Adams sought to recreate a monarchy and a nobility and only excused Washington from such ideas because of his past.[139] The Jay Treaty of 1796 forced even Joseph Fauchet, who as ambassador at Philadelphia had been a champion of improved relations, to admit that the Franco-American trade alliance was a dead letter. Republican solidarity was not evolving, and even the advantages that had been gained by Charles Gravier de Vergennes in the negotiations of 1778 were being eroded.[140] Moreover, the obstacles to the Franco-American alliance went far beyond the contingencies of politics. As Talleyrand argued, the hope that an independent United States would redirect its trade toward France had been entirely misplaced. England continued to dominate the American trade, and independence had helped by freeing England of the costs of governing the colony. Independence, "far from being a problem for England, has been advantageous to it in many ways."[141] Outside the wishes and desires of either Federalists or Democrats the nature of commercial relations determined that America would remain within the trading sphere of England. The chains of credit and the ties of taste bound them together. "Thus the American trader is tied to England not only by the nature of his business, by the need for the credit he will get and the weight of debt he has received, but even more by the irresistible law of the taste of the consumer."[142] The very nature of modern commercial relations, as currently constituted, integrated America into the British trading system. France could not hope for help from an element of the world with which it was at war.

Talleyrand's observations tended to support liberal rather than republican interpretations of the international trading system. The idea of a commercial republic might be intellectually coherent, and even rhetorically compelling, but could it be practically achieved? The core commitment of the commercial republic was to increase the freedom and the welfare of the population; its central claim was that democratic politics released productive energies. The happiness of the people was understood to mean this twofold flourishing. According to the liberal critique, the economy was a separate sphere, and to allow political imperatives to approach it was to corrupt its proper functioning. By 1799 even some whole-hearted republicans such as Charles

Theremin were accepting this view. The republic was an ideal generated by the aristocracies of the slave societies of Greece and Rome, and as such it was inapplicable to modern politics.[143] This contrasted vividly with his earlier argument that only a republic could create the theater within which citizens could exercise their political liberty.[144] What had changed in the interim was his appreciation of the consequences of this reading of Smith. While in 1797 he still took for granted that political liberty was meaningful in itself, by 1799 he had abandoned that faith. By then he was arguing that "the kind of republic that one might currently find must be subordinated to the system of political economy under which we live, just as that of the ancients was subject to their means of subsistence. The system of political economy is absolute and necessary, because it derives from people's needs, which nature demands to be fulfilled under pain of death. The political system is relative and arbitrary, because it depends on the infinity of combinations of which human intelligence is capable."[145] If he did not reject the republic outright, he did worse, in making it an irrelevance. Although there were some well-developed theoretical arguments that supported the idea of a high-wage republican economy, the facts of political economy on the ground were not easily reconciled to this vision. Commercial republican political economy was an alternative manner of conceptualizing political and economic development, but there were no absolute theoretical grounds on which its superiority to liberal ideas could be established. This debate could be resolved only in practice, through evaluating the effects and consequences of republican political and economic reforms. The trading world dominated by Britain was a fact. Could an alternative economy, organized around French peasant producers, become another fact?

The Directory and the Commercial Republic

The clearest picture we have of the practical policies of the commercial republic comes from the ministries of François de Neufchâteau. He is historically unusual because he was one of the main figures who elaborated the idea of the commercial, agricultural republic and then was charged with creating it. The transformation of France into a large agricultural republic, replacing England at the center of the world trading system, involved the Ministry of the Interior in a plethora of areas. One matter was, however, the sine qua non of any commercial society, republic or not: the creation of an adequate transport network. François de Neufchâteau directed most of his efforts into this network. In modern conditions nothing was possible without communications. "The two principal agents of general prosperity, as of that of individuals, are agriculture and commerce. The most effective means of developing these is freedom of communication, and ease of transport, either by water or by road."[146] François de Neufchâteau used a variety of expedients to foster communications. Since the coastal trade in French ships was made impossible by the actions of the Royal Navy he strongly supported allowing neutral countries, primarily the United States, to conduct it. "The greater the number of neutral carriers allowed to trade, the more our supply of colonial products will increase and the circulation of manufactured goods be facilitated."[147]

In his reports to the Directory he emphasized that too rigid a control of trade would deepen the trade deficit. The average consumption of 50 million francs worth of colonial goods was the major contributor to the deficit, and only increased exports could make up the difference.[148] He faced a difficulty in the conflict between the narrow military goals of the republic and the necessity for goods to move. The law of 29 Nivôse, Year VI, defined neutrality by the provenance of the goods carried rather than the flag. François de Neufchâteau argued against this definition on the grounds that a matching move by the British could destroy all French trade. He got around these difficulties as well as he could; he supported the colonial trade, for instance, by arguing that since Réunion and Guadeloupe were legally parts of the republic, he could authorize export to them as *de jure* cabotage.[149] This tension between the police arm of the state and the group around the Ministry of the Interior was endemic. For example, the Agricultural Council enthusiastically supported the export of mules to Spain from the fair at Beaucaire, reasoning that "the more they buy, the higher the price will go and the more mules will be raised; high prices and easy sales are the best bounty that can be offered to this kind of business."[150] But the trade had to be restricted because the local military authorities insisted on the application of a law restricting exports of horseflesh. Since the military needs were so urgent, the goals of the commercial republicans were attained through manipulating law more often than changing it.

François de Neufchâteau used such a manipulation to stimulate the grain trade in the Midi, which was suffering a localized shortage in Year VII despite the good harvest elsewhere. He used the law of 3 Fructidor, Year VI, allowing export of grain under license to support the armies, to grant licenses stipulating that for every five quintals exported four others had to be sold in the markets in the Midi.[151] To make speculation in the licenses impossible, they were granted for only two months.[152] He considered this measure a great success. The price of grain in the surplus-producing departments of the west, which had been so low that farmers were giving up their leases, rose from two to five francs per myriagram.[153] The effects were so beneficial, not least on the collection of taxes, that he proposed that trade in grain and cotton between France and Spain be freed on the same terms immediately. By allowing export, he argued, the Directory created a bounty for merchants, which compensated for the costs of the internal trade generated by the bad internal communications. Trade was the key to the success of the republic in the long run. "I will add to all these considerations, which have lost none of their urgency, those of our manufacturers for primary materials, needs which can only be filled by issuing money, which would be more unwise than ever, or by the exchange of the excess beyond our own needs, which in any case, is an aid to the balance of commerce."[154]

He also came up with some measures to support directly the manufacturing end of this cycle. Despite pleas from manufacturers, he, and Letourner before him, was adamant that the full force of state power, such as domiciliary visits, not be used to keep out contraband manufactures. As he pointed out, "experience has demonstrated that a prohibitive law that restricts peoples' freedom would be unduly severe and would not be applied.[155] Instead, an ad hoc industrial policy emerged. The ministry made direct cash grants to various industries to maintain production and provide alternatives to English imports. In Year VII, for example, the ministry granted 300,000 livres to the manufacturers of Amiens against their own commercial paper in order to keep their industries alive. In his letter explaining the grant to the minister of finance, François de Neufchâteau expressed the underlying strategic considerations. "One of the most effective ways of lowering the consumption [of English goods] consists of encouraging French production, particularly of those manufactures that can directly compete with the products of British industry."[156] Expedient as they were, these measures were still focused on creating the conditions for the commercial republic, but his efforts at promoting commerce went beyond expedients.

All of the measures discussed above were aimed at providing incentives to overcome the physical difficulties caused by the degradation of the transport system. François de Neufchâteau's policy was to get beyond expedients by restoring and improving it. The most pragmatic policy was the creation of toll roads through the institution of a road repair tax, passed into law by the legislature on 3 Nivôse, Year VI. The minister's correspondence was taken up with arrangements for collecting the tax and guaranteeing that its yield would be devoted to its object. Again he justified the tax as a paradigmatically republican measure: "The road repair tax will end those odious and unjust repair methods of the *ancien régime;* those disastrous corvées, a yoke imposed on the poor for the pleasure of the rich, that burdensome servitude which provoked the philanthropist to remark, at the prospect of the highway constructed by the corvée, I walk on the blood of the people."[157] This tax, which was to have a long future, solved the riddle of supporting roadworks that had bedeviled the monarchy. The failure to even consider such a rational system for maintenance of local roads illustrates the limitations imposed by political and environmental conditions on the efforts of the ministry. Communes, unable to raise local taxes, were driven back to the corvée to maintain local communications.[158] Despite the immediate utility of this measure, and for the movement of grain nothing but roads would do in many areas, the policy with the most far-reaching consequences was his canal policy.

François de Neufchâteau's work on the French waterways system exemplified his thinking on the commercial republic. The circulation of goods would be promoted by the waterways, and the circulation of information and ideas would in turn promote the creation of the waterways. He asked the departments to collect and forward every plan for the creation of canals they could find in their archives and libraries. He then proposed to have a study of each department's place in a national system written and sent on to them.[159] On the basis of this information he proposed to create commissions to implement the plan. The formation of these commissions directly reflected his ideas on the means of agricultural improvement: the sages equipped with the knowledge to make it work were the engineers of the Corps des Ponts et Chaussées, while the representatives of civil society were to be the leading members of the local communities, "savants, farmers, manufacturers, and merchants."[160] This marriage of civil society and state action was possible in a republic and allowed it to contemplate projects that "the chains of feudalism and the laziness of despotism" made impossible for the monarchy. In his plan for the financing of these proposed waterways François de Neufchâteau developed the view that political liberty, the republic, was the best system for the promotion of modern commerce. Capitalists could not risk their money on such huge and risky ventures, but a free state could turn a risky venture into a viable opportunity by having all the survey work and the preliminary engineering work done by engineers who would carry public authority and public confidence.[161] The action of the free state, through its agents, could turn private advantage to the public good by creating conditions in which private profits would produce public benefits. "They have only lacked this easy encouragement to turn their attention and their capital toward those kinds of enterprises that glorify those they enrich, by allying their personal interest with that of the Republic."[162] Political action by the republican state created the conditions for the resolution of the interests of all its citizens in the most direct way, and it created useful roles for its own agents. This particular proposal was to have a long life. It provided the model for the creation of the waterways, and later the railways, in France long after the political context in which it had been thought up had ceased to be relevant.

Of course, François de Neufchâteau's encouragement of the economic life of France was not an end in itself. The goal of the Directory was not to preside over an economy but to create the republic. The republic was the regime of political equality. As everyone including Smith had pointed out, however, modern commerce tended to produce inequality, to render an entire class unfit for political life. The problem of poverty was the central difficulty of the republic, and the minister set himself to finding some solution to it. "No government can end the existence of poverty; but the most dignified use of public authority is to aid the poor, to find a way to end indigence, which is the leprosy of states, and to prevent the disorders created by laziness and misery. Let us devote ourselves, citizens, to the solution of this political problem, perhaps the most intractable of modern legislation."[163] While no doubt this measure helped stop abuses, it did nothing to address the central problem of the institutions of public welfare, which was that they were broke. Given the terrible state of public finances, little could be done about that, though some measures were taken to assure at least some income to orphanages and hospitals.[164] In reality, bar hoping that the local administrations would intervene in the worst cases, little could be done in the short term, and François de Neufchâteau looked to long-term solutions. The strategy was, as ever, a variant on the association of private interest with the public good by allowing entrepreneurs to run the institutions of public welfare. "Who can doubt the improvement that will be generated by a system of enterprises, by allying private and public funds?" he asked.[165] Yet on reading his longest piece on the problem one cannot but be struck by the formulaic application of the model of the commercial republic to the issue.

The root cause of poverty, he felt, was political: the institutions of the monarchy had created a class that could not work because poverty had been seen as a virtue.[166] From a survey of poor relief in European countries he drew the predictable conclusion: all previous efforts had been misguided, and the English alternative was no better as it abandoned the poor to the greed of the rich.[167] It was up to the French Republic to regenerate the impoverished by offering them dignified labor rather than the servitude that had been their lot in all previous institutions. "One of the great disadvantages of the work in the old workhouses was that it was all the same. We must rectify this by establishing many simple workshops, where the weak and the old can work without distress . . . one must never degrade man by work, or work by man."[168]

Again, predictably, François de Neufchâteau argued that the one form of labor that respected the dignity of the poor republicans but was varied enough to be done by all was agricultural. In further application of the ideas of the commercial republic, he appended a model contract of twenty pages and fifty-eight articles stipulating the conditions for entrepreneurs running the institutions. Not surprisingly, this too was formulaic. The plain fact was that the state was in no position to dictate terms and was abandoning the care of the poor to anyone who would take it on. Reubell, for one, suspected that some entrepreneurs were tendering for these contracts in the hope of stripping the assets of the institutions.[169] There were some successes as a result of this policy: François Simonnet de Coulmiers and Gastady, for instance, used the freedom granted to them to promote a revolution in psychiatric care.[170] Pinel also took advantage of the moment to promote the application of the "moral treatment" beyond Bicêtre hospital and pressed the ministry to allow him to introduce it at the Salpetrière.[171] With these exceptions the institutions of public welfare could not be used to promote republican equality because the republic could not afford it.

All of these facets of the commercial republic, from transport to welfare institutions, were features secondary to its fundamental commitment to a reformed agriculture. Economic development, the extirpation of poverty and, more important, the creation of modern republicans depended on the improvement of agriculture. "Agriculture is either a pleasant or a useful occupation for everyone. It alone unites all the interests of the different classes of citizen."[172]

The ideal of the commercial republic and the commercial republican was derived from that of the independent farmer cooperating in a community of his like. The agricultural organization of France was far from ideal, but there was little disagreement on what should be done about it. Consolidation of properties, drainage, and the end of the three-field system were the prerequisites for the creation of a republican economy.[173] François de Neufchâteau's correspondents repeated this over and again. "The farmer awaits regulations and above all a law code appropriate to his needs and his prosperity. The division of common lands, the conservation of woods, an equitable method of consolidating property, the limitation of gleanage, if we decide to continue to tolerate it."[174]

The problem was that the entire ideological superstructure of the commercial republic depended on material changes, and these were difficult to effect. Overall the strategy was to reinforce the rights of property. Republicans in full possession of their rights would naturally associate their self-interest with that of the republic. François de Neufchâteau's efforts to encourage an end to the three-field system were hamstrung by the lack of a law defining how communities might reorganize themselves. Even years later he was still arguing that that subdivision was the curse of French agriculture and that legal action was necessary to remedy it. "One of the greatest obstacles to the progress of the first of the arts, is the disunion and subdivision of land. Badly organized farms underperform. The means of overcoming this is a prejudiced economic and political question that has not even been approached in a forthright way."[175] In lieu of a definitive law he was reduced to encouraging the local administrations to minimize the damage done to any enclosed holdings: "While awaiting a general, and rightfully severe, law that will protect property and agriculture from such attacks, it is your duty to apply at least those laws existing in this area."[176]

Juges de paix were particularly encouraged to protect enclosed pastures from communities that wished to exercise old rights of pasture on them.[177] Similarly, the minister sought to protect the rights of winegrowers to harvest their grapes at their convenience in enclosed vineyards and to maintain the rights of individuals to enter into leases under whatever terms and at whatever times they wished to.[178] While he could not bring about a wholesale reformation of French agriculture, what he could try to do was promote and protect a parallel reformed sector to encourage change by emulation and persuasion. "By revealing to farmers their self-interest, stimulating them unceasingly by the hope of profit, we will persuade some of them; their lands will work as a stimulus for the others."[179] François de Neufchâteau attempted to put the logic of self-interest to work to achieve things that political will had not.

The strategy of encouraging the creation of a new kind of independent farmer as the backbone of the republic through emulation was not restricted to the protection of consolidated farms. Emulation was the goal of a whole series of initiatives that François de Neufchâteau sponsored in Year VII. Central to the wider effort was his encouragement of the refoundation of agricultural societies. There had been twelve agricultural societies in France in 1789, but all had closed by 1793. The opportunity for a renewed agricultural society movement was presented by the radicalization of what was left of the Jacobin network. While some radicals, like Antonelle, were able to use the prosecution of the Babeuf conspiracy to rally an anti-Directorial left, the majority of the egalitarian and local democrats of France did not follow this initiative and needed to find some other institutional expression of their commitments.[180] The first effort to organize an agricultural society that came to the attention of the ministry was that of the department of the Creuse in Year VI. The Agricultural Council was enthusiastic about the idea, if nervous about its possible implications, reminding the administrators of the department to respect the laws on associations.[181] Their misgivings were overcome by the success of the idea: the new society was widely publicized, and by 1797 the ministry was attempting, with some success, to create a new network.[182] The agricultural society was imagined as the locus of the society of independent men, the community of research and mutual aid that agricultural improvement demanded. "There is a kind of work best done by a man alone. There are others, which require the collaboration and collective effort of many. The observations and experiments necessary to perfect agriculture are of the latter sort."[183] Just how different this kind of association was from the political sociability of the Jacobin clubs is highlighted by the metaphor used by the commissioner of the Executive Authority in his speech opening the society of the Nièvre. He told the members that by restricting their discussions to political economy they would show themselves to be good citizens. "The agricultural society should imitate the lovable sex, which is never as attractive as when it sticks to the affairs of the house."[184] It was rare to see this kind of conflation of the categories of citizenship with those of femininity.

François de Neufchâteau's goal was the creation of a national network with a central coordinating body, on the model of the English Board of Agriculture set up by act of Parliament in 1792. In his publicity for the societies he sought to establish how a network would forward the project of the commercial society. The idea was popular, and many societies were created. Late in Year VI *Rédacteur* reported that the Parisian agricultural society was invited to participate in the festival held to welcome the art of Italy to the Paris museums.[185] By Year VII forty departmental societies had been organized, and the minister could use them as a metaphor for the republic as a whole.[186] The founding of agricultural societies would ignite a virtuous cycle that would make the country rich, happy, virtuous, and glorious. Enthusiasts waxed lyrical at the thought of a prosperous land and a vigorous commerce "crossing every distance and uniting all peoples, enlightened *moeurs,* virtue respected, a vigilant justice overseeing the exercise of every right and the execution of all duties, the foreigner, attracted by our success and our glory, coming to enlighten and enjoy himself amongst us."[187] The agricultural societies were the institutional model and base for the commercial republic.

The agricultural societies were also central to the plans to improve the national livestock, especially the sheep herd. This was an ambitious plan aimed at stimulating both agriculture and commerce. The minister felt that the French textile industry had been retarded in comparison to those of England, Holland, and Germany for lack of supplies of good wool.[188] His plan was to exploit the terms of the treaty of Basel by sending an agent to Spain to buy 1,200 head of Spanish merinos. With a national sheep herd in the Pyrenees, the sheep could be acclimatized to French conditions and then sold to farmers at 50 francs a head, resulting in a steady improvement in the national herd. Gilbert was dispatched to Spain to achieve this end.[189] Sadly for Gilbert he died in Spain, his mission unachieved.[190] In fact most, if not all, of François de Neufchâteau's projects for the stimulation of agriculture through the creation of pockets of good practice met the same fate as that of the national sheep herd. Either they failed or their results were seen only after he left office. The first of the statistical accounts of the departments that he had encouraged appeared slowly and received little publicity at first.[191] The work, when circulated, was credited to Lucien Bonaparte and Jean-Antoine-Claude Chaptal in any case.[192] His own work on the improvement of the types of plow used in the country was not finished until Year IX.[193] Despite his best efforts he was even unable to increase the circulation of the *Feuille du cultivateur.* For lack of funds the ministry was forced to cut the subsidized run of the newspaper from 4,000 to 3,000 copies in Year VII.[194] The lack of money, and in the long run the lack of time before the outbreak of the War of the Second Coalition, undermined the concrete efforts to promote agricultural improvement.

The practical difficulties that were in the way of the development of the commercial republic should not obscure the political consequences of these efforts. The agricultural republic was not just a policy for the development of the country but a representation of the manner in which political liberty could be reconciled to the nature of modern commerce. Modern commerce of itself, in François de Neufchâteau's view, created a cycle of needs that was endless and threatened the possibility of the reconciliation of interests. "On the other hand, the communication established between every nation and all regions of the globe has created new needs, . . . what dike can we construct to protect us from this inundation? Where will it end? If in time, the needs generated from the progress of the arts and maritime trade continue to grow from century to century, as they have since the seventeenth century, what shall remain of our well-being?"[195] Agriculture was to be encouraged because it could create personalities who could have control over this cycle of needs. It was an occupation and a study that brought men back to their common interests and their social nature; "agriculture is fitting for everyone, either as a pastime or as an occupation. It alone unites the interests of the different classes of citizen, and because of that should be the usual guide of their thoughts and reflections. Every family should form an agricultural association."[196]

The minister could point to some examples of the regenerative power of agricultural activity. Much was made of the thirty-seven grape growers of Vesoul who devoted their leisure to harvesting the grapes of a colleague in the hospital. "The exercise of philanthropy is a harvest of liberty. Virtue is easy for republican souls, and this example of mutual aid is not the only one we have admired since the Revolution."[197] The civilizing effect of agricultural labor produced exactly the kind of civil culture that François de Neufchâteau imagined and that filled the pages of the *Bulletin décadaire:* "acts that will inspire civism and virtue . . . and instructive articles on agriculture and the mechanical arts."[198] The ideal of the agricultural republic was only consequently developmental; its goal was to harness the forces of commercial society to the task of building a democratic politics, of embedding competition in emulation.

Sadly for the project of the commercial republic such examples of cooperation as the Vesoul vineyard workers were few and far between. The opposed interests that manifested themselves compromised the representation of agriculture as a sphere that reconciled interests. François de Neufchâteau was inundated with complaints from landowners about the wage demands of agricultural laborers. "The departure of the second and third classes of conscripts has given the signal to agricultural workers to stop working and demand more money."[199] Some of these complaints merely asked that conscripts be released to perform the necessary labor, but most insisted that agricultural workers be coerced into working. On the other side were demands that a special levy be put on richer citizens to pay for a public works program.[200] The minister's projects were aimed at stimulating civil society through emulation, and thus his problem was that the commercial republican model of the state as an instrument of education and institutional change was not widely shared. From every side he had to meet demands that state power be used directly to achieve his ends. "You ask that the government enforce the planting of olive trees! The government should do nothing in this area other than to provide education and aid in useful experiment."[201]

The problem was more intractable than the contingent existence of people who did not accept the efficacy of "the victorious arena of persuasion." The model of the integration of rights-bearing individuals through communication was inimical to the actual political practice of whole areas of the state. As I have noted, commercial republicans could run afoul of military and strategic thinking. This tension was merely the most obvious of those between the political ideas of the commercial republicans and the arms of the state, committed as it was to constructing what Howard Brown has termed a security state.[202] The model of community that drove the political action of many administrators was that of the imposition of norms. Whether they were attempting to protect the practice of fixing the commencement of the grape harvest, and so carrying on a traditional practice, or transforming traditional practice by promoting individual herds, political actors were tempted to use the coercive power of the state as the best means of achieving their ends. The policy of promoting change in civil society through encouragement, persuasion, and example was not a central element of their political practice. This tension was most radically played out where the needs of internal administration ran up against those of the military. The fortunes of the Jourdan law (21 Fructidor, Year VI), making young men between twenty and twenty-five liable to conscription, illustrate the possible tensions. The law tried to reconcile the needs of the military to democratic goals by organizing conscripts in age classes, from twenty upward, calling each class as need demanded and refusing to allow conscripts to pay for replacements, the traditional escape route of the rich.[203] The system failed immediately, as recruits called to the colors by the law of 3 Vendémiaire, Year

VII, to prosecute the War of the Second Coalition deserted in droves.[204] The only solution to the military crisis this resistance created was the return to the old means of recruitment, setting quotas for departments that raised volunteers when they could and drew lots for the balance, all the while ignoring the trade in replacements.[205] The state, to survive, was driven to an alliance with local elites, which undermined its claim to promote a truly general welfare. The marriage of a new class of lawyers, professionals, merchants, and landowners, the *notables,* with the state may have been consummated under the authority of the empire, but the two began to fall in love under the Directory. The norms and values of commercial republicanism would not be transmitted by state institutions, especially after the Bonapartist coup. Thus to understand their long-term historical importance we must look to processes of social, economic, and cultural development in French civil society.

The Commercial Republic and Rural Economic Development

It is difficult to locate or evaluate the contribution of the Directory to the economic modernization of rural France. The Directory lasted only five years, and for two of these the commercial republican line of thought had to give way to the needs of war and foreign policy.[206] The commercial republicans dominated economic policy only after François de Neufchâteau became minister of the interior in 1797. Moreover, the environmental and fiscal restraints on their plans were enormous, to the point where little of the program for the transformation of the rural economy could be implemented.[207] It is impossible to pick out the direct effects of specific policies exercised for such a short period of time on processes of economic development that were long term by their very nature. The final difficulty of any purely economic assessment is the lack of agreement on the nature of economic modernization in any case. As Gilles Postel-Vinay remarks, twenty years of research has undermined our idea of an industrial revolution and, bar a stress on regional variation, has not replaced it with some other explanation of the economic transformation of Europe.[208] It is unsurprising that it is difficult to locate the Revolution in a process we do not understand.

Though our current state of research does not allow us to come to a global conclusion about the effects of the Revolution on French economic performance, we can come to some judgment about its effect on the rural economy. There are historians who concur with the pessimistic view of historians of trade and fiscal matters, such as François Crouzet and Florin Aftalion, but the consensus tends toward a more positive description.[209] While few agree with J. C. Toutain's claims that the Revolution and the empire promoted an enormous growth in agricultural productivity, it is clear that the stagnant rural world of C.-E. Labrousse, continually threatened by looming crises of production, did not describe the French countryside.[210] Even before the Revolution wages and subsistence goods prices rose together in regions that were integrated into market economies, by 60 percent between 1726 and 1789.[211] This growth in the rural economy continued during the Revolution, but with net gains for labor as wages rose by 36 percent between 1789 and 1810.[212] The effect of the increase in demand created by the rise in wages was concentrated in the provinces because of the movement of population out of the cities during the Revolution.[213] The high wages of the 80 percent of the population of the country living in rural areas, of which 30 percent were involved in nonagricultural activities such as transport, determined the trajectory of French economic development for the next century. French industrialists never had a large reserve army of low-cost labor on which to build an industrial economy.[214] The tendency toward supporting a rural population was intensified by the long-run effects of the sales of *biens nationaux*. Although the Revolution initially placed these lands in the hands of the urban bourgeoisie, they were on their way to ownership by the peasantry, who acquired them definitively in the nineteenth century.[215] By ending the historic process whereby the state and the elites had expropriated too much surplus from the countryside, the Revolution created the conditions in which the peasantry, and large farmers especially, could begin to invest.[216] The Revolution set the stage for what has rightly been called the golden age of the French peasantry.[217]

The prospect of a prosperous rural population would have brightened the eye of the commercial republicans, but it complicates the task of understanding French economic development. French growth rates per capita were indistinguishable from English during the nineteenth century, but many of the price incentives for innovation and higher productivity were missing in France. George Grantham has pointed out that the French agricultural sector grew by 2 percent per annum from 1820 to 1850, but this was not because of consolidation and a move to pasturage from tillage, the classic means of increasing productivity quickly, by lowering labor costs. There was no large urban market for the meat and dairy products of the new husbandry because of the continuity of the peasant population.[218] The economic effects of the Revolution had a self-reinforcing character and tended to widen the gap between the English and the French paths of modernization. Because of this gap, the English model, which explains the growth of the economy and productivity, is inapplicable to France. Given the configuration of the French polity, the innovations that created growth must have been centered on the agricultural sector, but the mechanisms that drove such innovations are difficult to discern.[219]

The work of Jean-Laurent Rosenthal and Judith Miller has revealed one of the mechanisms that clearly played a role, that of the state in reconfiguring economic institutions to foster growth. Rosenthal uses his study of water rights to argue that the state transformed the nature of property rights and the terms of political negotiation to facilitate irrigation schemes, land improvement, and canal systems. The imposition of simple property rules, buttressed by the authority of the state, which closed off the possibility of using the legal system to maintain unproductive relationships, created the institutional context for innovation and growth.[220] Miller's work reinforces these claims by revealing the political strategies used by the state to support these measures and the ideological commitment of state functionaries to reconfigure the country's economic life around markets and free trade.[221] In fact, the account of the development of a model of an agricultural republic by the commercial republicans fits easily into the narrative of economic and political learning by the state elites. However, while the agency of the state goes some way toward explaining the dynamics of the French economy, it does not provide a sufficient explanation. Much of this state program preceded the Revolution and had no success because of the social resistance to the risks and opportunity costs that would have to borne in any transformation. Agrarian individualism, in Marc Bloch's phrase, was a weak force and did not motivate farmers to entrepreneurial endeavors.[222] The ideal of economic relations organized around markets lacked social legitimacy; and while the Revolution destroyed the set of privileged legal relations that had been the major instrument of resistance to state-sponsored change, this change had not impeded social actors from creating other means of refusing to conform to market norms. The sans-culotte campaign for the *maximum* is an obvious example. To understand how state-sponsored institutional changes could have been successful we must understand how such social attitudes changed.

The idea of the modern republic and its associated rhetoric of commercial republicanism comprised just such a normative evolution. Its articulation of the productive citizen as the guarantor of collective *moeurs* fit with French social and political preferences. The norms comprehended within commercial republicanism could allow the articulation of interests, which in turn could express themselves within the new economic institutions created by the Revolution. The ethics of commercial republicanism offered an alternative kind of modern economic sensibility to agrarian individualism, the search for which has proven fruitless.[223] The hypothesis that emerges from a comparison of the culture of commercial republicanism with the outcomes of French economic development is that the long-term economic importance of commercial republicanism was its contribution of a republican political science. It bequeathed a lexicon for the defense of markets, small property, and political equality to the society, despite the effacement of commercial republicans and their policies by the Napoleonic state. This language of cooperation animated the small-scale, local markets that were the loci of development of rural France.[224] It promoted a form of economic modernization embedded in the ethical commitments of a social and political ideal, one that disposed economic actors to exploit the new institutional opportunities for investment, rather than take the opportunity for increased consumption or simply reduce production and maintain living standards on the back of higher prices. There is even some evidence that the lack of a republican culture could seriously hinder a region's efforts to come to terms with economic modernity. Tessie Liu's study of the area of the Pays de Mauges, in the antirepublican Vendée, describes the inability of small-scale industry to adapt to new conditions in the nineteenth century.[225] The politics of family, which animated weavers' struggles to maintain their role, left women in particular vulnerable to exploitative sweated labor in an effort to maintain traditional social structures.[226] Liu's rural artisans shared the economic situation of republican regions, but their political culture was different and hindered their capacity to negotiate change.

The simultaneous occurrence of commercial republicanism and French rural development is not sufficient evidence that the former was instrumental for the latter. Even the circulation of the propaganda of the commercial republic and the network of agricultural societies do not allow us to make any claims about the reception of this set of ideas. As Roger Chartier remarks of the Enlightenment, the context of reading determines the reception of cultural production. He argues, "it was the Revolution that 'made' the books, not the other way around, since it was the Revolution that gave a premonitory and programmatic meaning to certain works, constituted, after the fact, as origin."[227] To argue that the language of the commercial republic was co-opted by significant elements of the French rural population as their distinctive language of economic and political modernity we should have to find a mechanism or locus within the Revolution through which or in which the population could undergo the necessary social learning process. Such a locus was provided by the debate on *partage*, division of common land. This debate drove participants to consider the relationship of interests, norms, and institutions and forced them to acquire more powerful modes of understanding and explanation. As I shall make clear, this process created the context for the rural population to acquire the language of commercial republicanism and to occupy the new orientations toward economy, society, and politics that it contained.

CHAPTER 4

Big Theories and
Small Farms

The agricultural republic needed agricultural republicans: independent peasant proprietors, or strong tenant farmers, who would be the backbone of the republic and the example of a new species of virtue. Rural conditions in eighteenth-century France did not tend to promote the independent yeoman on his consolidated holding. While much land changed hands over the course of the Revolution, primarily in the form of *biens nationaux,* there were few, if any, sustained efforts to transfer land to the peasantry or to consolidate what holdings they already had. The exception to this general rule was the movement for the breakup of common land, *partage,* which began in 1789 and ended only after 18 Brumaire. The *partage* movement occasioned a long national debate that confronted the central issue of the relationship of economic organization to political liberty for the audience of French rural dwellers. *Partage* was the issue that took agrarian radicalism from the assembly and the journal and returned it to the fields.

Peasant Revolutions and Capitalism

Partage is difficult to approach because it has been a pawn in the great historical debate over the nature of the peasant revolution and its relationship to long-term economic change. Lefebvre thought the movement highly ambiguous. The provisions of the law of 10 June 1793—which mandated division of village commons on an equal basis among all inhabitants of a commune, including women and children—were both too individualist for his vision of a rural world resisting capitalism and too egalitarian to be considered part of the bourgeois assault on that world.[1] Enclosure on the English model was the only possible road to the future for Lefebvre, much as he may have regretted it, and so *partage* was never a historically relevant option and did not merit attention in itself.[2] Soboul and Ado, unconvinced of the existence of a homogeneous anticapitalist and anti-individualist peasantry, were more sympathetic to a history of *partage*. For them it became a feature of the general trend of the peasant revolution to institutionalize petty capitalism.[3] The most sustained local studies of the division of the commons were inspired by this approach and revealed a complex world of negotiation and new approaches to modern economic life within the world of the peasantry.[4]

Unfortunately, the insight that the peasantry, or at least significant elements of it, sought to integrate modern forms of commercial and economic life into the revolutionary transformation of France has been lost. An opposing consensus holds that the Revolution as a whole was categorically opposed to any form of economic modernization. Simon Schama argues that the Revolution, far from embracing economic and political individualism, was actually in revolt against it. He asserts that "while the *cahiers* of the liberal nobility offered an alluring picture of a briskly modernizing France that would consummate the great alterations of the 1770s and 1780s by shaking off restrictions like a butterfly emerging from a chrysalis, those of the Third Estate wanted, very often, to return to the cocoon."[5] Schama's neoconservative interpretation of the sociopolitical meaning of the Revolution is shared by many who might not share his sympathies. William Sewell, in a seminal work on the political consciousness of artisans, has argued that they understood the Revolution as the extrapolation of the moral economy of the trade to the level of the nation. Richard Andrews sees premodern patriarchalism even in the organization of the *sections,* the backbone of the sans-culotte movement.[6] Capitalism and individualism were not the moving forces of history contested over by different social formations, as Soboul and Lefebvre had argued. Rather, they were saved by the actions of what Judith Miller has termed the "stealth state."[7] Bar some notable individuals, French society at every level in the Revolution was antimodern. Only the liberal nobility and state reformers had an interest in creating economic rationality.

This view, characteristic of some political and cultural historians, finds much support among their economic colleagues. François Crouzet, in his generally critical comparison of the French economy with the British in the eighteenth century, characterizes the Revolution as a "national catastrophe."[8] René Sedillot argues for the deformation of the French economy due to the demands of the revolutionary and imperial wars, a point taken up by Guy Lemarchand, who further argues that the effects of war were amplified by the neglect of agriculture by the revolutionary assemblies.[9] The interpretation of the Revolution as a setback in French economic development finds its apogee in economic historians' views on fiscal matters and trade. The Revolution destroyed the French Atlantic trade, especially with Saint-Domingue, and ended the dominance of Marseilles in the Levant.[10] Nantes and Bordeaux, for most of the eighteenth century the most dynamic ports in France, hit a decline from which they did not recover until well into the nineteenth century.[11] With France's once thriving trade sector destroyed, entrepreneurial energies turned to extracting the spoils of war; the notable economic figures of the latter part of the Revolution for economic historians are the *fournisseurs,* military suppliers who made a profit on supplying the army.[12]

However deleterious the effects of the Revolution on trade and the economy, economic historians argue that the revolutionaries plumbed the depths of irrationality in their handling of the state's finances. The Revolution was provoked, if not caused, by a crisis in the state's finances, but the Revolution turned an annual budget deficit of 93 million livres in 1788 to one of 998 million livres by 1792. Having been called to allay the country's budgetary problems, the Estates General succeeded only in deepening them. The only economic historian to have attempted a full-blown interpretation of the Revolution through this optic, Florin Aftalion, argues that their mishandling of the money supply was the greatest contributory factor of the revolutionaries to the destruction of the French economy.[13] He argues that the revolutionaries inherited a country that was undertaxed, by comparison with Britain, and yet refused to increase taxes. Through an ill-prepared scheme for the nationalization of church property and the creation of a paper currency they managed to drive good specie out of circulation, provoke massive inflation, and tie up the working capital of the country in land speculation.[14] The subsequent economic crisis led to the Terror, itself a sign of the failure of the Revolution to create a modern politics based on a culture of rights. For many contemporary economic historians France achieved economic modernization despite rather than because of the French Revolution. In the face of this consensus the details of any revolutionary land settlement would seem to be of antiquarian interest.

The idea that the Revolution was both anti-individualist and sought to resist modern economic structures has been criticized by a group of scholars who have looked at the interactions of the fields of politics, economics, and culture. The search for alternative approaches has been fuelled by the knowledge that the catastrophic interpretation of the effect of the Revolution on French development is difficult to sustain in even a medium-term perspective. Patrick O'Brien and Caglar Keydar have long established that though gross national product may have dipped during the revolutionary period—and they stress that this was largely due to the difficulties in the colonial trade—French growth rates matched those of England right through the nineteenth century.[15] Had the Revolution destroyed fundamental economic institutions, such as markets, these growth rates would have been impossible. Close attention to the fortunes of particular economic and fiscal policies reveals no sustained attack on economic modernization. Eugene White has established that the assignats were not doomed to failure on economic grounds and that the fiscal horrors of the Revolution were the result of a tax strike, which was a political phenomenon.[16] White's assertion that the fiscal history of the Revolution cannot be apprehended without paying attention to the political and cultural environment in which economic measures were proposed is fully supported by Michael Sonenscher's analysis of the pamphlet debate on financial reform.[17] White's and Sonenscher's arguments underline the necessity of looking at particular debates and the development of particular institutions in order to understand the global significance of the Revolution for the economic organization of France.

The particular features of revolutionary economic history cannot be captured by macroeconomic cost-benefit analysis. What was at stake in the Revolution was the creation of the institutional forms that would differentiate France from the other advanced economies for the next hundred years. The institutions that were to distinguish nineteenth-century French capitalism from the paths followed in Britain, the United States, and Germany were all forms of organization created in the Revolution itself or strengthened in the revolutionary decade.[18] The model of the market discussed in the preceding chapter, the forms of wage labor, the archetype of property, the ideal of the small unit of production, and the industrial community, all emerged in that period. Measuring inputs and outputs assumes a fundamental similarity among French, English, and American paths of modernization; by contrast, the institutional approach, which is sensitive to the political, social, and cultural conditions of economic life, explodes those assumptions. In particular it captures the "framework of values and objectives" that are necessary to make any credible judgments of performance.[19] The institutional approach allows us to understand the rationality behind the economic choices made by individuals and communities in France, instead of obscuring specific rationalities behind unwarranted assumptions about the universal nature of economic behavior.[20]

Viewed from this perspective the history of *partage* assumes a new importance.[21] The waste and common lands were, in many areas, the cornerstone of the traditional organization of production, had many social rights (collectively termed *vaine pâture*) inscribed in their use, and had been the occasion of disputes within communities and between communities and seigneurs throughout the century.[22] The *partage* movement thus opened an issue with economic, social, and political ramifications. The two laws that enabled *partage*, of 14 August 1792 and 10 June 1793, provoked a blizzard of correspondence, petitions, and proposals, all of which had the effect of moving local contests over land and rights into national debates on political and economic organization. Florence Gauthier and Kathryn Norberg, both of whom have looked at the general significance of local responses to the *partage* law of 1793, have noted the radical and sometimes surprising reactions to the new provisions for dividing up communal resources.[23] Poorer peasants, long thought to have been attached to commons as a means of assuring subsistence, were largely in favor of division. Stockkeepers, producing for the market, were largely opposed, claiming commons were necessary to maintain herds. Thus we have the curious phenomenon of a capital-owning group defending a communal feature of production against the landless poor, an as yet unforeseen outcome of a moral economy. This first finding should alert us to the enormous complexity of the debate on division, and to its pliability. Participants in the debate clarified their interests, and acquired the languages and concepts to further them, in the debate itself.

The revolutionary situation created new contexts of negotiation, as well as new areas of conflict, over common land. It also created new, previously unthought of criteria, such as the rights of citizens, to adjudicate such conflict. Peter Jones's pioneering efforts to trace the place of the *partage* movement in the peasant revolution have uncovered precisely this interaction of national themes and local concerns.[24] In his study of the effects of land reform in twenty-five villages in the district of Versailles, he remarked on the attachment of the poor peasantry to both common rights and individual plots of land and asked, "was this enthusiasm perhaps the first stirrings inside the rural community of the modern conception of property?"[25] His article addresses exactly the right question, but one that cannot be answered only in terms of property. Rather, the *partage* debate must be read for a whole panoply of economic and political values that were not merely acquired but actively constructed by the participants.

The archival sources left by the *partage* debate offer us a unique perspective on development and modernization in the French Revolution.[26] The departmental sources, exploited by Jones, Norberg, and Gauthier, offer a clear picture of concrete change in particular situations. They reveal the continuing relevance of the Revolution to the evolution of local communities, and the revolutionary transformation of local politics, until 1799 at least.[27] The petitions collected at the national level are documents of another feature of the Revolution, of the appropriation of new modes of political discourse, and new categories of self-understanding, by rural society. Petitions sent to the national level addressed local needs but justified particular measures with reference to the general good and in general terms. In 1988 Roger Chartier noted how the revolutionary situation provided the opportunity for individuals and communities to understand themselves in new national contexts and to develop the cultural resources, such as literacy, to participate in these new contexts.[28] The *partage* debate, which occurred at the nexus of politics and the economy, demanded that all levels of rural society, from day laborers to stockbreeders, learn to express their interests in the modern languages of politics and commerce, to acquire a language of interest.[29] The debate therefore offers us the opportunity to investigate the extent to which the concerns of the commercial republicans, and the hopes they rested on agriculture, found any echo in rural France.

Creating a Reform Community: The Early Debate on *Partage*

Prerevolutionary economic reformers all agreed that breaking up common land was a prerequisite for the economic development of France. Turgot thought that commons helped sustain undercapitalized and unproductive forms of agriculture.[30] Arthur Young was merely repeating a commonplace of agronomists when he observed that if one found a poor peasantry in the more affluent regions of France, "it is twenty to one but that it is a parish which has some commons that tempt the poor people to have some cattle, to have property, and in consequence misery."[31] Few outside the small community of reformers around Turgot shared this manner of conceiving of the issue of the commons, and so the problem of common land was to be one of the least cited concerns in the parish *cahiers* of 1789.[32] People outside the state structures or the agricultural societies had little reason to acquire the developmental view, which demanded of groups and individuals that they think of their particular interests in long-term and grand geographical perspective.[33] The idea of privilege, which still dominated economic and social relations, reduced negotiations of interest to a zero sum. In the absence of institutions to negotiate interests, there was no incentive to compromise any advantage held, even in the hope of benefiting from a general improvement.[34] Diderot's disenchantment with physiocracy as a response to the troubles that faced France was motivated by exactly these concerns. He rejected André Morellet's idea of a pristine economic sphere and opinion that economic reform could occur in France without political reform: "your property right is a chimera that has not been, is not, and will not be respected by anything less than a government of angels."[35] Self-government could, ideally, do away with the need to find angelic governors, by allowing the latent possibilities for cooperative change to express themselves, but the habits and assumptions learned under the political and economic conditions of the late monarchy did not disappear with the Bastille.

The first inquiries into the feasibility of wholesale reform of the common land were the circular letters of October 1790, November 1791, and March 1792, all asking departments and communes to declare their views on whether commons should be divided and if so, how.[36] The issue, at first glance, was not complicated. Either one was for or against division. There were only three bases for division that might be contemplated: by head, in equal portions to every member of the commune; by hearth, to every family; or in proportion to tax paid, that is, effectively in proportion to the amount of property already owned. But this conceptual clarity was at odds with the complexity of claims on commons themselves. Common land was not ordinary property; it was subject to a variety of rights, such as wood collecting, which private property did not bear. Moreover, there were different sorts of commons throughout the territory of France. In Normandy there were no free commons; all users had to pay rights of entry to the local seigneur. It was an interesting legal point to ascertain whether he was therefore the owner of the land and the users his lessees. In Alsace rights of commonage were the jealously protected privilege of the bourgeois. It was far from clear if their rights in the commons were a form of property, and so protected, or a feudal privilege, and so abolished. Before responding to the issue at hand the various departmental administrators had to figure out how to make these legal determinations. More difficult than all these issues were the politics of division that predated the Revolution. The right of *triage* accorded in 1669 gave one-third of the common to the seigneur in any division. *Triage* itself was abolished along with all other feudal privileges, but what was the status of the lands previously acquired under it and possibly sold on to third parties? Conflict on this issue had been rife even before 1789. Florence Gauthier notes 128 denunciations of usurpations of commons by seigneurs in Picardy alone.[37] No land settlement that simply left the lands acquired under the terms of *triage* in their current hands could hope to survive the antiseigneurialism of the peasant revolution.[38] Finding a means of reconciling the interests around that issue was a delicate political task.

From the responses of the departmental authorities to these early circulars it is clear that the majority of departmental administrations did not have the cultural resources to conceptualize the issue of *partage* as an issue in itself and to derive criteria on which to decide it. The context for a debate based on economic development had not been constructed, and basic understandings were not in place. For instance, departments argued both for and against the principle of *partage* on exactly the same grounds. The departmental authorities of the Haut-Rhin, Meurthe, and Seine-Inférieure argued for it on the grounds it would consolidate the tax base, while those of the Seine-et-Marne, Jura, and Var all argued against it for precisely the same reason.[39] Therefore, it is impossible to understand anything about the authorities' assumptions about economic development from their support for or resistance to division in and of itself.[40] Through an examination of their responses, however, we can reconstruct the intellectual and cultural contexts into which they placed the question on division. Their reasoning, the kinds of arguments they made, and the vocabulary through which they expressed themselves reveal the ideals and assumptions this important level of French society held not only about *partage,* but about the possibilities of transforming French economic, social, and political life.

The absence of a common lexicon within which to conduct a national debate on the future of the commons did not mean that the departmental responses to the circulars lacked sophistication. The respondents placed the issue of *partage* within several contexts of developed moral public argument. One of the strongest lexicons used to respond to the issue was that of the moral economy.[41] The departmental authorities of the Ariège, Oise, Aube, Gers, and Nièvre all argued that the fundamental issue in *partage* was fairness toward the interests of the poor. Their colleagues in the Haute Garonne, Haute-Saône, Loiret, and Basses-Pyrénées went further in arguing that some element of redistribution toward the poor should be a part of any scheme for division.[42] The limit of this moral economy discourse was its ascription of paternalistic supervision to the authorities; its model of stable social order was exactly what the Revolution challenged. The clearest early example of this

feature was the proposition made by the administrators of the Landes arguing for the exclusion of farm servants and propertyless laborers from any division, because for them to acquire property would disturb the natural social
order.[43] The connection between the paternalism of the moral economy
ideal and its implied vision of a natural social order became more explicit
as subaltern elements of rural society began to make more demands. The
Haute-Garonne, which had been in favor of *partage* in April 1791, came out
against it in March 1792 because the *journaliers* had taken division into their
own hands and so "the fields now only offer the somber prospect of domestic disorder."[44] The rhetoric of the moral economy was not calibrated to
manage the stresses and strains of social and political transformation.

Another strong theme in the departmental responses was the rhetoric of
legality. The idea of legality, as Hilton Root has established, was highly contested in the French countryside; the differences of understanding of the
concept of law, such as those put forth by opposing groups in prerevolutionary Burgundy, continued and intensified during the Revolution.[45] The department of the Haut-Rhin made possibly the strongest defense of legality as
settled practice. The common grazing in Alsace had been defended from
seigneurial encroachment for centuries by the bourgeois, the free citizens,
and they should now benefit from their defense of their legal rights.[46] This
idea of particular rights in communal property was strong enough that department officials were trying to persuade the Constituent Assembly to allow them to rent out the commons to meet communal debts rather than to
divide. This system would have saved the richer taxpayers from higher rates.
As late as September 1792 the district of Altkirch was trying to defend what
it understood as the property rights of the local freemen against the landless
laborers or *manouvriers,* by proposing that the corps of freemen acquire the
right to grant bourgeois status from the seigneur.[47] By widening the corps to
those *manouvriers* worthy of participating in its dignity, they would balance
legality with a tincture of revolutionary equality. The incomplete transition
from a notion of legality based on privilege to one based on universality of
application was not confined to Alsace. Several departments supported the
rights of commoners, that is, those with preferential access to the fruits and
grazing in waste and common land.[48] The argument from continuity of possession of rights was reinforced by the conflation of the new category of
active citizens with those who had enjoyed privileges. Several departments
argued that *partage* should be enacted among property owners (active citizens), or at least should grant them preferential status.[49] The idea of legal

continuity did not always favor large landowners; the Yonne and the Marne both defended the smaller users of the commons against those with legal right to them claiming usage generated right. Oddly enough, both arguments proposed no change in actual practice. Only the departmental administrator of the Côte d'Or saw through the confusion generated by the mismatch of notions of legality. He baldly stated that any model of division would either have to dispossess those who used the commons in favor of those who had rights in them, or vice versa.[50]

Related to the competing conceptions of law, but logically separate from any of them, was the rhetoric of economic efficiency. Contrary to what one might imagine, and to the views of economic reformers, this rhetoric defended traditional agricultural practice. The departments of the Yonne, the Ardennes, and the Vienne argued that the maintenance of the herd demanded that of the commons. This position, of course, was exactly what agricultural reformers most strongly contested. Reformers held that common grazing made breeding of better stock impossible and took away the incentive to introduce new fodder and root crops. Only the administrators of the department of the Gard developed their view from this argument. In fact, their submission was remarkable precisely because it placed the issue of division in the context of the development of the French economy as a whole and argued for the structural benefits of *partage,* definitely a minority view. Even those who admitted in principle that common land in its undivided form anchored an inefficient form of agricultural production defended it in practice for ad hoc reasons. The administrators of the Vosges and the Hautes-Alpes pointed out that mountain regions could practice no other form of agriculture, and those of the Hérault and the Landes were taken up by the inconveniences that would ensue if woods were to be split up. The hand of local self-interest can easily be seen behind these arguments. Many departments, even some who favored the status quo, admitted that the rich—that is, the stockholders—rather than small landowners or laborers derived greatest benefit from the commons.[51] Only the department of the Var seriously argued that the commons were in truth the patrimony of the poor.

The departmental administrators tried to control the issue of *partage* within a diversity of traditional discourses of social and economic order. There was no one discourse that organized the issues of *partage,* and every argument they developed tended toward inertia. Those elements of a moral economy discourse that seemed sympathetic to an egalitarian division of common land were undermined by the imperative to control the peasantry built into the set of ideas. There seemed to be no vocabulary with which to express the hope of a dynamic transformation of rural economic practice and rural society. The English option, of enclosure by landlords, was conspicuous by its absence from public debate. Only one department argued that a wholesale expropriation of all commons in favor of the rich would be of benefit to the country as a whole: "the indigent classes are tempted away from the path of morality, by the hope of pleasure without effort, and toward the taste for independence and laziness" through the existence of the commons.[52] The idea of stripping away the overlay of political and social illusions that obscured the reality of productive relations had few takers.

Administrators of districts and communes, as well as individuals who took an interest in the debate on division of the commons, shared many of the same contexts for understanding the issue as did the departmental administrators. Petitions defending or promoting *partage* as a means of defending the tax base of the country, of securing the moral economy, and of maintaining agricultural productivity were plentiful.[53] Indeed, the debate could become even more scattered at this level; some concerns, such as the maintenance of woodlands, which were barely mentioned by departmental administrators, were central for petitioners from the communes.[54] Yet the communal and individual petitions in this early debate did not converge on inertia the way the departmental contributions did. Some of the differences were marginal, if significant. The vocabulary of political rights, which was entirely absent in the departmental replies, was deployed in certain instances as the criterion for navigating through the *partage* issue. Relying on the universality of French citizenship, the town of Montcornet-sur-Serre in the Aisne asserted the right of its citizens to share in the division of the commons of the surrounding villages, though it had no common of its own.[55] Less self-servingly, a body of the inhabitants of the town of Roquefort built their claim to a share in the division of the cheese caves on their duty to enact their political rights.[56] They argued that the monopoly on the cheese caves, effectively exercised by the three families who rented them from the municipality, robbed the other inhabitants of the town, which had no other productive work of any means by which they could attain active citizenship. A *partage* of the economic resource was necessary to ensure equal participation in political life. Another precocious sign of the introduction of the vocabulary of rights into all areas of public life was the petition in favor of division from the Jacobin club of Saint Sever Cap in the Landes.[57]

Nevertheless, petitions animated by the older understanding of rights as privileges heavily outnumbered these fleeting appropriations of universalistic languages of political identity across the country. Chopin, a judge writing from the department of the Ardennes, became a clear and representative example of this understanding of the issue when he asserted that there could be no question of a commune deciding to divide its commons as that would negate the rights of commoners.[58] Collective rights, or privileges, were also defended. The village of Buffon, in the Côte d'Or, asserted its right to the second crop in the seigneur's enclosures, and the municipality of Paris rejected selling off the commons to help meet debts.[59] The possibility of deriving a reform policy from the premises of revolutionary change was glimpsed but not exploited fully.

The real differences between the departmental petitions and the local varieties derived from local references to particular controversies. Local communities and particular individuals, some with long memories, saw the *partage* debate as a tactical opportunity to win long-standing land disputes, and in some cases to reverse legal defeats. Communities such as Guemont in the Haute-Marne and Luzanger in the Loire-Inférieure argued that they could not contemplate division until the commons had been reestablished in their entirety. This meant regaining a wood lost in a 1763 case for the first and the reacquisition of a meadow alienated by the marquis de Grandeville for the second.[60] These local disputes did not necessarily lend structure to the debate on *partage* or inspire communities to acquire new ways of understanding themselves and the political context. The citizens of Luzanger did send their petition to the National Assembly, but they addressed it on their knees as loyal subjects of the king, hardly a novel posture. When these sorts of legal battles were conducted in areas where economic change was under way, however, the variety of interests deployed could, potentially, undermine the meaningfulness of older languages of politics and promote genuine innovation.

A new pattern was created and a new context for the debate on rural land reform was outlined in the parts of France where efforts to change agricultural practice had already altered social relations and occasioned dispute over land use. Two zones were primarily affected: some highly productive northern departments (especially in areas that provisioned Paris) which had integrated into the market economy; and some southern departments, which were facing a crisis of production.[61] In the south conflicts between *métayers* (sharecroppers) and landlords were the impetus for a partial transformation of the debate. In regions where there was substantial sharecropping and where the productive capacities of the local economy were under strain, the legalistic and moral economy frames for the debate on division were shattered.[62] Sharecropping had developed as an institution that provided poor small farmers with a hedge against radical fluctuations in the price-wage ratio and that guaranteed landlords against default by indigent lessees.[63] The hedge was imperiled in the Revolution as the southern region suffered disproportionately from rising food prices.[64] The rise in prices for basic foodstuffs caused sharecroppers to withdraw further from the market into autarky, which required more land. One would thus expect them to have been massively in favor of *partage*.[65] The head of the administration of the Saint Porquier canton explained the imperatives at work in this situation to the Parisian authorities.[66] Since work was so scarce and prices so high, the *journaliers* and artisans of the department had to be supported by work schemes *(ateliers de charité)* instituted by the department. The only alternative, was a *partage*. Every petition from the *journaliers* or report that mentions them notes their support for *partage* as a measure that would allow for their preference for autarky, just as the administrator explained. The petitions from the poor of Pontac and of Mont-de-Mersan were typical.[67] The first argued that there could be no reasonable impediment to putting land under the plow and rejected the needs of the stockholders. The second asked for a quick and cheap procedure for reintegrating common lands alienated by ci-devant nobles. Both were animated by the goal of acquiring the means of withdrawal from labor and commodity markets for a community threatened by their dysfunction.

As the sharecropping and landless poor aligned their interests with a policy, their rationality imposed shape and direction on the other participants in the debate on *partage* in this region. The concerted efforts of the poor to divide the commons either by head or by household provoked landowners, and perforce stockholders, to a defense of their interests. A series of petitions defended the rights of stockkeepers to their pasture. Some of these defenses were highly political in nature: I have already noted the petition by the departmental administrators of the Landes that only property owners be allowed to participate in the debate on division.[68] This course would have defended stockholder interests by silencing any others. The more general expression of landowner interests was an appeal to legality. Goulard, from Bressels in the Haute-Gironde, argued that the commons of his village could not be divided since he held the lease for their use.[69] Similarly, the administration of Gondrin pointed out that the commons had been sold in lots in

1756 to meet village expenses and thus, even if unfenced, was private property.[70] In short, in the southern debate we find that interests, social identity, and policy were aligned in a negotiable array. The poor cited their needs in favoring division, while the rich cited their legal rights in opposing it. This alignment of interests led to conflict but also to clarity in the debate. Of the thirty-five petitions sent in from this sample area between 1790 and 1793, only four did not express a clear preference either for or against *partage*. Also, as the debate developed, participants sought to understand and combat the reasoning behind their opponents' views, seeking a better and more complete understanding of the issue. Thus the Société des Amis de la Constitution of Saint Sever acknowledged that the local seigneur and the rich opposed the division because they feared it would compromise their interests but simultaneously argued that such interests had less weight than the equality guaranteed by the constitution.[71] Intermediary groups sought to capture the force of both arguments to defend their own interests. The *laboureurs* of Saint Jory in the Haute-Garonne were enthusiastic about the possibility that the *partage* law would allow them to assert their right to a common over which they had been in conflict with the local seigneur since 1444; but they still denounced any "illegal *partage*."[72] The particular position of the subaltern group, the sharecropping *journaliers,* provided the impetus for the debate.

Its very premises limited the possibilities of developing this debate on *partage*. The economic horizon of the *journaliers,* autarky, was technically impossible and economically retrograde. Subdivision of the commons could not supply enough land for autarky; indeed, in some areas the mere prospect of division threatened to splinter the land into completely unproductive units. The departmental administration of the Gers proposed that there be no division in any area where the lots would average less that half an *arpent,* still a lot less than the five hectares minimum for self-sufficiency.[73] Moreover, even those supporting the *journaliers'* case acknowledged that their actual goal was unrealizable. The town of Pau, complaining of the resistance of the local administration and seigneurs to division, admitted that some commons would have to be left undivided to provide pasture for the pigs. These pigs were the main support of the local economy, and the exception reflected an awareness that there was no real possibility of escaping market relations.[74] The *journaliers* seem to have been aware that there was a mismatch between the recognition of their interests and their expression of those interests as policy or preference. The debate in the southwest revealed how interests might express themselves and align with policy in a manner that pointed past older symbolic organizations, but the debate did not develop a fully articulated lexicon of rights and interests. Only in the north, where society was not so simply divided between the landed and the landless, would the debate acquire a genuinely novel rationality.

In the south the needs of one group, *journaliers,* imposed structure on communication; in the north it was an institution, enclosure *(defrichement),* that organized opinion on *partage.* The politics of *defrichement* predated the Revolution; the monarchy had passed *arrêts* allowing division from the 1760s, and the predictable struggles for control of land and resources had followed.[75] The right of *triage* was particularly resented by rural communities, and so predisposed them to antiseigneurialism, but the simple opposition of communities to their feudal lords was only one element in a complex mix. In Picardy, for instance, where enclosure issues were reinforced by the difficulties of the local textile industry, the *cahiers de doléances* of 1788–89 were already demanding an end to all feudal privileges in order to assist agricultural production and the return of all alienated common lands.[76] The consensus around antiseigneurialism could not be sustained, however. The *partage* issue revealed differences within the village communities themselves, the effect of which was a sophistication of the arguments over division. The debate on *partage* fractured the united front of antiseigneurialism of the peasant revolution. Rural elites and subaltern elements had to find new languages to represent their differing interests and to promote their conflicting projects for the commons.

The first stage of community participation in the debate was the effort of various villages to have the effects of the previous enclosures rolled back. They ranged from the example of Ivry, in Seine-et-Oise, which had attempted to enclose under the old rules, to those of Velaune or Mandeville, which demanded the reintegration of meadows alienated by nobles and religious orders into their commons. All elements of rural society could agree on regaining the commons before they began to disagree about what to do with them.[77] Rural communities were aware themselves of the conditions that fostered disagreement. The smallholders of Coulonbiers in Calvados explained to the Paris authorities that the invitation to discuss the commons had created a three-way dispute.[78] In a region where considerable investment had already been made in the quality of lands, the large landowners argued that they should be rewarded for their investment in the community by having the commons shared on a basis equivalent to the property already owned. The old seigneur, by contrast, argued that he should retain the lands he had already acquired under the right of *triage* and maintained that he had a claim on the entire common, which was legally his property and had only been let in usufruct to the community. The small landowners, who wrote the petition, asked the authorities to reject all these arguments in favor of the formal equality of all claimants in the regenerated community. Within these communities the debate over the division of the commons could not be a blind clash of interests. Parties to dispute had no difficulty in representing the position of their interlocutors to themselves and reacting strategically to it. A good example is the community of Pontpoint in the Oise; the large landowners of the community wrote to the National Assembly protesting the proposal to divide the commons.[79] The petition argued that the proposal was a factional initiative supported by those who had rejected a previous effort at a division and aimed at dispossessing the nonresident landowners and the poor. The counterpetition, from the village assembly, did not contest the content but questioned the form of the first petition.[80] It argued that the defense of nonresidents and the poor was an entirely strategic maneuver designed to protect, by obscuring, the domination of the large stockholders whose herds monopolized the common. The complex social structures and sophisticated cultural resources of these communities created the conditions for an intricate, and dynamic, debate on the future of the commons.[81]

The *partage* issue brought participants in the debate to a clear-eyed appreciation of the possible relationships between political and economic power. Local groups reiterated the necessity for national oversight of any arrangements if they were not to have perverse results. The inhabitants of Annet-sur-Marne denounced their own village administration as a cabal that used its new power to deny access to the commons to anyone other than its members.[82] The departmental administrators of the Oise explained that several communities had divided their commons in proportion to the property held without waiting for any enabling law. This was because local landowners wished to put as much land as possible under the plow as quickly as possible, to take advantage of the high grain prices.[83] The department argued that the needs of agriculture, especially maintenance of the herd, and the interests of the poor demanded that the state act quickly. The local effects of this dynamic were a steady alienation of the poor from richer rural inhabitants. The municipality of Ronquerolle, for instance, came to demand that the rich be excluded altogether from any *partage*.[84] Since *partage* was configured within these communities as an issue of the modalities of enclosure, it created the conditions for social groups to recognize themselves, and others, as organized around a series of interests, which could be promoted, contested, compromised, or negotiated. The difference between the northern farmworkers and smallholders and the southern day laborers and sharecroppers was that the northerners were maneuvering in order to share in the profits of an agricultural region well integrated into market relations, while the southerners were trying to protect themselves from the possible collapse of fragile local arrangements. The demand that the rich be excluded from *partage* was therefore best understood as a move within the negotiation of new arrangements, which would have to have at least minimal consensual acceptance within the community. This move was in turn met with the predictable defenses of the richer rural dwellers against egalitarian division: that it would traduce established legal rights, undermine the basis of the agricultural system, and perversely punish those who had already invested in land improvement.[85] The challenge was to find modes through which these positions could move from recognition to negotiation.

In theory, national institutions of representation were to do the work of integrating these differing expressed interests. But in reality the participants themselves were left to reconcile the differing ideas in play. The departmental and district administrators understood the problem to be that of reconciling justice with efficiency and believed they saw the remedy in the evil itself. As the district administrators of Saint Omer put it, "it is proven that the commons are of benefit only to the landowners close to them and to the rich stockbreeders"; therefore the obvious solution was to make those individuals pay for the benefit they had previously had for free.[86] If the commons were put up for sale, those landowners who needed them for their herds would be forced to buy them. In addition, strict justice could be served by using the proceeds of the sale to indemnify those who had lost their rights of usufruct.[87] A similar effort was that promoted by the village assembly of Vassens in the Aisne.[88] It proposed a compromise whereby not all the commons were divided, leaving some land for the common herd. More interesting, it stipulated that anyone could enclose a portion of the land, at his own expense, but that he would acquire usufruct only in his enclosure, which he would retain as long as he paid the *contribution foncière*. Thus, communal and individual goals could be pursued without conflict. Both these proposals displayed flexibility and imagination. Even though both had obvious faults, the first because there was unlikely to be a market for marginal common land when so much good land was for sale as *biens nationaux,* and the second because administrating the scheme would involve great difficulties and costs, they revealed the ability of local political groups to mediate conflicting imperatives, such as strict legality and local need.

Both the ideas discussed above were ultimately conservative in inspiration: their scope was the preservation of rural communities, the organization of agriculture in its existing form, and the maintenance of legal continuity in landholding. A more radical approach to the issue, and one more clearly inspired by the revolutionary experience, was to ask how greatest benefit for the community might be derived from these "common" lands, and effectively to replace legality with utility as the most relevant norm for apportioning these resources. Several communities promoted an approach along these lines, sometimes for local and specific reasons. The village of Marchienne argued in this way because the land in its area was so bad as to require a substantial investment of time and effort, an investment worthy of reward.[89] The *agronome* Longuet, responding in the name of the agricultural society of Caen, stressed that the most important issue was dividing up the commons into small, but viable, units, to which could be applied the best agricultural techniques.[90] The most radical version of this approach was that taken by the district administrators of Avranches. They argued that the most efficient farm was the small consolidated landholding, and that in consequence the National Assembly should not restrict itself to encouraging improvement through division of the commons but should institute a wholesale redistribution of the productive land of the country.[91] From the context of the petitions it is clear that what the administrators had in mind was not an equal distribution of all land, an expropriation, but a legal instrument that would oblige landowners to consolidate their scattered holdings into economically productive and meaningful units. This support for the smallholder could not have been further from the idea of autarky. It was grounded in the idea of efficiency, of successful participation in market relations. Most important, it was a progressive vision, one that was not a simple reflex of the interests of any group. It demanded a change in land use and agricultural practice and, in truth, broke the bounds of the *partage* debate to engage with the wider issue of the economic and social effects of the Revolution.

The Avranches petitions were the high point of the early debate in the northern departments, the most consistent application of a universalizable principle, utility, to the concrete problem before them. However, it is important not to isolate this one example from the general debate. The southern and northern debates reveal that communities were able to learn new dispositions toward the changed circumstances of political contest in the Revolution. They could find ground from which to begin integrating the various principles and ideas at stake and work out how to express their own interests within these new configurations. While the *métayers* of the Basses-Pyrénées and the administrators of the Manche were precocious in the subtlety and complexity of their responses, they were fully representative of the manner in which the French rural population might manage the process of transformation of its most basic productive relations. The social and cultural elements of a reform community existed. For this process to mature, however, it required the national debate to be as rational as the local. The legislators would have to show as much subtlety and intelligence in their framing of the laws that would enable *partage* as had the rural populations that would actually conduct it. *Partage,* which began as a challenge from the administration to the population, would end up as a challenge to the political class from civil society.

The Carnival of the Interests

There can be few more graphic examples of the failure of the political class of France to understand and guide the Revolution than its mishandling of the *partage* issue in 1792 and early 1793. The Code Rurale, enacted as the Constituent Assembly closed, had nothing at all to say about common land and offered no guiding principles to help resolve the issue. The law of 14 August 1792, despite the detailed discussion that had preceded it, simply stated that the commons would be divided after the harvest. Every difficult question of the procedure for partitioning, of who might be eligible to receive land, and of what might be done with lands with doubtful title was simply ignored. The Legislative Assembly promised that a method and law on division would follow within three weeks. The supplementary law of 28 August, sponsored by François de Neufchâteau, sought to clarify matters by granting communities the right to seek to reintegrate lands lost to *triage* appropriations in the previous forty years. The redistributive intention behind these measures was underlined by the pendant laws of 14 August and 2 September allowing the confiscation of émigré estates and their sale in four-*arpent* holdings.[92] These measures, which sought to take some of the uncertainty out of the issue, turned out to make matters worse. The Convention, which came into being on 23 September 1792, did not turn its attention to a definitive law and preferred simply to suspend the 14 August measure on 11 October, and no law establishing a procedure for breaking up émigré holdings was passed until June 1793. Communities and individuals were left in limbo: no one could doubt that some measure would eventually be passed, but the shape it might take was entirely obscure. The community of Montdragon voiced the suspicion that the interests of rural France might not have been at the forefront of the minds of their representatives; that the pressure exerted by "the sections of Paris, who are refused nothing," meant that "meanwhile we farmers, some two hundred leagues distant from the National Convention, see that we are forgotten, and that it is always a question of the sections of Paris, of the Paris Commune, of the Paris municipality, or even of the Paris theaters."[93] Since the state and the institutions of national representation would not guide and direct the debate, its terms were ruptured, submerging rationality around the issue in suspicion and fear, and a "war of attrition" for control of rural resources began.[94]

The terrible effects of the indecision of the state authorities were obvious in rural France and were quickly communicated to Paris. There was a steady rain of letters from all over the country, from every kind of institution and assembly, pointing out that in the absence of clear principles to guide the movement for division it threatened to become totally anarchic. Departmental administrators from the Aisne to the Gard, communal assemblies, Jacobin clubs, and *sociétés populaires* all demanded a definite mode of division on clear principles.[95] The danger was that without norms in place to govern the debate on, and the reality of, division, individuals would take matters into their own hands and unleash social conflict across the country. The promise of *partage* without a method heightened conflicts without allowing any way for them to be mediated and resolved. The effects escalated as time went on. In the early winter communities still appealed to the Convention to settle disputes. Seven and a half pages of signatures accompanied the petition from the farm laborers of the Haut-Rhin against the continuing use of the distinction between bourgeois and *manans* for access to commons.[96] They warned that matters threatened to degenerate: "there are those who seek to excite their just indignation in order to foment a civil war." Clearly, the ground for compromise between the local administration seeking to defend the bourgeois ownership of the commons and the popular challenge to that domination was disappearing. As winter wore on local populations took matters into their own hands. The administration of Montigny asked what it was to do about *attroupements,* which were invading the common and dividing it at will.[97] The *société populaire* of Nîmes informed the convention "that many uneducated citizens, thinking themselves authorized by law to take the harvest of those who have rented out common land, now look on every enlightened patriot who opposes their designs, and even the constitutional authorities, as an enemy and an aristocrat."[98] The day laborers of Saint Hilaire complained of the opposite phenomenon. They had taken the promise of *partage* at face value and invaded the common, only to find that the district administration denounced their occupation as illegal and evicted them. The burning of their huts by the local landowners added a touch of malice to the situation.[99] The collapse of social relations due to the insecurity of the norms of social and economic life struck the district administrators of the Vosges. They complained of conflicts between individuals and the authorities, "individual disputes between farm laborers and big landowners, vexatious divisions, partial sales of commons to avoid the coming legislation."[100] The competition for scarce resources threatened to degrade the fabric of rural social life. The communal authorities of Larrey, in the wine-producing region of the Côte d'Or, described the situation created by the indecision of the legislators in Hobbesian terms. Not a scrap of land had gone uncultivated in the village for the last thirty years, but often the title to any part of the vineyards was informal. The proposed *partage* had turned every man against his neighbor, protecting his own self-interest and holding what he could, out of fear of what the other might do.[101] Insecurity fed paranoia. A landowner in the Aveyron wrote to the Convention predicting that if there was a *partage,* a civil war of rich and poor would follow, and the poor "will demand the agrarian law."[102]

The failure of the representative institutions to create a means for differing interests to negotiate a compromise on the fate of the commons removed any incentive to develop mediated or hybrid positions. The effect was a polarization of opinion, most obviously seen in the petitions that now called for expropriation of this resource. Harcourt simply informed the Convention that it had appropriated the commons and divided them as the community saw fit.[103] The district of Andelys called for the immediate partition of all one-time commons, and of the harvest that stood on them, a policy mirroring that of Charres, which decided to knock down any hedges less than forty years old and to distribute the lands on an egalitarian basis.[104] In fact the temptation to expropriate your neighbor's land for fear he might do the same to you proved difficult to resist. Twelve petitions to the Convention between September 1792 and June 1793 called for the expropriation of all land that had been removed from the commons without any compensation, even for any investments. Only two argued that reintegration would have to acknowledge both antecedent rights and investments.

The seeds of a shared lexicon of rights—utility and function—which existed in the debate on *partage* before August 1792, did not germinate. Instead, exclusive languages of denunciation and justification began to dominate the petitions. The poor of Langry asserted their need to divide the common land as a response to the rich, "who look on the poor as something akin to the dogs they pass in the street."[105] There was no place to represent the legitimate interests of others in this kind of absolutizing language. Even lexicons, such as that of legality, which were technically open, could be closed to rhetorical effect. The district of Donjon asserted that there could not be any commons, and so no question of dividing them, since constitutionally all property was individual, and thus the pasture was the property of those in possession of it.[106] The state had created a situation where it was assumed that everyone was playing beggar my neighbor. Woodlands were a particularly fraught object of this way of thinking. The Paris Jacobin club, in a petition that tells us more about the structure of negotiation that the various interests found themselves in than it does about actual conditions in the countryside, reported as fact that the one-time nobility were systematically chopping down woodlands in an effort to stop them from falling into any other hands.[107] No woods were safe: the competition to grab resources was intense enough that at least three communities seriously proposed to the Convention that they be allowed to harvest all their woods and share the proceeds among the villagers.[108] That such a proposal could be voiced, despite the state's historical role in protecting woodlands from peasant encroachment, shows the absence of rational norms governing the debate. Some awareness that the legitimacy of productive relations and the coherence of rural communities was under threat penetrated the Convention, and on 13 March 1793 it responded by passing a law making it a capital offense to promote a *loi agraire,* a forcible redivision of landed property.[109] This was just a gesture, promoted in this case by Barère, toward stabilizing a republic in crisis and was no substitute for actually working out a means of reconciling the differing principles at stake.

Even as political communication in many communities degenerated into systematic suspicion, other communities entered the debate and sought to bring order to it. Few petitions were presented from southeastern departments before the 14 August law; only two came from the Drôme, for instance, even though the departmental authorities admitted that there were extensive commons in the department.[110] The *partage* movement in this department developed from revolutionary politics rather than preexisting struggles over land use, and was organized as a political campaign, itself a genuine innovation.[111] The backbone of the *partage* movement in the Drôme was the local Jacobin clubs. Indeed, the inspiration for a campaign seems to have been imported from the more highly politicized department of the Gard.[112] The first big petition from this region, demanding an egalitarian *partage* and claiming more than thirty thousand adherents, came from the district administration of Uzes.[113] The following day a club in the Drôme, at Châteauneuf-du-Rhône, asked for an egalitarian *partage*. Its petition became the model for eight others sent to Paris in one week.[114] As with any other well-organized campaign, the fundamental message was simple and easily communicated. The end of the commons could be a final overthrow of feudal relations, and so the division of the commons was the logical outcome of the antiseigneurialism that had characterized the Revolution from the first. Every one of these eight petitions used this idea, but we can see the transformative possibilities presented by this novel engagement with a practical question of political economy if we look at how some clubs developed the notion. The club of Châteauneuf-du-Rhône was not content with antiseigneurialism and teased out the economic consequences of citizenship, which it saw as paying progressive taxes on property and income. The Bouchet club, in a vocabulary taken directly from commercial republicanism, described *partage* as one piece of the "succession of the century of industry to that of indolence" under the republic. The citizens of Saint Paul argued that the long term goal of the *partage* movement had to be to generate a modern economic order "by directing citizens to industry and individualistic farming." What all of these petitions had in common was their attempt to construct a context for *partage* that would make it a rational economic policy in pursuit of valid and rationally grounded public goals. What none of them could do, of course, was make the national representation act, and the momentum of the movement was soon lost. In January of the following year the departmental authorities were lamenting that not one village had divided its commons, "because of local disagreements of every kind."[115]

Local Jacobins sought to arrest the slide of the debate on division into rancorous attempts at mutual spoliation, not just in the Drôme but across the country. Jacobins sought to clarify the intuition of natural justice that should govern a *partage*. They were among those most alert to the confusion and suspicion generated by the lack of a procedure to divide up the land, and all of them demanded a law.[116] Jacobins, unlike departmental administrations, did not simply ask for the re-creation of order. Rather, they sought through *partage* to promote egalitarianism.[117] They were disturbed by what they saw as the perverse effects of the republican state's defense of law: "under the reign of the law and justice, the usurper harvests in peace the fruits of his crime, while the poor cannot get back their property."[118] This tension between the aspiration to protect liberty and equality and the persistence of opposed interests troubled the Jacobins, and the movement found it difficult to find ways of understanding the dispute that did not reduce to the most paranoid forms of antiseigneurialism. The Paris club's suspicion that the one-time nobility were deliberately destroying the woodlands of the country is a case in point.[119] Where the Jacobins were not immobilized in this way the logic of their position drove them to identify the interests of the republic with the interests of the poor. They began to argue that the redistribution of the common land was not only a matter of economic efficiency but also one of political justice. The republic, to be meaningful, had to transform the economy of France by releasing the pent-up energies of its poorer citizens. "We have strong arms that only await the signal of the law to make the waste land, which up to now has been used to the exclusive benefit of the rich, bloom."[120] *Partage*, which had been understood in terms of local interests, the maintenance of the moral economy, economic development, or the dilemmas of law, was turned, in the hands of this section of the Jacobin movement, into another facet of the drive toward political equality. Jacobins pursued an egalitarian division of common land through the logic of their investment in the ideal of citizenship. As the citizens of Saint George explained, "while you are free and we are the slaves of poverty, it is your duty to rescue us from this state."[121]

The idea that *partage* ought to contribute to the creation of political equality informed the law of 10 June 1793, which finally laid out a mode for dividing the commons. The law prescribed that if one-third of the members of the commune were in favor of the measure, then the land should be divided. Such division should be by head, that is, equal portions ought to go to every inhabitant regardless of sex or status. Similarly, the vote on division should be open to all the members of the village, not just men. This was a consistent application of Jacobin principles. The solution to the problem of bringing order to the process of reform was to be found in political process, a vote. Moreover, since this issue was primarily a social and economic issue, the arguments against female participation did not hold, and women could vote. Finally, a commune could decide to rent or sell off the village commons if it saw fit.

Needless to say, the 10 June law completely transformed the politics of the movement for division. It was one of a series of measures, including the law of 3 June, which provided a means to break up émigré estates, that formed part of the Jacobin campaign for agrarian reform.[122] These were the rural equivalents of the *maximum,* though, of course, the second policy seriously undercut the first. But in the summer of 1793 the internal tensions that would destroy Jacobin social and economic policy were not apparent, and the rigorous application of political principles to social and economic problems seemed to hold promise for a reformation of life for even the poorest citizen. The law of 10 June had some particular advantages. It reconstituted the issue as one of local politics, as evidenced by the fact that only 88 petitions to the Convention are preserved from the date of the promulgation of the law until 1795, indicating the issue was no longer an object of contention in national politics. It turned communities and individuals away from arguments for and against the principle of *partage* and toward its actual implementation or refusal. The simplicity of the law, and its unswerving adherence to one principle to adjudicate the issue, removed all uncertainty from the minds of rural dwellers. Though they might agree or disagree with the principle of political equality that was invoked, they at last had a concrete proposal around which to organize themselves.[123] The law of 10 June 1793 did not acknowledge all the principles that were at stake in the debate on *partage.* The notion of legal continuity in property ownership was not confronted. But by using a universal principle to address the problem, the law restored the possibility of rational conflict as opposed to simple expropriation. The Jacobin moment transformed the ground on which such debates could occur, even though the Jacobin movement itself failed. Its intervention in the *partage* debate ensured that any eventual solution would have to accede to the Jacobin demand for clear, universally applicable principles. The carnival of interests initiated by the procrastination of the Legislative Assembly and the Convention was ended by the new alliance of left Jacobins and the popular movement in the summer of 1793.

Opinion is much divided about the concrete effects of the law. Lefebvre emphasized the extreme variation in responses to it even within one department, the Nord, where in the districts of Quesnoy and Valenciennes there was considerable enthusiasm for division, while in Avesnes and the Cam-brésis communities preferred either to sell or to leave arrangements as they were.[124] Supporters of the thesis of a "peasant route" to capitalism, such as Florence Gauthier and Guy Robert Ikni, argue that the high rates of division in such departments as the Oise, and in the old province of Picardy gen-erally, are evidence of a modernizing peasant movement in embryo.[125] How-ever, even they acknowledge that far more divisions were projected than actually carried through. Kathryn Norberg attributes this outcome to the re-sistance of stockholders, who used whatever means they could to impede the application of the law, a view supported by the fact that of the few peti-tions sent to the Convention, those complaining of obstruction were the sec-ond most numerous category.[126] Peter Jones asserts that the law itself was flawed, since division imposed large administrative costs on the communes, and that in any case the peasantry tried to protect communal forms of prop-erty.[127] Nadine Vivier points out that the confusion and anxiety of the years of Terror make it difficult for us to pick out the effects of one law.[128] We can-not come to any secure judgment of the measure since it was only opera-tive for three years, and three very difficult years at that. The administra-tion was, in many cases, unable to organize or even inform the population for this major economic and social innovation. The Conseil Général of the Ardeche reported in 19 Germinal, Year II, that it still had not even had a re-sponse from any district to the original circular informing them of the law.[129] What is clear is that whatever the costs and difficulties created by this law—and complicated by the demand, reiterated in another law of 24 August 1793, that villages clear all debts before they be granted permission to di-vide—the suspension of the law on 21 Prairial, Year IV, arrested the transfer of considerable amounts of property that was still under way.[130] The law of 10 June 1793, despite its deficiencies, was the benchmark of republican egalitarianism and the measure around which the debate on division would turn until 1799.

The republican egalitarianism of the law clearly exceeded the populist va-riety that informed the peasant *partage* movement. One of the few clusters of petitions from the countryside to the Convention questioned the scope of those who should participate in any division. Several communities were unconvinced that the legislators could really have intended servants to have a share.[131] Some communities argued that certain occupations should be ruled out of participation. The village of Grey, for example, asserted that cus-toms officers should derive no benefit from the community's resources.[132]

Other social categories whose participation was queried were female servants, orphans, and children born outside marriage.[133] The Montagnard-inspired law did not acknowledge the informal codes of respectability and status that might have conditioned different communities' ideas of which persons should properly benefit from a land-reform measure. Although the measure was unquestionably calculated to buttress peasant support for the regime in the aftermath of the coup of 31 May 1793, its claim to legitimacy was not that it satisfied the desires of poorer rural citizens but that it was a universal measure derived from principle not factional interest. In the end the 10 June law did not settle the *partage* issue. Through its reassertion of the principle of universal application, and its reliance on at least an understanding of a principle in its adjudication of the issue, however, it allowed the continuing debate on *partage* to recover the rationality that it lost in 1792–93.

The Commercial Republic and *Partage*

In 1793 and 1794 the Revolution consolidated itself through an alliance of the state with the Jacobins. The clarity and principle brought to bear on the *partage* issue was one example of the benefits that accrued to the country, beyond simple military survival, from this alliance. The costs were enormous. The Jacobins became state actors and lost their mooring in civil society. Whereas in the early stages of the Revolution they had provided a ground for mediation and communication, between 1793 and 1794 they were the agents of Terror.[134] Jacobinism became a form of political fundamentalism that threatened the plurality of French society and the possibility of democratic politics. The fall of Robespierre in Thermidor, Year II, could not restore the Jacobins as a social movement; the moment for that kind of political mobilization had passed. In the absence of Jacobin politics it remained to be seen if the republic could find a ground of legitimation, a problem I addressed in earlier chapters, and if it could sustain its newly created social and economic institutions. The debate on the elimination of the commons thus survived the fall of the Montagnards and continued to be a defining issue for the French Republic. The rural smallholder became the iconic figure of commercial republicanism, but could the political means to create smallholders be defended in the aftermath of Terror?

In the immediate aftermath of the fall of Robespierre arguments for land redistribution based on the rights and duties of citizens ceased to be compelling. Instead, a new kind of universalism was brought to bear on the problem of *partage*, that of universal property rights. Petitions sent to the Ministry of the Interior in 1795 and early 1796 claimed that the law of 10 June 1793 was effectively criminal. This was not because it had traduced particular rights and privileges, but because it had undermined the right of property, which was the foundation of society.[135] Unlike previous critics of *partage*, these petitioners did not oppose the economic and social needs of the country to established rights. Rather, they sought to reinterpret the goal of reform in terms of the protection of property rights. The idea of privilege was abandoned and replaced with a new notion of a right as a guaranteed enjoyment of a possession. Where the law of 10 June had understood the promotion of citizenship as the goal of public policy, this new understanding argued instead that public policy should promote respect for the fundamental right to property. Petitioners arguing from this ground held that the mode of division mandated by the law was a facade for expropriation.[136] The petitioners from the town of Magnac, for instance, described the law "as subversive of the right of property, and . . . without any doubt the precursor of an agrarian law."[137]

The claim that the law of 10 June 1793 had traduced the right of property was buttressed by the argument that it had also undermined the procedural rationality of the law by including provisions for forced arbitration.[138] The law had removed disputes over ownership of the common from the purview of the courts and created a system in which disputes were settled by the departmental administration on the basis of written arguments submitted by the disputants. Creating a means through which those whose property had been expropriated in this manner could find legal redress was the issue through which the new debate on *partage* began to effect policy.[139] The rapporteur of the proposed amending legislation, Jean-Philippe Garran-Coulon, offered an entirely new understanding of *partage* to the members of the Council of Five Hundred.[140] Garran-Coulon's strategy was to contrast the clarity of the idea of property with the confusion that surrounded the concept of common land. He reconstructed a speculative history to illustrate his point. Commons had properly been the mode of organization of the farmlands of the antique city, where property and political rights were coterminous and so the city assembly might conveniently make whatever arrangements it saw fit for agricultural production.[141] Modern commons were the result of the efforts of monarchs to re-create cities in imitation of the antique form. Their legal status had always been dubious, however.

They were not property in the strict sense and so had been subject to the legislative whim of monarchs and were corrupted by the appropriations of feudal lords. "Because of this," Garran-Coulon explained, leaving aside the bad faith that motivated any manner of usurpation, it was a most difficult affair to distinguish between true common land and common usages, and in turn between those and simple toleration of entry or the rights of gleaning, which were prevalent throughout France, on fallow land and even on cultivated land after the harvest."[142]

This confusion had been exploited by the "municipal anarchists" of the summer of 1793 to create a law that had unlimited potential for expropriation. Garran-Coulon's suggested resolution to the problem of stimulating agricultural improvement was to reverse the priority of community and property. Since there was no way that secure communal title to commons could be established, because for the most part it did not exist, the solution was to begin with those who had any title to land and subtract that land from the commons.[143] Possession was not to be nine-tenths of the law; because there was no real principle to appeal to outside possession, it was to be the tenth as well. This was a remarkably evenhanded resolution to the problem, since it would protect those who had gained land under the terms of the 10 June law as well as those who may have alienated a common in the thirteenth century.[144] Opposition to his proposal—on the grounds that the Council of Five Hundred should effectively draw a line under the current state of land ownership while working out a system to distribute whatever remained in common ownership—centered on the perceived injustice of allowing criminals to profit by their deeds.[145] This opposition was overcome, and his proposal was passed into law on 21 Prairial, Year IV. From that date the provisions of the law of 10 June 1793 were suspended until a better system could be passed into legislation.

The mutual interrogation of political elites and elements of civil society marked every stage of the debate on *partage*. This interaction revealed the value and meaning of the new terms and ideas that were brought to bear on the issue of transformation of rural economic and social life in the period. So it was that the internal tensions in the conciliatory package of legality and property put together by Garran-Coulon were revealed by the pressure exerted as his ideas were put into circulation. One of the first petitions that explicitly supported Garran-Coulon's proposal unwittingly revealed its problems. The petitioner from Sauverney entirely agreed with the priority of property but argued that since the law of 10 June did not acknowledge property rights, it was illegal and its effects should be nullified.[146] The principles of property and legality were at odds with each other. As numerous petitioners complained, the law of 10 June was so contrary to natural justice that there could be no proper title to land acquired under its provisions, and so they asked for a redress of the injustices committed under it.[147] There were two ideas of procedural legality available. To defend their *partage* several petitioners appealed to this adherence to republican forms. Their opponents rejected the idea that the procedure laid down in the 10 June law could ever have been truly legal. For every petition, such as that of Brisy of Sanspoux, who complained of the expropriation of land he had bought, appealing to natural justice to be allowed to reopen cases settled under forced arbitration, there were several asking that definitive title be granted for land acquired under the forms of the law of 10 June.[148] The *partage* debate came to be structured under the premise of assuring a rational regime of property holding. This opened up the problem of the status of property, either as a right prior to political association or as one guaranteed under the constitution, and spoke as much to the status of *biens nationaux* as it did to one-time commons.

The new debate on *partage* was further complicated by the reassertion of the state's interest in securing its tax base, protecting its resources from appropriation, and rationalizing its operations. In Thermidor of Year IV the Ministry of Finance asked the legislature to confirm that the portions of common land that had belonged to émigré nobles and religious houses were *biens nationaux* and not available for division.[149] This classification intensified the process whereby specific claims on the one-time commons threatened to frustrate any redistributive efforts whatsoever. If the claims of the state, the needs of communes to cover debts through land sales, and the preexisting rights of property owners were all acknowledged, it was difficult to imagine there being any common left to divide. Garran-Coulon's revised legislative proposal reflected the tendency of the property principle to override all others. All enclosures, all claims of debtors, and the state's interest in *biens nationaux* were given explicit recognition in his bill, as were all *partages* effected before August 1792.[150] The legality of divisions enacted since was to be determined by their agreement with the new conditions, and any future divisions would need an absolute vote of the male electors. The previous provision that women should have a right to vote on economic matters that affected their lives was rejected. It was a short step from this proposal to the complete rejection of the fundamental elements of 10 June by Jean-

François Barailon and François Rivaud. Barailon argued that the commons were an extension of private lands and therefore 10 June 1793 "was in fact an agrarian law, promoted by anarchists and levelers."[151] Rivaud's language was less extreme, but his principles were the same. There could be no way to divide the common other than in proportion to the property already held in the area: "the rights of usage and division in the common are a property of the same sort as every other property."[152] Even though he admitted that the effect of the earlier legislation had been to accelerate the trend toward sowing new fodder crops in areas such as Flanders and the Beauce, he decried its other effects of destroying the social order in sharecropping areas. He was particularly critical of involving women in the deliberative process. In short, he felt the law should be replaced and its effects overturned.[153] The debate in the Council of Five Hundred followed this line of argument and rejected Garran-Coulon's bill because it was not sufficiently distant from the law of 10 June 1793. It was sent back to committee with the demand that it be replaced by another proposal more respectful of property rights.[154]

The use of property as the key term to adjudicate the difficulties of the *partage* issue had all the strengths and weaknesses of the previous, Jacobin, use of citizenship. It was formally rational—clear and consistent rules for the settlement of disputes could be derived from the position—but it spoke only to the material interest of one element of the society, in this case the rich stockkeepers. The economic and social reality remained that large farmers used the commons to support archaic, but profitable, forms of agriculture.[155] Within forms of thought that polarized public and private good, rights and common interest, it was difficult for these other interests to express themselves. As the discussion of a measure to remedy the defects of the law of 10 June 1793 worked its way through the Council of Five Hundred, it became clear that using proprietarian premises the council would simplify matters by allowing partition in every commune in a manner proportional to the quantity of land each household already owned. In a debate in Prairial of Year V the council agreed to add Jean-Baptiste-Michel Saladin and François Godefroy Sainthorent to the commission drawing up the new bill on *partage* with the explicit instructions to pursue this goal and to eliminate all the provisions of the 10 June law.[156] The possibility of social conflict, which the council understood had been encouraged by the old law, was to be avoided by reinforcing property and social standing. The objective of the new law would be to defend the social order and the structure of property ownership. These were essentially understood to be the same thing. As a member put it in the debate in Fructidor of Year IV, the original *partage* law had "banished good faith from the countryside, enclosures had been violated, fences torn up, properties invaded; on all sides there was nothing but violence and rapine, and no man could call himself the master of the heritage of his fathers and grandfathers."[157] Property was a heritage, and respect for that heritage was the fundamental condition of the social order. In any case, it was argued, the idea of commons was a feudal absurdity, since property could only be private, by definition. The so-called commons were in fact unfenced extensions of private property. The proposal in hand allowed only property owners to vote on whether or not to partition the commons and called for division strictly according to tax status.[158] Landowners would not have to be resident to benefit from these measures. Economic efficiency would be promoted, social structure reinforced, and conflict obviated by one wise measure.

Pierre-Jean-George Cabanis was the most eloquent advocate of this strategy and explained its rationality in terms highly indebted to physiocracy. To give land to the poor was only to offer a temporary palliative to their misery: "the real treasure of the poor is work, but fruitful work, not that wasted on infertile fields which would demand investment beyond their means . . . The best circumstance for the poor, is if there are capitalists who are investing and who need them. Its great interest is that all the big industrial and commercial enterprises are flourishing."[159] Cabanis's thinking was reflected in a group of petitions that used the same language of economic development. The village administration of Schlestatt in the Bas-Rhin argued that egalitarian division would merely reduce production even further by diverting elements of the scarce labor force out of the labor market.[160] A petition from the Creuse applauded Cabanis's intervention in the debate, as did the commissioner of the Executive Authority of the Meurthe, who added that freeing the export of grain would make obvious the need for large efficient farms.[161] Citizen Rey of Paris made explicit that the commons should be broken up by enclosure rather than division. The most efficient form of agriculture was in large units; thus lands should accrue to large landowners.[162] Physiocracy provided an economic rationale for the distribution of common land to large landowners. These large landowners would provide the basis for social and political order in the countryside.

Late in December 1798, as the last piece of business after a long day, Antoine-François Delpierre rose to his feet in the Council of Five Hundred to defend what would seem by then to have been a lost cause.[163] Speaking in the debate on the third reading of the new *partage* bill, he wished to offer "two propositions, whose basis, as well as the principal dispositions, differed from those of the commission."[164] Delpierre's response to the neat conjunction of social, economic, and political power was to denounce it as an offense to "ideas of equity, ancient usages, and the views of any wise popular administration."[165] While the bulk of his words addressed the errors of the commissioners, such as mistaking the terms of the *parcours* with those of the *communaux*, the core of his argument attacked the values and principles that grounded the measure.[166] He argued that the supposed basis in political economy for this measure was entirely fictive, since there was no reason to suppose that large landowners contributed to the enrichment of the republic. The near universal resistance of *laboureurs* (large farmers) to partition was based on their desire to maintain their domination over the *manouvriers* (agricultural laborers).[167] Since *partage* the agricultural laborers had "learned the importance of their work . . . they now placed greater value in their sweat, since they were no longer under the pressure of dire necessity."[168] Partition took free land and cheap labor away from landowners and forced them to be efficient; "I am convinced," he said, "that in an infinity of communes, they would never have created artificial meadows [*prairies artificielles*], notwithstanding their incalculable advantages, if not for the division of the commons." He summarized his defense of this Jacobin law, originally passed in the heat of the ejection of the Gironde from the Convention, with a metaphor developed from the image of the tree of liberty:

> it would be a big question in political economy, to work out if it is appropriate to a republican government, or even to the spirit of agriculture, to expand large farms, to encourage the careers of some particular people, while restricting the possibilities for others. In the place of three giant trees, which suck the life out of three acres, while casting their murderous shade, you could plant fifty more vigorous varieties, which would produce excellent fruit, and whose branches would not break in the wind nor call down the lightning.[169]

In place of the proposed law, which would thrust the rural poor into "the class of proletarians," he then offered his own, which amended rather than abandoned the egalitarian premises of the law of 10 June 1793.

Delpierre's intervention in this debate is fascinating for many reasons. It is educative to see an egalitarian defense of land reform in the late eighteenth century that uses arguments from political rather than moral economy.[170]

Delpierre's reasoning on welfare and opportunity makes him an ally of such British agrarian radicals as Thomas Spence, echoes Paine's *Agrarian Justice* and Thelwall's *Rights of Nature,* and is one more aspect of the international nature of the revolutionary dynamic.[171] The most important element of Delpierre's intervention, however, was its success. His demand that any partition scheme respect the value of equality was accepted by the council and formed the backdrop to a debate lasting another year and a half on what practical measures should be taken. Delpierre's central rhetorical strategies—of making property equivalent to egalitarian citizenship and arguing that democracy best served economic development—became the premises for that debate. How are we to reconstruct the context of moral public argument of the latter half of the Revolution to understand how egalitarianism might be a dominant value?

It is clear that Delpierre's egalitarianism, around which the debate turned, was not that of the sans-culottes or of Year II. Rather, it followed the model of commercial republican citizenship: "the maxims of democratic government demand that the legislator devote himself to forming citizens and not subjects, owners not beggars . . . Knowledge and ownership, these make a man free."[172] Liberty, he argued, was the principle upon which any secure government rests and that which motivates men to act to the fullest extent of their powers. "But by the side of that prime mover," he added, "nature has placed an indispensable auxiliary: property. That is the link that unites citizens to one another and to the country."[173] Delpierre developed the notion that property ownership was a secondary, but necessary, attribute of citizenship and political rights, rather than the precondition for political life, in his eulogy of the high-wage economy. In reply to those who argued that high wages would put pressure on large landowners, he stated, "I believe that it is no business of the representatives of a free people to create a system that establishes the prosperity of one part of the French people on the suppression of the other."[174] Tellingly, he called this form of domination "an attack on society," thus emphasizing the role of property as a social condition of republican liberty.[175] The normative power of this ideal of the right to property as a condition of participation in society and of acquisition of citizenship was so strong that Delpierre argued that the conditions of the law of 10 June 1793 did not go far enough. By leaving the decision whether to divide the commons to the commune, it went against the rights of the poor. The rich would never agree to a measure that would deny them use of a resource they monopolized for free, by having larger herds than anyone else.[176] Therefore, he was driven to propose that division be mandatory, since any opposition to it would be opposition to citizens' acquiring the basic condition of their citizenship.

Delpierre's exposition of the scope of land reform went unchallenged by the majority of the participants in debate. He captured the idea of property for the republicans and challenged the physiocrats' program by accusing them of representing monopolistic interests, which were illegitimate even under their own norms. Those opposed to him were dragged onto his ground of debate. Those who did agree with him could not finds words strong enough to express how "in the execution of this insight of political economy . . . he has found a perfect accord between principle and practice, from which great public happiness will ensue."[177] Dissension was most notable among those who thought his proposal not egalitarian enough. Charles-Antoine Mansord was only one who felt that by demanding residence and dividing by household rather than by head "the day-worker, the farm laborer, the farm servant, who own no habitation but live and sleep where they can" would be unjustly excluded.[178] Others argued that the measure was likely to be self-defeating, since many of the poor were likely to sell the plots they might acquire and so were unlikely to derive the long-term social and psychological benefits of land ownership. Instead, they proposed, village commons should be let and the proceeds invested in local primary education.[179] Only one participant in the debate denied the egalitarian yet individualistic premises laid down. François-Augustin Trumeau called forthrightly for the social and political domination of the countryside by large landowners, asking, "what is the social state in which reciprocal duties and services are not recognized? It will be or should always be the case that one class gains the services it needs from another, as long as it can pay for them."[180] His illustration of the desire for ranks and domination merely reinforced Delpierre's fundamental argument.

The success of Delpierre's intervention, and the coherence of the long-term debate that followed, demands explanation. There were purely political conditions that gave him support. The political atmosphere after the coup of Fructidor, Year V, was far more open to egalitarian ideas. Moreover, he had been deputy for the Vosges to the Legislative Assembly along with François de Neufchâteau, who was then minister of the interior and a known supporter of division on an egalitarian basis. Their political collaboration was to continue into the Napoleonic period.[181] Indeed, Delpierre's discussion of the older laws on landholding of commons could have been taken from François's files.[182] Yet the authority of the minister and the change in political circumstances could not have conditioned the terms of an argument in this way. Rather, the terms of this debate, and the preference for a particular political economy based on small-scale property ownership, came from the reflections of republican thinkers and administrators on the forms of a specifically republican market economy. As he developed his arguments, Delpierre was not innovating but quoting the ubiquitous literature and an ongoing debate. His political success was based on his exploitation of the ideal of the commercial republic and its iconic figure, the independent farmer. That success is illustrative of the extent to which the commercial republicans achieved their goal of instituting a compelling account of how modern economic and social behavior could be integrated into the practices of a democratic republic.

The lexicon of the commercial republic had popular appeal as well as intellectual power. The idea that citizenship established a right to property as the condition of economic development was the central thrust of several petitions supporting *partage*.[183] Even the very language of *industrie,* which expressed the core commitment of the commercial republic to labor as the defining mark of the citizen, turned up in the petitions. The inhabitants of Saint Quentin in the Pas-de-Calais supported an egalitarian *partage* because it would "save the poor from the corruption of *moeurs* created by inactivity."[184] Those of Genainville made the political commitments of the republic even more explicit. They pointed out that the law of 10 June had "given a political existence to a mass of citizens" and embedded their sentiments in the nation by granting them property.[185] Local interests reached a new level of participation in the national debate. The canton of Rousillon stated that the importance of the Fructidor coup was that it broke the resistance to egalitarian *partage*.[186] The commune of Bressols supported egalitarian *partage* because that would promote citizenship of the poor; it specifically commented on how reassured it had been by Delpierre's intervention in the debate in the Council of Five Hundred.[187] The terms of debate set by Delpierre exploited the power and coherence of a political lexicon that sought to master the revolutionary experience, comprehend the various interpretations of the idea of liberty released by that revolutionary experience, and achieve some of the utopian aspirations of the revolutionaries. Moreover, his use of this revolutionary ideal found a response outside the realm of formal politics.

While the negotiations of rural communities with national representatives were important, the changes in the terms under which such negotiation took place were even more significant. Where previously the frame for the debate on *partage* had been the configuration of particular communities, we find communities articulating their interests through a genuinely national vocabulary. The most important change was the general apprehension that politics, in the sense of ongoing institutional negotiation of interests, had a direct effect on everyday life. Simon Dubos, a day laborer from Ferte, wrote to the Council of Five Hundred to gain protection from the "rich egoist" who threatened his enjoyment of his allotment, relying on the "republican morality" of the legislators to give him justice.[188] He appealed not to their sense of charity but to what he saw as their political sense that the rich, the enemies of the republic, were also the enemies of division. This identification of the republic with the interests of the poor, and hence with egalitarian division of the commons, informed a mass of petitions from all over the country.[189] Participation in the *partage* debate allowed rural communities to acquire a development perspective and the cultural resources to appropriate universal ideals, such as rights. Several petitions sought to embed enjoyment of the newly divided land not in statute but in right and asked for a legal instrument to guarantee such rights.[190] The village of Gasny used this idea of the mutuality of political and property rights when it asked the council either to make this kind of property immune to legal query or to restore the title the community once had in the commons.[191] In either case title would be secure. The petition of the village of Saint Laurent Daigon was the most comprehensive statement of the commercial republican disposition.[192] It sought to defend legal rights, particularly those acquired through the law of 10 June. It buttressed the claim to rights with a political claim, that the best support for the republic was the smallholder. Finally, it invoked the utilitarian principle to make sense of the whole: the best government was that "which made the greatest number of people happy," and it did so by releasing the productive energies of the people. The republic and its social base were speaking the same language.

Partage after the Republic

Delpierre's success in the debate on land reform was based on the creation, by the Directorial republicans, of a language of modern republicanism, a task that had been beyond the powers of the Gironde and the Montagne. Assessing the historical importance of this language is difficult, given the

collapse of the regime shortly afterward, one effect of which was to termi-
nate the debate on *partage* that concerns us. Despite the continuities in some
administrative practices, the political and social goals of the Directory did
not survive "a man who talks only of himself" as Constant put it.[193] The final
law on *partage* was that of 9 Ventôse, Year XII, which sought to annul divisions and reinstitute commons where it could.[194] In effect, it was a retreat
beyond the ideas of Garran-Coulon to a simple alliance of the state with the
rural elite. The long-term effects of the debate on division of the commons
could not be the actual division of the commons, given the social and economic priorities of the Napoleonic regime. Instead, the debate left behind
the apprehension of new modes of political discourse, universalistic models
of political and economic language, and the aspiration to marry modern economic forms with democratic political practice.

The last of these is of the first importance to an understanding of the evolution of democratic political culture in France. One of the most famous, and
durable, observations in political science is the simultaneous occurrence of
democracy and prosperity.[195] There is also a consensus that capitalist development in and of itself is not a sufficient condition for the creation of democratic norms. Social equality, understood as equality of status and respect for
individuals regardless of economic condition, is as important to the long-
term success of democracy as economic development.[196] Commercial republicanism was, in effect, a development theory that harnessed aspirations to
equality of dignity to economic development. The Revolution allowed the
subaltern classes to acquire the new perspectives that released them from
fruitless and systemic opposition to capitalist development and equipped
them to act as the most articulate proponents of democratic political reform
in the nineteenth-century French polity.[197] The centrality of agriculture and
the independent peasant proprietor to commercial republicanism reinforced
its democratizing effects. While the working class has historically been the
most active proponent of political democracy, the social base for democracy
has been an independent peasantry enjoying relative equality of landholding.[198] Impoverished laborers working *latifundia* do not make good democrats, though they may make excellent revolutionaries. Commercial republicanism reinforced the French peasantry, encouraged its acquisition of the
lands made available by the Revolution, and offered it a systematic understanding of the place of the peasantry in the economic and political transformation of France. The veteran revolutionary Arthur O'Connor, son-in-
law to Condorcet, commented on this long-term effect in the aftermath of

the 1830 revolution. By ending primogeniture and opening up the land market, the first revolution created conditions in which "the whole property of France is, by its continual action, nourishing equality."[199] The eclipse of the institutions of the republic has obscured the profound transformations in social and cultural values promoted by those institutions. The republic created the forms of popular modernity.

It is worth noticing that every effort to formalize the market as a central institution in French economic life had failed up to this point. After the innovation of the language of the commercial republic, social struggles over the economy expressed resistance to monopoly rather than to the market principle itself. Hilton Root has pointed out the institutional deficits that had existed in politics and made true markets impossible; the absence of political structures for the negotiation of interests made it imperative for economic actors to retain whatever privileges they had.[200] They could not respond to any institutional encouragement to innovation for fear that the free market created today might be legislated out of existence tomorrow.[201] The creation of representative structures could not overcome this problem, so long as the republic lacked a culture through which the subaltern elements of society could represent their interests. A republican political science with a lexicon for the defense of markets, small property, and political equality allowed the subaltern elements of society, which had innovated to create new structures of neighborhood and new repertoires of protest, a means to express their modernity without surrendering their agency to large property owners and physiocratic schemes for economic restructuring.[202] Economic modernity could attain legitimacy because it need no longer be the project of an administrative class.

The existence of a language of democratic capitalism may also help us understand some of the features of French political economy in the nineteenth century. Amartya Sen has alerted us to the dependence of modern economic relations on moral codes and relations of trust that are based on noncommercial logics.[203] While the thrust of his own work is to challenge the dominant paradigm of explanation in economics, rather than to offer a new interpretation of specific paths of economic development, we can usefully capture his insight to explain some paradoxes of French economic history.[204] Classical political economy has found it difficult to reconcile the relatively high growth rates in the French economy in the nineteenth century, the resistance to corporations in the modern sense, the consensus in favor of state intervention, and the dominance of the small firm and the industrial neighborhood. William Reddy's fine study of the textile industry exemplified the gap between the assumptions of paradigmatic economic development and the real nature of economic relations, going so far as to argue that the entrepreneurial functions in the French economy were carried out by artisans and small producers. Only they bore risk.[205] Yet Reddy's story of the imposition of political economy on a differently structured reality underplays the extent to which the subaltern classes had access to an alternative model of markets and production, what Charles Sabel and Jonathan Zeitlin call "high-skill, universal machine economies."[206] If Sen makes us anticipate a shared moral world that will allow for relations of trust as a prerequisite for modern commercial relations, then the existence of republican political science fulfills that anticipation in the French case, whose most successful sectors were precisely of this sort.

What the study of the *partage* debate reveals is that republican political economy was not restricted to the world of the artisan, that it could be directed toward phenomena far from that area of economic life. If further work was to support the contention that a democratic economic culture was one of the outcomes of the French Revolution, and at least a partial determinant of French economic development, then Delpierre's victory may well have been far more than rhetorical. We cannot say that French economic development took place despite the French Revolution. More to the point, without the Revolution, France could not have created its economic culture or its political culture.

CHAPTER 5

Learning to Be Free:
The Educational System of
the Commercial Republic

The meaning of democracy was established as administrators and citizens struggled to create working institutions. The creation of a democratic idea of market economics was a central contribution. The people did not pursue their happiness only in social and economic institutions, however. The welfare of the population, and the capacity for autonomy of its members, depended on participation in state institutions as well, none more than the educational system. As one might imagine, modern republican thinkers under the Directory were particularly exercised by the possibilities of formal education. Teachers were vital agents, for example, in the education in moral sentiment envisaged by François de Neufchâteau: after 18 Fructidor he told the teachers of the central schools, "the nation rests its hopes in you: it has charged you with the preparation of our children for the vocation of liberty, the perpetuation of our taste for knowledge and useful work, the preparation of the coming generation for public life, through passing on the heritage of enlightenment and virtue that we owe to posterity. You must make the human species aware of the precious features of the capacity for self-improvement that it has been granted by nature."[1] Formal education was understood to have a central role in the integration of political liberty into modern life.

Implementing these ideas required overcoming numerous practical and political obstacles. The administrators and legislators of the Directory inherited a troubled educational system. The national system established in the dying days of the Convention did not work, and it could not work since its goals were so unclear. In education, as in every other feature of social life, the early confidence of the revolutionaries in their mission of regeneration had been quickly undermined. The first great statement of revolutionary goals for education, Talleyrand's report and law proposal to the Constituent

Assembly on 11 September 1791, gave easy assurance that the application of fairly obvious principles would guide the creation of a rational system.[2] Following Sieyès's views on modern social life, Talleyrand defined the duty of the state to be the creation of an educational system that met evident social needs: primary schools for the poor and advanced schools for the rich. A little over a year later, Condorcet's reports reflected the growing awareness that modern social life and the institutions of a free state could not be so easily resolved.

Whereas Talleyrand saw education as the provision of skills to persons in particular social situations, Condorcet understood education to be a systemic element that could stabilize the dynamic and evolving world of modern social life. He perceived that the very process of enlightenment and development, which he argued was the central tendency of modern history, could self-destruct without properly calibrated systems of education.[3] The immanent rationality of modern life, and its capacity to fulfill everybody's needs, was not obvious even to the people who could benefit from its effects and could be destroyed "if natural inequality was not rendered meaningless, relative to the happiness derived from the social state and from the exercise of the rights common to all."[4] This problem, of making evident the rationality of a system comprised of individuals to the individuals themselves, was the fundamental logical dilemma of democratic government, and much of Condorcet's thinking on voting systems was inspired by it.[5] His views on education were haunted by an even deeper problem: the possibility that modern social life might produce not individuals roughly equal in their intellectual and moral capacities but utterly different species of human beings.

The division of labor, which, following Smith, Condorcet thought to be the principal mechanism driving the progress of modern societies, threatened to create a new inequality of the intellect, in effect creating two different types of person.[6] The repetitive, simple tasks that a perfected productive process demanded would make operatives stupid, "and so the perfecting of the arts will become, for some of the human race, a cause of their stupefaction, and create, in every nation, a body of men incapable of recognizing any interests above the most base."[7] Smith himself, in arguing for public provision of education, had noticed this effect of the division of labor and made it the cornerstone of his case for universal primary schools.[8] Condorcet's originality lay in his insight that these differential effects of the division of labor were injurious even if one seemed to benefit from them. Unadulterated repetitive labor would dull the moral intelligence of the poor, but those who tried to make political power "a patrimonial possession, by devoting them-selves to certain professions," corrupted themselves just as surely.[9] The con-sequences of Smith's thinking on the absolute necessity of a universal edu-cational system to stabilize a modern polity drove Condorcet to draw the radical conclusion that without such a system, which would allow even the poorest inhabitants of a country to understand their rights, the only possibil-ities were "the creation of an eternal war of avarice and duplicity . . . be-tween the different classes of the same people" or a demagogic state "where one can only maintain the shadow of a false equality by sacrificing to it lib-erty and security."[10] Education was not a preferential social policy or a politi-cal strategy for Condorcet, but a structural necessity for stabilizing a modern social and political order.

Condorcet developed this conclusion from his reading of Rousseau, espe-cially the "Discourse on the Origins of Inequality." Rousseau, more than any other, had explained precisely why there could be no legitimate division into rulers and ruled, "and this merits the glory of being placed among those truths that can be neither forgotten nor denied."[11] His influence was also ev-ident in Condorcet's distinction between a citizenry that had been educated to a rational love of the laws, "without which the desire for liberty is a pas-sion and not a virtue," and one that saw the law as an externally imposed limitation on action.[12] The Rousseauian background to Condorcet's peda-gogical speculations allowed him to link two models of instruction, *éducation nationale* and *instruction publique,* which were normally seen as alternatives to each other. The citizen had to be autonomous in civil society and in his political participation, so the educational system had to attend to both sides of his nature. The actual system was the formal embodiment of the universal commitment to knowledge that was supposed to characterize a modern so-ciety and guard against the degenerating effects it could produce.[13]

Any appropriation of Rousseau in defense of formal education was not a simple matter; Lakanal was to remark that Rousseau's writings on education were "the most useful to read, but the most dangerous to imitate."[14] Con-dorcet illustrated the truth of that observation. He could not succeed in ex-plaining just how the ideal of universal education might be institutionalized. There were too many ideas of universality at play in his texts, each an alter-native to the rigor of the society of the social contract that Rousseau himself had theorized as the solution to the problems he identified. At various points in his writings on education Condorcet cited three different warrants for the progressive nature of his ideas. He variously invoked the universal assent of the enlightened men of Europe to the validity of the curriculum, the participation of the enlightened French citizen in the drama of the perfection of the republic, and the universal benefit of an enlightened public culture for that republic.[15] The very centrality of education to the possibility of a free society made it difficult to conceive of any particular educational system, curriculum, or generalized popular culture that could fulfill all these ideals of universality. Too much ideological weight was placed on the idea of education, making it next to impossible for any system to carry this philosophical load. Condorcet could not supplement his insights into the role of the idea of public education with a credible practice of a public school system. It is hard to see how the demands of these contexts would be filled by a graduated scheme of public schools without guaranteed access, which was what Condorcet proposed. While the role that Condorcet foresaw for education in a regenerated society was far more extensive than that envisaged by Talleyrand, in the end the institutions they both recommended were not that different.

The gap between the vision of the universal function of education in a free state and the actual institutions that the republic eventually set up was widened by the circumstances of their creation. Despite the endless discussions of education by the committees of the three assemblies, the definitive laws on education, of 3 and 4 Brumaire, Year IV (25–26 October 1795), were last-minute acts of the Convention, "a crippled child of its senility," as Luminais put it.[16] None of the difficult decisions that needed to be made to create an effective educational system were confronted in this set of laws. The provision for primary education, with one school envisaged for every canton, fell far short of actual needs. The second level of education, the central schools, had already been established by the law of 7 Ventôse, Year III (25 February 1795), and the Daunou law, as the Brumaire acts were termed, simply acknowledged them and attempted to organize their curriculum.[17] What it did not do was integrate the planned primary schools with the central schools; there was a three-year gap between the highest level of primary instruction and the lowest rung of the next level. As Daunou himself stated, in a later report, the lack of coordination among the schools was mirrored by the haphazard nature of the curriculum of the central schools themselves, which was not truly progressive. There was no clear reason for following a year of language study with a year of mathematics. Moreover, the role of the central school was confused; it was not clear if it replaced the older college or the university.[18] This was the reason he proposed the creation of nine *lycées* to provide true higher education in the arts and sciences, a proposal that did not even get a hearing.

The Daunou law has attracted attention because it became the defining revolutionary law on education, but its goals were in fact modest. The law was conservative in inspiration. It responded to the perception, voiced by an orator at the Lycée des Arts in Prairial, Year II, that the Revolution, though inspired by men of letters, threatened to destroy letters.[19] The law recognized the reality of the central schools, instead of creating new institutions, and limited rather than enhanced the number of primary schools. It reflected the counsel of despair from the Executive Committee on Public Education, which in its final report had essentially abandoned any attempt to establish primary education.[20] The committee's only advice had been for the republic to exert a benign neglect, try to distribute books, and hope that parents would improvise measures to educate their own children. It is therefore completely understandable that the central thrust of the education law was the creation of the Institut National, not as an educational institution but as a research foundation, a modernized academy. The most striking element of the Daunou law was its aspiration to preserve the personnel of French cultural life rather than to found a new system that would transform French political culture.

The institutions of French culture life were in crisis by 1794. As Dupont de Nemours pointed out to Bernardin de Saint-Pierre, when pressing on him his scheme for a national library system, the government recognized that the book trade had collapsed and that the state was going to have to support men of letters and scientists.[21] The deregulation of the book trade had made the publication of books too risky and redirected the industry toward periodical literature.[22] A grand total of 69 new books had been published in France in 1793, and only 396, of which 178 were of songs, were published in 1794.[23] The creation of the Institut National and the reinforcement of the central schools was a stopgap, of a piece with the pensions for intellectuals introduced by Grégoire, until a proper functioning of literary and artistic life would allow men of genius to benefit from the copyrights newly accorded them.[24] The Daunou law could not save teachers, legislators, and administrators of the republic from the Sisyphean task of fashioning an educational system to inculcate and support liberty, because it was only a defensive and ad hoc response to crisis. In fact, the very distance between the ideal system and the provisions of the law would be the major impediment to their resolution of this problem. Given the difficulties, then, the creativity and to some degree success of the republicans' effort to create a modern, demo-cratic set of educational ideals and institutions is more striking than the more frequently remarked upon vista of "phantoms soaring over ruins."[25] Republican educational institutions were not to survive the republic, but the work invested in creating a republican educational system created new models and contents for popular education. Guizot's own laws in 1833 were the real foundation of the French public school system, but his institutional achievement would have been unthinkable without the creation of educa-tional goals in the Revolution.[26]

That All Might Learn

The weighty political and cultural problems that lurked in the educational system did not make themselves apparent to the legislators and administra-tors of the Directory at once. This was hardly surprising, since as Pierre Benezech, the minister of the interior, reported to the Directors in his first overview of the state of the country, only the medical schools and the Ecole Polytechnique were in operation. Issues of justice and access could hardly arise when there were no institutions to which one might have access.[27] This was something of an exaggeration, since the central schools were beginning to organize themselves, but it expressed the essential truth that the prob-lems being confronted were those of setting up a system, rather than run-ning it.[28] As Ginguené, writing as head of the education section of the Minis-try of the Interior, put it, "you have said everything about education when you have said that everything remains to be done."[29] Understandably, the matters that concerned the councils and the ministry in the first year of the Directory had more to do with the local politics of education than with its central principles. As with every set of revolutionary foundations, towns competed for the economic advantages that the new schools would bring.[30] Tarbes, Rodez, and Langres, for example, petitioned to move the central schools to their towns from the *chef-lieu* of the department. Places with a long history of educational institutions, such as Douai, reacted angrily to the pretensions of new rivals, in this case Mauberge, and other towns asked to be allowed to set up a supplementary central school.[31] Local administrations also tussled with the problem of raising funds for the new schools, especially when it seemed as if they were debarred from using the old college buildings for them, as these were now *biens nationaux*. The members of the Council of Five Hundred drew on their years of parliamentary experience and refused

to allow themselves to be distracted by minutiae, by debarring any such petitions and by quickly deciding to allow such use of the old colleges.[32]

The unfinished business of the Convention, rather than the administration of the new schools, reminded members that considerations of principle
could not be postponed indefinitely. The results of the competition for textbooks, announced to the Council of Five Hundred, were one leftover element of the universal educational project that had been abandoned by the
Daunou law, and no one was more closely associated with that project than
the rapporteur, Lakanal.[33] Lakanal's plan for republican education, introduced to the Convention on 26 June 1793, had been a consistent application
of the principle of universality of access and provision to the problem of republican education.[34] While Le Peletier de Saint-Fargeau's proposal for militarized boarding schools looked like a more radically republican program, it
was never a serious proposal and had been read into the record as an act of
recognition of one of the martyrs of the republic.[35] Lakanal's plan, supported
by Sieyès and Daunou, was simple. It proposed that the republic found a primary school for every one thousand inhabitants and that all further education be funded privately. To found institutions of higher education in the
larger cities would be an offense to equality and would only "change the
forms of oppression."[36] Instead, the public purse should ensure that teachers' salaries were high enough to make teaching an attractive career and
that the benefits of education were extended to women. Other than primary schools for all, the only educational initiative foreseen in the Lakanal
plan was a series of national festivals. Though this proposal was rejected by
the Convention, its fundamentals, particularly the single tier of instruction,
were incorporated in the Bouquier law of 29 Frimaire, Year II (19 December
1793). In fact, this law went even further than Lakanal's original proposal to
provide universal public education by promising to pay teachers proportion-
ally to the number of students they taught and by allowing the creation of a
school by anyone holding a *certificat de civisme*. This law, partly amended on
the initiative of Lakanal in Brumaire, Year III, to fix salaries, instituted the
idea of a right to primary education as the fundamental educational promise
of the Revolution. And despite the difficulties that primary education en-
countered, the idea of such a right retained its force.[37]

In bringing up the question of elementary textbooks, Lakanal reopened
the debate that the Daunou law had effectively avoided. Lakanal had attempted to resist the law in the first place, arguing that the Institut National
was nothing other than a revised corporation. If there were to be state-

funded central schools, then the teachers should be drawn from among those who had already given years to the instruction of the young in the primary schools.[38] There were political impediments to raising the issue of republican schooling. The support for universal public education by the neo-Jacobins in the *Journal des hommes libres* and the *Orateur plébien* made education a dangerous issue. Moreover, the form of education was prescribed in the constitution. Despite these difficulties, Lakanal easily reopened the question of the provision of republican instruction.[39] The need was too obvious to be denied. As Dupont de Nemours wrote to Boissy d'Anglas, Lakanal was "bringing water to the river,"[40] simply contributing to an already powerful force. The specific source of the debate was soon lost, as the Directory resisted paying for the mass printing of books that had been approved by the previous regime, but for which it could see little use. This resistance was politically unimportant, as the discussion broadened into a revisited debate on the use and nature of the primary school.[41] On 29 Frimaire, Year V (15 December 1796), Roger Martin of Toulouse made the lack of regard for primary schools the cornerstone of his attack on the Daunou law.[42] He pointed out that the gap in the system undermined its rationality. In addition, he said, the focus on the higher levels of education ignored the fact that "nothing is of greater importance to the legislators of a republic than the means by which the great mass of people acquire the knowledge necessary for them to play their role in the political order."[43] After his speech he was appointed to the council's committee on education and so became the rapporteur for the first general report on the primary school system, delivered on 12 Priarial, Year V (1 May 1797).[44]

Roger Martin's report established the arguments put forward by Directorial republicans for a universal primary school system. They exploited the resources of the language of moral sentiment and the ideal of the communicating citizen to construct their vision of democratic education. The school, they argued, was the institution that could inculcate the habits of body, soul, and mind necessary to live the life of a citizen in a modern republic.

> In effect, it is this wise institution that, embracing the whole of a person at an age when he is subject to the most profound and durable impressions, can give him his first social identity, develop at the same time his physical, moral, and intellectual faculties, . . . inspire in everyone, from infancy, those happy dispositions, those sacred principles of justice and morality, which can at times be overwhelmed by the passions, but which sooner or later recapture their salutary rule.[45]

The core mission of the primary school was to prepare children for life in a democratic society. In addition to literacy and numeracy, children had "to develop in the heart honest, generous sentiments, and to learn to feel the ills of others," in other words, to develop the faculty of moral sentiment.[46] Martin and others teased out the consequences of an education aimed at generating the sentiments proper to social life, "as a product of civil society, and a source of the benefits of civil society."[47] It had to be provided to both sexes, since both were equal participants in society.[48] Most crucial, the form the education took had to be compatible with the values of the modern republic, of which it was supposed to be the exemplar. Léonard Bourdon, one-time radical Jacobin and headmaster of a school for orphans, developed this theme and proposed that the primary schools be self-governing. The schools had to reflect republican liberty; "the man and the child are alike in this one point: the one and the other are brought to the performance of their duty through the enjoyment of their rights."[49] As the rapporteur of the project for the Directory neatly summarized it, schools should not teach students the rights and duties they would someday be responsible for, but rather should operate on their basis. Republican schools should teach by example, "so as to change the state of servitude of the student into one of freedom, into a free education that would stimulate the faculties of the soul, instead of constricting them, and channel the passions in a useful direction, rather than tormenting them."[50] Such a free institution would release the young from all the "moral and physical prejudices that enchain their reason and oppress their hearts," and in so doing create the modern individuals fit to be modern republicans.[51]

The idea that children could not learn to participate in free social life unless their education was modeled on it was one of the favorite themes of the minister of the interior, François de Neufchâteau. Twenty years before the Revolution, he had condemned contemporary teaching methods as a torture dealt out in "gothic institutions" designed to break the spirit of liberty natural to youth.[52] Heavily influenced by the educational theory and practice of Jéremie-Jacques Oberlin, with whom he was friendly, he proposed that the principle of liberty be applied to even the most mechanical and elementary tasks of the primary school.[53] He argued that the manner in which the young were taught to read and write was so wrong-headed that all it succeeded in doing was giving them the impression that "reason and science were arbitrary and totally dependant on caprice."[54] Instead of teaching the alphabet, which did not contain all the sounds of French, he argued for teaching from a phonetic system of thirty-four elements, associated with symbols and the words of which they were characteristic. Under this system, students could rationally deduce the meanings of words and learn to compose. This method would teach rationality and allow students to learn together: "through these combined exercises, diversified and spread out over some time, progress is certain, because you will allow the children to correct themselves and one another, which will encourage a useful self-love."[55] Learning to read and write would become a model for the collective learning and immanent rationality of republican society, and form the basis for a totally republican education.

The proposal Roger Martin made in Prairial, Year V, reflected these aspirations toward democratic education but carried a stronger imprint of political and financial necessity. While he argued that in the long run a universal system based on republican principles of equality was necessary, the budget of the republic could not support even the teachers for such an ambitious system at that time. Of the 30,000 teachers that would optimally be involved, the republic could afford 9,000,[56] thereby creating one school for every 3,000 persons in the country. Although this proposal represented a big increase in the number of schools envisaged by the law of 27 Brumaire, Year III, it was still a compromise between the wider views of the democrats and those of the critics of any national system. After the coup of 18 Fructidor, Year V, the political impediment to a more thoroughgoing overhaul of the educational system no longer existed. Education became one element in the project of creating specifically republican institutions as a means of generating the social basis for the regime.[57] The opportunities opened up by the coup provoked the committee, and Roger Martin in particular, to a more daring plan.

A second proposal put forward by Roger Martin confronted the great shortcoming of the Daunou law, the gap between primary schools and the central schools.[58] His plan was to halve the number of central schools and use the money saved to create three or four secondary schools in every department. The curriculum for these proposed schools manifested the educational ideas of J. H. Hassenfratz, who had argued for technical education in the arts, agriculture, and trade, allied to a grounding in ancient and modern literatures.[59] The redeployment of resources suggested that the republic did not need to give too much support to education in the honorable and liberal professions. These were so attractive that people would prepare themselves for them in any case. Instead, the idea was to spread among "the classes of the people least favored by wealth, those hitherto least served by education, those simple and useful types of knowledge, without which the benefits of our kind of government will remain unrecognized or unknown to the greater number of the population, political equality but an illusion, and liberty a vain name."[60] This is another example of the commercial republican strategy of integrating social mechanisms of emulation and ambition with collective provisions ensuring relative equality. In characterizing the constituency he thought would be attracted to the new schools as "the greater part of the artisans in the towns, and smaller landowners in the countryside,"[61] Martin hammered home the point that his project aimed to consolidate the democratic basis of the republic. Both Condorcet's thinking about the functions of schools and his four-tier system of education were revived in this plan, with the difference that Martin could imagine democratic education in a concrete way rather than as a formal demand.

Supporters of the new plan emphasized its democratic possibilities. Luminais, in particular, argued that the new institutions would align universal provision with access to universally valid culture, while providing an adequate number of institutions of higher learning and research.[62] By creating secondary schools the republic could make the sciences the common heritage of all rather than the privilege of a minority.[63] However, the debate on the proposition revealed the lack of consensus on the meaning of universal educational provision. François Maugenest and Jean-François Ehrmann both pointed out that creating one primary school for every three thousand inhabitants would still mean only one school for every seven communes on average, making the secondary schools an irrelevance.[64] It seemed preposterous to them to create secondary schools unless the primary schools were healthy and well supported. The real criticisms came from those opposed to any dilution of the central schools and unconvinced of the practicality of providing another level of school. Opponents of the scheme, such as Alexis-François Pison-Dugalland and Jean-François Barailon, were skeptical of the very idea of an intermediary kind of popular science and of the possibility of *gens de cabinet* (pointy-heads) teaching practical skills.[65] Other speakers reminded the council that they were not inventing an educational system for a country that had never known one. Anthelme Marin argued that they had to meet the expectations of parents that the schools would tutor their children and inculcate habits of self-discipline and hard work, rather than lecturing them from within a systematic understanding of the world of knowledge.[66] The debate attained clarity through Pison-Dugalland's intervention. He pointed out that while those who disagreed with the scheme for secondary schools supported the idea of universal primary education, they argued that limited further education was not an offense to equality. Neither did differentiated education threaten the political rights of those who did not participate in it; such education was a natural feature of a complex modern social system:

> Nature and necessity spontaneously create farmers and artisans. Self-interest and the taste for riches spontaneously give rise to commerce. Accumulated riches create the arts and luxury, they promote the contemplative disposition, which in turn produces the sciences and the art of government, which, in a free state, ought to be the most important among them. In this process all I see is the effect of nature, and little of the intervention of the legislator.[67]

Of course, the deputies of the council could not find any reasonable grounds on which to discriminate between these two views of the nature of modern society. It was simply impossible to tell how far universal common education should extend to ensure the basis for democratic politics and how much specialization was necessary to promote the progress of the arts and sciences. Faced with a well-defined dilemma they fudged, by rejecting the idea of secondary schools while at the same time entertaining Mortier-Duparc's proposal that model primary schools with an extra year of instruction be established.[68]

The proposals for secondary schools and reformed primary schools marked the limits of the legislative imagination on the issue of universal provision of education. Understandably enough, the councils could find no way past this impasse. Although the discussion of primary education was reprised in Years VI and VII, no new proposals were introduced and the council became more interested in a series of laws penalizing private schools.[69] Projects to achieve the goals of republican education were limited to discussions of improving teachers' salaries.[70] The executive was as inactive on the primary schools as the legislature in the latter half of Year VI and in Year VII.

In fact, one effect of the rapprochement between the councils and the Directory after the Fructidor coup was the revelation to the deputies of what administrators had long known: that the effort to create primary schools had been an almost total failure. The replies to the circular of 20 Fructidor, Year V, looking for information on the educational foundations of the Revolution, made depressing reading.[71] The departments that gave any information on primary schools all depicted a disaster. In Cantal only 30 of the mandatory 143 schools were even in operation, and the Ardèche had none of its 42.[72] Even departments with high rates of literacy had no great success in establishing schools; "very few" schools were in operation in the department of the Meurthe, where 80 percent of the population was literate, while the Eure, whose literacy rate was 70 percent, had only 50 of the 250 primary schools proposed.[73] The agents of the Directory in the countryside reported that the primary schools could not even replicate the old pattern of the *petites écoles*. Rather than finding an increase in winter, as children were released from farm tasks to attend school, agents recorded a decline in the numbers of children attending school in that season in 1798–99.[74] In some departments primary schools were closing for lack of students. A common desire for educational provision had united the warring factions in Nîmes, and they had set up their own primary schools in 1793, but even these were inoperative by Year VI.[75] Ginguené, in a message in reply to the request for information from the councils, stated bluntly that with few exceptions in most departments the primary schools did not exist.[76]

The reasons for the failures of the republican primary schools identified by Ginguené—ranging from the lack of adequate salaries for teachers, through a prejudice on the part of the rural population in favor of religious education, to the gap between primary schools and the central schools—doubtless had their effects. But more profound social processes impeded any project to "ground the republic in the primary school," as Heurtault-Lamerville proposed.[77] The literate elites who conducted the debates and made up the plans for education conceived of literacy as a quasi-natural attribute of a human being. To be illiterate was to lack a vital social sense. This attitude did not acknowledge the extent to which the attainment of literacy was promoted by particular contexts and needs. The accumulation of social practices centered on literacy in Paris made illiteracy a real handicap to members of the popular classes; as Daniel Roche explains, the man in the streets of Paris more or less had to read.[78] Paris was exceptional in that regard, and nowhere else was literacy a prerequisite for everyday life. The early years of the Revolution, by making politics national, had created such a need, and correspondents bewailing the lack of *esprit public* yearned for the time when reading the news from the poster-newspapers was a daily enthusiasm.[79] Yet this was precisely the kind of mobilization for politics that the republic now rejected. Since the Directors had good reason not to promote those kinds of energies, the project of literacy was subject to more paradoxical social conditions. For instance, the only agency that had promoted peasant literacy and numeracy in the eighteenth century had been that bastion of superstition, the church, but the church was understood to be the antithesis of republican education.[80]

Few participants in the debate realized that if the republic's efforts were to have any success, the new schoolteacher would have to fulfill a set of social roles parallel to those once played by the priest, while simultaneously introducing villagers to new contexts of literacy. Maugenest, with his suggestion that the schoolteachers also run small local agricultural societies, seems to have had an inkling of the forces that actually promoted literacy.[81] There was also an interesting suggestion by Jean-François Ehrmann that the council approach the issue of mass education not through principles and theories but by investigating the methods of systems that did seem to work. He recommended they take up the example of the margravate of Baden.[82] Ehrmann was also exceptional in underlining the need to provide primary education in tongues other than French if local populations were to be enticed into the world of education.[83]

Interventions like these, which went beyond generalities and adverted to the specific, local conditions that determined the success or failure of the educational institutions of the republic, were few and far between. Majority opinion was far closer to the view of Barailon on this topic, when he advised that the republic adhere to its responsibilities under the Daunou law but abandon more ambitious projects. In the face of the resistance of the population, which he put down to its lack of good will, its poverty, the labor shortage, the lack of good teachers, and the lack of respect shown those they could find, he could see no possibility of creating a workable system.[84] Barailon's rejection of the population's fitness for general education also marks the beginning of the process through which the anxieties and difficulties generated within the debate were projected out into the population; the emerging construct of social class was already beginning to make its effects felt.

The primary school, which at first seemed to be the institution most suited to the goals of a republican education, proved to be an intellectual cul-de-sac. There was no general demand for universal civic education, especially in the countryside, and the state was unwilling to exercise wholesale coercion to force children into the schools. It could, and did, insist that its own agents send their children to its schools, and would attempt to stifle any form of instruction it thought avowedly counterrevolutionary, but would not utterly abandon the constitutional principle of freedom of religious instruction.[85] Since neither society nor state was willing to act, the discussions of primary education were fruitless. And though the goal of universal primary education was never challenged, its attainment became indefinitely postponed. The most concrete achievement of the debate on the primary school was not a set of institutions but another integration of the modern republican model of the citizen into a feature of a modern society, in this case mass education. The debate on republican education laid down markers for the future. It provided another example of the idea that the republic was to be understood as fundamentally egalitarian. However, the problem of education, science, and the humanities remained unresolved for, and without an institutional place in, the democratic republic.

Modern Literature and the Modern Republic

Universal primary education seemed to be an obvious consequence of modern republican principles, but the ideal was undermined by inattention to the social and cultural obstacles that hampered the creation of a new educational system. Advanced schools posed problems and offered opportunities that were the opposite of those generated by the primary schools: they were theoretically problematic but pragmatically productive. Their selective entry and abstruse subjects were difficult to reconcile with egalitarian principles; in the absence of a properly functioning primary school system they could become the ground for a political aristocracy, as Condorcet had feared.[86] As it turned out this fear was somewhat misplaced. While the central schools were filled with the children of liberal professionals, administrators, and merchants, these elite groups did not dominate the new institutions any more than they had the old.

Still, the principled issue retained its worrying edge.[87] The relative success of the central schools, relative since they never had more than a quarter of the number of students of the old *collèges*, made them the institution in which the consequences of the application of republican principles to the educational system were worked through. The network of central schools was a fixture by 1798 and allowed teachers, administrators, and legislators to stop "occupying themselves with new theories on public education, most of which have been fruitless, and instead apply themselves to real issues."[88] In their work with the schools the administrators, teachers, and legislators developed a practice of republican education. This practice escaped the initial premises of the political debate and created a new understanding of the role of formal education, the sciences, and the arts in the construction of the modern citizen. The schools had this strategic effect because of their political importance to the regime. After Year VI the central schools became the institution of the republican state that *commissaires* pointed to when they outlined their hopes for the future, even as they complained of the disasters they faced in other spheres. Their monthly reports emphasized that only the central schools compensated for the problems in the other republican educational institutions.[89] They also acknowledged that the achievements of the central schools were due to the teachers: "every day the number of students increases, and for this due praise must be given to the majority of teachers who devote themselves to the schools and the prosperity of republican education."[90] The schools, and the teachers who staffed them, had cultural and political consequence; every project for their reform had to be a negotiation by the republican state, anxious to preserve these assets.

The need for reforms was obvious. There were two species of problems that beset the central schools. The organization of the school system as a whole was incoherent. Entry to the first cycle of the central school came at age twelve, but primary education sought only to teach "reading, writing, basic arithmetic, and the fundamental notions of republican morality," a task that was normally completed by age eight or nine.[91] There was no educational system worthy of the name, since the first element did not prepare students to enter the second. The secondary schools proposed to fill in this gap did not make the problem disappear. And it was only the most glaring of the organizational problems. The ad hoc nature of the original legislation left basic issues, such as the professional status of the teachers, their remuneration, and the terms of their appointment, undefined. These organizational problems had to be solved if the system was to function.

In addition, there were glaring pedagogical issues. Even Daunou, who gave his name to the law that created the system, thought the curriculum of the schools made no sense.[92] The system admitted students to two-year cycles of subjects, but with no internal progression. Languages, for instance, were studied between ages twelve and fourteen, and then abandoned until two years later, when the final cycle again took on belles lettres and history, a system Roger Martin condemned as "nothing less than eliminating the study of languages from public instruction."[93] The middle cycle, for children aged fourteen to sixteen, consisted of mathematics, physics, and chemistry, but there was no mathematical preparation in the first cycle, whose only scientific content was in natural history. Some on the council defended the principle of modular education. Letourneur, for example, argued that the students who were stimulated to appreciate the fundamental principles of learning would be "better prepared for the diverse situations and occupations of society" than those more closely schooled in another system.[94] Nevertheless, this defense of the principle provided no defense of a particularly incoherent version of it.

All of the discussions of education under the Directory circled around these two sets of concrete problems. The Council on Public Instruction was created as an instrument of the executive by François de Neufchâteau during his second term as minister of the interior in 1798 and 1799. Its mission was to impose a design on the educational system where the legislature had failed to do so.[95] Originally charged with ensuring the republican content of the textbooks used by the teachers, the council soon widened its remit to the organizing principles of the entire system.[96] The textbooks would have to be rewritten, but only after the philosophical principles of a republican education had been identified. Though the drawing, mathematics, physics, and natural history classes were generally reported to be productive, the council was instructed to reform the course designs to conform to the principles they would enunciate.[97]

This singularity of intent was reinforced by the coherence of the personnel. The initial council of six had three members (Jacquemont, Garat, and Le Breton) who were members of the Ideologue circle, and they were reinforced when Destutt de Tracy was appointed in Ventôse, Year VII.[98] Palmer has argued that the Ideologue group dominated the thinking of the council and gave it direction. Certainly, they were consciously acting to further an Ideologue agenda.[99] Destutt de Tracy was appointed to the task of rewriting the general grammar syllabus, the strategic center of the central schools' curriculum from the point of view of the Ideologues.[100] Their ambitions even motivated them to petition the minister to commission Garat to write a "text for the young concerned with the sciences termed ideological," which would be a primer for the primary schools.[101] A reorganization of the school curriculum around general grammar was clearly the preferred strategy of the Ideologues to bring coherence and progressivity to the schools of the republic, despite the fact that this course was the least attended course in the curriculum.[102] But this policy proposal was based on even more profound commitments in their understanding of the function of education in a republic.

The Ideologues did not accept the modern republican model of education for citizenship. They did not share the republican understanding of the psychology of sentiment that was the foundation of arguments for democratic education. The ideal of a unified and egalitarian education, which structured the opposition of *éducation nationale* to *instruction publique*, was in their view based on a misapprehension of human behavior. They argued that the desire for a common political education reflected an anachronistic belief in the common capacities of humans and misidentified the real communities in which men and women participated, which were differentiated by role and function. As consistent environmentalists they did not agree with the Scottish position that moral judgment was an independent faculty of humans, the view that provided the foundation for arguments for social and political equality.

Their argument developed from the thoughts of prerevolutionary educational reformers such as Chatolais and Nicolas Baudeau, who had criticized the unified curriculum of the old colleges and called for education to match social position.[103] The Ideologues reinforced this view by holding that attachment to education in common revealed an unscientific commitment to a psychology of the rational soul, which had been exploded (in their view) by moral realists such as Helvétius and Saint-Lambert.[104] The old college course had ignored completely the real contexts that had formed the cognitive capabilities and aptitudes of the students, and those in which they would use their minds after their education. They were also highly critical of the ideal of education developed from the writings of Rousseau. The notion of self-creation through education seemed preposterous to them. Reflexive knowledge of the social system was available to different members of society depending on the level of abstraction of which they were capable. The most general form of knowledge, and therefore the most appropriate for a republican elite, was general grammar: this was the master discipline from which the structure of the curriculum would be derived and the most exclusive course taught in the upper cycle of courses.[105] This powerful functionalist vision also responded to the problem of the teaching profession's status. Teachers were to be instruments for the expression of the rationality of the system, exemplars of the formal rationality that animated the educational institutions. They were to be the channels through which the rationality of the curriculum was transmitted, rather than independent agents themselves. Just as social position determined who should be taught, so the state would determine how students should be taught. Curiously, this marriage of form and function echoed the arguments of the proponents of democratic education, such as Léonard Bourdon, who had argued that the republican function of education had to be immanent in its form, and so sought the greatest latitude possible for teachers and pupils. A different notion of system produced a different idea of function.

One can easily follow the deliberate manner in which the Ideologue members of the Council on Public Instruction sought to promote school reform within this understanding of its nature and function. The most explicit theoretical exposition of their ideas was provided by Destutt de Tracy in his final statement on their work in 1801.[106] He argued that social position and cognitive capacity were equivalent and derived from the inexorable laws of society. Since social nature had divided men into two classes, laborers and property owners, the school should reflect that division. The education of the first should be short, so as not to deprive families of the fruits of young labor, while that of the second should be the best possible. The education system should do nothing to confound the two classes, which were different, "morally, in their capacities and in their natures."[107] The initiation of the elite into the rational and scientific apprehension of society had to be carefully controlled since the future of the regime depended on it. For that reason Destrutt de Tracy was suspicious of the ritual invocation of Condillac by teachers of general grammar.[108] He suspected them of putting up a smoke screen for literary studies rather than properly teaching analysis of understanding, followed by grammar and then logic—a strict genealogy designed to fashion the consciousness of the students and to turn them into analysts of society.

New plans for the function of general grammar in the education of a republican elite were paralleled by the new role envisaged for history. In the old colleges history had not established itself as a core subject; it was a supplement to rhetoric, the heart of the old Jesuit curriculum.[109] The new model of the training of a republican elite envisaged a greatly expanded role for history: no longer the record of particular civilizations, it would "concern itself with the documents of every society and of the epochs they represented."[110] History would be the last subject taught, "the crown of the edifice," where the students could perceive the working of the laws of social development that they had learned from their previous courses.[111] The Ideologue members of the committee felt so strongly about this program that they petitioned the minister directly to instruct the history teachers to structure their courses around the work of Constantin-François de Chasseboeuf, comte de Volney, and Edme Mentelle, even in advance of the final report of the committee.[112] Similarly, the jurisprudence course was not to be a training in French law but a grounding in the philosophical principles of natural law.[113] The policy of school reform proposed by the Ideologue members of the council followed consistently from their philosophical commitments. They proposed to reform the upper levels of the curriculum in order to make the schools what other people feared they might be, the seedbed for a republican elite. Their policy was to fashion the brain of the body politic and trust the brain to control and direct the rest of the organs and limbs in a rational manner. They were inventing a new kind of *ratio studiorum,* based on the social sciences rather than on rhetoric as the original Jesuit *ratio* had been, but equally calibrated to make an elite.[114]

In making their reforms, the Ideologues consistently applied the notion that the basis of a modern republic lay in a society of orders. They used the same idea of a social division of labor that had inspired Sieyès as their central informing conception for how a republican polity could be constructed, but they supported the idea with a more developed social psychology and a pedagogy. Despite the individual brilliance of some of the Ideologue writers and their powerful position within the educational bureaucracy, however, their efforts to control the curriculum were almost completely unsuccessful. We can calculate the ineffectiveness of their efforts using a remarkable source: the replies to François de Neufchâteau's circular to the teachers of Fructidor 20, Year V.[115] These documents, and the course descriptions appended to them, relate the syllabi, reading lists, and numbers of all the classes in the central schools, along with professional data on the teachers themselves. The model courses and syllabi sent in by the teachers reveal that they refused to implement the program of the council.[116]

Surprisingly, the general grammar curriculum was the least successful. Teachers in that subject never cited Helvétius as one of their core authors, and Garat's text was used by only two teachers out of the seventy-six that sent in returns. Claude Désirat and Tristan Horde, who have conducted the most systematic study of this subject in the schools, have even argued that there was a pattern in the teachers' resistance to the imposition of a curriculum in this field. Their resistance was not unstructured; rather, they substituted another curriculum firmly based on a competing notion of literary instruction.[117] The failure of *idéologie* in general grammar was a spectacular reversal, since general grammar was by definition an Ideologue subject. The pattern of failure to affect actual teaching practice was replicated across the entire range of courses, so much so that Martin Staum has concluded that the teaching of the central schools bore no imprint of *idéologie*.[118] Staum has suggested that the teachers' resistance was based on their previous pedagogical commitments. Many of them had been members of the disbanded religious teaching orders, and given this religious background they were predisposed to reject the imposition of materialist, and atheist, Helvétius as a model of moral science. This would make the story of republican advanced education converge with that of republican primary education: both were wrecked on the reef of long-run processes that they did not understand, on social and cultural dispositions held in place by the structures of civil society. The republican state confronted attitudes in civil society, in this case a traditional understanding of education, and lost. Neat as this pattern would be, it does not describe the fortunes of the central schools. Staum is clearly correct in identifying one element of the motivations of the teachers, but this is only part of the story. What it cannot explain is why the same teachers who were rejecting Helvétius and Garat as texts for their general grammar courses were happy to use the modern philosophical texts of Condillac and Locke and the new grammars of James Harris and Urbain Domergue.[119]

The modern curriculum of the Ideologues was not resisted in favor of the old classical curriculum of the colleges. Rather, it was changed and negotiated in pursuit of a different modern curriculum. This curriculum is a little more difficult to identify, because it was not worked out in one place in the educational hierarchy. We can see it developing through the interaction of educational administrators, the deputies in the councils, and the teachers. This particular deliberation on revolutionary education was remarkable because it hammered out a compromise between the conflicting imperatives that had asserted themselves around the educational system. This is one of the few revolutionary intellectual controversies in which the discussion of principle resulted in a change in practice. By its conclusion the participants had found a role for the central schools in a democratic conception of republican education.

The key social basis for an alternative agenda for educational reform was the teachers. They had the confidence to engage as a group and to assert their ideas and their interests because they had ceased to be a corporation and were taking on the character of a profession. This process had begun well before the Revolution. The expulsion of the Jesuits between 1762 and 1768 had stimulated a debate on the nature of the teaching profession, the educational background necessary to join it, and the kinds of certification necessary to guarantee competence. The most systematic reply to this set of issues was that of the Parlement of Paris, which proposed turning the Lycée Louis-le-Grand into a teacher-training college of the University of Paris and instituting a new certificate of competence in teaching, the *agrégation*.[120] Instituted in 1766, the *agrégation* created a new kind of professional identity for scholars and teachers, outside their membership of teaching orders, and separated competence for public instruction from religious discipline, a development that was resisted by the heads of the Paris colleges.[121] The professionalization of particular subject areas was rapid; by 1789, 75 percent of the *agrégés* in belles lettres and 80 percent of those in grammar were not clerics.[122] Clerics continued to dominate only in philosophy and theology, two areas that were not to do well during the Revolution. Professionalization was intensified by the Revolution.[123]

The teachers of the central schools came from the old colleges, the free teaching institutions (such as the *lycées*), and some revolutionary circles. Thus, they married professional competence to political acuity. Consider the teachers of general grammar and belles lettres: of the 144 who replied to the ministerial circular, 91 had taught in the Old Regime colleges and universities (one had been a fellow of Balliol College in Oxford).[124] These men were not new entrants to the profession for the most part; their average age was forty-two. They shared the new institutions with personnel who had criticized the colleges and provided the alternative to them under the monarchy, the teachers of private courses and free societies. Of these teachers 16 had taught in institutions such as the Lycée de Lyon and the Institut de Nantes. Moreover, there was a smattering of men whose pedagogical formation had been heavily influenced by the revolutionary experience itself. For instance, 7 of the teachers had attended the Ecole Normale of Year III. More important yet, for some of the personnel membership in the central schools was only one element in a distinctly republican career in education. At least 8 teachers had transferred within the central school system, and even more strikingly 4 teachers had been promoted from the primary schools. A republican career still meant a career in education. Only 4 teachers in all cited previous service to the republic in spheres such as departmental administration as their qualification for teaching. In fact, of the belles lettres teachers, 56 of the 77 had no participation in any institution of the republic other than the schools.

Another marker of professionalization was the commitment of the teachers to scholarship and publication. Among teachers of belles lettres, 36 mentioned that they had published in the field. Most of this work was poetry or drama, and so expressed the identity of the teachers as men of letters as well as scholars and teachers. Similar patterns can be seen in the sciences, which were less dominated by the notion of the man of letters and which had been less well institutionalized in the colleges. For instance, of the 24 teachers of natural history who replied to the census, 9 had publications in the field of the life sciences.[125] The new institutions profited from a transformation in the manner in which teachers organized themselves. As a profession, rather than a corporation, the teachers could promote their knowledge areas and their social interests in a way that would not conflict with the revolutionary distrust of political faction. They formed an element of a republican civil society.[126]

The deputies of the councils also saw teachers as professionals, in a new kind of collectivity. The Council of Five Hundred accepted a petition that teachers' salaries be calculated according to their total years of service to the profession, not just since the Revolution, acknowledging their autonomy from purely political considerations.[127] The principle that the profession was autonomous was reinforced by the nature of the tenure teachers came to enjoy. They could be dismissed only on the unanimous recommendation of the local educational board *(jury d'instruction)*, the departmental administration, and the Directory, thus "surrounding the beautiful role of public instruction with an aura of respect."[128] Teachers' salaries were pegged to those of departmental administrators, and both the councils and the Directory defended them against efforts by local administrators to divert funds to other uses.[129] Challenges to the principle that teachers' salaries should be equivalent to those of public officials arose from fears that this arrangement eroded professional status. L. S. Mercier cited Smith and "his immortal work *The Wealth of Nations*" in arguing that by paying teachers out of public funds the state undermined their professional improvement.[130] As Smith explained, professionalism and insecurity of income, if not of tenure, went together: "in some universities the salary makes a part, and frequently but a small part, of the emoluments of the teacher, of which a greater part arises from the honoraria or fees of his pupils. The necessity of application, though it is always more or less diminished, is not in this case entirely taken away."[131] This particular derivation of the professional principle was not applied, but the attempt to even raise the issue in these terms reveals the importance attributed to fixing the nature of the teaching profession.

In fact, the idea of a professional status for teachers was taken so seriously that the council seemed to confuse teaching with serving a public function and considered making it illegal for a teacher to hold any other public post.[132] L. B. Guyton, a deputy and physics professor, explained that to pass such a law would be to overextend the salutary principle of the specialization of intellectual labor.[133] Even this regulatory proposal was the unwitting result of the success of the teachers in creating a general acceptance of their value as a collective group, as a profession. Of what area of life other than education could a republican have asserted that "it had taken on that aura of philosophical independence, which long before the Revolution had characterized the literary institutions"? In what other field could republicans wish, "in the creation of institutions of public instruction, to profit to our advantage from the lessons of experience and reconcile certain old habits, recommended to the wise by the opinion of nations, to republican forms"?[134] The notion of teachers as members of a profession, endowed with a competence that had to be respected and that was relatively independent of political concerns, committed the deputies of the Council of Five Hundred to negotiate a reform of the schools rather than impose it.

On 13 Messidor, Year IV, a message from the Directory, requesting that the councils consider setting up chairs of modern languages in the Paris central schools, was sent to the Council of Five Hundred. The way in which the council responded illustrates how thoroughly it accepted this idea of teaching as a profession.[135] The committee appointed to study the idea was enthusiastic about the teaching of foreign languages but suspected that language teachers would be more useful than professors of language. It was frankly suspicious of the ministry's direction: "the men qualified to teach the young are more numerous than ever; but these are independent men who do not wish to submit themselves to the direction of pedants."[136] The issue of language teaching opened up the possibility of a general attack on the organization of the central schools and their demotion of language and literary instruction in favor of the sciences. Mercier's satire on professors of "human understanding, legislation, history, political economy and morals, so many professors and no students," was the humorous beginning of a reconsideration of the nature of the curriculum.[137] Frédéric Lamarque defined the issue in the clearest way: while French might be the language of universal reason, he said, actual French people had to communicate with other peoples in the commerce and interaction that constituted the modern world.[138] The study of languages and literature created the imaginative sympathy among students that made them capable of understanding the historical genesis of their own institutions and of comprehending those of others.[139] Rather than organize the schools around a speculative philosophy of history, the council should organize them around the product of history, the languages that had been created by the particular experiences of the peoples of the world through time.

Roger Martin put this theoretical defense of the study of language and literature at the center of a modern curriculum and combined it with the history of education in France. He completely accepted the critical point that general grammar was not a suitable subject to ground a general education and that literature should replace it in that role.[140] He concluded that the classics would have to be restored to their central importance; despite their well-known limitations, they were a proven basis for a general educational system.[141] More concretely, he proposed that a second classics teacher be appointed in every school and that language and literary instruction be introduced at every level of the schools, not just the first.[142] Carrying out this reform would also demand introducing belles lettres into the middle cycle rather than the last. This proposal was very attractive. Even Daunou, who as author of the Daunou law might have had some attachment to the original plan of studies, endorsed it, and it was incorporated by the Directory into the suggestions to the councils for reform.[143] This proposal was also, on first sight, quite conservative; it appeared to retreat to the curriculum of the disbanded colleges.[144] Respect for the professional competence of teachers on the part of the deputies seemed to demand abandoning any specifically reformist approach to the curriculum.

Neither the teachers nor the educational administrators in the Ministry of the Interior interpreted literary studies as conservatively as did the deputies. Where the deputies saw an opposition between the modern curriculum promoted by the Council on Public Instruction and the classical curriculum associated with the teaching profession, the actual profession and those close to it sought to reconstruct the literature curriculum to make it appropriate for modern citizens. The administrators clearly did not see the function of the central schools as drilling the youth of France in Latin. Letourneur's list of prize books for Year VI is the first evidence we have of the ambition to define a modern set of classics, one that would embody the values of the republic rather than simply reproduce a literary *patrimoine*.[145] The authors he nominated as those appropriate for presentation to students formed a national canon, one that could even integrate religious authors, such as Fénélon.[146] This school of the virtues is interesting as much for what it does not include, especially Rousseau, as for what it does. It was most closely aligned with the ideal of French culture represented by the third class of the Institut, as opposed to that of the second. More interesting was the second list of books recommended by Letourneur, texts in the political and moral sciences. Here he compromised between the modern republican taste for moral sentiment theory and the Ideologue fascination with a more deterministic form of social science. The first was represented by Filangieri, Aristotle, Montesquieu, and Rousseau, while Beccaria, Saint-Lambert, and Holbach stood for the second. Smith's *Wealth of Nations* was shared between them. This list of Italian, English, and French authors replicated the major references of modern republican writing. A further eight categories of books were offered as supplements to these core categories of republican books, all making up an imagined library for a citizen of the modern republic.[147]

Letourneur's list reveals the ambition to construct a new literary culture that could encompass rather than reject the human sciences, but this was just a list after all, exploiting the culture rather than creating anything new. Ginguené's bureaucratic maneuver as head of the fifth section of the ministry was more creative. He used the excuse of the tardiness of the Council on Public Instruction to create another parallel body directly under his control charged with producing an interim curriculum while waiting for the report of the full council. This body was remarkable because it included none of the Ideologue members of the council but several of the republicans. The group was commissioned to produce a series of textbooks for use in the schools.[148] Ginguené himself was to write the text on moral theory. He underlined the shift away from moral science by including the preachers Bourdalou and Massilon among his moral exemplars, along with more predictable figures such as Cérutti.

The most striking innovation was the introduction of the most distinctively modern form of prose—and the epitome of sentimental literature—the novel, into the school. Bernardin de Saint-Pierre was commissioned to write a series of supplementary volumes to his *études de la nature*. These were to be *harmonies de la nature*, novels to provide a complete course in moral theory and practice for the primary schools as well as function as training manuals for teachers.[149] Erneste-Désiré Desforges de Parny was appointed to produce a poetry anthology. These men also had an influence on the teaching of history. While they did not wish to remove philosophical history entirely from the course, they assigned Joseph Lavallée to write a collection of exemplary civic actions to stand as a pendant to Mably's *Abrégé des observa-*

tions sur l'histoire de la France. This request came directly from François de Neufchâteau, whose historical imagination had been redirected while sharing Jacques-Guillaume Thouret's cell in the Luxembourg Palace.[150] Thouret had passed the time before his death editing Dubos's *Histoire des Gaules* for the use of his sons. Finally, they put the task of writing a fundamental philosophy text into the hands of Joseph de Maimieux, rather than any of the well-known Ideologues who were more qualified for the task. In terms of the institutional politics of the Directory, one might say that this was the revenge of the members of the third class of the Institut on those of the second class. A modern literature was to replace a modern philosophy as the keystone of higher education.

The shape of this modern culture, the proposed source for republican education, can be appreciated only from the reading lists of the social sciences and literary studies. In the schools, the politics of the institutions of culture were not as pressing as in Paris, and more complex accommodations between different understandings of a republican education were possible. If we look at the recommended reading in the two social sciences, history and jurisprudence (sometimes called legislation), we can discern the lineaments of just such a compromise. The most cited authors in the history curriculum were (in order of popularity) Millot, Condillac, Mably, Mentelle, Voltaire, Montesquieu, Rollin, Blair, and Priestley.[151] These can be broken up into a series of categories. Millot's and Rollin's works were textbooks, fundamental but without any significant ideological color. The citation of Condillac is interesting: he was the only author mentioned by significant numbers of teachers in every field, and he was clearly the foundational writer for every pedagogical tendency. Mably and Mentelle represented opposed political ideas, classic republicanism and Ideologue social science, respectively, but three of the authors were from the modern republican group: its inspiration, Montesquieu, and two British authors central to that understanding of the modern world, Blair and Priestley.

The importance of modern republican social science to the form of social science taught in the central schools is even more vividly illustrated by the preferences of the teachers of jurisprudence. Here the favored texts clustered around natural law theory (Pufendorf, Locke, Hobbes, and Burlamaqui) and political economy (Filangieri, Smith, and Garnier), with an important representation of explicit republicans (Rousseau and Mably) and social theorists (Montesquieu, Ferguson, Saint-Lambert, and Condillac). The intersection of natural rights theory with political economy was obviously the site on which modern republican theory was developed, and the notion of a republican society was the central concern of modern republicans. There are other clues to the dominance of modern republicanism in this subject: Filangieri, the most important modern republican political economist, was cited twice as often as Smith, despite the latter's authority in the field. What is excluded is almost as important as what is included. The twenty-seven authors cited twice or less by the teachers included Aristotle, Cicero, Machiavelli, and Plutarch, core constituents of classic political theory. They were all rejected in favor of the explicitly modern—that is, seventeenth-century and after—theorists of natural right. Finally, it is interesting to note that contemporary authors in the modern republican vein, such as Vandermonde, Lacratelle, and Maublanc were also used, though by few teachers. A new canon was beginning to be supplemented by current work.[152] If we synthesize the most cited authors from both subjects, we can see that the cores of the disciplines were constructed around a canon of French authors. Condillac, Rousseau, Montesquieu, and Mably were the most important, but these were surrounded by the Anglo-Dutch theorists of natural law and the Anglo-Italian political economists to generate a political and social theory canon for a modern republic.

Of course, very few students would actually be exposed to the history and jurisprudence courses; the majority would receive a literary education. One might suspect that though a modern curriculum was created for history and political science, the same was not true for belles lettres. Certainly the classical authors retained a place in the belles lettres curriculum that they did not in political science and legal scholarship. The orators Cicero and Quintilian, for instance, were respectively the fifth and seventh most regularly recommended authors to the students in belles lettres, and the standard classical history of Rollin was the fourth most cited text.[153] Horace's writing was as popular as Dumarsais's *Les tropes,* and Aristotle was cited as a literary theorist ahead of Boileau. However, the version of the classics that was promoted in the belles lettres curriculum was particular. The imperial authors were almost nonexistent: Virgil was recommended only once, as was the staple of the prerevolutionary Latin course, Plutarch. Caesar was never used, and even Livy was used by only one teacher. This was not the teaching of the classics as authorities in politics and in the art of living but the selection of classical authors compatible with the search for the forms of communication in modern life that would perform the political function of rhetoric in ancient times. The most cited authors were not classical but firmly modern:

Batteux, who had published his *Principes de la littérature* in 1772 and his *Réflexions sur la langue française* in 1778, and the novelist Marmontel. This was not a retreat to a classic curriculum, though of course it shared certain elements with it. Rather, it was an elaboration of Lockianism, sensationalist aesthetics. There were French exponents of this field, notably Dubos and Diderot, but the text that developed a theory of literature from this ground, and invented literary studies as we know them, was Hugh Blair's *Essays on Rhetoric and Belles Lettres.*

Blair's basic argument was that the study of literature achieved for the moderns what the study of rhetoric had for the ancients: it prepared the greatest number for the exercise of public duties.[154] It achieved this by educating the taste of youth, taste being the faculty most appropriate to the middle nature of modern persons, "between the pleasures of sense, and those of pure intellect." By exercising and developing the taste of students, work or teacher exercised and developed their moral sense: "the exercise of taste is, in its native tendency, moral and purifying."[155] Blair's arguments made the teaching of literature the appropriate general study for a modern, democratizing society. His book was recommended in every model curriculum sent out by the Ministry of the Interior after year V. While the injunction to use other texts, such as *Système de la nature,* was ignored, Blair enjoyed a remarkable vogue among teachers. Of forty-four teachers of belles lettres who replied to the circular, twelve were recommending Blair to their students and using his *Essays* as a textbook. This is particularly remarkable since there was no French translation of the book, nor even an English-language French edition until 1801. Blair's examples of prose writing are all English, with many taken from Addison, and though his philosophical history of language owes most to Rousseau, that did not narrow the language gap that had to be traversed to use Blair as a text. No other contemporary foreign author is mentioned as often as Blair, not even Locke or Bacon. Indeed, if we look through the texts recommended by the teachers we can see that this reorientation of the schools toward literary studies understood in this way was a general phenomenon. Even among the general grammar teaching staff the specifically Ideologue authors were little used. Garat's textbook was totally overshadowed by Dumarsais's *Théorie des tropes,* used by fifteen teachers, and even by Domergue's and Harris's writings, used by seven and fifteen teachers, respectively. The promotion of a curriculum based on the literature of the moderns was a success in the classrooms as well as in the Paris ministries.

How did this development meet the ideological problems of education? The rationale for a literary education was that it trained the most universal capacity of humans, that of sentiment. The psychology of the sentiments was an egalitarian response to the hierarchical model of the materialists. As Adam Smith's *Theory of Moral Sentiments,* republished in France in a new translation by Sophie de Grouchy in 1796 put it, modern society was not best imagined as a machine in which the individual elements maximized their utility. It was better understood as a sentimental exchange, a system of emulation in which individuals were brought to an awareness of their ethical identity. Literature, which spoke directly to those sentiments, was the great pedagogical tool and the most distinctive product of that society. By focusing the teaching of the central schools on literary studies the republicans sought to reflect the universalizing and egalitarian tendencies of modern society rather than those that alienated modern individuals. In addition, the stress on literature promoted the integration of the primary schools with the central schools. Students who had already mastered basic reading, writing, and arithmetic, as well as the elements of republican morality, were capable of entering the higher schools, which continued this study by supplementing it with ancient languages but without introducing general grammar until the third cycle. Moreover, many of the texts in preparation, such as Bernardin de Saint-Pierre's work, were to be used at both levels.

The victory for the modern republicans was complete when, in the final report of the council, and against the opinion of Destutt de Tracy, it recommended that the entry age to the schools be reduced from twelve to nine, thus easing the transition from the lower to the upper.[156] Finally, literary studies were the most useful for anyone going on to a career in teaching, and so helped the schools fulfill one of their stated functions as teacher-training colleges. In a practical way the schools would be institutions that served the goals, however long term, of universal education by producing teachers, the lack of which had been one of the main reasons for the failure of the primary schools. Modern literary studies, as the pedagogy of a teaching profession, provided concrete answers to the difficult questions that had been asked of the educational system in a democratizing republic.

William Reddy has identified the sentimental novel as the repository of what he calls a "counter-tradition" to the dominant code of honor that sustained male identity in the early nineteenth century.[157] Reddy points out that the rejection of the sentimental novel as a significant voice in moral pedagogy was achieved by gendering such novels as "female." By rejecting the sentimental novel as a significant public voice in this way the dominant culture of the early nineteenth century was also rejecting a democratic pedagogy. Honor replaced sentiment as the defining characteristic of a public person, but to do so it had to efface the educational efforts of the Directory. The novel was marked as the democratic literary form not only because it was popular and accessible but also because its reception required acquisition of the qualities of the modern republican citizen. Auber, giving the speech to open his course in literature, described the perfect reader precisely as a "republican . . . who can tell simplicity from lowliness and taste from naiveté," and whose own expression was "the faithful mirror of his thoughts and sentiments."[158] This man of sentiment was the inverse of the man of honor. The man of sentiment lived in society "because of the need he had for his fellow being"; only in society could he generate "the moral existence that depends on the reciprocal opinions of his fellow beings."[159]

Depending on the opinions of others to create moral identity was a characteristic shared by modern republicans and women but antithetical to the self-defining male.[160] The teachers and educational reformers of the Directory created a genuinely democratic educational ideal, one that did not implicitly exclude women. The republican curriculum was useless as a basis for the defense of privilege, even gender privilege. It pointed the way to the destruction of hierarchies of culture and to its democratization. The Rights of Man might pose paradoxes of inclusion, but the republican novel did not.

CHAPTER 6

Dance Like a Republican: Public Culture, Religion, and the Arts

In the aftermath of violent revolution, Louis-Sebastien Mercier, the great chronicler of the life of Paris, seemed to be absolutely certain what the proper relationship between politics and culture should be: "Parisians, my dear Parisians, may you dance or go to mass, go to mass or dance, may you even dance and go to mass at the same time, but for the love of God don't go into politics."[1] Mercier was not just making an ironic comment on the 118 dance halls in the capital; he was advertising a categorical division between culture and politics, between social life and public life, a division that has become second nature to modern Western cultures but that, for Mercier, was a recent invention.[2] Public and private were only two of the many categories used to describe social space.

Public and Private

Mercier's polarity between politics and dancing has been extended to a series of contrasts—between public and private, ancient and modern liberty, the public arena of self-presentation and the private sphere of intimacy—that are fundamental to the conceptual architecture of the late twentieth century. The historiography of the Revolution of the last twenty years has been dominated by the view that it was the failure of the revolutionaries to respect these categorical divisions that drove the revolutionary dynamic.[3] The Revolution can thus be understood as an illustration of Isaiah Berlin's dictum that only negative liberty is coherent and that all forms of positive liberty are ill-conceived.[4] Virtue, the stoic disregard for self-interest, and pleasure, the individual's fulfillment of his or her desire, could not be reconciled in the institutions of the republic because virtue and pleasure represented two opposed conceptions of freedom. From this point of view the

198

failures of schemes for universal education, analyzed in the last chapter, were the predictable results of trying to force pleasure-seeking moderns to act like self-abnegating ancients.

Modern culture and republican political forms would, on this reading, seem to be incompatible; it was impossible to dance like a republican. It is surprising then to read Mercier, who was generally critical of the cultural forms of the republic, praising the Festival of the Federation of 1790 as "a type of public show [*spectacle*] so original, that it was impossible for even the most cynical to remain unmoved."[5] Mercier's use of the term *spectacle,* rather than *sollenité* or even *fête,* is telling in this regard. *Spectacles* were the pleasurable pastimes of modern people, specifically the pleasures cultural entrepreneurs had invented so creatively in eighteenth-century Paris.[6] At one point *spectacles* had been banned from the stages of Paris precisely because they were not virtuous. Fiction gave way to revolutionary reenactment as popular entertainment in 1794.[7] If the polarity between culture and politics was a real one, it was simply nonsense to call any revolutionary fête, especially the Festival of the Federation, a *spectacle.*

In fact, Mercier rarely used the polarity of public and private to analyze the life of Paris, defining it preeminently as the city of hybridity, of mixed categories. The private individual was purely an effect of self-presentation; in Paris even the most private experience, the instincts, became plastic and publicly negotiable: "All the actors who play their roles in this grand and noble theater will force you also to become an actor. Good-bye to tranquillity; desires become stronger, superfluities become necessities, and the needs of nature become infinitely less tyrannical than those inspired in us by opinion."[8] Paris dissolved differences, including social differences, and its confusion of social ranks made it the perfect habitat of all middling creatures, those of middling fortune, who could live there in better style than anywhere else. It was especially kind to those who lived in the garret but walked among the great, the *hommes des lettres.*[9] The Revolution itself had been the work of these odd creatures; "great mediocrities, and that is perhaps why everything worked out. There is no error as dangerous as that of a man of genius. At least one can recover from our mistakes."[10] The idea of a difference between public and private certainly existed for Mercier and his contemporaries, but the majority of their social institutions, particularly the most innovative, were hybrid and could not be organized within it.[11]

Some contemporary cultural historians have noticed that the master division between public and private cannot organize the social experience of late-eighteenth-century France. The paradigm for the hybrid institutions that escaped the polarity was the restaurant, which Rebecca Spang has characterized as "a publicly private space," one in which diners could enjoy the experience of displaying their most intimate and private sensations to a select public.[12] The restaurant was invented in 1767, and its success resulted from the way it met these many demands. Michelle Root-Bernstein has argued that the great innovation in the theater of the 1780s, the *drame bourgeois* of the boulevard theaters, was another hybrid that subverted the social hierarchy of genres.[13] The theater was not the only realm in which older organizations of culture were subverted to express new civic experiences. Thomas Crow has shown how Jacques-Louis David revivified the conventions of historical painting to exemplify the values of the new urban public.[14] David's output of intensely individuated portraits and grand historical narratives reflected the contrasting tendencies he was trying to master. The figures in his *Oath of the Horatii* and *M. and Mme. Lavoisier* were both efforts at expressing the values and the dignity of the new kind of person who existed in the middle ground between publicity and privacy. The process of hybridization was not monopolized by middling elements of social life seeking their representations. The strategy was also used by social elites, the most well known case being the appropriation of the crowning of the rose-girl of Salency by the local nobility in the 1770s.[15] Jean Starobinski has tried to understand the whole revolutionary process as a hybridization of the hopes of "the man of pleasure . . . with a famished people."[16] The oath, a strong revolutionary theme, was for Starobinski the institution used to fuse these disparate elements in the revolutionary syncretism.[17] The cultural history of the late eighteenth century is littered with strategies of appropriation and hybridization that sought to conjoin ideas of antiquity and modernity, publicity and privacy, intimacy and transparency. The revolutionaries made every effort to use these strategies in their attempted reconstruction of French social and political life. The failures of the cultural projects of the Revolution occurred when the revolutionaries tried to divide the world into purely private and public arenas and ignored the dominant hybridity of the cultural forms of the era.

We must be mindful of the complex task facing republican thinkers, politicians, and administrators when they addressed the problem of creating a culture for a modern republic after 1794. The animating idea of the republic was that private persons could achieve self-fulfillment only by collective public action. Thus, the cultural world they sought to create would have to find space for the canonically private, the utterly public, and the intermediary areas that articulated the relationships of all. A republican dance would be a complex pattern.

A Sacred Republic?

Mercier posited two alternatives to politics, dancing and going to mass. Mercier's opposition of politics to religion would have seemed stark to contemporary French people. Religious ceremonials, in particular, were too important to public life for religious practice to be relegated to private devotion. The conflation of politics and religion was most obvious in the revolutionary festivals. As Mona Ozouf has pointed out, every reflection on public culture during the Revolution included some suggestions for the place of festivals in public education, and, in turn, every design for the festivals embodied a particular understanding of the republic.[18] The festival was understood as an enactment of the collective life of a regenerated people. It was also understood as the antidote to the elements of modern life that threatened the possibility of a republic. As the chevalier de Moy put it, "Without festivals only commercial relations connect us to one another, but these sorts of relations do not properly connect us. Left this way, circumscribed within our own social circles, and each one closed off within our own coterie, we will live strangers to one another, without knowing or esteeming one another."[19] Though there were great variations in the types and meanings of particular festivals during the Revolution, every festival was understood to be an instrument for the self-education of the French people into the new habits and assumptions, or *moeurs*, necessary for a free people. Even Boissy d'Anglas, who was far from being a republican, argued for the necessity of these cultural institutions in the life of the nation. Only by retaining its religious institutions had the Jewish nation retained its coherence, despite having been endlessly oppressed, he observed.[20] The monarchy had been abolished more easily than Catholic religious services, because the people had need of the emotions and values produced by its ceremonies.[21]

Boissy's ideas are emblematic of one central line of reflection on festivals: the possibility of aligning religious sentiment around the new regime through such public ceremonies. The festivals could be appropriated as part of a civic religion, one that quoted civic ceremonial practices of the antique republics and responded to Rousseau's ideas. By Year II this process was well under way and revolutionary festivals had transformed themselves from

spontaneous practices open to many uses to the central institution of a Jaco-
bin-inspired civil religion, the cult of the Supreme Being.[22] There was no de-
termining logic that compelled the revolutionaries to contrast civic festivals
with religious sentiment; celebrating 14 July (the taking of the Bastille)
would not normally drive the citizens of a modern republic to a repudiation
of their other faiths, after all.[23] But in the circumstances of 1793–94, during
which time the most radical feature of sans-culotte politics was their anti-
Christian campaign, the difference between a civic and a transcendental
faith could not be sustained.[24] In the meaning given to it by Robespierre, in
particular, the Festival of the Supreme Being, more than elections or actual
political participation, became the essence of popular sovereignty.[25] It was
the site upon which the ideas of society, the state, sovereignty, and democracy were gathered together under an aura of sacrality.[26] The calendar of festivals, also regulated by the law of 3 Brumaire, Year IV, continued the ideological escapism of the Jacobinism of Year II—the replacement of politics
with rhetoric and representation.[27] This rhetorical republicanism, of which
the festival was but one element, came to be understood as the antithesis of
the genuine politics of the republic to which the Directory was committed.
Dupont de Nemours could assert that "a revolutionary or counterrevolutionary religion would be the greatest atrocity that could dishonor the human race."[28] However, this perception did not impede certain elements of
the regime from continuing the effort to create a revolutionary religion.

The conflation of sovereignty and sacrality in a civic religion, while clearly
a possibility in all early modern revolutions, was particularly threatening to
any effort to create a free state founded on ideals of individual liberty in
France. One of the most important achievements of the early years of the
Revolution had been to disentangle the different kinds of religious and secu-
lar authority gathered together in the person of the king. Sieyès's *Qu'est-ce
que le Tiers Etat?* had developed new premises of sovereignty for the French
Revolution, a notion of popular sovereignty ultimately located in the population but wholly represented by the deputies elected under due constitutional process. While the novelty of Sieyès's idea of national sovereignty has
long been noted, the contrast with the common understanding of sovereignty against which his concept was deployed in 1789 has been under-
played. Sovereignty in the French political tradition did not mean ultimate
authority; it meant a particular type of ultimate authority, one that was
undivided, absolute, and analogous to the authority of God over creation.
Moreover, while in England the concept of sovereignty was considerably di-

luted in the seventeenth and eighteenth centuries, exactly the opposite effect occurred in France. There, constitutional doctrine and political practice tended to merge the two bodies of the king as the centuries progressed.[29] Sarah Hanley has argued persuasively that, beginning with the minority of Louis XIII and culminating in the personal rule of Louis XIV, the efficacy of any notion of public law or of the separation of the monarch from the monarchy was lost to a doctrine of total and absolute personal representation of the polity by the king.[30] Such practices of this form of monarchy as the removal of the king from public sight to Versailles and the bureaucratization of rule have been well noted; what is less remarked on are the ideas that held this form of rule in place. The phoenix and sun images used to buttress the notion that the king never dies were supplementary to the idea of a Bourbon *mystique du sang*, the idea that sovereignty in the strict sense inhered in the actual blood that moved in the veins of the legitimate monarch. Thus Bossuet's claims for an absolute sovereign power, coeval with that of God over creation, were not made for the mystical body of the monarch, to be transferred to and diluted in the mystical body of the nation. Rather, they were made for the actual physical body of the king. Ultimate power and religious authority were gathered together in one sovereign body.

Moreover, that ideal and practice of sovereignty was not seriously challenged throughout the eighteenth century, despite the obvious political struggles that dominated the period after 1750.[31] The Parlements never claimed to represent the sovereign nation; rather, they claimed to represent the Estates General in abeyance. Before 1789 there was no doctrine of the sovereignty of the Estates General. That body represented the interests of the corporate bodies, from guilds to provinces, that made up the nation.[32] Neither party in the great religious controversy between Jansenists and Dévots ever questioned the sovereign powers of the monarch, or the extension of those powers to church organization.[33] No more vivid example of the seriousness with which the ideal of the sovereign monarch was taken could be found than the horrible execution of Robert François Damiens in 1757. As Reinhart Koselleck put it, the monarch's sovereignty was intact in 1789—it was the efficacy of that sovereignty that stood in question.[34] Indeed, as late as 1791 the abbé Emery republished Bossuet's work on sovereignty as the most efficacious antidote to the radicalization of the Revolution, asserting in the introduction the traditional understanding of the nature of the sovereign: "This doctrine of popular sovereignty and of an original contract with kings is fallacious: and, understood in its vulgar interpretation, it is an erroneous and pestilential doctrine, capable of pitching every government into confusion and of inundating the world in tears and blood."[35]

In enunciating a doctrine of national sovereignty Sieyès was not simply performing a tactical maneuver of stunning brilliance that met with instant success, though he was doing that. He was also trying to secularize what remained a fundamentally theological concept, in the French context, and change its meaning all at once. Crucially, as Lucien Jaume has pointed out, the notion of the sovereign implied that of the subject, not that of the citizen. To be a subject meant not participation in a free state but submission to the sovereign, whether king or nation.[36] The sovereign nation was potentially as much of an impediment to Sieyès's ideal of individual self-realization in an empowered state as the monarchy had been.[37] To locate sovereignty in the nation was to threaten the possibility of a representative system, organized by a constitution. Moreover, as hostile as Sieyès was to supernatural and theological concepts, he could not by wishing it or writing it alone divorce the notion of sovereignty from that of religious authority.[38] To claim that the nation was sovereign was implicitly to grant it the right to reorganize the spiritual life of the country and to contribute to the fusion of the political and regenerative goals of the Revolution. By positing that the goal of the Revolution was the regeneration of the sovereign nation, Sieyès unwittingly contributed to what early-nineteenth-century historians like Michelet and Quinet recognized as a religious movement, the creation of a new man, embedded in a civic religion, itself supported and guaranteed by the state.[39] Sieyès, and other reformers of his ilk, faced the difficulty that the very tools they used to loosen the monarchy's grip on power threatened the project of creating a modern polity, to which they were committed, by turning political questions into metaphysical or theological questions.[40] This retreat from politics to metaphysics had happened in the festivals of 1794 and had created another paradox for the practice of republicanism. Shared political life demanded festivals, but festivals as part of a civic religion symbolized the end of politics.

Given this history it is entirely understandable that the musings of Director La Révellière-Lépeaux on the possibilities of a civic religion in 1797 should have led him to be dubbed "the pope of the republic."[41] His ideas were particularly threatening since he was responsible for the internal policy of the republic and because he voiced them just before, and in the immediate aftermath of, the coup of 18 Fructidor, Year V.[42] Certainly La

Révellière's presentation of his ideas did nothing to undermine the notion that he wished to institute "a political inquisition in France, to make it a vast tomb for the living, like the prisons of Genoa, over the doors of which is written, derisively, the word *libertas*."[43] He berated the population of the country for failing to live up to the standards of republicanism and for listening to those who "defamed the republican spirit in order to reestablish the yoke of priests and kings."[44] François de Neufchâteau, the minister under his authority in the section of the interior, seconded La Révellière's lecture by interpreting the coup, and the purgation of deputies from the councils, as the reeducation of the people "deceived by a faction, the enemies of liberty."[45] Both François and La Révellière exhorted the departmental authorities to do everything in their power to reanimate the festivals: "those who fear their influence deride them; yet the people always are filled with the sweetest feelings when they take part in them."[46] The didactic, and self-deluding, Jacobin politics of Year II seemed to have returned. La Révellière's statement that "without some dogma and some form of external rite, you can neither inculcate the principles of morality into the people, nor get them to practice them," taken at face value, seemed to herald a return of the cult of the Supreme Being.[47]

Yet the parallel between the actions of the Committee of Public Safety and the Directory, between La Révellière-Lépeaux and Robespierre, and between the cult of the Supreme Being and theophilanthropy cannot be sustained. La Révellière-Lépeaux's project was not to conflate sacrality, legitimacy, and sovereignty in a total civic experience but to disaggregate them. In every speech and pamphlet that he issued during Fructidor he was at pains to distance current events from those of 31 May 1793 and of Year II.[48] His great fear was that republican forms would fail to organize the political life of the country and that there would be a return to anarchy and a violent, uncivilized understanding of the meaning of the republic, a fear that some supporters thought exaggerated.[49] Supporters of the Directory, such as the editors of the *Décade philosophique,* considered the unconstitutionality of the coup a superficial and temporary breakdown of political life.[50] But La Révellière, while a convinced republican, was not an optimistic republican, and he did not resort to those kinds of circumstantial arguments. Instead, in his reflections on the coup and its meaning he developed his idea of the republic as a historically fragile and rare form of government. In his speech for the Festival of the Republic he denied that Rome had ever been one, and eulogized the free city-states of the Mediterranean as the only (if ephemeral) model of the form that had ever existed.[51] Moreover, he was fully aware that republican forms could easily be co-opted or degenerate; he observed that the stated admiration of any politician in the Revolution for the position of *juge de paix* had been the rhetorical gesture most indicative of the corruption of the speaker.[52] Legislative assemblies, in particular, he thought susceptible to losing sight of their goals and becoming enamored of impossible projects. As he put it, tensions among will, passion, and intellect tended to dissolve the identity of one person, so much more so the identity of assemblies made up of many persons, and in consequence they tended to become irrational.[53] His mind turned to civil religion as one of a set of institutions able to stabilize the public culture of the republic and ensure its rationality.

La Révellière-Lépeaux argued that the republic should comprehend a civil religion, civic ceremonies, and national festivals.[54] He was at pains to emphasize that these were three different institutions and could not form one total organization. His views on ceremonies, such as marriage and interment, and festivals were widely shared; his most distinctive contribution to the articulation of republican institutions was his interest in civil religion, specifically theophilanthropy.[55] Theophilanthropy had been founded only seven months before Fructidor, Year V. Its main sponsor was the ex-Terrorist Valentin Hauy, but its theorist, and the man most closely identified with the movement, was J. B. Chemin-Depontès.[56] Theophilanthropy was the latest in a long line of natural religions, but it was the first that explicitly tried to use deist ideas as an antidote to the violence of the Revolution. As Chemin-Depontès explained its goals, "the sole aim was to create a useful institution, which would heal the wounds of the Revolution, resolve all hearts by preaching mutual understanding and the forgiveness of all grievances, which would unite all sects in universal tolerance, by giving morality, the sweetest ever professed, a sanction above all criticism, and unite the people in a genuine fraternity."[57] The forms of theophilanthropy were highly syncretic; its texts mingled sacred and profane authors with abandon. For example, the first forty-two lessons of the theophilanthropist reader were taken from the Bible, and the rest from the histories of ancient and modern republics.[58] These syncretic forms were fashioned into a sort of coherence by Chemin-Dupontès's perception that the *moeurs* of the republic were best understood as social rather than political virtues. As he explained, politics were so factionalized during the period when the cult was organized that the best basis for the republic no longer seemed to be the state but a religious institution that would profess a universal morality.[59] The social and domestic, rather than political and public, basis for theophilanthropy drove Chemin-Depontès to stress fraternity, a social rather than political quality, as the basis of republican morality: "It has often been said that there cannot be a republic without virtue. This is because there cannot be a republic without fraternity, and that fraternity, properly understood, is the basis of all the other virtues that make up a republican."[60] Theophilanthropy made explicit the reversal of moral priority, which replaced the public with the private virtues that had been implicit in the political theory of the republic.[61] It based the universality of the republic not on its political forms but on the social ethics that informed them. Political virtues were derived from the fundamental commitment to fraternity and social equality, rather then being seen as foundational in themselves.

Theophilanthropy was an attempt to define a moral stance based on a utilitarian ethic that retained the civic commitment of the Jacobin ideal by casting that utilitarian ethic in a religious frame. Happiness, rather than virtue, was seen as the highest good. Man's social nature, in the view of the theophilanthropists, meant that he would rationally love his country.[62] Under their heavy rhetoric that commitment was imagined in two ways: the good citizen was a laborious citizen, who made his home a religious site, and that citizen was prepared to serve his country directly in case of war.[63] In the aftermath of Fructidor this rather vague and sentimental religious movement not only attracted the support of the directors, La Révellière-Lépeaux in particular, and that of many republican theorists, like Thomas Paine, but also recruited a massive public following.[64] La Révellière-Lépeaux saw in theophilanthropy an institution that could produce the kinds of public religious ceremonies that would sacralize the affective and social relationships among human beings in society.[65] The affection of La Révellière for the new religion made it a target for victims of 18 Fructidor such as Carnot. He denounced it and the Directory's religious policy as nothing more than a reworking of the cult of the Supreme Being of 1794.[66] Nothing could have been further from the truth. The Directory colonized and supported theophilanthropy precisely as a bulwark against a renewed total revolutionary religion, which at the same time could, the directors hoped, satisfy the desire for religious expression apparent in even the most republican departments. Thus theophilanthropy provided a locus through which the regenerative project of the Revolution might be located and redefined. It operated as the second wing of the Directory's politics, the first of which was the foundation of a republican constitutional order. Theophilanthropy provided a means of sacralizing the republic without attributing to it the religious characteristics of sovereignty.

Although the difference between a civic, or more properly a social, religion and a system of civic ceremonies might have been clear to La Révellière-Lépeaux, in practice the difference was not sustained. As Mona Ozouf has remarked, the revolutionaries seem to have underestimated how much the traditional organization of time, especially the seven-day week, was embedded in the organization of work and leisure, and the extent to which, by attempting to change civic ceremonies, they threatened symbolic relations and identities.[67] Olwen Hufton has stressed that women, in particular, resisted the elements of republican civic ritual because it did not acknowledge their social roles.[68] Our understanding of the relationship between the Revolution and religious institutions and sentiment, however, is not furthered by the thesis that the consequence of the difficulties of Directorial religious policy was the failure of a transference of sacrality.[69] As noted above, the Directorials were well aware that the legitimation of the republic by a monolithic ideal of sacrality would be self-defeating. A more differentiated and empirically sensitive approach to the problem of legitimation is necessary to understand the evolution of political practice. There was no blanket resistance by civil society to the changes in everyday life proposed by the republicans, when the Directorials paid attention to the real sources of anxiety. For example, metric weights and measures were resisted in the markets not because of an atavistic attachment to the older measures but because the change, and the lack of model measures to ensure uniformity, allowed unscrupulous merchants to cheat.[70] For once the revolutionaries did not make an ideological issue out of a social problem and adapted republican desire to social practice. They abandoned the idea of using conversion tables for calculation from the old measures to the new and distributed model measures freely.[71] Model measures, being of a piece with the practices in French markets, were acceptable, and the new measures and weights were introduced without too much trouble. The problems of legitimation occurred where these adaptations to social practice either were not found or were not to be found.[72]

Nothing created so much friction between the regime and population, and so discredited the republic, as the campaign to replace Sunday observance with the *décade*.[73] The central informing idea of the *culte décadaire* was to celebrate the republic as the institution of the social virtues, "to encourage the precious instinct of sociability, which drives men to communicate their sensations, their joys, and their pleasures."[74] The principal architect of the ceremonies, François de Neufchâteau, emphasized that republican mayors and commissioners should not interpret resistance to the *décade* as nostalgia for church and king, but put it down to old habits. Moreover, he called for local festivals to be held on what had been local saints' days and for local fairs to be held on traditional dates as well. His idea exemplified the meliorative politics designed to maximize the potential for a commercial republic: "these festivals were more sentimental and commercial than religious. Dissipate the aura of fanaticism and conserve the institution, and more easily since prejudice and need are allied in maintaining them."[75] As minister of the interior he attempted to control the meaning and use of the cult and to guide it in this direction. He instituted rest periods and entertainments in the workhouses of the poor on the *décade* and advised the commissioner in Besançon not to coerce artisans working in their shops behind closed doors on the day into observing it fully, since "one cannot achieve our goal by violent means."[76] To the mind of the minister there should have been no reason for tension between the civil ceremonies of the republic and any religion, republican or not.

These hopes proved to be naive. Pacific intentions could not dissolve the logic of confrontation built into the program of creating new forms of civic life. The *décade* became a new object of contention in areas of France, such as the south, where local political life was already polarized and factional, and reanimated the well-known process of attracting the support of the central state to win local disputes.[77] By creating these weekly festivals the republic gave new targets to clerical critics, at which they quickly took aim, in turn provoking anticlerical actions by local authorities.[78] Of course, some local authorities, especially in disturbed areas, used the *décade* campaign as another stick with which to beat local opponents. The central administration of the Bouches-du-Rhône was particularly enthusiastic about the institution, despite the worries of P.-J.-Marie Sotin, the minister of police, that it might just aggravate matters.[79] François reprimanded the commissioner of the Allier for even suggesting that he be allowed to coerce the priests of the department to hold mass on the *décade* but did not investigate too deeply when congratulating the municipality of Monsigny on persuading the local clerics to do the same.[80] Inevitably, observance of the *décade* became a measure of political loyalty; despite his view that participation in the *décade* cult should be voluntary, the minister asked for a report on the failure to implement the republican calendar in Paris as early as Floréal, Year VI.[81] Commissioners' monthly reports took for granted that they could gauge the public spirit of a department by its support for or neglect of the new institutions.

The collated report for Messidor, Year VI, for instance, argued that the lack of support for the republic in the country was due to "religious prejudice."[82] In any case, whatever the views of the minister, the Directory quickly decided that observance of the *décade* would be enforced if necessary and demanded that fairs and local festivals deliberately avoid the old saints' days.[83] So insistent were they that the *décade* supplant all other ritual calendars that they even demanded that fish markets avoid Fridays.

The campaign to institute the *décade* as an obligatory observance mingling republican politics with anti-Catholicism created the kind of confusion between religion and politics that La Révellière had hoped to avoid. In the short term it undermined whatever utility theophilanthropy might have had by making it one more element in the *décade* controversy. In later years Chemin-Depontès complained that the government's patronage destroyed the movement by attracting into it careerists, by forcing it to expand in numbers too quickly, and by encouraging it to stage its ceremonies in churches, thus bringing it into conflict with the constitutional clergy.[84] By politicizing, or more accurately factionalizing, the theophilanthropists, the directors fashioned a rod for their own backs. During Year VII the movement was increasingly pulled toward the neo-Jacobin opposition, and one of the most effective *libelles* written against the Directory in the elections of that year was written by Goupil-Préfeln, a leading theophilanthropist.[85] In the longer term it rendered two of the three institutions identified by La Révellière-Lépeaux as capable of creating the moral basis of the republic, civil religion and civil ceremonies, useless. Moreover, this failure was not contingent on the actions of the government itself, even though the authoritarian tendencies of Reubell did nothing to help the new institutions retain a liberal image. Rather, any set of civil ceremonies would have inevitably confronted the transcendental claims of the various clergies and again have involved the republic in an unwinnable struggle over the meaning of sacrality. A modern regime could not be sacralized; it had to be legitimated. If the republic was to have institutions that could do the work of education by representing the nature of the modern republic for its population, then they would have to be revolutionary festivals that were closer to the profane pleasures of the stage than the sacred illumination of the church.

A Spectacular Republic

It is no surprise, therefore, that in the aftermath of the coup of Fructidor, Year V, Director La Révellière-Lépeaux, in addition to pondering revolution-

ary religion, should have mused on the possibilities of creating revolutionary *spectacles,* specifically modern revolutionary festivals. He perceived that
efforts at creating a new public culture had been as much aesthetic as political failures. From the beginning of the republic, "our theaters have seemed
to me ludicrously petty, and the repertoire so stuck in such narrow genres
that none of it matches up to our new ideas and the current state of
things."[86] The inadequacy of the theaters was surpassed by only the "horrible confusion of the eternal Maratist processions," which characterized the
revolutionary festivals, utterly incapable of "inspiring the souls of the citizenry, softening their hearts, and fastening them to the nation."[87] The sublimity and moral excellence of the republic was not represented in any way.
Yet La Révellière-Lépeaux's proposed solution to the problem he had identified revealed that he could not imagine a genuine response to it. His idea
was to make a giant roofed theater of the Champs de Mars, where the people could be led in communal singing to celebrate the festivals.[88] This proposal developed the hopelessly discredited analogy of the French Republic
with its specific ancient exemplars. But even in Athens the participants in
the theater festival had not been obliged to form the chorus. Jean-Baptiste
Say had rejected the same proposal by his colleague Amaury Duval, asserting that "those sorts of popular entertainments were fine for the ancients.
There an idle citizenry could parade its laziness at the festivals given by mag-
istrates eager to curry favor," an arrangement unsuitable for industrious
moderns who abhorred the slaveholding that supported the ancient city.
"Let us abandon the hope of making our citizens a people of Greeks and
Romans. We can be far better than that."[89] The mimicry of the ancients was
less than useless as a guide to the construction of a republic. Yet La Révellière's one concession to modern life was to insist that there should be lots of
refreshment stalls in his giant stadium.[90]

La Révellière could see that a modern republican public culture would
have to use some form of *spectacle,* but he did not further question the meaning of *spectacle.* The relatively unknown de Moy, by contrast, understood that
spectacles, like restaurants, were institutions necessary for modern social life.
"Thus, theatrical entrepreneurs are the restaurateurs of the mind, or, if you
like, are merchant proprietors of shops for those commodities necessary to
satisfy our moral appetites, to assuage the hunger of the soul and the intellect. These restaurateurs are necessary to a people, particularly in the great
cities."[91]

Festivals would, of necessity, have to conform to the nature of *spectacles,*
because *spectacles* were the modern form of festival, "given to a paying pub-

lic, by entrepreneurs; thus a commerce is made of festivals, as of every other need."[92] The old distinction between a festival and a *spectacle*—that in the first the participants expressed their own feelings, whereas in the second actors feigned them for an audience—had collapsed.[93] Jacques Delille argued that the collapse of the distinction between festival and *spectacle* had led to some of the worst excesses of the Revolution. The love of *spectacles* had habituated the French to "violent sensations," and in public life they sought to satisfy this need. "One often saw public assemblies degenerate into theatrical representations, speeches into declamations, the tribunes into theater boxes, from which furious boos and applause alternated; even the streets had their scenery, their plays, and their actors."[94]

Spectacles had created their own form of action for the population, and whatever the festival, at least in the cities, it would have to be a show for the people and a show by the people. De Moy also laid his finger on the difficulty inherent in taking the analogy between festival and *spectacle* too far; one paid for a *spectacle,* but a festival had to be free. The public entertainment needed to entertain and educate a large population could not be confined to the commercial stage but would have to be open to all as a public festival.[95] Replicating the experience of the restaurant or the stage as a public festival posed enormous pragmatic difficulties, however. The institutions of criticism, taste, connoisseurship, and privileged access (in other words, the process of self-distinction) were central elements of participating in an audience or ordering a meal. Diderot might have delighted in the idea of social life as a universal theater, but real theaters had tickets, seats, and ushers.[96] How could the most individuating experiences be universalized?

De Moy was not the only person to reflect on the possibilities of republican *spectacles* and the manner in which they might be brought closer to the population. Even the original planners of the festival cycle had made a distinction between the purely political festivals (14 July, 10 August, 31 January, 1 Vendémiaire, 9 and 10 Thermidor, with 10 Fructidor added in Year VI) and the moral festivals (Youth, Old Age, Marriage, Thanksgiving, and Agriculture).[97] When it quickly became apparent that the moral festivals were far more attractive to the population, especially those in the cities, Letourner set as the first goal identifying the attraction of the moral festivals and extending it to the political versions.[98] The attraction of the moral festivals may well have been explained by the poor management of the political festivals. Ginguené had successfully persuaded Benezech, the minister of the interior at the time, that the festivals would be most efficiently run under unitary authority.[99] The man appointed, Lachabeaussière, did not fulfill these expectations. Short of funds, he had to recycle costumes from the old royal costume store, and even so, faced competition from the opera; he was eventually accused of embezzling funds.[100] In any case, his task was hopeless since Benezech clearly thought the exercises a waste of time and advised administrations to spend as little money on them as possible.[101] Parsimony threatened the festivals with ridicule. Even La Révellière, who was an enthusiast for republican simplicity, thought that Barras's suggestion that the directors walk through the unpaved streets of the left bank of Paris to the festival celebrating the execution of Louis XVI would only erode their authority by making them mud-spattered and tawdry.[102] The lack of imagination and enthusiasm at the administrative center was reflected around the country. Orators who used the festivals to eulogize their own administrations or to rehearse their fears of anarchy and royalism, the hardy perennials of Directorial propaganda, were hardly providing uplifting entertainment to a republican people.[103] The moral festivals, conceived of on simpler lines, could hardly have been worse than all this.

The success of the ceremony for Louis-Lazare Hoche's funeral, in Vendémiaire, Year VI, prompted a reconsideration of the form of the festivals.[104] The ceremony was well attended and well received, in a way that only celebrations of military victories had been up to then. But commissioners in the departments recognized that the enthusiasm for military victories was no indicator of support for the republic and was, in fact, a continuation of an older national sentiment.[105] Hoche's funeral was different in many respects. It was properly funded; a *spectacle* had to have something of the spectacular about it after all.[106] More important, the theme of the ceremony was not Hoche's military prowess, nor his loyalty to the republican regime, but his personal virtues, his peaceful nature, and his upright character. Hoche's funeral was used as an occasion to emphasize the virtues of a republican rather than the qualities of the republic. Delivering the valedictory address La Révellière was moved to tears by the pathos of his own sentiment of grief.[107] Hoche was mourned as a loss to the sentimental community of the nation, rather than as a military leader and servant of the state. The ceremony was a melodrama, and like the most effective melodramas of the period, it depicted the private costs of public life. The *Oath of the Horatii* or the *Lictors Returning the Sons of Brutus* would not impart their message without the female figures in agonies of mourning in the frame. Hoche's heroic self-affirmation might be admired, but as the possessor of the domestic virtues, dying in pursuit of his civic duty, he epitomized the elevation of private qualities to the dignity of the most noble public self-sacrifice. The Hoche ceremony colonized the new ideal of the disclosure of intimacy, which had formed so much of the appeal of Rousseau for his readers, to the purpose of the legitimation of the republic.

Republican publicists explored the idea that the best way to institute a republican public culture might be to create a *spectacle* of intimacy. The idea that there might be an alternative *esprit public,* one found not in the theaters and cafés but in domestic gatherings, was explored in *Le conservateur.*[108] Just how one might "hear merchants who have their suppers together" or find "medical students who talk of the republic before discussing medicine" was not elaborated, but the idea that the republic and the domestic virtues should be harnessed to one another was clearly well established. The most vivid enactment of this notion was another funeral ceremony, this time that for the French negotiators assassinated by Austrian hussars after the collapse of the peace talks at Rastatt.[109] The assassination was a catastrophe. It meant the resumption of hostilities for a France that could not afford it, forestalling the economic and social measures that were the best hope of consolidating the regime. Worse again, it revivified fears that war would not be conducted within its laws and could degenerate into an annihilatory struggle.[110]

Despite the obvious parallels with the first military crisis of the republic, rather than reenact the forms of popular mobilization of 1792, the funeral ceremony for the dead negotiators was conducted as another exercise in sentimental *spectacle.* The procession in the Champs de Mars focused attention on the families of the dead and the survivor.[111] Family members appeared at the center of a cortege with no armed troops, only drummers and standard bearers, preceding the directors. No effort was spared in the attempt to create the tableau of domestic suffering. The daughters of the dead men were dressed in black, while those of the survivor, Jean Debry, wore white.[112] In a final touch, Debry's blood-stained clothes were carried aloft in the rear of the procession. The meaning was clear: Austria had not only broken the laws of nations but had destroyed families, and in a war with Austria, France would be defending not just itself but the very sentiment of humanity.[113] In his speech Marie-Joseph Chénier picked up all these themes and appealed to the participants to respond to the plight of widows and orphans, and to take vengeance for them.[114] His appeal to sentiment was reinforced by his use of the pathetic fallacy in describing the landscape of the atrocity: "Two rows of poplars that line the road deepen the shadows: on one side down the Marg, closed within a canal, flow waves of sadness; on the other, meadows end in a wood; dark clouds loom on the horizon."[115] Chénier fused sentimental *spectacle* with the techniques of sentimental literature to generate the awe and sadness proper to family tragedy. The visual effect was reinforced by the strong pressure being placed on German states to side with the French against the Austrians. Sentimental *spectacle* was not for home consumption only, and so the meaning of the festival was exported by printing translations of Mercier's attack on the Austrians for distribution in Germany.[116]

The practices of sentimental *spectacle* might offer more effective techniques for festivals, but they could not provide a systematic rationale for a republican public culture. Without such an understanding of festivals they would become a simple adjunct to the failed project of creating a civil religion.[117] The idea of a *spectacle* of intimacy could provide such a rationale, by featuring the moral festivals over the political, but asserting the primacy of the moral festivals demanded a reversal of the understanding of their nature. Even François de Neufchâteau, who was committed to the idea of a modern republicanism, had argued from the position that that the political festivals were primary because they represented the universal basis of the rights of citizens.[118] The point of the moral festivals was to represent particular virtues appropriate to particular moments in the life of a citizen. Promoting the moral festivals over the political festivals demanded a different insight into the universal appeal of the republic.

The Festival of Agriculture facilitated a new understanding of festivals. Agriculture, as detailed in Chapter 3, was the sector in which the politics of the republic were played out most clearly. Imagined as a profitable activity— indeed, a way of life—that was inherently virtuous, agriculture recalled the moral core of the ancient republics while providing the basis for the most modern forms of commercial organization. Agriculture synthesized the pursuit of private interests with that of public goods. Accordingly, its festival connected the moral and political celebrations: "The republic will not achieve the level of glory, prosperity, and wealth to which it is susceptible, unless there is not one citizen who is not convinced that agriculture ought to occupy the first place in the sources of national prosperity, and that liberty is the first element, the indispensable element, for the prosperity of agriculture."[119] The test of the prosperity (private happiness) and liberty (public virtue) of a society was the state of its agriculture. Hence the Festival of Agriculture was to exemplify the fundamental attributes of republican prosperity, comprised of political liberty, social emulation, and commercial development.[120]

In short, the Festival of Agriculture dramatized the connection between political liberty and the moral disposition of the citizen; as François de Neufchâteau put it, "this institution, proper to a great people, aims to create public prosperity, and so underlines the simplicity and purity of *moeurs*."[121] Where the properly commemorative festivals recalled the moments when the people regained their rights, the Festival of Agriculture solemnized the dispositions of character and social institutions that made a regime of liberty possible, the *moeurs* of the republic. The two cycles enshrined different models of the history of the republic. The first replayed the political reenactment of the contingent moment when the action of the people founded the republic. The second portrayed the historical conditions that made the republic a timely institution.

The use of the Festival of Agriculture to assert the primacy of social organization over political form was facilitated by its date. Held on 10 Messidor, it broke up the sequence of political festivals from 14 July to 1 Vendémiaire.[122] Full advantage was taken of its summer date in Year VII. Plans to establish the festival in the Bois de Boulogne had to be abandoned, but the Champs de Mars was transformed into what we would call a theme park.[123] A commercial village was built around the stadium, where merchants could install themselves so that "both rural and urban dweller can find things to delight their eyes, meet their needs, and feed their desire [*fantaisie*] of the moment."[124] The traditional processions and award ceremonies were supplemented with dancing and fireworks in the stadium at night, and the whole event lasted nine days. The festival became a summer celebration of the social life of the republic and the morals and mores it exemplified. The idea that both festival cycles might be articulated through the theme of the sentimental and commercial *moeurs* of the republic was a flexible and powerful new understanding of republican public culture. It allowed for precisely the reversal that was needed to create a new understanding of the historical meaning of the republic. In his circular alerting local administrators to the upcoming festival season of Year VII, François de Neufchâteau could offhandedly note that in ordinary circumstances the political festivals had only an indirect effect compared to the moral festivals, which sought "to stimulate the virtues into action, to ground their effect in the sensations and so to prepare the education of a large people by the most effective institutions."[125] It was clear that the most effective institutions were now seen to be the moral festivals, because these directly enacted the moral virtues and modes of life that made the republic possible, while the political festivals commemorated the historic moments when republican values had institutionalized themselves.

The idea that both political and moral cycles of festivals should be understood as different aspects of the celebration of republican *moeurs* had consequences for both cycles. The moral festivals, which had been established to exemplify a natural morality, now carried political valence. The minister of the interior recommended that the Festival of Marriage, for instance, honor both the natural virtues of the family bond and "those internal, modest virtues, of order, decency, economy, etc., which are particularly associated with republican government."[126] The moral festivals were reimagined as an ongoing cycle of spectacles of intimacy, where the domestic and sentimental virtues were enacted for a republican audience so that they could be practiced by a republican people. The most explicit statement of this project was François de Neufchâteau's circular for the Festival of Thanksgiving [*reconnaissance*], again in Year VII.[127] The ideas of remembrance and gratitude were used by the minister as placeholders for that of sociability, the fundamental disposition of humans to exist in society. According to Pufendorf and the theorists of natural law who followed him, sociability became the ground of moral consciousness. Thus the festival was more properly understood as a festival of society, which "only exists in the mutual services rendered to one another by men; it is a commerce of good actions."[128]

The function of the festival was to reanimate the republican *moeurs* of the population and so to invigorate republican society with the spirit of fraternity, the political principle that expressed the reality of sociability. The vision of fraternity would strengthen sensibility and turn citizens to good works through remembrance of the hardships they had themselves faced, to philanthropy in order to give to the species what could not be given to individuals, and to every quiet virtue, every tender and consoling sentiment.[129] François recommended such scenes as those of children stretching their arms out to their old nurses, of vines draped around oaks and giving their fruit, and of flowers clustered around the source of a spring as those most descriptive of the virtue being celebrated.[130] In the latter part of the circular he emphasized that he was not recommending to administrators a mere set of techniques to produce a response, but that the idea of intimate disclosure implied a series of values. The sentimental republic was the inverse of the military republic. The military republic was the scene of the self-deification of the citizen-soldier. The thanksgiving of the sentimental republic should be given to the domestic "solid virtues, and not to those of seductive talents, to the virtues of an entire life, and not [to] those of a year, a day, or a moment."[131] Actions deserving recognition were those that promoted a "philanthropic emulation" and taught the citizens of a commercial republic how to enjoy "a patriotic luxury," something known only in free states. Thus citizens who had donated a public fountain or opened a roadway or a factory were to be recognized.[132] The Festival of Thanksgiving was idealized as a form of symbolic action, creating an antiheroic ideal of a commercial society, which would be the basis of a commercial republic. Rather than a politicization of domesticity, this festival was part of a project for the domestication of politics.

The project of the domestication of politics, of interpreting political virtues through those of civil society, had greater effect on the political cycle than on the moral cycle of festivals. Some of these changes, such as the reinterpretation of the Festival of the Execution of Louis XVI as a solemn reflection on the perfidy of perjury, or the celebration of 18 Fructidor as a return to "happiness and social peace," were somewhat superficial and clearly designed to meliorate difficult memories.[133] The Festival of Pluviôse especially could not be assimilated into a celebration of the social bases of the republic, since it marked the definitive end of monarchy in the person of the monarch, by definition a contingent, historical moment. However, even here citizens were reminded that the monarchy gave way to "the elements of happiness, that double guarantee of every social liberty, the division of powers and the representative system."[134] The Festival of the Sovereignty of the People was another special case that resisted reinterpretation. Coming as it did just before the elections, it had to be used as a form of electioneering in favor of the Directorial candidates. Thus old icons of revolution such as the fasces, used to signify unity, could not be eliminated from the ceremonies, much as the minister might have wished to.[135] Again though, even in as pragmatic a festival as this one, the minister still requested the constitutional principles of Rousseau's *Social Contract* be rehearsed as an antidote to the "tumult of joy, the impetuous drunkenness of the heart and the spirit," which might misunderstand the nature of sovereignty.[136] The memory of the violence of the Revolution constantly threatened these festivals, so much so that administrators were counseled, "could anyone reproach us for an honorable moderation? Let us avoid anything that might relight the half-damped flames of hatred and division."[137] A real festival would reject all memory of violence in favor of the pleasing images of "security, order, abundance, and all that peaceful and sharing system of improvements, of industrial and agricultural developments, which can only flourish in prosperous times."[138]

The Festival of the Foundation of the Republic, held every year on 1 Vendémiaire, was the celebration most successfully transformed to meet this new ideal. In Year VI the festival was totally divorced from the events it celebrated and turned into a monument to fraternity. As the minister of the interior instructed the departments, the political moment of sociability, "which forms the indissoluble links between all the elements of the social pact, is the power of democratic states, and while remaining the most powerful nerve of the body politic, provides the majority of the pleasures that a man may enjoy under the empire of the laws."[139] That fraternity was understood to be a social and domestic value was underlined by the list of qualities that were associated with it, particularly those of fulfilling the métier where one best expressed one's *industrie* and exhibiting hospitality, compassion, and moderation.[140] The duality of fraternity and *industrie*, the ideological core of the commercial republic, could not be represented through the usual forms of the revolutionary festival: processions, allegorical performances, and athletic competitions. Instead, a *spectacle* was made of embodied *industrie*, the products of work and ingenuity. The foundation of the republic was to be celebrated through a five-day industrial exhibition, a "*spectacle* of a new sort" of the fruits of social life, to display in the most vivid fashion the real origins of the republic in the elaboration of civil society.[141]

The industrial exhibition was a profoundly hybrid form of celebration of the republic. On the face of it, the exhibition seemed to be an effort to efface the revolutionary violence that had founded the regime and to put forth an *encyclopédiste* eulogy of technology: "Those arts which sustain man, provide for all his needs, and augment his natural faculties by the invention and use of machines are at the same time society's bond, the soul of agriculture and commerce, and the most fertile source of our joys and wealth."[142]

Administrators and citizens were encouraged to forgive any wrongs that may have been committed in the past and to leave them to historians. The most obvious interpretation of the festival, therefore, is as a form of deliberate obfuscation and forgetting, of a piece with the later erection of a giant elephant in the Place de la Bastille by Napoleon. Yet in the circulars organizing the exhibition and the festival the history of violence in which the republic was implicated was rehearsed, indeed emphasized. At the moment the republic was born, "enemy armies were at the gates of Paris, the English had

Toulon, Dunkirk was threatened, and the counterrevolution unsheathed its daggers throughout the west."[143] The republic was completely identified with the mobilization of the country to defeat these forces. Even the violence of the Terror was acknowledged as a tyranny equivalent to that of kings, "when the blood ran from the scaffold and famine stalked our walls, when every day brought us new crimes and new tears."[144] The violence of politics could be acknowledged, indeed had to be acknowledged, to the people who had suffered it, because what was being celebrated was their endurance, their sacrifice, and their ability to survive the privations of revolution. The violence was not republican; true republican virtue was displayed in the moral rectitude of those who lived in society and suffered violence without succumbing to its allure. Endurance sanctified even the guillotine:

> It is no longer a theater of crime and shame,
> It becomes an altar, when innocence climbs it.[145]

The violence of the Revolution was providential. It had tested the French people, and they had proved themselves capable of liberty: "If God made us to exercise virtue, he made us to be free. How often have we proved it?"[146] The light of the republic showed up more clearly against the dark of the violence from which it had emerged.

Representing the moral qualities of those who exhibited such loyalty and endurance posed problems nonetheless. The traditional iconography of military virtue was obviously inadequate, and no artist had yet solved the problem of the depiction of the energy of a modern population in movement.[147] Even La Révellière, as noted above, was aware that the classical allegories so favored by the designers of the festivals were empty, but there was no other iconography at hand. The ambiguities and tensions felt about the representation of the quotidian virtues of a republican can be read from the speech of La Révellière's successor as president of the Directory, Charles Treilhard, at the festival: "it is a consoling sight to see the bloody swords of victorious generals sheathed, as they visit the monuments of the industry of nations."[148] How were the qualities of the "simple country-dweller, the timid bourgeois unused to the exercise of arms," who had saved the country and created the republic to be represented?[149] The industrial exhibition solved this problem by representing the citizens of the country to themselves as workers. "The freest nations are necessarily the most industrious": thus in displaying the works of hand and mind, the fruits of industry, the republic was displaying the concrete elements of liberty.[150] The elaboration of liberty

and the perfection of the arts would make the same history, and the attainment of democratic equality for the citizenry would be reflected in the suppression of the illegitimate division between the mechanical and liberal arts:
"industry is daughter of invention and sister of genius and taste: as the hand
fashions, the imagination creates and reason perfects. The most common
arts, in appearance the most simple, will enlighten themselves in the home
of the light of the sciences."[151] Just as modern citizenship transcended the
ancient model, so the standards of classical workmanship were to be emulated and surpassed. By displaying the works of human artifice, the exhibition attained the quality of transparency that was appropriate to a revolutionary festival while providing the participants with the entertainment of
a *spectacle*. All the exhibits, from the Durand hand mills at arcade fifty-five
to the ballooning display at the end of the day, were the work of French
citizens, of the republic.[152] There was no separation between viewer and
viewed, between audience and performance. The show was an autoportrait
of the industrious citizen, with his or her essential qualities displayed as
work. The particular exhibits were the work of particular men and women,
but the ingenuity and labor they represented were the common heritage of
all republicans. Again, this representation of the meaning of the republic
could be extended to areas outside the economy. François de Neufchâteau
argued that the real triumph of the republic over its enemies would come
when it had surpassed their commerce, not when it had defeated them mili-
tarily.[153]

The exhibition was a success. It had to be extended by five days to accom-
modate the crowds trying to attend, and extra fireworks displays and con-
certs had to be improvised. Admitted François, "we have no more money,
but that is not important."[154] It achieved such success because it quoted and
syncretized the exigencies of politics and the nature of social life; the imme-
diacy of the festival and the artifice of the *spectacle;* the industry of the working citizen and the "pleasure of loitering in the arcades," as one might on a
city street.[155] It succeeded in making a *spectacle* of modern life and of the
modern republic. The success of the festival was the best possible background for the launch of the *Bulletin décadaire,* the official publication that
would seek to promulgate the model of the industrious, commercial republic. Its prospectus concluded with an epigrammatic statement of the central
inspiration of the new regime: "It is most important to generate and inculcate good moral habits, because the Republic has greater need of citizens
than heroes, of *moeurs* than victories."[156]

The Festival of the Foundation of the Republic was so popular that the industrial exhibition was turned into an annual event. Moreover, the interpretation of the foundations of the republic as the useful arts of civil society was successfully instituted as the meaning of the festival as a whole. Daunou, for instance, praising the festival in his capacity as president of the Council of Five Hundred, enumerated "benevolent laws that reanimate agriculture, honor and encourage industry, and open the sources of social prosperity" as the successes of the republic.[157] Daunou recognized the festival as a type of "those institutions which among the most progressive peoples consecrate and make the constitution live, and sometimes act in the place of it."[158] The festival, and the revision of the festival cycle in general, showed that a specifically modern form of political culture for the republic could evolve, but that it had to be syncretic and novel if it was to work. It remained to be seen, though, as Daunou himself noted at the end of his speech, if the prototype of the festival could be generalized as a form of public culture that would "regenerate *moeurs*."[159] While the designers of the festivals had shown that an accommodation between the needs of the republic and modern cultural proclivities was possible, the more general problem of the reconciliation of the arts and sciences with democratic politics remained unsolved. The idea of civil society, and the behaviors proper to it, as the ground of such a reconciliation was a useful insight for the design of festivals, but could it ground a more extensive politics? More specifically, could the republic embrace the useful and decorative arts as the basis of its legitimation without doing violence to the autonomy of civil society?

A Republic of Artists or Republican Art?

By depicting the republic with the arts of civil life the organizers of the Festival of the Foundation of the Republic revisited the site of a disaster. The central insight of the festival was that republican liberty was based on the exercise of the arts. However, the history of the relationship of the republic, and indeed the Revolution, to the arts was unhappy. There was a fundamental problem reconciling the social differentiation generated within civil society with republican equality. Policies such as the promotion of universal primary education and a civil religion did not answer this structural problem, and indeed tended to exaggerate it. The more concrete relationships between the republican state and the expressive and plastic arts had, if anything, been even more difficult. The contrast between utopian hopes invested in the arts and practical difficulties (of patronage, standards and modes of public art, and artistic heritage) generated massive incoherence in revolutionary artistic policy.[160]

There were some fixed points amid the confusion: all parties agreed that artistic genius should be schooled by nature, that the community which exemplified the marriage of genius and liberty was the city-state of Greece, and that the antithesis of a natural, regenerated art was luxury.[161] No one could derive a practice, either administrative or artistic, from these premises. Even as lucid a journal as the *Décade philosophique* could in one issue carry a glowing account of the foundation of the Lycée des Arts, a society for the preservation of the arts from revolutionary vandalism, and in another call for the destruction of "the theater boxes where one seems to hide from the sight of one's fellow citizens."[162] The incoherence of attitude merely reflected the incoherence of practice, which was always present in the relationship of politics to art in the Revolution. The Constituent Assembly, even in 1790, had found itself inaugurating revolutionary vandalism, by demanding the removal of the statues of the enslaved nations from the foot of the statue of Louis XIV. Almost simultaneously it laid down the foundations for the *patrimoine national,* by creating the Commission des Monuments to preserve the works of the past.[163] The revolutionaries' failure to differentiate the principles of cultural expression from those of political representation meant that negotiations between the two realms always threatened to harness artistic production to the needs of the state—to reduce art to propaganda.[164] The utility of the arts to the project of the commercial republic depended on the maintenance of the difference between civil society and politics so that the pursuit of the arts in civil society could provide a content for the formal category of liberty, which politics was to defend. The representation of the population of the republic as an industrious citizenry required a discourse that could organize the relationship between the arts and the republic rather than collapse them into one.

As in other areas, the very disasters of 1793 and 1794 were a spur to innovation and to rethinking this problem. One of the most innovative essays in the reconsideration of the relationship between the arts and public life was Abbé Grégoire's on vandalism.[165] In coining this rhetorical term, Grégoire lay responsibility for revolutionary iconoclasm, and revolutionary violence generally, at the feet of the *ancien régime,* which had trained the people in infamy. The true enemy of the arts and sciences was not the virtuous republican but the degenerate subject of the monarchy, who shared his master's hatred for learning and the freedom it promoted.[166] The denomination of a degenerate population, created by the monarchy, as the cancer of vandalism that fed on the body of the Revolution had tremendous currency as a defense of the republic from the charge of barbarism.[167] Yet, while the discourse of vandalism could rescue the Revolution from the imputation that it was essentially inimical to modern forms of cultural expression, it could not solve the central problem of reconciling citizenship with the arts. The review of Grégoire's speech in the *Décade philosophique* acknowledged this failure and even admitted that one consequence of Grégoire's arguments was the inapplicability of any ancient model, not just rustic Sparta, to the construction of a modern polity. One might admire the simplicity of the Greeks, but it was irrelevant to contemporary France, where "new thoughts and original ideas continually spring up."[168] The incompatibility between ancient simplicity and modern complexity created precisely the kind of confusion that allowed vandals, destructive of all social and artistic life, to pass themselves off as republicans. The urge to destroy could mask itself as the urge to simplify and purify. Yet the release from the antique model was not quite the liberation it might seem to have been. The most authoritative statement of the hope that a democratic state would naturally be the home of an artistic renaissance, Quatremère de Quincy's *Considérations sur les arts de dessin en France*, had built its argument and its aspiration out of a reflection on ancient Athens.[169] The arts of Athens were the arts of free men and as such could teach how to live freely and beautifully. They reconciled nature and regeneration. To deny this particular classical model its universal validity was to provoke hard questions indeed.

The displacement of classical artwork from the peak of cultural value opened up some interesting perspectives, even if the view was somewhat vertiginous. This process penetrated deeply and quickly into the cultural life of France. In a review of an Italian work on art criticism the *Rédacteur* stated as obvious truth the notion that good work was original, that it communicated a personal vision. Neoclassical standards were abandoned: "philosophy is also for independence and not given to routine, it is not the domination of accredited opinions that determines its judgment, but nature."[170] Nature, which had been safely constrained by its identification with the classical world, was here let loose as individual judgment. Just what followed from the invocation of nature in this manner and what sort of artistic originality should provide the model of a public culture remained moot. J. B. Leclerc tentatively explored the idea that a republican art might be built out of popular culture, from the bottom up as it were. He suggested that village poets should immortalize the lives of those who lived exemplary lives in the vernacular forms and that these should form the historic memory of the villages of France.[171] Gabriel Olivier argued for a different kind of universality as the basis of a republican art, for the universality of music "as the language of the soul."[172] In language that directly quoted the moral sentiment theorists he argued that the effect of good music was to provide "a proof of the truths of sentiment and to dissipate any of our anxieties."[173] Although the idea was insightful, and developed some of Diderot's thoughts on the potential for music to enhance social integration, it was impossible to imagine the cultural institutions that would follow.[174] The plastic, written, and visual arts were the inescapable ground on which this debate had to be played out.

One interesting line of argument was to sever completely the ties that bound culture to politics, to accept the conclusions of Grégoire's argument (that political and artistic expression had to inhabit different spheres), and to argue that the maintenance of liberty was the maintenance of the categorical difference. Letourneur and Daunou took up this line of thought in declaring that public service of the arts should maintain their pristine independence. There was no instrumental or institutional relationship between the forms of republican liberty and the arts; rather, the freedom of the arts was one of the results of republican liberty, one of the signs of its flourishing.[175] This was a creative idea: rather than seek another model of universality to replace the impossible classical model, Letourneur and Daunou heralded the specificity and self-legitimation of the arts. For all the clarity this approach might have brought to the relationship between the arts and the evolution of republican liberty, however, its potential was severely constrained by the actual condition of the arts. No sphere of creativity, or even of the economy, could, in the conditions of the late 1790s, have survived without the active help of the state. The perilous conditions of the publishing industry (discussed in the previous chapter) replicated themselves in the plastic arts, theater, and other forms of literature. The Revolution might have incarnated the principles of the men of letters, but it had destroyed the institutions, such as the academies, that had fed them.[176] The republican state could not simply respect the autonomy of aesthetic expression and point to that realm as a model of liberty. It had to directly support aesthetic expression, in the forms of pensions, subsidies, and, most important, commissions, and so had to have a more mediated cultural policy. Artistic expression might be free in principle, but in practice it would have to be paid for by the republic.

This troubled ground, where principles met historic institutions with which they did not quite fit, had long been occupied by men such as Daunou, Mercier, and François de Neufchâteau, who were now running the cultural policy of the French state. In the mid-1770s Mercier and François, in the pages of the *Journal des dames*, had vigorously opposed the "tyranny" of the sole stage for drama in Paris, the Comédie Française.[177] The goal of their campaign was to overturn the effective censorship exercised by the members of the troupe over the presentation of drama in the capital, and to establish proper communications among authors, the public, critics, and performers.[178] Mercier had laid out the fundamental principle of the property of the author in his text in *Du théâtre*, and François used the principle as the basis of his case for Lonvay de la Saussaye against the Comédie. François lampooned the troupe for having effectively stolen the intellectual property of another by not paying him the author's share for the five productions of his *Alcidonis* and, worse yet, for having disfigured the piece through their self-interested rewriting of it.[179] The critics of the Comédiens did not restrict themselves to a defense of individuals. They demanded a reorganization of the troupe. Their goal was to set authors free of its internal regulations. In later stages of their campaign they demanded a second theater, so that competition would force the Comédie to respect talent rather than faction.[180] The campaign was a failure and collapsed when the support of the publisher Charles-Joseph Panckoucke was withdrawn, but the experience of mediating the needs of cultural institutions with the demands of principle would linger for participants in the debate, and the ideas generated retained their potency. In the following decade Daunou, then finding his literary and political feet, would reflect these notions when lauding Boileau for his independence in giving law to literature and contrasting him with the state of literary faction, "which hoards talent, ends useful communication, and substitutes hatred for emulation."[181] Ten years later, this time as commissioner for the collection of art treasures in Italy for Parisian institutions, that earlier education in the interaction of public life, arts, and politics was still with him. On being asked if it was practical to take Trajan's column from Saint Peter's Square, he replied that it certainly would not be wise and reminded La Révellière-Lépeaux that "it is neither just nor politic to take too much material of this sort; the best patriots of this country look on these events with some pain, as would we in their place."[182] The language of public policy and the arts was one in which commercial republicans were well versed.

The entanglement of the republican state in artistic policy is best illustrated by the attempts to revive the Paris theaters and the opera. A decree of 13 January 1790 had removed all controls on theater ownership, and in 1792 the Paris Commune had removed the opera from the purview of the state and given the lease to Francoeur and Celerier for a thirty-year period. They lasted seventeen months.[183] When the artists tried to run it themselves, they did no better. The institution could not be self-sustaining. It had to have a subvention, and this need pulled the state into areas it would rather not have treaded. The replacement of the administrators with François de Neufchâteau's friend Ignace-Frédéric Mirbeck in Year VI did stabilize matters, and he was able to announce that the repertoire would be printed since he could guarantee future productions.[184] But even he could do nothing about the technical bankruptcy of the institution; at the end of Year VII its assets of 416,127 francs were overshadowed by debts of 577,359 francs.[185] Nor was the opera, always a money-losing operation, the only institution that needed support. The Comédie, now renamed the Théâtre de la République et des Arts, also needed money. The sterling efforts by Augustin Sagaret to open both the Odéon and the Salle Faydeau failed in Year VII, and François de Neufchâteau had to pay off his debts and restore the company to its home rent-free.[186] A fire in the Odéon and demands by star actors such as Molé and Fleuri for more money before they would return to the stage were only two of the events that piled unforeseen expenses on an already chronic financial situation.[187] The minister may have wished the major companies to be as self-sufficient as their brothers and sisters of the boulevards, but circumstances conspired against this, and he found himself embroiled in company details. The involvement of the republican state in the world of culture opened it to requests for jobs in theater administration and, in one case, the demand for the donation of an entire theater.[188] The need to avoid expense if at all possible also put the minister in the position of effectively censoring theatrical production. A request from Italian theatrical entrepreneur Varisco that he be allowed to found a comic opera was turned down, precisely because the possible losses it might have made could in turn undermine the financial position of the main opera.[189] The corrupting touch of patronage could go a long way toward undermining the theater as a sphere of liberty. Despite this, figures who were committed to the future of the Paris stage could see no other way to support it. In Year VI Chénier argued that the freedom of the theaters had created nothing but trouble, explaining, "now that exclusive privileges have been annulled we confront the inconveniences of an unlimited variety [of theaters], which destroys the dramatic arts, real competition, social *moeurs,* and the legitimate interests of the government."[190]

Giving financial support to the theater created ideological as well as financial challenges. The theaters of a commercial republic were supposed to contribute to the welfare of those who could not afford to attend their productions. In Year V a whole series of measures had sought to hypothecate funds from theater box offices for the support of the indigent. Administrations were invited to encourage local theaters to give benefit performances for local projects.[191] In Paris it had even been hoped that the sectional charity boards would be funded by a 10 percent tax on theater tickets, a tax systematically resisted by the directors of the houses.[192] This alignment of privilege with fraternity was utterly reversed by such measures as the request to the Council of Five Hundred to raise the Paris toll charges *(octroi)* by 10 percent to supply funds for the theaters.[193] It was vitally important for the regime to clarify to itself and to the population the possible grounds on which such a priority might be made of the arts and the likely benefit that would accrue to the population.

Even if the more obvious public functions of the theater were called into question by their financial situation in the late 1790s, the Directory at least consistently maintained its adherence to the principle of the primacy of the author or artist.[194] As François de Neufchâteau stressed, in his instruction to local administrators to ensure that copyright fees were paid for theatrical performances, the theater was an aid to public instruction and would help solidify republican *moeurs.* This could be achieved only if the "long study, meditation, and care of that class of citizens who often have no other property but that which they have created from their own abilities" was protected and rewarded.[195] The idea that the model of independence portrayed by the individual author or artist was an inspiration for republican liberty, and so deserving of the protection of copyright, was the principle that François de Neufchâteau used to discriminate between the artistic policy of the state and the protection of art by the state. Again, he did not have tremendous room for maneuver. In the visual arts, for instance, he found himself beset by demands that he honor commissions made during the Convention.[196] The suggestion that he effectively hand over control of the state's commissioning policy to the Institut National—which Philippe-Auguste Hennequin proposed would evaluate the works already in hand, under David's direction, and then lay out a future strategy for support of artists—provoked François to defend the state's own interests. If the state, through the

Institut, were to attempt to control the art world in this fashion, he argued, it would corrupt the artists and severely harm the state's interests.[197] Though the republic had already re-created the Ecole Nationale de Peinture et Sculpture (the Beaux-Arts) and the free drawing school, and had also reinstituted the Prix de Rome, to do more than this would be, in effect, to recreate the Academy of Painting, which would be intolerable.[198] Instead, he argued, a clear distinction needed to be drawn between the liberty of the artist to create whatever he wished and the liberty of the state to commission whatever it needed. Moreover, "in a time in which the greatest need is to support the constitution and republican institutions by every means, it behooves us not to ignore that medium whose influence is greater because it is emotional and exerts itself with force, but without violence."[199] François was effectively saving the independence of artists from themselves. A commitment by the state to guarantee the support of artists might give them security, but a republic that bought works rather than bought men was the best guarantee of artistic liberty. "Under the monarchy the arts were slaves," he recalled; "for a republic they are instruments and supports. One does not injure their freedom in this way: it remains entire."[200] Total support for the arts would amount to censorship, so artists would have to live with the dangers that went along with their liberty. Even in the last month of his ministry, when subject to extreme criticism in the Council of Five Hundred for insufficient republican zeal, François continued to defend this position at personal cost. Required to propose amendments to the opera *Adrien,* he expressed his extreme displeasure at having to undertake "this sort of censorship" and reminded the directors that if one wanted masterpieces, "one cannot encourage writers on the one hand and torture them on the other."[201] The freedom of artists had to be respected and protected by the republic. The free artist would then become the model republican, his creativity the model for emulation by the industrious citizen, his free writing and speaking the model for liberty.

The idea of the free artist as the model of the republican citizen was exploited and developed by François de Neufchâteau in a series of speeches. The best known of these was his speech welcoming the art works collected in Italy in the wake of the republican armies to Paris, a speech that Edouard Pommier has identified as the most important statement of the understanding of republican France as the *patrimoine* of liberty.[202] François figured the great artists of the past as republicans before their time, "lost in the centuries of slavery," whose works bequeathed their vision of liberty to the future.[203]

The works of liberty had now come home to the land of liberty: "you made these works for France. Now they have found their destination."[204] François moved his speech beyond a somewhat sophistic justification for the acquisition of so many works of art into a more profound discourse on the nature of the republic by pointing out that even as the French people deserved custody of the works of the free men of the ages, that custody imposed duties on them. The most obvious were the duty of care and that of making these treasures available to the regard of the world as a model of virtue for all who would come to see them. More important, these works of art represented a series of exemplars to live up to. The artists of the past had no doubt "foreseen the destinies of peoples; and their sublime pictures were the inheritance through which they bequeathed the spirit of liberty."[205] These works of art incarnated the true sprit of liberty, and it was from them that the French could learn to be true republicans: "art, for a free people, is the principal instrument of social happiness."[206] As the works of industry exemplified the actual liberty of the French, so the masterpieces of the past outlined the achievements of freedom to which they might aspire. The arts deserved public support because they were the school of liberty.

The idea of the artist as the model of the republican citizen was a powerful image that had application beyond the problem of the relationship of the world of the arts to the state. It was the ground upon which the idea of self-command, a notion central to the neostoic premises of republicanism, could be recuperated for the modern republic. In his speech to the students of the Conservatory of Music, François de Neufchâteau pointed out that the republic supported their institution because it fostered independence, which was the basis of "genius, elevation of spirit, and magnanimity of heart."[207] He elaborated on the independence that he hoped was fostered in music education by his depiction of the itinerant musicians who had the misfortune to live under the *ancien régime*, "too constrained in palaces, untamed by gold or disdainful caresses, throwing themselves into the happiness of independence, traveling throughout Europe, without a homeland, because liberty was nowhere to be found . . . republican nomads, looking in vain for the virtues they might sing and so satisfy their talent."[208] The authentic voice of the artist, his originality, cried out for liberty; his refusal of tainted honors was due to his independence. Independence and originality of expression were harnessed as the meaning of republican liberty. The ideal of a musical education nurturing moral consciousness as well as talent was extended to scientific education for the students of the Ecole Polytechnique. Their self-mastery was based on "the power of the sciences on the morality of a man. They do not desiccate the heart, . . . they regulate the action of men and direct it toward the good in things."[209] François repeatedly made the point that the moral dignity and self-mastery of these students was not an individual attainment but was made possible by the regime of liberty. They enjoyed moral peace, "that peace of the heart, tranquillity of the soul," because they did not face the terrible choices of the sages, artists, and musicians of old, torn between praise and glory without honor, or freedom with hardship.[210] The peaceful domestic virtues, rather than the heroic dispositions of the republicans lost in time, were those proper to a citizen of the French Republic. Finally, the vision of a universal republic, based in the practice of the arts and in the slow work of civilization, could be glimpsed as a historical possibility: "He is virtuous whose work embraces all nations, and gives fruit useful to his contemporaries, and which future generations will also enjoy; who recognizes no national rivalries, nor conflicts of place, time, or opinion, which can rob men of the benefits of their experience; and whose work can be given to the peoples of the world to the best of his ability."[211]

The French Republic was, as Condorcet had written in his *Esquisse*, the culmination of the history of civilization. What Condorcet could not have imagined was how tortuous, but ultimately fruitful, the marriage of the republic and the arts, of liberty and civilization, would be. Only in the late days of the republic would its elites create a language capable of retaining the long-held intuition that liberty and the progress of the arts were intertwined, expressing the relationship between the spheres of cultural creativity and political representation, and maintaining the difference between them. Through the practices of administration and negotiation the inchoate ideas that animated the republic were given form and the principles of a modern liberty adduced. In the confused, and often frustrating, interactions of a complex politics and a diverse social order a new representation of the democratic subject as the self-mastering creative artist was generated and another aspect of republicanism adapted to the exigencies of modern life.

The institutional innovations around the idea of the citizen artist were lost with the republic, just as the educational institutions of the republic were closed by Napoleon. However, just as the notion of a shared literature as the ground of a shared political culture survived the collapse of the *écoles centrales*, the idea of the citizen artist also survived the political eclipse of its adherents. The idea of the citizen artist was not lost; it transformed itself into the most dramatic ground of political critique of the nineteenth century, to become eventually the ancestor of the politics of the avant-garde. Of course, the analogy of democratic freedom to artistic self-expression took some unpredictable turns. For one man, Charles Fourier, the idea of a harmonized social, economic, and political order came with the force of a revelation in April 1799.[212] Fourier's writings were highly critical of the Revolution, arguing that it had portrayed the inutility of the ideals of both political liberty and capitalist economics.[213] The third part of his first published work, *The Theory of the Four Movements,* of 1808, was devoted to a critique of the Directory's religious and economic policies. Theophilanthropy was "a soul without a body," and the "mercantile systems of the philosophers" were chimeras in the face of the real logic of economic development represented by the "insular monopoly."[214] Yet Fourier himself seems to have been unaware of the extent to which some of his insights were indebted to the political culture of the commercial republic. His condemnation of the revolutionaries for having "forgotten the chief and only useful right among them, the right to work," sits uneasily with the commercial republican emphasis on *industrie* as the primary characteristic of the republican citizen.[215] Even Fourier's anti-metropolitan idealization of the joys of horticulture echoed the agricultural ideal of the commercial republicans.[216] Most important, though, his central norm, in the name of which he condemned contemporary social and political arrangements, was a development of the ideal of the free citizen as the self-mastering creative artist. The repression of *passionate attraction* made frustrated and unhappy bourgeois out of men and women who could have been free and fulfilled; despite the denial of the passions by civilization, "the germ of their existence continues to live in our souls, tiring or stimulating us according to individual levels of activity. That is why so many civilized men spend their lives in boredom, even though they may possess everything that they desire."[217] Fourier's description of the splendors of the combined order portrayed participation in the arts, alongside gastronomy and membership in the amorous army, as the antithesis of the boredom of civilized life. The citizens of the harmonized order would all be natural artists, dramatists, singers, and poets. "If every phalanx has a minimum of seven or eight hundred actors, musicians and dancers, it will be able to provide itself with all the entertainments enjoyed in a great capital city like Paris or London."[218] This was a far cry from trying to scrape together the money to keep the Salle Faydeau open.

Fourier's ideas, and their later development, obviously went far beyond the bounds of commercial republicanism. What the example of Fourier reveals is the enormous critical and cultural potential built into the speculations and institutional experiments of the commercial republicans. The historical difficulty I started with was to explain how the Revolution could be the origin of the idea of political democracy in Europe when the Revolution itself had been so besmirched with political violence, foreign war, and terror. I hypothesized that the revolutionaries had created a civic culture, a store of social capital, despite the opposing tendencies within the Revolution itself. What we see as we follow the development of the notion of the citizen artist is that the civic culture created in the Revolution exceeded the institutional logic for which it was intended. The revolutionaries sought to ground the republic in the purified *moeurs* that would sustain a democratic republican order. They succeeded in creating the ground for forms of critique—ideas of individuality and notions of politics that went beyond anything they could have imagined. They created the dynamic problems and opportunities for a whole new century.

Conclusion

Between 1795 and 1800 a new democratic republicanism was elaborated. Before 1795 Jacobins and sans-culottes had tried, and failed, to create a polity in which universal rights did not corrode all particular freedoms. After the Terror the republicans at the heart of the Directory laid the basis for such a regime. French men and women, acting in the spheres of culture and politics, produced fundamentally new normative orientations for their society; they generated the social capital that democrats would exploit for the next century. The languages of sentimental psychology and of *industrie* were embedded into civil life. These democratic ideas were woven into mundane experiences and institutions, such as the market, giving social life in France a set of values distinct from other European countries in the nineteenth century. The revolutionary context provoked French society to substantial and profound innovation, but the experience also generated ideas and social forms inimical to the democratic republic.

Democratic values were to be far from dominant in nineteenth-century France. The new values generated under the republic were not strongly enough represented to ensure its survival, and so democratic republicanism had to survive in a hostile environment. The Directory itself lasted only five years, until the coup of 18 Brumaire replaced it with a dictatorship of a new sort. Benjamin Constant wrote to Sieyès the day after the coup to point out the dangers inherent in Napoleon Bonaparte. The balance of forces was now uneven, he wrote, as "he has the generals, the soldiers, the aristocratic population, and all those who are enthused by the appearance of power; the Republic has only you, which is something, and the representatives, which, good or bad, will always be a defense against the plans of any individual" and especially against "a man who talks only of himself."[1] Constant's fear that the Bonapartist coup would usher in a new kind of regime with a social and institutional base antagonistic to the values of the republic proved to be

correct. The creation in 1802 of the *lycées,* for example, reversed the informing ideals of the education system in favor of the creation of a military-
bureaucratic elite for state service.[2] The direction the new order of things in
this sphere would take had been clear from the very first days, when the
new minister of the interior took away all funding from the development of
the humanities curriculum.[3] This pattern of draining the republican state of
its content, and substituting a new alliance of the state with social elites, was
repeated across the range of the state's competencies. The Directory may
have promoted the development of the political culture of the democratic
republic, but after its failure nearly a century would be required to rescue its
institutional form.

We can see the discontinuities created by the Napoleonic regime through
the reactions of the liberal constitutionalists to it. The novelty of the Consulate and the empire came as a shock to men such as Sieyès who had connived
at a coup against the Directory confident that they would control the regime
that would emerge from it. Those who thought that modern liberal values
would be secured under authoritarian rule were soon disabused of their illusions. In 1804 Carnot, returned from exile after Brumaire, protested in the
Tribunate against the idea of hereditary rule in principle—"if this citizen has
restored political liberty, brought safety to his country, is it a reward to offer
him the sacrifice of that very liberty?"—and from constitutional legality,
since the declaration of 22 September 1792 made even proposing a monarchy illegal.[4] Roederer, an ally of Sieyès's, replied that the provision was void
and had been made out of hatred for the monarch, not for the monarchy.[5]
Monarchy and republican *moeurs* were, in principle, perfectly compatible.
Roederer was one of four commissioners who organized the transition to
the empire in good faith.[6] His reward for this revealed to him the real understanding of the nature of power that Bonaparte represented. As a recom-
pense Bonaparte offered him a golden box he had first received from the city
of Milan, encrusted with 20,000 francs in diamonds. Reflected Roederer, "I
understood from this that he had all the pride of a sovereign, who believes
he honors a subject by presents, or that of a private man, who believes he
acquits himself of all obligation through paying his account, and treating me
as one would a lawyer or a doctor."[7] In his two examples Roederer captured
the nature of the social and political relations fostered by the Napoleonic regime—patriarchal authoritarianism overlaying modern economic forms—
precisely the mixture that liberals had argued was an absurdity, and therefore impossible.

The Napoleonic experience would be a chastening one for the anti-

Jacobins who brought Napoleon to power and their friends. Dupont de Nemours, for one, was driven to clarify his political thinking as a result of his experience. In the early days of the regime Roederer wrote to him in America, pressing him to return to France, inviting him to join his friends in the re-creation of the country.[8] Ironically, he in turn encouraged Germaine de Staël to do the same: "surely you will not stay at Coppet when France has been given a final chance?"[9] She was entirely skeptical from the very first: "I firmly believe that we will have a monarchy in 1801."[10] Her timing and nomenclature may have been inaccurate, but the analysis was sound. By contrast, Dupont de Nemours remained of the opinion that the Consulate solved all the problems of the Revolution.[11] He most approved of the institution of notability, "an elective and graduated nobility, to which anyone with distinguished talents or eminent virtues can aspire . . . with this beautiful and fundamental institution, whatever the form of government, there is the Republic, there is even democracy."[12] We can gauge the extent to which democracy had established itself as a norm when Dupont de Nemours was driven to try to argue the proposition that notability was democratic. The only problem he saw was the fragility of the first consulship, since the incumbent might be removed by assassination. He thought this inconvenience could be overcome by electing an alternate, who would rule if any harm came to Napoleon.[13] By 1814 he recognized that his notion that liberal values could survive, or even be protected, by authoritarian political structures and a society of ranks was wrong: "I do not believe in republics with emperors. Not even that of England, which has a king and peers by birthright."[14]

The observations of liberal theorists were reinforced by those of a less reflective nature. A. C. Thibaudeau became prefect of Bordeaux and then Marseilles under the Consulate; he heartily approved of Bonaparte, claiming, "he was not perfect, no god, but in his head and his soul there was as much perfection as is compatible with human nature."[15] He also approved of the coup, which dispersed the confusion of the Directory and created new political conditions: "there was a real enthusiasm to create a new regime, as there was at the beginning of the Revolution to overturn the old."[16] Yet though Thibaudeau had no strong ideological commitments that would have driven him to be critical of the regime, he recognized its goal was to replace politics with deference and domination. He argued that the court was the instrument of this policy, and it was a sorrow for him to see "the care taken to make the elite of all the talents of the nation ready for servitude, and to have it put back on the hateful yoke of superannuated forms more quickly than it had rid itself of them."[17] By 1804 new institutions had created new habits of thought and new expectations. Among the men of the Revolution, some saw they could not stop this development and stayed quiet; others consoled themselves for the wreck of the republic with the personal advantages the new monarchy offered them. One could no longer talk of liberty without being marked down as an Ideologue, a Jacobin, or a Terrorist.[18]

Another marker of the radical change in the political elite was Grégoire's eulogy of Port-Royal.[19] Grégoire, whose defense of the constitutional church was undermined by the concordat, staged his critique of Napoleon in the politically charged ruins of the convent destroyed by Louis XIV. Grégoire found his principle of opposition in the Jansenist tradition; his Jansenist republicans were charged to "set up a double barrier to the encroachments of political and ultramontane despotism."[20] He cited Pascal to rally their resistance: according to Pascal, "it was a great evil to introduce a king into a republican state and to take way from the people the liberty that God had given them."[21] Yet this was a retreat to the sources of opposition to the crown, effectively ignoring the Revolution, and it revealed just how quickly the terms of political and social identity had changed. Jansenism as opposition implied the monarch on the throne. One of the directors, writing much later, also understood how the Consulate and the empire created new social facts that in turn demanded what he considered a total misrepresentation of the Directory. In La Révellière-Lépeaux's view the only period in the Revolution that had been truly republican was the Directory; before it had come anarchy, and after it despotism.[22] Why then, he asked, was the Directory the object of the scorn of both the enemies of liberty and "of a crowd of people who call themselves excellent liberals?" The answer was the evolution of their social interest; during the Revolution they were motivated by jobs, money, credit, fame; while the republic brought these to them they supported it, and after, as the political situation demanded, they changed their values to follow their interests.[23] Having rallied to Napoleon they had to denigrate the regime they had betrayed. Caught between their principles and their interests they pursued their interests.

This destruction of the republic was made possible by the directors themselves. The emerging rationality of political life in France was not capitalized on by the executive. Instead, in a series of coups in Years V and VI, the executive managed to delegitimize the republican state. To many observers the directors' actions lacked any rationality other than a struggle for factional advantage and seemed a perversion of the meaning of the republic. Yet in the spring of 1797 political life had seemed stable enough to the editors of the *Décade philosophique* that they thought it worthwhile to educate their readers on the groups that made up the Council of Five Hundred.[24] The journal broke the council into three parts; those who thought the constitution insufficiently democratic; those who thought the constitution well conceived but found particular laws against royalists necessary; and those who, while sincerely committed to the constitution, favored the repeal of all measures against royalists. The *Décade* argued that this last position was unrealistic, that the "constitutional moderates" *(constitutionnels modérés)* misunderstood the nature of royalism, and that the correct course for the Directory was to sustain its support among the centrists and the democrats. The analysis went on to argue, though, that the very existence of a constitutional opposition was a benefit to the republic, that its interrogation of the executive contributed to the development of a more rational and coherent polity.[25] Two things are important about this analysis. The very acknowledgment of a legitimate form of principled opposition to the republican executive goes against the common opinion that republican ideology could not tolerate such internal division.[26] More important, the mutual interrogation of constitutional moderates and republicans was evidence that moderates and republicans shared a normative ground copious enough to allow for plural political values to inhabit it. This glimpse of a possible way of stabilizing the regime was lost in the coup of Fructidor, Year V. The republican directors, convinced that a royalist plot was brewing in the legislature, arrested and exiled the suspected deputies to forestall their action. By undermining the integrity of the constitutional structures the directors made the republic vulnerable to a crisis like that of 1799. By Year VI the coup had become a normal part of the repertoire of political action; the police spies of Barras were reporting to him that in Paris it was assumed that Barras and Napoleon, having attacked every political faction in turn, would make a bid for dictatorial power out of fear of worse.[27] The political elite was taught the politics of the coup by the directors themselves. Judgment of the Directory has turned on this action ever since.

A line of argument that focuses solely on the personal qualities of the directors as an explanation for the failure of republican political forms in 1799 is highly unsatisfactory, however. The crisis of 1799 did not come out of thin air. The neo-Jacobin revival in the legislature, which provoked the coup of 18 Brumaire, was due to the bad showing of French armies in renewed warfare. The final crisis of the Directory was, in essence, due to foreign policy failures. Moreover, these failures were not contingent but were inscribed in the very nature of the regime. This is not to say that the Directory was inherently expansionist. Even Albert Sorel, who was critical of the war aims of the directors and argued that they never negotiated for peace in good faith, did not claim the republic was inherently expansionist.[28] The old canard that the directors conducted war as an economic concern, financing the army on loot, has also been exploded. Howard Brown has shown that war was not a paying proposition for the regime, and that the Directory needed peace to rein in debt and gain control of army provisioning.[29] The Directory was not committed to war; it just could not find the way to make peace. Its intellectual resources did not extend to a useful understanding of international power politics. The weakest feature of commercial republicanism was its understanding of the nature of a world of separate and competing states.

French thinking about the congress between the German states of the empire and France at Rastatt in the winter and spring of 1797–98 illustrates the problem. French goals at Rastatt were not unreasonable, and France's position was strong. Austria had been forced to sue for peace at the treaty of Campo Formio (17 October 1797) and had reached a secret understanding with France to give up the left bank of the Rhine in return for Venice. The consequent dramatic withdrawal of the Austrians from Mainz in December 1797 undermined the resistance of the smaller German states to a Franco-Austrian reorganization of the empire.[30] The French plan was to use secularized episcopal territories in Germany to compensate those who were displaced by the new arrangement.[31] French ministers were mindful of the existing international agreements that governed the composition of the empire, which would have to be respected, and even understood that though they might wish to aid the Poles, there was no pragmatic way of doing so.[32] Their most forward goal was to assure the futures of the Cisalpine and Batavian republics. The seeming convergence of interests between France and Austria on mutual aggrandizement in Germany and Italy, and promotion of these interests within the Austrian camp by Johann Ludwig, Count Coblentz, created an opportunity to end war on the Continent, release France from crippling military expenditures, and allow it to concentrate on consolidating the republic. As the minister of the interior put it to the Directors in one of his monthly political reports, "peace alone will revive the confidence and tranquillity that are the bases for every commercial venture. Then, we will be able to inspire the resolution of particular interests with the general good, giving manufacturing and agricultural France the role among the nations assigned to it by the fertility of its soil, its large population, and its taste for agriculture and the arts."[33]

The creation of the Roman and Parthenopeian republics, on 19 February and 24 November 1798, respectively, destabilized this balance. Talleyrand, as minister for foreign affairs, was of the opinion that these republics should be abandoned, since they could not be defended, but as Sieyès pointed out, they were not a French creation but a consequence of the instability of Italy.[34] To abandon the new republics would cause chaos, which could present a situation even worse than the current one. The problem for French foreign policy was immense. Even so, some accommodation between French and Austrian interests might have been possible, but in the continuing correspondence among Talleyrand in Paris, Sieyès in Berlin, and Treilhard at Rastatt the situation was analyzed in terms of the commercial and political competition with Britain, not the resolution of states' interests on the Continent. As the tensions rose Talleyrand began to argue that the real moving hand behind Austrian resistance to a final settlement was England. He told Treilhard that he was trying to establish an understanding with the Prussian authorities to counterbalance the Anglo-Austrian front.[35] Talleyrand further explained his thinking to Sieyès: the war would continue only as long as England had the financial means to support it, which England could maintain through its commercial monopoly.[36] Talleyrand and Sieyès agreed that the best way to combat England was to ally all the European nations around France in a commercial league.[37] The commercial and strategic logic that informed this thinking was compelling, but it ignored the immediate military and strategic effects such maneuvers would have on the Austrians. A commercial alliance against England was indistinguishable from a military alliance against Austria, and so the Austrians had no option other than to ally with the Russians, the very outcome the French were most anxious to avoid. Russian troops under General Suvorov pushed the French out of Italy and threatened France with invasion by the summer of 1799. There could be no more compelling lesson in the differences between state and society, between military and economic power, than that administered by the Russian forces. The commercial republican insight that modern social and political relations were grounded in economic relationships created problems for the republic in this sphere, because the economic understanding was not aligned with a parallel understanding of the modern state, particularly its military and strategic nature.

The lack of understanding of the states system had domestic repercussions. The poisonous divisions within the Directory were derived, at least in part, from confusions and disagreements caused by differing views of France's strategic and economic interests. The coup of 18 Fructidor itself was provoked by dissension among the directors over the line to take with English negotiators at Lille in Year V. As Madame de Staël recognized, these negotiations should have been a triumph for France.[38] England was riven with internal political discord, the fleet was immobilized owing to the Spithead and Nore mutinies, and even the cabinet thought the war lost. As Foreign Minister George Canning wrote, "we cannot and must not disguise our situation from ourselves. If peace is to be had, we must have it . . . For my part, I adjourn my objects of honour and happiness for this country beyond the grave of our military and political consequence, which you are now digging at Lisle."[39] Peace would have allowed the directors to break the stranglehold their critics in the legislature held over finances by relieving themselves of the burden of maintaining the armies. Success abroad would have resolved the crisis caused by the election of a majority of anti-Directorials to the councils in Year V. However, while the difficulties of England did give the directors a breathing space, the prospect of peace only complicated existing political tensions. Within the Directory Barthélemy was already in agreement with the legislative majority. Though Carnot was by no means an ally of Reubell, La Révellière-Lépeaux, and Barras, he was too committed to a strong executive and the existence of the republic to cave in entirely to the councils on internal policy. The peace negotiations clearly split him from the triumvir; Carnot argued against Reubell and La Révellière-Lépeaux that the republic should be willing to cede Mantua and Venice to Austria and to give up the right bank of the Rhine.[40] He felt that the Directory could create a majority in the councils around a peace policy of this sort, and thereby create the ground for wider compromise.[41] His Directorial colleagues clearly did not understand the subtlety of this position: La Révellière-Lépeaux was confused but suspicious, while Reubell was convinced that Carnot was plotting with the royalists.[42] Indeed, his policy may have been overly subtle for ignoring the fact that the majority of the councils were using the peace issue as a stalking horse for their attack on the Directory. Dumas in his pamphlet on the negotiations damned the directors as international terrorists: "this tornado of destruction, which menaces all civilized peoples with being sucked into the abyss of revolution, only survives amongst us through abuse of power."[43] The confusions and tensions within the Directory were played out in spectacular fashion, if Reubell's manuscript note written five years after the event is to be believed. In a sitting of the Directory La Révellière-Lépeaux could no longer contain his anger at Carnot's perceived treachery and burst out, "how is it possible . . . that you will abandon your colleagues to unite against them with those wretches who have never shown their civic commitment or made sacrifices for the Revolution?"[44] This confusion and distrust split the Directory entirely and gave Barthélemy his opportunity to frustrate the plans of his colleagues. He opened secret channels of communication to the earl of Malmesbury and thenceforward kept him informed of the plans of the Directory.[45] Soon he was exploiting the disarray within the Directory to the extent that he and Malmesbury were acting in efficient concert against all other forces.[46] The most spectacular success of this strategy was the frustration of the proposed Franco-Portuguese treaty that would have closed Portuguese ports to English vessels. The more profound effect was to make the Fructidor coup inevitable. A united Directory might have weathered the storm; a divided executive was prone to desperate measures.

Carnot broke with the triumvir over the commercial clauses of the proposed treaty. On the face of it Malmesbury's terms were generous: Britain was prepared to recognize the acquisition by France of Belgium, Liège, Luxembourg, Avignon, and Nice and to return to France and Holland all of their colonies save Trinité and the Cape of Good Hope. Britain was even prepared to compensate Holland for the cape with Ceylon.[47] The matter turned on the question of the cape. Initially, the Directory, concluding that this was a price worth paying for peace, informed the new Batavian Republic that it would have to be prepared to accept its loss.[48] On reflection, the directors came to the conclusion that the treaty as framed would be fatal to the commercial republican project of replacing England as the dominant center of world trade with a republican trading bloc. To cripple the Dutch by permanently ceding the cape to their commercial rivals in the Pacific would be to allow the British to snatch commercial victory from the jaws of political defeat. In Year V France was running a colonial trade deficit of 120 million francs.[49] In that year colonial imports from Hamburg, Copenhagen, and Prussia amounted to 72 million francs, and the vast majority of these goods were of English origin. The only alternative to the English as a supplier of such goods was the Dutch: imports from Amsterdam amounted to 61 million francs in the same period.[50] The Netherlands was potentially the colonial pole of a republican trading system of which France would be the supplier of agricultural and manufactured goods. To recommence normal trading relations under the conditions of the proposed peace would be to abandon to the English "the commerce of the entire world, which they have hoarded for so long."[51] As a report to the directors at the beginning of Year V had argued, within the current configuration of colonial trade the British fleet always had, and always could, strip France of all its colonies at the outbreak of war.[52] That report had identified the Cape of Good Hope specifically as the key to the colonial system and controlling it as the means through which the republic could improve its strategic position. Giving it away would mean that any attempt at creating the commercial republic would be hamstrung. Resistance to the idea of surrendering the cape carried with it an implicit commitment to the creation of a new trading order of republican states.

Carnot was literally incensed at this manner of conceiving of the problem of the Lille negotiations. He thought his one-time colleagues on the Directory were utterly confusing fact and right. The position they were taking had coherence, but as a consequence "the republic will never have a commerce, Martinique will be definitively lost, the West Indies conceded without anything in return to Great Britain; our allies will be totally sacrificed *in fact*, even though, *in law*, they will not have lost, nor us either, the smallest bit of territory."[53] Carnot's criticism pinpointed the weakness in the vision of the commercial republicans. Their notion of replacing England in a transformed commercial order was a projection of their ideal of the commercial republic, but norms such as utility, happiness, and *industrie*, which had a real social and institutional basis in domestic politics, had none in the sphere of international relations. Relations between states had an irreducibly Hobbesian quality; they were mediated by interest, and only marginally by norms. The commercial republican concern with legitimacy was calibrated to the complex interactions of a modern society, not to the more naked calculations of interstate relations. There was no set of concepts through which to articulate the norms of the democratic republic with the facts of international relations.

Without the tools of rational communication, the introduction of these issues to the already fragile political situation ended the possibility of a constitutional settlement to the crisis. Clear heads understood that it was the confusion and total lack of understanding by one side of the other that was driving the polity toward a logic of coup d'état. This was clear even to the pamphleteers: "fear of royalism predisposes the majority of the directors to violent measures; fear of anarchy leads the councils in their ill-considered direction; fear puts them both in a state of war."[54] The same clear-eyed observer's description of the political conflict served only to underline how deep-rooted that mutual incomprehension and the attitudes based on it had become. What hope for compromise could there be while the legislature seemed "only to care for priests, émigrés, and anything to do with the enemies of the state, while the pay of its defenders was not assured"?[55] At the same time the clumsiness of the Directory turned every hand against it: "they can offer only extreme remedies for the ills of the country."[56] The situation degenerated into that state of fear, and consequent incoherence, described by Mercier. "Fear has played such a big part in our revolution, its arena has been so vast, that one has often attributed to politics, to ambition, to deep strategy, that which was done only to disconcert an enemy and to impress on him also fear and terror."[57] The nexus between formal constitutional politics, democratic political culture, and international affairs produced destructive irrationality, and eventually destroyed the coherence of the regime.

Despite the disastrous mistakes of the directors, the potential of the institutions of the Constitution of Year III did not absolutely recede from the historical memory of political actors. Seventeen years after the coup of 18 Fructidor, in 1814, one of the constitutional moderates, Dupont de Nemours, reflected on the lessons to be drawn from his experience. He was not a man one might expect to be overly enamored of the Directory and its institutions. He had been saved from deportation after Fructidor only through the intervention of Madame de Staël and La Revellière-Lépeaux. Even then he was unhappy to have been spared for being thought old and harmless. The situation in 1814 brought him back to that of 1797. It was again a moment of crisis: Bonaparte had fallen, and the Senate, of which Dupont de Nemours was a member, found itself at the center of events. As he wrote later to Carnot, in the vital six days between the fall of the empire and the accession of Louis XVIII, the Senate, as the last authority in the country and because of its control of the National Guard, had the power to remake the constitution.[58] His analysis of the situation facing the Senate was grim. The Bonapartes had no credibility as a focus of stability and legitimacy, and the Bourbons, who retained an aura of legitimacy, were "too dangerous. Mediocre in themselves they have been surrounded for the past twelve years by the weakest, most hateful and least moral elements of their old court."[59] Their return would threaten the property settlement at the base of any order that might be hoped for in France. His solution to this dilemma was to return to the institutional structure of the republic: "A wise, humane and well thought through republic is the last resort for the Senate and the nation."

The Constitution of Year III was the first stage of such a regime, where the Conseil des Anciens was an institution in the nature of a Senate, and the Conseil des Cinq-Cents was like the Legislative Body.[60] In his draft for a Sénatus-Consulte to implement his ideas, Dupont de Nemours even introduced the startling constitutional idea that the entire government of the country had been illegitimate since the coup of Fructidor, Year V: "this constitution remains in force because it was only through violence that it was overturned on 18 Fructidor."[61] He argued that, in consequence, Carnot and Barthélemy, the directors who had been ousted by the coup, represented the legitimate executive, and that they should complete their interrupted terms. The only task that faced the Senate was to amend the constitution to ensure that the executive could never become so divided against itself that some element of it might resort to unconstitutional action.[62] After twenty-five years of political turmoil, and despite his own fate in the period, Dupont de Nemours identified the Directory as the regime whose institutional structure seemed to offer the greatest hope of stability and legitimate government.

Practical politics undermined whatever hopes Dupont de Nemours might have had that his ideas would form the template for the reconstruction of the French polity in 1814. Against his better judgment he supported the friends of Talleyrand who thought a constitutional monarchy the best resolution possible.[63] Soon, the idea of a member of the political elite seriously proposing the republic as a viable political project would seem absurd. The republicanism of the Directory was receding as a theory of the institutional possibilities for France, to be replaced with the historic memory of the republic of 1793–94. As George Weill put it, "for the upper classes the republic was Jacobinism, it was the guillotine, it was 1793."[64] He might have added that for the lower classes the republic became as open an idea, but one filled with more hope. Republicanism was about to become systemically oppositional. What was effaced was the new republicanism of the Directory. It was to reappear, in the 1848 revolution, after which republicanism began its transformation into the positivist creed of Jules Ferry and Léon Gambetta.[65] Republicanism would have its élan and its relationship to the Revolution restored to it only through the efforts of the historians of the Third Republic.

The weakness of republicanism contributed to the political instability of France in the nineteenth century, but this weakness at the level of formal politics has obscured the vital contributions made by republicanism, and the republic, to the possibility of French democracy. Republicans between 1795 and 1799 were fully aware that the integrity of a republican constitution depended on the *moeurs* of the population, on its cultural resources and social capital. The institutions of democracy could function only if citizens were motivated to consider themselves as active communicating participants. The irony is that the commercial republicans did succeed in creating a democratic political culture but could not discipline the actual political system. The Directory collapsed from the top down, even as it was building its base. The case studies of *partage*, the educational curriculum, and public festivals all show a consistent pattern of negotiation between the republican state and elements of civil society, whether peasants, teachers, or artists. These negotiations used the vocabulary of utility and happiness as the ground of communication and produced institutions, events, and reforms. The most important effect of the new republicanism was the creation of an idea of modern life that could circulate and inform the rural dwellers of France.[66] The rhetoric of the agricultural republic meshed peasant and farmer cultural and social preferences with the exigencies of markets and of modern communication. It allowed new values to penetrate rural society, which would allow it in turn to master processes of modernization and democratization. The republic bequeathed to the village the languages through which it might negotiate the modern world.

The nexus of modern republicanism with rural life in France was to have a long history, and the peasant was to be the social as well as the cultural backbone of the Third Republic. We should not collapse the idea of French democracy into its social formations, however. The critical components bequeathed to democratic political culture by the republicanism of the Directory were as important to nineteenth-century developments. The promotion of vernacular prose, and of the novel in particular, as the paradigmatic literature of democracy was a prescient move. As Linda Orr has shown, a "popular romanticism" underlay subaltern political involvement, especially in the early part of the century, while Jacques Rancière has highlighted the extent to which the democratic aspiration was generated in the nighttime reading of the urban worker.[67] The politicization of popular culture was a feature of the entire Revolution, but the notion of the democratizing effects of the novel was a specific development of the new republicanism. Finally, the critical ideal of self-expression or self-realization, was a development beyond the initial premises of commercial republicanism. The idea of work as self-expression and as the defining characteristic of the republican citizen developed in the republican festivals but inspired a whole new approach to the articulation of culture, society, and politics. Fourier may not have acknowledged his debt to the hated French revolutionaries, but it was there.

Vivid images of the French Revolution remain compelling. The storming of the Bastille, the trial of the king, the volunteer armies of 1792, even the Terror—all are dramatic and serious, in some cases wonderful, images of the capacity of humans to make their history, for good or ill. Faced with this color and drama, with difficulty we turn our attention to the slow processes of civilization, of the creation of social bonds, of the possibility of symbolic communication, of work and learning. These less dramatic processes have to be understood in order to comprehend the full historical stature of the Revolution. History was not made only with a gun or a speech in hand during the Revolution. The contingencies and possibilities that unfolded before French society were as much social and economic as political. Revolution could be made with a spade or a memorandum. This is not a banal point once again reminding us of the ubiquity of the local and the everyday. Rather, the Revolution was so profound that the norms and values of these profound areas of human experience were opened up to human agency. We are at the disposition of our sources as to how far we can penetrate the depth of social experience, but what information we can get, such as the petitions on land division, reveal to us rapid and profound changes. The transformation in the way farmers and peasants talked about their land was of more significance than any constitution: it marked the end of an immemorial world of thought and experience. Old and strong forces were woken by the Revolution, they began to know themselves in a new way, and they changed the world.

Notes

Introduction

1. It is curious that natural history and geology have embraced the explanatory power of contingency: see Stephen Jay Gould, *Wonderful Life: The Burgess Shale and the Nature of History* (New York, 1989); and Walter Alverez, *T-Rex and the Crater of Doom* (New York, 1998).
2. This is not to deny a radical democrat strand to the Anglophone tradition. See Benjamin R. Barber, *Strong Democracy: Participatory Politics for a New Age* (Berkeley, Calif., 1984).
3. Michel Foucault, *The Order of Things: An Archaeology of the Human Sciences* (London, 1970), 221.
4. For some comments on the problems of a nonreductive history, see Geoff Bennington and Robert Young, "Posing the Question," in *Post-Structuralism and the Question of History* (Cambridge, 1987), 3–15. For a nuanced effort to incorporate new epistemological demands, see Joyce Appleby, Lynn Hunt, and Margaret Jacob, *Telling the Truth about History* (New York, 1994).
5. On this specific conjuncture, see Richard J. Evans, *In Defence of History* (London, 1997), 244–245.
6. Georges Lefebvre, *The Coming of the French Revolution,* trans. R. R. Palmer (Princeton, N.J., 1967), 100.
7. François Furet, *Marx and the French Revolution* (Chicago, 1988), 31.
8. The original, and still classic, critique of the utility of the Marxist category of class in the eighteenth century is Alfred Cobban, *The Social Interpretation of the French Revolution,* (Cambridge, 1968). Some other classic works include Colin Lucas, "Nobles, Bourgeois, and the Origins of the French Revolution," *Past and Present,* 60 (1973); George Taylor, "Non-Capitalist Wealth and the Origins of the French Revolution," *American Historical Review* (1967); and Guy Chaussinand-Nogaret, *La noblesse française au XVIIIe siècle, de la Féodalité aux Lumiéres* (Paris, 1976).
9. See Timothy Tackett, *Becoming a Revolutionary: The Deputies of the French National Assembly and the Emergence of a Revolutionary Culture (1789–1790)* (Princeton,

N.J., 1996), and Harriet Applewhite, *Political Alignment in the French National Assembly, 1789–1791* (Baton Rouge, 1993).

10. See François Furet, Jaques Julliard, and Pierre Rosanvallon, *La république du centre* (Paris, 1988).

11. See François Furet and Mona Ozouf, eds., *A Critical Dictionary of the French Revolution,* trans. Arthur Goldhammer (Cambridge, Mass., 1989), specifically Furet, "Terror," 146.

12. François Furet, *Interpreting the French Revolution,* trans. Elborg Foster (Cambridge, 1981), 45.

13. Ran Halevi, "Estates General," in Furet and Ozouf, *Critical Dictionary,* 52; Ran Halevi, "La monarchie et les élections: Position des problèmes," in Keith Michael Baker, ed., *The French Revolution and the Creation of Modern Political Culture,* vol. 1, *The Political Culture of the Old Regime* (Oxford, 1987), 387–402.

14. Furet, "Terror," 148.

15. Mona Ozouf, "Regeneration," in Furet and Ozouf, *Critical Dictionary,* 790.

16. I avoid the differentiating the terms "radical democracy" and "totalitarian democracy" advisedly as these refer to differing positions within the one research paradigm. See Ferenc Féher, *The Frozen Revolution: An Essay on Jacobinism* (Cambridge, 1987), 22.

17. Keith Michael Baker, "Public Opinion as Political Invention," in Baker, *Inventing the French Revolution: Essays on French Political Culture in the Eighteenth Century* (Cambridge, 1990), 172; Pierre Rosanvallon, *Le sacre du citoyen: Histoire du suffrage universel en France* (Paris, 1992), 106–109.

18. Gail Bossenga, *The Politics of Privilege: Old Regime and Revolution in Lille* (Cambridge, 1991); Sarah Maza, *Private Lives and Public Affairs: The Causes Célèbres of Pre-revolutionary France* (Berkeley, Calif., 1993).

19. There are variant versions of this interpretation, such as Ran Halevi's, which argue that the project of democratization, or the creation of the virtuous state, was that of a small elite who acquired a central role in 1789. This reading, dependent on Augustin Cochin's work on Burgundy, is merely a conspiratorial version of the more general thesis and is no more credible than any other conspiracy theory. See Halevi, "Estates General," 52, and Augustin Cochin, "La campagne électorale de 1789 en Bourgogne," in Cochin, *L'esprit de Jacobinisme: Une interprétation sociologique* (Paris, 1979), 49–76.

20. Keith Michael Baker, "Sovereignty," in Furet and Ozouf, *Critical Dictionary,* 850.

21. Kaja Silverman, *The Subject of Semiotics* (New York, 1983), 237.

22. Roger Chartier, "The Chimera of the Origin: Archaeology of Knowledge, Cultural History, and the French Revolution," in Chartier, *On the Edge of the Cliff: History, Language, and Practices,* trans. Lydia G. Cochrane (Baltimore, 1997), 59.

23. Charles Taylor, *Sources of the Self: The Making of the Modern Identity* (Cambridge, 1989), 285–302.

24. Philip Nord, *The Republican Moment: Struggles for Democracy in Nineteenth-Century France* (Cambridge, Mass., 1995), 190–191.

25. Sudhir Hazareesingh, *Political Traditions in Modern France* (Oxford, 1994), 75.

26. Furet, *Interpreting the French Revolution,* 45.

27. Keith Michael Baker, "Fixing the French Constitution," in Baker, *Inventing the French Revolution: Essays on French Political Culture in the Eighteenth Century* (Cambridge, 1990), 305.

28. Furet, *Interpreting the French Revolution,* 45.

29. See Reinhart Koselleck, *Critique and Crisis: Enlightenment and the Pathogenesis of Modern Society* (Cambridge, Mass., 1988), 127–189, for a classic development of this theme.

30. See Anthony Giddens, *A Contemporary Critique of Historical Materialism,* vol. 2, *The Nation-State and Violence* (Cambridge, 1985), 94–99; Rogers Brubaker, *Citizenship and Nationhood in France and Germany* (Cambridge, Mass., 1992), 35.

31. Patrice Higonnet, "The Harmonisation of the Spheres: Goodness and Dysfunction in the Provincial Clubs," in Keith Michael Baker, ed., *The French Revolution and the Creation of Modern Political Culture,* vol. 4, *The Terror* (Oxford, 1994), 117–137.

32. Suzanne Desan, *Reclaiming the Sacred: Lay Religion and Popular Politics in Revolutionary France* (Ithaca, N.Y., 1990), 11; David A. Bell, "Lingua Populi, Lingua Dei: Language, Religion, and the Origins of French Revolutionary Nationalism," *American Historical Review,* 11, no. 5 (December 1995), 1403–1437.

33. John Hardman, *French Politics, 1774–1789: From the Accession of Louis XVI to the Bastille* (London, 1995); Munro Price, *Preserving the Monarchy: The Comte de Vergennes, 1774–1787* (Cambridge, 1995); Julian Swann, *Politics and the Parlement of Paris under Louis XV, 1754–1774* (Cambridge, 1995).

34. Philippe Reynaud, "American Revolution," in Furet and Ozouf, *Critical Dictionary,* 595–597.

35. See Barry Alan Shain, *The Myth of American Individualism: The Protestant Origins of American Political Thought* (Princeton, N.J., 1994).

36. Isser Woloch, *Jacobin Legacy: The Democratic Movement under the Directory* (Princeton, N.J., 1970).

37. Isser Woloch, *The New Regime: Transformations of the French Civic Order, 1789–1820s* (New York, 1994); Suzanne Desan, "Reconstituting the Social after the Terror: Family, Property, and the Law in Popular Politics," *Past and Present,* 164, no. 1 (August 1999), 81–121.

38. Pierre Rosanvallon, *L'état en France de 1789 à nos jours* (Paris, 1990), 38–45, 122–132.

39. Michael Walzer, "Intellectuals, Social Classes, and Revolution," in Walzer, *Democracy, Revolution, and History,* (Ithaca, N.Y., 1998), 133.

40. Niklas Luhmann, *Love as Passion: The Codification of Intimacy,* trans. Jeremy Gaines and Doris L. Jones (Cambridge, 1986), 2.

41. David D. Bien, "Old Regime Origins of Democratic Liberty," in Dale K. Van Kley, ed., *The French Idea of Freedom: The Old Regime and the Declaration of Rights of 1789* (Stanford, Calif., 1994), 23–71.

42. Barrington Moore, *The Social Origins of Dictatorship and Democracy* (Boston, 1966).

43. Gabriel Almond and Sidney Verba, *The Civic Culture: Political Attitudes and Democracy in Five Nations* (Princeton, N.J., 1963).

44. Theda Skocpol, *States and Social Revolutions: A Comparative Analysis of France, Russia, and China* (Cambridge, 1979).

45. Dietrich Rueschmeyer, Evelyne Huber Stephens, and John D. Stephens, *Capitalist Development and Democracy* (Chicago, 1992), 271. For an important corrective, see Ruth Berins Collier, *Paths toward Democracy: The Working Class and Elites in Western Europe and South America* (Cambridge, 1999).

46. George Ross, Theda Skocpol, Tony Smith, and Judith Eisenberg Vichniac, "Barrington Moore's *Social Origins* and Beyond: Historical Social Analysis since the 1960s," in Skocpol, ed., *Democracy, Revolution, and History* (Ithaca, N.Y., 1998), 14.

47. This view has cogency over a tremendously long time-frame; see Ellen Meiksias Wood, *Peasant-Citizen and Slave: The Foundations of Athenian Democracy* (London, 1988).

48. For an account of the Russian Revolution from this perspective, see Orlando Figes, *A People's Tragedy: The Russian Revolution, 1891–1924* (London, 1996).

49. Ross et al., "Barrington Moore's *Social Origins*," 9.

50. Almond and Verba, *The Civic Culture*, 3.

51. Ibid., 243.

52. Robert Putnam, *Making Democracy Work: Civic Traditions in Modern Italy* (Princeton, N.J., 1993), 107; Thomas Ertman, *Birth of the Leviathan: Building States and Regimes in Medieval and Early Modern Europe* (Cambridge, 1997), 10–19.

53. Putnam, *Making Democracy Work*, 167.

54. Seymour Martin Lipset, "The Social Requisites of Democracy Revisited," *American Sociological Review*, 59, no. 1 (February 1994), 1–27. For the integration of game theory with this cultural approach, see Barry R. Weingast, "Democratic Stability as Self-reinforcing Equilibrium," in Albert Breton, Gianluigi Galeotti, Pierre Salmon, and Ronald Wintrobe, eds., *Understanding Democracy: Economic and Political Perspectives* (Cambridge, 1997), 11–46.

55. Bernard Gainot, "Les troubles électoraux de l'an VII: Dissolution du souverain ou vitalité de la démocratie représentative," *Annales historiques de la Révolution française*, 297 (July-September 1994), 447–462.

56. Gabriel Almond, "The Intellectual History of the Civic Culture Concept," in Almond and Verba, eds., *The Civic Culture Revisited* (London, 1989), 29.

57. Putnam, *Making Democracy Work*, 126.

58. Almond and Verba, *The Civic Culture*, 6.

59. Putnam, *Making Democracy Work*, 179.

60. Joe Foweraker, *Making Democracy in Spain: Grass-Roots Struggle in the South, 1955–1975* (Cambridge, 1989), 247.

61. For the thematics of nationalist culture, see Tom Garvin, *The Evolution of Irish Nationalist Politics* (New York, 1981), 50–52.

62. Tom Garvin, *1922: The Birth of Irish Democracy* (New York, 1996), 26.

63. Seymour Martin Lipset, *Political Man: The Social Bases of Politics* (Baltimore, 1981; orig. ed. 1959), 27–56.
64. For a dynamic account of this process through the nineteenth century, see Jean-Claude Caron, *La nation, l'état, et la démocratie en France de 1789 à 1914* (Paris, 1995), 205–217. See also the essays in Biancamaria Fontana, ed., *The Invention of the Modern Republic* (Cambridge, 1994).

1. Modern Republicanism and Revolution

1. See A. M. Wilson, *Diderot* (Oxford, 1972), 618–619, for Diderot's disinclination for travel.
2. Anthony Strugnell, *Diderot's Politics* (The Hague, 1973), 136.
3. This was also the only position he ever shared with Gabriel Bonnot de Mably, see Keith Michael Baker, "A Script for the French Revolution: The Political Consciousness of the Abbé Mably," in Baker, *Inventing the French Revolution: Essays on French Political Culture in the Eighteenth Century* (Cambridge, 1990), 104–105.
4. Denis Diderot, "Mélanges pour Catherine II," in Diderot, *Oeuvres,* vol. 2, *Politique* (Paris, 1995), 213. Unless otherwise noted, all translations from the French are my own.
5. See Dale K. Van Kley, *The Religious Origins of the French Revolution: From Calvin to the Civil Constitution, 1560–1791* (New Haven, Conn., 1996), 249–302, for a developed account of this process.
6. Diderot, "Mélanges pour Catherine II," 225.
7. Gerolamo Imbruglia, "From Utopia to Republicanism: The Case of Diderot," in Biancamaria Fontana, ed., *The Invention of the Modern Republic* (Cambridge, 1994), 82–85.
8. On the Italian roots of this ideology, see Quentin Skinner, *The Foundations of Modern Political Thought,* vol. 1, *The Renaissance* (Cambridge, 1978), 6–11, 70–107; Ronald Witt, "The Rebirth of the Concept of Republican Liberty in Italy," in Anthony Mollo and John A. Tedeschi, eds., *Renaissance Studies in Honor of Hans Baron* (Florence, 1971), 173–200.
9. The central text here is J. G. A. Pocock, *The Machiavellian Moment: Florentine Political Thought and the Atlantic Republican Tradition* (Princeton, N.J., 1975).
10. J. G. A. Pocock, "Virtues, Rights and Manners," in Pocock, *Virtue, Commerce, and History* (Cambridge, 1985), 39, 47.
11. Skeptics about the coherence of classical republicanism as a tradition include Joyce Appleby, "Republicanism in Old and New Contexts," *William and Mary Quarterly,* 3d ser., 43 (January 1986), 20–34, and Isaac Kramnick, "Republican Revisionism Revisited," *American Historical Review,* 87 (June 1982), 629–664.
12. For a critical understanding of the failure of civic humanism in England, see Steven Pincus, "Neither Machiavellian Moment nor Possessive Individualism: Commercial Society and the Defenders of the English Commonwealth," *American Historical Review,* 103, no. 3 (June 1998), 705–736. For a revision of the un-

derstanding of republicanism in that context, see Alan Craig Houston, *Algernon Sidney and the Republican Heritage in England and America* (Princeton, N.J., 1991).

13. See Herbert H. Rowan, "The Dutch Republic and the Idea of Freedom," in David Wootton, ed., *Republicanism, Liberty, and Commercial Society, 1649–1776* (Stanford, Calif., 1994), 339; Eco Haitsma Mulier, "The Language of Seventeenth-Century Republicanism in the United Provinces: Dutch or European," in Anthony Pagden, ed., *The Languages of Political Theory in Early Modern Europe* (Cambridge, 1987), 192–194.

14. Blair Worden, "The Revolution of 1688–89 and the English Republican Tradition," in Jonathan I. Israel, ed., *The Anglo-Dutch Moment: Essays on the Glorious Revolution and Its World Impact* (Cambridge, 1991), 269.

15. Hagley Library, Wilmington, Del., w/2/a/38, Dupont de Nemours to Marquis de Mirabeau, 18 December 1774.

16. Thomas L. Pangle has asserted that the very idea of a coherent "classic republicanism" makes no sense given the heterogeneity of the sources from which it is supposed to have been constructed: Pangle, *The Spirit of Modern Republicanism: The Moral Vision of the American Founders and the Philosophy of Locke* (Chicago, 1988), 35–36.

17. The jeremiad could and did, of course, have considerable political effect. See Sacvan Bercovitch, *The American Jeremiad* (Madison, Wis., 1978), 93–129.

18. Gabriel Bonnot de Mably, *Entretiens de Phocion sur le rapport de la morale et de la politique* (Caen, 1986), 7.

19. Ibid., 48.

20. Nicolas Louis François de Neufchâteau, *Le désintéressement de Phocion: Dialogue en vers* (Nancy, 1778), vi–vii.

21. Franco Venturi, *The End of the Old Regime in Europe, 1776–1789*, vol. 2, *Republican Patriotism and the Empires of the East*, trans. R. Burr Litchfield (Princeton, N.J., 1991), 459–496.

22. Linda Kirk, "Genevan Republicanism," in David Wootton, ed., *Republicanism, Liberty, and Commercial Society, 1649–1776* (Stanford, Calif., 1994), 304–305.

23. See the essays in John Robertson, ed., *A Union for Empire: Political Thought and the British Union of 1707* (Cambridge, 1995).

24. Colin Kidd, *Subverting Scotland's Past: Scottish Whig Historians and the Creation of an Anglo-British Identity* (Cambridge, 1993), 78, 109–110.

25. On "The Dominion of Providence," see Richard B. Sher, "Witherspoon's *Dominion of Providence* and the Scottish Jeremiad Tradition," in Sher and Andrew Smitten, eds., *Scotland and America in the Age of the Enlightenment* (Edinburgh, 1990), 46–64. Witherspoon was James Madison's teacher at Princeton.

26. *The Continentalist*, no. 6 (4 July 1782), in Harold C. Syrett ed., *The Papers of Alexander Hamilton* (New York, 1961–1979), 3, 103, cited in Paul A. Ruhe, "Antiquity Surpassed: The Repudiation of Classical Republicanism," in David Wootton, ed., *Republicanism, Liberty, and Commercial Society, 1649–1776* (Stanford, Calif., 1994), 238.

27. W. Paul Adams, "Republicanism in Political Rhetoric before 1776," *Political Science Quarterly,* 85 (1970), 397–421.

28. Shelley Burtt, *Virtue Transformed: Political Argument in England, 1688–1740* (Cambridge, 1992), 8–9.

29. Johnson Kent Wright, *A Classical Republican in Eighteenth-Century France: The Political Thought of Mably* (Stanford, Calif., 1997), 46–47.

30. Abbé Mably, *Observations sur le gouvernement et les lois des Etats-Unis d'Amérique* (Amsterdam, 1784), 74.

31. Ibid., 15.

32. Ibid., 20–21, 32.

33. Ibid., 5

34. For obvious reasons the American debate on the nature of their new republic was more nuanced and extensive than the European, however it falls outside the remit of this discussion.

35. A. R. J. Turgot, *Mémoire sur les colonies américaines, sur leurs relations politiques avec leurs métropoles, et sur la manière dont la France et l'Espagne ont dû envisager les suites de l'indépendance des Etats-Unis de l'Amérique* (Paris, 1791), 7. The memoir was originally written in 1776.

36. A. R. J. Turgot to Richard Price, Paris, 22 March 1778, in Richard Price, *Observations on the Importance of the American Revolution and the Means of Making It a Benefit to the World, to Which Is Added, a Letter from M. Turgot, Late Comptroller-General of the Finances of France* (London, 1785), 118.

37. Etienne Clavière and J.-P. Brissot, *De la France et des Etats-Unis ou de l'importance de la Révolution de l'Amérique pour le bonheur de la France* (London, 1787), 7.

38. Jacques Pierre Brissot de Warville, *Examen critique des voyages dans l'Amérique septentrionale, de M. le marquis de Châtelleux* (London, 1786), 102–103.

39. Filippo Mazzei, *Recherches historiques et politiques sur les Etats-Unis de l'Amérique septentrionale où l'on traite des établissements des treize colonies, de leurs rapports et leurs dissentions avec la Grande-Bretagne, de leurs gouvernements avant et après la révolution,* 4 vols. (Colle, 1788) 1vi.

40. Ibid., 1:166–167, 2:24–26.

41. Honoré G. R. Mirabeau, *Considérations sur l'ordre de Cincinnatus ou imitation d'un pamphlet anglo-américain par le Comte de Mirabeau* (London, 1784), 10.

42. Condorcet, *Lettres d'un bourgeois de New-Haven à un citoyen de Virginie, sur l'inutilité de partager le pouvoir législatif entre plusieurs corps* (Colle, 1788), 267.

43. Ibid., 268.

44. Ibid., 276–277.

45. Price, *Observations,* 72.

46. Ibid., 10–13.

47. John Adams, *A Defence of the Constitutions of Government of the United States of America against the Attack of M. Turgot in His Letter to Dr. Price,* 3 vols. (Philadelphia, 1797), 1:x.

48. William Vans Murray, *Political Sketches Inscribed to His Excellency John Adams Min-*

ister Plenipotentiary from the United States to the Court of Great Britain (London, 1787), 5. Murray wrote the pamphlet while a law student in London. He would later be instrumental in negotiations between Napoleonic France and the United States. See Peter P. Hill, *William Vans Murray—Federalist Diplomat: The Shaping of Peace with France, 1797–1801* (Syracuse, N.Y., 1971), 5–7.

49. Mazzei, *Recherches historiques,* 1:173.

50. David Wootton, "Introduction—The Republican Tradition: From Commonwealth to Common Sense," in Wootton, ed., *Republicanism, Liberty, and Commercial Society, 1649–1776,* (Stanford, Calif., 1994), 7.

51. Adams, *Defence of the Constitutions,* 1:xviii.

52. Ibid., 87.

53. Murray, *Political Sketches,* i.

54. For Sieyès's political thought, see William H. Sewell, Jr., *A Rhetoric of Bourgeois Revolution: The Abbé Sieyès and What Is the Third Estate?* (Durham, N.C., 1994).

55. Archives Nationales (hereafter cited as AN), Paris, 284 AP 5, dossier 5, f. 7, "Réflexions morales, politiques, littéraires, 1792–93."

56. Nannerl Keohane argues that civic humanist values gave way to individualism by the early seventeenth century in *Philosophy and the State in France: The Renaissance to the Enlightenment* (Princeton, N.J., 1980), 83–116. See also J. H. M. Salmon, "Cicero and Tacitus in Sixteenth-Century France," *Renaissance and Revolt* (Cambridge, 1987), 27–53.

57. For the Genevan revolution of 1782 and its aftermath, see Franco Venturi, *The End of the Old Regime in Europe, 1776–1789,* vol. 2, *Republican Patriotism and the Empires of the East,* trans. R. Burr Litchfield (Princeton, N.J., 1991), 459–496.

58. Monique Cottret, "Aux origines du républicanisme janseniste: Le mythe de l'église primitive et le primitivisme des Lumières," *Revue d'histoire moderne et contemporaine,* 31 (January–March).

59. David Bell, "Lawyers into Demagogues: Chancellor Maupeou and the Transformation of Legal Practice in France, 1771–1789," *Past and Present,* 130 (February 1991), 107–141.

60. See Richard Tuck, "The 'Modern' Theory of Natural Law," in Anthony Pagden, ed., *The Languages of Political Theory in Early-Modern Europe* (Cambridge, 1987), 99–119.

61. See Richard Ashcraft, *Revolutionary Politics and Locke's Two Treatises of Government* (Princeton, N.J., 1986), 165, 252–259.

62. For his classic account of the derivation of political legitimacy, see John Locke, *Two Treatises of Government* (Cambridge, 1988), 330–349.

63. Ibid., 288.

64. Ashcraft, *Revolutionary Politics,* 165.

65. Ian M. Wilson, "The Influence of Hobbes and Locke in the Shaping of the Concept of Sovereignty in Eighteenth-Century France," *Studies on Voltaire and the Eighteenth Century,* 101 (1973), 55.

66. Darlene Gay-Levy, *The Ideas and Careers of Simon-Nicolas-Henri Linguet: A Study in*

Eighteenth-Century Politics (Champaign-Urbana, Ill., 1980), 47–50; Sarah Maza, "'Innocent Blood Avenged': Emplotting Judicial Reform, 1785–1786," in Maza, *Private Lives and Public Affairs: The Causes Célèbres of Prerevolutionary France* (Berkeley, Calif., 1993), 212–262.

67. For a full account of their partnership, see Richard Whatmore and James Livesey, "Etienne Clavière, Jacques-Pierre Brissot, et les fondations intellectuelles de la politque des Girondins," *Annales historiques de la Révolution française*, 3 (October 2000), 1–26.

68. J.-P. Brissot and E. Clavière, *Le Philadelphien à Genève, ou lettres d'un Américain sur la dernière révolution de Genève, sa constitution nouvelle, l'émigration en Irlande, etc., pouvant servir de tableau politique de Genève jusqu'en 1784* (Dublin, 1783), 68.

69. AN, T* 6461, Clavière to de Gelière, 29 November 1782.

70. Hagley Library, w/2/a/2/292, Dupont de Nemours to Clavière, 16 June 1787.

71. Bibliothèque Nationale (hereafter cited as BN), Paris, N.Aq.Fr. 9534, f. 397, Clavière to Mirabeau, 25 April 1788.

72. Robert Darnton, "A Spy in Grub Street," in Darnton, *The Literary Underground of the Old Regime* (Cambridge, Mass., 1982), 41–69. For vigorous dissention from Darnton's views, see Frederick A. deLuna, "The Dean Street Style of Revolution: J.-P. Brissot, *Jeune Philosophe*," *French Historical Studies*, 17, no. 1 (Spring 1991), 159–190; Leonore Loft, "*Le Journal du Lycée de Londres:* A Study in the Pre-Revolutionary Press," *European History Quarterly*, 23 (1993), 12–13.

73. AN, 446 AP 1, d'Ivernois to Brissot, 20 March 1782.

74. AN, 446 AP 9, Dupaty to Brissot, 20 January 1781.

75. AN, 446 AP 8, Mirabeau to Brissot, 5 October 1786.

76. Robin Blackburn, *The Making of New World Slavery: From the Baroque to the Modern, 1492–1800* (London, 1998), 324.

77. Brissot, *Examen critique des voyages dans l'Amérique septentrionale*, 120.

78. Blackburn, *New World Slavery*, 442–443.

79. Leonore Loft, "J. P. Brissot and the Evolution of Pamphlet Literature in the early 1780s," *History of European Ideas*, 17, nos. 2/3 (1993), 275.

80. Daniel P. Resnick, "The Société des Amis de Noirs and the Abolition of Slavery," *French Historical Studies*, 7, no. 4 (Fall 1972), 559.

81. Robin Blackburn, *The Overthrow of Colonial Slavery, 1776–1848* (London, 1988), 172.

82. Yves Bénot, "Comment la Convention a-t-elle voté l'abolition de l'esclavage?" *Annales historiques de la Révolution française*, 242/243 (1993), 349–361.

83. J.-P. Brissot, *Observations d'un Républicain sur les diverses systêmes d'administrations provinciales, particulièrement sur ceux de MM. Turgot et Necker, et sur le bien qu'on peut en espérer dans les gouvernements monarchiques* (Lausanne, 1788), 141.

84. Ibid., 155.

85. Brissot, *Examen critique*, 120.

86. Maurizio Viroli, *From Politics to Reason of State: The Acquisition and Transformation of the Language of Politics, 1250–1600* (Cambridge, 1992), 238–280.

87. Judith Shklar, "Montesquieu and the New Republicanism," in Gisela Bock, Quentin Skinner, and Maurizio Viroli, eds., *Machiavelli and Republicanism* (Cambridge, 1990), 265–279.

88. See Jean Cohen and Andrew Arato, *Civil Society and Political Theory* (Cambridge, Mass., 1992), 83–91, for a brief synopsis of the evolution of civil society as a theoretical object. Their account is conceptually usefully but understates the contribution of explicitly republican themes. See Ernest Gellner, *Conditions of Liberty: Civil Society and Its Rivals* (London, 1994), 61–80, for a discussion of Adam Ferguson's relationship to the tradition.

89. For extended discussion of this theme, see John Brewer, ed., *Consumption and the World of Goods* (London, 1996).

90. For a survey of the use of the idea of *bonnes moeurs,* see Claudine Haroche and Ana Montoia, "Former et réformer les moeurs: Une question morale et politique," in *Les bonnes moeurs* (Paris, 1994), 191–213.

91. David Hume, "Of Civil Liberty," in Hume, *Essays Moral, Political, and Literary* (Indianapolis, 1985), 93.

92. David Hume, "Of Refinement in the Arts," in Hume, *Essays Moral, Political, and Literary* (Indianapolis, 1985), 269.

93. David Hume, *Enquiry concerning the Principles of Morals* (Oxford, 1975), 256–257.

94. Tzvetan Todorov, *On Human Diversity: Nationalism, Racism, and Exoticism in French Thought,* trans. Catherine Porter (Cambridge, Mass., 1993), 369.

95. Montesquieu, *The Spirit of the Laws* (Cambridge, 1989), book 11, chap. 3, 155.

96. Ibid., book 11, chap. 6, 156–166, and book 19, chap. 27, 325–333.

97. See Thomas L. Pangle, *Montesquieu's Philosophy of Liberalism: A Commentary on the Spirit of the Laws* (Chicago, 1973).

98. For an account of Rousseau's combat with the *philosophes* over the meaning of autonomy, see Mark Hulliung, *The Autocritique of Enlightenment: Rousseau and the Philosophes* (Cambridge, Mass., 1994).

99. This was a revelation for Kant and the point of origin for his moral theory. See J. B. Schneewind, *The Invention of Autonomy: A History of Modern Moral Philosophy* (Cambridge, 1998), 487–492.

100. J.-J. Rousseau, *Du contrat social* (Paris, 1964), 191.

101. Montesquieu, *Spirit of the Laws,* book 19, chap. 27, 326.

102. J.-J. Rousseau, *Fragments politiques* (Paris, 1964), 377.

103. Rousseau, *Du contrat social,* 290.

104. Rousseau's criticism of the creation of false needs through the system of appearances in modern life has been most fully analyzed in Jean Starobinski, *Jean-Jacques Rousseau: Transparency and Obstacle* (Chicago, 1988).

105. J.-J. Rousseau, *Discours sur l'origine et les fondements de l'inégalité parmi les hommes* (Paris, 1971), 253.

106. See Johann P. Arnason, "The Theory of Modernity and the Problematic of Democracy," in Peter Beilharz, Gillian Robinson, and John Rundell, eds., *Between Totalitarianism and Postmodernity* (Cambridge, Mass., 1992), 50–52, for a good

explanation of the conceptual difficulties with the idea of totalitarian democracy.

107. Adam Smith, "Letter to the Edinburgh Review," in W. P. D. Wrightman, ed., *Essays on Philosophical Subjects* (Indianapolis, 1982), 254.

108. Legend has it that when the Irish Brigade broke through the British lines, he threw away his collar and went into the battle.

109. Ernest Gellner, *Conditions of Liberty: Civil Society and Its Rivals* (London, 1994), 55; Michael Walzer, "The Civil Society Argument," in Ronald Beimer, ed., *Theorizing Citizenship* (Albany, N.Y., 1995), 170.

110. Jean Cohen and Andrew Arato, *Civil Society and Political Theory* (Cambridge, Mass., 1992), 83.

111. Adam Ferguson, *An Essay on the History of Civil Society* (Cambridge, 1994), 245.

112. AN, F12 798c, "Précis du prospectus de l'établissement des assurances sur la vie."

113. Ibid.

114. Etienne Clavière, *Réponse au mémoire de M. Necker concernant les assignats et à d'autres objections contre une création qui les porte à deux milliards* (Paris, 1790), 15–16.

115. The Atlantic perspective has not been much in vogue of late, but see the classic R. R. Palmer, *The Age of the Democratic Revolution: A Political History of Europe and America, 1760–1800*, 2 vols. (Princeton, N.J., 1959–1964).

116. For Thelwall, see Gregory Claeys, ed., *The Politics of English Jacobinism: Writings of John Thelwall* (University Park, Pa., 1995).

117. Harold T. Parker, *The Cult of Antiquity and the French Revolution* (Chicago, 1937), 124.

118. Marcel Gauchet, *La révolution des droits de l'homme* (Paris, 1989), 136–198; for Baker's critique, see Keith Michael Baker, "The Idea of a Declaration of Rights," in Dale Van Kley, ed., *The French Idea of Freedom: The Old Regime and the Declaration of Rights of 1789* (Stanford, Calif., 1994), 189–196.

119. John Markoff, *The Abolition of Feudalism: Peasants, Lords, and Legislators in the French Revolution,* (University Park, Pa., 1996), 563–569.

120. Ted W. Margadant, *Urban Rivalries in the French Revolution* (Princeton, N.J., 1992), 84–110.

121. Michael S. Lewis-Beck, Anne Hildreth, and Alan B. Spitzer, "Y-a-t-il eu un groupe girondin à la Convention nationale (1792–1793)?" in François Furet and Mona Ozouf, eds., *La Gironde et les Girondins* (Paris, 1991), 171.

122. Lynn Hunt, *Politics, Culture, and Class in the French Revolution* (Berkeley, Calif., 1984), 63–64.

123. See Antoine de Baecque, *The Body Politic: Corporeal Metaphor in Revolutionary France, 1770–1800* (Stanford, Calif., 1997), for a full account of the presence of this metaphor.

124. Marie-Hélène Huet, *Mourning Glory: The Will of the French Revolution* (Philadelphia, 1997), 94.

125. Dorinda Outram, *The Body and the French Revolution: Sex, Class, and Political Culture* (New Haven, Conn., 1989), 90–105.

126. Ferenc Feher, *The Frozen Revolution: An Essay on Jacobinism* (Cambridge, 1987), 104.

127. Ibid., 104.

128. Patrice Higonnet, *Goodness beyond Virtue: Jacobins during the French Revolution* (Cambridge, Mass., 1998), 205.

129. Sarah Hanley, *The Lit-de-Justice of the Kings of France: Constitutional Ideology in Legend, Ritual, and Discourse* (Princeton, N.J., 1983), 319–320.

130. Gary Kates, "The Transgendered World of the Chevalier/Chevalière d'Éon," *Journal of Modern History,* 67, no. 3 (September 1995), 586.

131. Lynn Hunt, "Pornography and the French Revolution," in Hunt, ed., *The Invention of Pornography: Obscenity and the Origins of Modernity, 1500–1800* (New York, 1996), 324–325.

132. Roger Chartier, *Les origines culturelles de la Révolution française* (Paris, 1990), 162.

133. Hunt, "Pornography and the French Revolution," 313.

134. Philippe Reynaud, "Y-a-t-il une philosophie girondine?" in François Furet and Mona Ozouf, eds., *La Gironde et les Girondins* (Paris, 1991), 296–297.

135. See Pierre Rétat, "The Evolution of the Citizen from the Ancien Régime to the Revolution," in Renée Waldinger, Philip Dawson, and Isser Woloch, eds., *The French Revolution and the Meaning of Citizenship* (Westport, Conn., 1993), 3–15, for an analysis of the underspecified model of popular authority in the Revolution.

136. Alphonse Aulard, *The French Revolution: A Political History, 1789–1804,* 4 vols. (London, 1910), 3:124.

137. J. P. Brissot de Warville and Etienne Clavière, *Nouveau voyage dans les Etats-Unis de l'Amérique septentrionale fait en 1788,* 3 vols. (Paris, 1791), 1:xx–xxi.

138. For an argument that antinobilism was the central motivating dynamic of the Patriot party, see Timothy Tackett, *Becoming a Revolutionary: The Deputies of the French National Assembly and the Emergence of a Revolutionary Culture (1789–1790)* (Princeton, N.J., 1996), 293–296.

139. Patrice Gueniffey, "Cordeliers or Girondins: The Prehistory of the Republic?" in Biancamaria Fontana, ed., *The Invention of the Modern Republic* (Cambridge, 1994), 86–106.

140. Cohen and Arato, *Civil Society and Political Theory,* 16.

141. Crane Brinton, *The Jacobins: An Essay in the New History* (New York, 1930).

142. The best account remains R. R. Palmer, *Twelve Who Ruled: The Year of the Terror in the French Revolution* (Princeton, N.J., 1941). On engineers in the period, see Ken Adler, *Engineering the Revolution: Arms and the Enlightenment in France, 1763–1815* (Princeton, N.J., 1997), 253–319.

143. Richard Cobb, *The Police and the People: French Popular Protest, 1789–1820* (Oxford, 1970), 176.

144. For Soboul's reading of sans-culotte political rhetoric, see Albert Soboul, *The Parisian Sans-Culottes and the French Revolution, 1793–4* (Oxford, 1964), 18–43; for a critique of Soboul's conclusions, see Richard Mowbray Andrews, "Social Structures, Political Elites, and Ideology in Revolutionary Paris, 1792–94: A

Critical Evaluation of Albert Soboul's *Les Sans-Culottes Parisiens en l'an II*," *Journal of Social History*, 19, no. 2 (Winter 1985), 71–112. Andrews overstates Soboul's insensitivity to the problem of social typology.

145. On the local contexts for urban popular politics, see Morris Slavin, *The French Revolution in Miniature: Section Droits de l'Homme, 1789–1795* (Princeton, N.J., 1984). Controversy rages on the nature of "work" as understood by the sansculottes and its place in their political consciousness. See William H. Sewell, Jr., *Work and Revolution in France: The Language of Labor from the Old Regime to 1848* (Cambridge, 1980), 62–142; Michael Sonenscher, *Work and Wages: Natural Law, Politics, and the Eighteenth-Century French Trades* (Cambridge, 1989).

2. Happiness Universal?

1. For the classic statement of the position that the Terror was the hidden mainspring of all discussion, see Mona Ozouf, "The Terror after the Terror: An Immediate History," in Keith Michael Baker, ed., *The French Revolution and the Creation of Modern Political Culture*, vol. 4, *The Terror* (Oxford, 1994), 3–18.

2. Isser Woloch, *Jacobin Legacy: The Democratic Movement under the Directory* (Princeton, N.J., 1970).

3. Ibid., 152.

4. Pierre Serna, *Antonelle: Aristocrate révolutionnaire, 1747–1817* (Paris, 1997), 369.

5. On the Cercle Social, see Gary Kates, *The Cercle Social, the Girondins, and the French Revolution* (Princeton, N.J., 1985); on the Courrier de Provence group, see Jean Bénétruy, *L'atelier de Mirabeau: Quatre proscrits genevois dans la tourmente révolutionnaire* (Geneva, 1962); the Lycée Républicain has yet to find its historian, but there are some interesting remarks in R. R. Palmer, *The Improvement of Humanity: Education and the French Revolution* (Princeton, N.J., 1985), 151–154.

6. Keith Michael Baker, "Introduction," in Baker, ed., *The French Revolution and the Creation of Modern Political Culture*, vol. 4, *The Terror* (Oxford, 1994), xxvi.

7. Martin Staum, *Minerva's Message: Stabilizing the French Revolution* (Montreal, 1996), 95–117; John C. O'Neal, *The Authority of Experience: Sensationist Theory in the French Enlightenment* (University Park, Pa., 1996), 225–244.

8. For Condillac's semiotic theory, see Etienne Bonnot de Condillac, *Essai sur l'origine des connaissances humaines* (Paris, 1973), 125–132.

9. See Kenneth Margerison, *P. L. Roederer: Political Thought and Practice during the French Revolution* (Philadelphia, 1983), 97–102, and Emmet Kennedy, *A Philosophe in the Age of Revolution: Destutt de Tracy and the Origins of "Ideology"* (Philadelphia, 1978), 67–73.

10. Ch.-F. de Saint Lambert, "Discours préliminaire," in *Oeuvres philosophiques* (Paris, Year IX), 1:35–37.

11. Ch.-F. de Saint Lambert, "Le catéchisme universel," in *Oeuvres philosophiques* (Paris, Year IX), 2:5–10.

12. Martin Staum, *Cabanis: Enlightenment and Radical Philosophy in the French Revolution* (Princeton, N.J., 1980), 161–167.

13. Louis-Claude de Saint-Martin, "Réflexions d'un observateur sur la question: Quelles sont les moyens les plus propres à fonder la morale d'un peuple? Sujet du premier prix de la classe des sciences morales et politiques de l'Institut national de France, pour le 15 messidor an VI de la République," in Robert Amadou, ed., *Controverse avec Garat, précédée d'autres écrits philosophiques* (Paris, 1990), 163.

14. Ibid., 143–144.

15. Louis-Claude de Saint-Martin, *Eclair sur l'association humaine* (Paris, Year VI), 14.

16. Louis-Claude de Saint-Martin, "Lettre à un ami, ou, considérations politiques, philosophiques, et religieuses sur la Révolution française" (Paris, Year III), in Robert Amadou, ed., *Controverse avec Garat, précédée d'autres écrits philosophiques* (Paris, 1990), 56–64.

17. Ibid., 103–104. Saint-Martin's writings exemplify the difficulties with the concepts of "public good" and "sovereignty" identified in Lucien Jaume, "Citoyenneté et souveraineté: Le poids de l'absolutisme," 518, and Pierre Rosanvallon, "L'utilitarisme français et les ambiguités de la culture politique révolutionnaire (position d'un problème)," 438, both in Keith Michael Baker, ed., *The French Revolution and the Creation of Modern Political Culture,* vol. 1, *The Political Culture of the Old Regime* (Oxford, 1987).

18. O'Neal, *The Authority of Experience,* 3.

19. Jean-Jacques Rousseau, "Notes en réfutation du livre de l'esprit, d'Helvétius," in *Oeuvres complètes de Jean-Jacques Rousseau* (Paris, 1851), 3:287; Mably, "Doutes proposées aux philosophes économistes sur l'ordre naturel et essentiel des sociétés politiques," in *Oeuvres complètes* (London, 1789), 11:43–50.

20. The literature here is simply enormous, but the two vital texts on this topic are Joan De Jean, *Tender Geographies: Women and the Origins of the Novel in France* (New York, 1991), and David J. Denby, *Sentimental Narrative and the Social Order in France, 1760–1820* (Cambridge, 1994). For a definitive account of the development of this aspect of the novel in France, see Orla Smyth, "La réhabilitation de l'affectivité et l'évolution du roman, 1670–1770" (Ph.D. diss., Ecoles des Hautes Etudes en Sciences Sociales, 2000).

21. See Dale Van Kley, *The Religious Origins of the French Revolution: From Calvin to the Civil Constitution, 1560–1791* (New Haven, Conn., 1996), 249–303.

22. Anne C. Vila, *Enlightenment and Pathology: Sensibility in the Literature and Medicine of Eighteenth-Century France* (Baltimore, 1998), 26.

23. O'Neal, *The Authority of Experience,* 14.

24. Destrutt de Tracy, "Mémoire sur la faculté de penser," in *Mémoires de l'Institut national des sciences et des arts-sciences morales et politiques* (Paris, Year VII) 1:401–410.

25. C. Leclerc, *Traité des maladies morales qui ont affecté la Nation française depuis plusieurs siècles* (Paris, n.d.), 42.

26. T. Giraudet, *De la famille, considérée comme l'élément des sociétés* (Paris, Year V), 6; J. A. Perreau, *Considérations physiques sur la nature de l'homme, ses facultés, etc.* (Paris, 1799), v.

27. François de Neufchâteau, "Notice littéraire sur M. Emmanuel Kant et sur l'état de la Métaphysique en Allemagne," *Le conservateur,* 2 (Paris, Year VIII), 38.

28. AN, 27 AP 13 (5), "Discours prononcé par le ministre de l'intérieur, à la séance d'ouverture des cours de l'Ecole polytechnique, le 7 pluviôse an VII."

29. François de Neufchâteau, *Recueil des lettres circulaires, instructions, programmes, discours, et autres actes publics, émanés du Citoyen François (de Neufchâteau) pendant ses deux exercises du ministère de l'intérieur,* 2 vols. (Paris, Year VII), hereafter cited as *Recueil;* see specifically "Discours prononcé par le minstre de l'intérieur à l'Ecole veterinaire d'Alfort," 10 Germinal, Year VII, 2:313.

30. "Observations de Adrien Lézay, sur le PROJET DE PAIX PERPETUELLE, d'Emmanuel Kant," *Journal d'économie publique, de morale, et de politique,* 1, no. 5 (20 Vendémiaire, Year V), 240.

31. Sophie de Grouchy, "Lettres à Cabanis sur la théorie des sentiments moraux," in Adam Smith, *Théorie des sentiments moraux, ou essai analytique sur les principes des jugements que portent naturellement des hommes,* 2d ed., trans. Sophie de Grouchy (Paris, 1830; orig. ed. 1796), 312.

32. Cabanis, "Considérations générales sur l'étude de l'homme, et sur les rapports de son organisation physique avec les facultés intellectuelles et morales," in *Mémoires de l'Institut national des sciences et des arts-sciences morales et politiques* (Paris, Year VII), 1:42.

33. Destutt de Tracy, "Mémoire sur la faculté de penser," 361.

34. Adam Smith, *The Theory of Moral Sentiments* (Indianapolis, 1982), 52.

35. Sophie de Grouchy, "Lettres à Cabanis," 356.

36. Ibid., 333–337.

37. Ibid., 317.

38. Ibid., 325.

39. Ibid., 331.

40. Ibid., 386.

41. Ibid., 387.

42. Ibid., 326.

43. Ibid., 362.

44. Ibid., 378.

45. Perreau, *Considérations physiques,* 116.

46. Guillaume le Febure, *République fondée sur la nature physique et morale de l'homme* (Paris, 1798), 46–47.

47. Benjamin Maublanc, *Considérations sur l'homme* (Paris, Year V), 19.

48. B. E. Manuel, *Des institutions sociales* (Paris, Year VII), 4.

49. Louis-Marie de La Révellière-Lépeaux, *Réflexions sur la culte, sur les cérémonies civiles, et sur les fêtes nationales* (Paris, Year V), 4.

50. Maublanc, *Considérations sur l'homme,* 84.

51. Jean-Baptiste Say, *Olbie, ou essai sur les moyens de réformer les moeurs d'une nation* (Paris, Year VIII). For a reading of *Olbie* in this light, see Philippe Steiner, "Comment stabiliser l'ordre social moderne? J. B. Say, l'économie politique, et la Révolution," in Guy Faccarello and Philippe Steiner, eds., *La pensée économique et la Révolution française* (Grenoble, 1990), 173–179.

52. Say, *Olbie*, 24.

53. Ibid., 29.

54. Ibid., 31.

55. Bulard, *Instructions élementaires sur la morale: Ouvrage qui a été jugé propre à l'instruction publique par le jury des livres élémentaires et le corps législatif* (Paris, Year VII), 8–9.

56. Ibid., 55.

57. Maublanc, *Considérations sur l'homme*, 137.

58. AN, 29 AP 12, J. B. Salaville to Roederer, 7 Prairial, Year VII. For his views of the historical significance of the revolution, see Salaville, *De la Révolution française, comparée à celle de l'Angleterre, ou, lettre au réprésentant du peuple Boulay (de la Meurthe), sur la différence de ces deux révolutions, pour servir de suite à l'ouvrage publié par ce réprésentant sur celle de l'Angleterre* (Paris, Year VII).

59. Jean-Baptiste Salaville, *L'homme et la société, ou, nouvelle théorie de la nature humaine et de l'état social* (Paris, Year VII).

60. Ibid., 33.

61. Ibid., 138–139.

62. Adam Ferguson, *An Essay on the History of Civil Society* (Edinburgh, 1767), 8, 12–15.

63. Ibid., 16.

64. Daniel Gordon's assertion that the Scots provided the French with a language of society that could put aside all political reference is too narrowly focused on Jean-Baptiste Suard and André Morellet. Salaville is but one example of a radical reading of the Scots. See Daniel Gordon, *Citizens without Sovereignty: Equality and Sociability in French Thought, 1670–1789* (Princeton, N.J., 1994), 160–176.

65. Smith, *The Theory of Moral Sentiments*, 226.

66. Ferguson, *Essay on Civil Society*, 28.

67. Salaville, *L'homme et la société*, 254.

68. Ibid., 44.

69. Ibid., 77.

70. Bulard, *Histoire abrégée des républiques anciennes et modernes, ou, l'on voit leur origine et leur établissement, et les causes de leur décadence et de leur ruine* (Paris, Year IV) 1:14.

71. Bulard, *Instructions élémentaires*, 37.

72. Ibid., 54.

73. Manuel, *Des institutions sociales*, 2. For Destrutt de Tracy's views on law, see his *Quels sont les moyens de fonder la morale chez un peuple?* (Paris, Year VI), 4–10.

74. M. J. Satur, *Les préjugés constitutionnels de l'an VI: Digression sérieuse et nécessaire sur la liberté politique* (Paris, Year VII), 12.

75. "Plan du Bulletin décadaire," *Bulletin décadaire de la République française*, 1 (first ten days of Vendémiaire, Year VII), 2.

76. P. S. Dupont de Nemours, *De l'origine et des progrès d'une science nouvelle* (Paris, 1768).

77. Jean-Claude Perrot, "Nouveautés: L'économie politique et ses livres," in Henri-Jean Martin and Roger Chartier, eds., *Histoire de l'édition française*, vol. 2, *Le livre*

triomphant, 1660–1830 (Paris, 1989), 278; William Scott, "The Pursuit of 'Interests' in the French Revolution: A Preliminary Survey," *French Historical Studies,* 19, no. 3 (1996), 811.

78. Jean-Claude Perrot, "Condorcet: De l'économie politique aux sciences de la société," in *Une histoire intellectuelle de l'économie politique (XVIIe–XVIIIe siècles)* (Paris, 1992), 366–367.

79. Marcel Dorigny, "La formation de la pensée économique de Sieyès d'après ses manuscrits (1770–1789)," *Annales historiques de la Révolution française,* 60, no. 271 (1988), 17–34; Manuela Albertone, "The Difficult Reception of James Steuart at the End of the Eighteenth Century in France," in Ramon Tortajada, ed., *The Economics of James Steuart* (London, 1999), 47–51.

80. The fundamental works on this body of writing are Guy Faccarello and Philippe Steiner, eds., *La pensée économique pendant la Révolution française* (Grenoble, 1990), and Richard Whatmore, *Republicanism and the French Revolution: An Intellectual History of Jean-Baptiste Say's Political Economy* (Oxford, 2000).

81. For an overview, see Staum, *Minerva's Message,* 191–210.

82. Germain Garnier, *Abrégé élémentaire des principes de l'économie politique* (Paris, Year IV), 16.

83. AN, 284 AP 5, dossier 1, f. 7.

84. An early approach to the problem was François Crouzet, "Les conséquences économiques de la Révolution: A propos d'un inédit de Sir Francis d'Ivernois," *Annales historiques de la Révolution française* (April–June 1962), 186–217.

85. On this fascinating group of Genevans, see Jean Bénétruy, *L'atelier de Mirabeau: Quatre proscrits genevois dans la tourmente révolutionnaire* (Geneva, 1962), xli.

86. P. L. Roederer, "De l'état politique et économique de la France sous la constitution présente, ouvrage traduit de l'Allemand," *Journal d'économie publique, de morale, et de politique,* 1 (Year IV), 126–127.

87. Jacques Mallet du Pan, *Correspondance politique pour servir à l'histoire du républicanisme français* (Hamburg, 1796), 24–25.

88. François d'Ivernois, *A Cursory View of the Assignats and Remaining Resources of French Finance,* trans. P. Byrne (Dublin, 1795), 4.

89. M. de Montlosier, *Des effets de la violence et de la modération dans les affaires de la France* (London, 1796), 51.

90. Joseph Barnave, *Power, Property, and History: Barnave's Introduction to the French Revolution and Other Writings,* trans. Emmanuel Chill (New York, 1971), 103.

91. François d'Ivernois, *Table historique et politique de l'administration de la République française pendant l'année 1797, des causes qui ont amené la révolution du 4 septembre et de ses résultats* (London, 1798), 210.

92. British Library ADD MS 34448 (Auckland Papers) f. 313, "Considérations sur la manière de concerter le plan d'épuration, qui doit terminer les inquietudes des Puissances de l'Europe relativement à l'état actuel et aux suites de la Révolution française," [1793].

93. [Mallet du Pan], *Lettre à un ministre d'état sur les rapports entre le système politique de la République française et celui de sa révolution* (London, 1797), 11, 31.

94. Ibid., 246–248.

95. Raynal, *Tableau philosophique de la Révolution de France en 1789, où l'on dévoile l'origine et l'accroissement progressif du despotisme qui régnoit sur les peuples de cet empire et les causes de l'oppression sous laquelle ils ont gémi si longtemps* (Marseilles, 1790), 18.

96. Roland-Gaspard Lemerer, *Appel à la nation française par Roland Gaspard Lemerer, député d'Ile et Vilaine au Conseil des cinq-cents* (Toulouse, 1797), 18.

97. AN, 29 Ap 110, ff. 329, "Voltaire il a été républicain."

98. B. F. A. Fonvielle, *Essai sur l'état actuel de la France, 1 Mai 1796* (Paris, 1796), 27.

99. Grégoire listed Bitaubé, Thillaye, Cousin, LaHarpe, Vandermonde, Ginguené, la Chaubeaussière, La Metherie, François-Neufchâteau, Boncerf, Oberlin, Volney, Laroche, Sage, Beffroy, and Vigée, in Henri-Baptiste Grégoire, *Rapport sur les destructions opérées par le vandalisme, et sur les moyens de le réprimer* (Paris, Year II), 14

100. "Littérature: Les vosges, poëme récité à Epinal, dans la fête de la fondation de la République," *La décade philosophique*, 11, no. 8 (20 Frimaire, Year V), 467–468.

101. Marmontel, *Le peuple et le sénat traités comme ils le méritent* (Paris, Year VI).

102. Morellet, *Mémoires* (Paris, 1988), 416–420.

103. Hans-Jürgen Lüsebrink, "Le rôle de Raynal et la réception de l'*Histoire des deux-Indes* pendant la Révolution française," *Studies on Voltaire and the Eighteenth Century*, 286 (1991), 89.

104. Anon., *Le 18 fructidor, ou, anniversaire des fêtes directoriales* (Hamburg, 1798), 18–19.

105. Ibid., 11–15.

106. Anon., *Liberté, égalité, fraternité: Journée de 18 fructidor*, (Paris, Year VI), 15.

107. Charles Theremin, *De la situation intérieur de la République* (Paris, Year V), 58.

108. B. Barère, *De la pensée du gouvernement* (Paris, Year V), 184.

109. Condorcet, *Esquisse d'un tableau historique des progrès de l'esprit humaine* (Paris, 1988), 149.

110. "Littérature-philosophie: Oeuvres de Diderot, publiées sur les manuscrits de l'auteur, par Jacques-André Naigeon," *La décade philosophique*, 16, no. 15 (30 Pluviôse, Year VI), 335.

111. Maine de Biran, *Journal intime de Maine de Biran de l'année 1792 à l'année 1817* (Paris, 1927), 27.

112. Ibid., 63.

113. Charles R. Sullivan, "The First Chair of Political Economy in France: Alexander Vandermonde and the *Principles* of Sir James Steuart at the Ecole Normale of the Year III," *French Historical Studies*, 20, no. 4 (Fall 1997), 635–664.

114. *Séances des Ecoles normales recueillies par des sténographes et revues par les professeurs*, rev. ed. 9 vols. (Paris, Year IX), 1:304.

115. Ibid., 307–308.

116. Ibid., 354–355.

117. AN, F17 1232, dossier 1, f. 5, "Rapport présenté au ministre de l'intérieur," 27 Ventôse, Year IV.

118. Herrenschwand, *De l'économie politique moderne: Discours fondmental sur la population* (London, 1786), 1–6.

119. Roederer, "De l'économie politique moderne—suite du discours fondamental sur la population, par Herrenschwand," *Journal d'économie publique, de morale, et de politique,* 1, no. 8 (20 Brumaire, Year V), 345.

120. AN, F17 1232, dossier 1, f. 13, "Rapport présenté au ministre de l'Intérieur," 8 Pluviôse, Year IV.

121. AN, F17 1338, Dossier 4, "Le ministre de l'Intérieur aux profeseurs des écoles centrales," 24 Messidor, Year VI.

122. Gaetano Filangieri, *La science de la législation, ouvrage traduit de l'italien d'après l'édition de Naples de 1784,* 6 vols. (Paris, 1786).

123. Ibid., 1:26–27.

124. Ibid., 214–216.

125. Ibid., 2:118.

126. Paine anticipated this appropriation of Italian political economy through his interest in the work of Dragonetti: see David Wootton, "Introduction—The Republican Tradition: From Commonwealth to Common Sense," in Wootton, ed., *Republicanism, Liberty, and Commercial Society, 1649–1776* (Stanford, Calif., 1994), 36.

127. Germain Garnier, *Abrégé élémentaire des principes de l'économie politique* (Paris, Year IV), 16.

128. Ibid., 32.

129. "De l'état politique et économique de la France sous la constitution présente, ouvrage traduit de l'Allemand," *Journal d'économie publique, de morale, et de politique,* 1 (Year IV), 124.

130. A. J. R. Turgot, "Réflexions sur la formation et la distribution des richesses," *Oeuvres,* ed. Dupont de Nemours (Paris, 1808), 5:35, 104.

131. Adam Smith, *An Inquiry into the Nature and Causes of the Wealth of Nations,* ed. R. H. Campbell and A. S. Skinner, 2 vols. (Indianapolis, 1981), 1:86–87.

132. Simone Meysonnier, "Aux origines de la science économique française: Le libéralisme égalitaire," in Gérard Guyot and Jean-Pierre Hirsch, eds., *La Révolution française et le développement du capitalisme* (Lille, 1989), 111–124.

133. Salaville, *L'homme et la société,* 254.

134. There was also a socially conservative version of the relationship of labor to politics: see Thomas E. Kaiser, "Politics and Political Economy in the Thought of the Ideologues," *History of Political Economy,* 12 (1984), 141–160.

135. Clavière, *Lettres écrites à M. Cérutti* (Paris, 1790), 8.

136. Cérutti, *Idées simples et précises sur le papier monnaie, les assignats forcés, et les biens écclésiastiques, suivies d'une réponse à M. Bergasse et à M. de Montlosier, et terminées par une note importante sur M. Burke* (Paris, 1790), 10–11.

137. For an excellent account of the politics of the bankruptcy, see Eugene Nelson White, "The French Revolution and the Politics of Government Finance, 1770–1815," *Journal of Economic History,* 55, no. 2 (June 1995), 227–256. The effect of the coup on the national debt was well understood even at the time. See

anon., *Des finances publiques de la France avec un mot sur le sort du Directoire Exécutif* (n.p., [1797]), 3.

138. Saint-Aubin, *Est-il conforme à un bon système de finances de traiter les terres comme l'on a fini par traiter les assignats?* (Paris, Year VII), 5–10.

139. Jules Gautier, *Essai sur la restauration des finances de la France et sur l'organisation générale et administrative de l'agriculture et du commerce* (Paris, Year VII); Gérome, *Nouvelle théorie des finances fondée sur la propriété* (Paris, Year VII).

140. This was developed from the earlier proposal of 18 March 1793; see Jean-Pierre Gross, "Progressive Taxation and Social Justice in Eighteenth-Century France," *Past and Present,* 140 (August 1993), 111.

141. Lecoulteaux, *Essai sur les contributions proposées pour l'an sept, sur celles qui existent actuellement en Angleterre, et sur le crédit public* (Paris, Year VII), 21.

142. Ibid., 15.

143. Ibid., 32–34.

144. Joseph de Maistre, *Considérations sur la France* (Paris, 1980), 54; Jean-François LaHarpe, *Du fanatisme dans la langue révolutionnaire, ou, de la persécution suscitées par les barbares du dix-huitième siècle, contre la religion chrétienne et ses ministres* (Paris, Year V), 34.

145. "Happiness" was a troubling idea for an eighteenth-century sensibility. See the debates outlined in Robert Mauzi, *L'idée du bonheur dans la littérature et la pensée françaises au XVIIIe siècle* (Paris: Armand Colin, 1965).

146. William Scott, "The Pursuit of 'Interests' in the French Revolution: A Preliminary Survey," *French Historical Studies,* 19, no. 3 (1996), 811.

147. Linda Colley, *Britons: Forging the Nation, 1707–1832* (New Haven, Conn., 1982).

148. For an interesting discussion of some of these issues, see Dror Wahrman, *Imagining the Middle Class: The Political Representation of Class in Britain, 1780–1840* (Cambridge, 1995), 8–9.

149. For an account of the Revolution that argues for a similar revolution in structures of public communication as its enduring legacy, see Immanuel Wallerstein, "The French Revolution as World-Historical Event," in Ferenc Fehér, ed., *The French Revolution and the Birth of Modernity* (Berkeley, Calif., 1990) 117–130.

150. For a slightly different take on the comparison I wish to make, see Günther Lottes, "Radicalism, Revolution, and Political Culture: An Anglo-French Comparison," in Mark Philp, ed., *The French Revolution and British Popular Politics* (Cambridge, 1991), 78–98. Lottes argues that the revolutionary transformation of political culture was the creation of the individual as the normative ground of political debate.

151. The original essay of 1971 is reprinted as E. P. Thompson, "The Moral Economy of the English Crowd in the Eighteenth Century," Thompson, *Customs in Common* (London, 1991), 185–259.

152. E. P. Thompson, "Moral Economy Reviewed," in *Customs in Common,* 269–271.

153. Thomas Paine, *The Rights of Man* (New York, 1973), 446.

154. For an elaboration of the difference between the old and the new arguments in favor of commerce, see Albert Hirschmann, *The Passions and the Interests: Political Arguments for Capitalism before Its Triumph* (Princeton, N.J., 1975), 69–88. On Smith's ambivalence, see Richard Whatmore, "'A Gigantic Manliness': Paine's Republicanism in the 1790s," in Stefan Collini, Richard Whatmore, and Brian Young, eds., *Economy, Polity, and Society: British Intellectual History, 1750–1950* (Cambridge, 2000), 135–157.

155. William Godwin, *The Enquirer: Reflections on Education, Manners, and Literature in a Series of Essays* (Dublin, 1797), 1.

156. Ibid., 161.

157. Ibid., 216.

158. Thomas Paine, *Agrarian Justice Opposed to Agrarian Law and to Agrarian Monopoly; Being a Plan for Meliorating the Condition of Man by Creating in Every Nation a National Fund*, in G. Bell, ed., *The Pioneers of Land Reform: Thomas Spence, William Ogilvie, Thomas Paine* (London, 1920).

159. Ibid., 188.

160. Ibid., 182–183.

161. On Thelwall, see principally Gregory Claeys, ed., *The Politics of English Jacobinism: Writings of John Thelwall* (University Park, Pa., 1995); E. P. Thompson, "Hunting the Jacobin Fox," *Past and Present*, 142 (1994), 94–140; and Ian Hampshire-Monk, "John Thelwall and the Eighteenth-Century Radical Response to Political Economy," *The Historical Journal*, 34, no. 1 (1991), 1–20. On Spence see Malcolm Chase, *The People's Farm: English Radical Agrarianism, 1795–1840* (Oxford, 1988).

162. John Thelwall, *The Rights of Nature, against the Usurpations of Establishments: A Series of Letters to the People of Britain, on the State of Public Affairs and the Recent Effusions of the Right Honourable Edmund Burke*, 2 vols. (London, 1796) 1:76.

163. The argument that Thelwall was procommercial is developed in Gregory Claeys, "The Origins of the Rights of Labour: Republicanism, Commerce, and the Construction of Modern Social Theory in Britain," *Journal of Modern History*, 66 (June 1994), 249–290. Claeys argues that the evaluative horizon of Thelwall's ideas was independence, as will become clear I think that independence was for Thelwall a secondary principle.

164. Thelwall, *The Rights of Nature*, 2:55.

165. Ibid., 89.

166. John Thelwall, *The Tribune* (1796), 1:8.

167. Thelwall, *The Rights of Nature*, 1:73.

168. John Thelwall, *Peaceful Discussion and Not Tumultary Violence the Means of Redressing National Grievance* (London, 1795), 4.

169. Thelwall, *The Tribune*, 1:49.

170. Thelwall, *The Rights of Nature*, 2:79.

171. Ibid., 1:21.

172. Ibid., 1:13.

173. Ibid., 2:48.

174. For the Friends of Peace, see J. E. Cookson, *The Friends of Peace: Anti-War Liberalism in England, 1793–1815* (Cambridge, 1982).

175. See Donald Winch, *Riches and Poverty: An Intellectual History of Political Economy in Britain, 1750–1834* (Cambridge, 1996), 253–254.

176. For an account of the evolution from Spencean radicalism to Owenite socialism, see Gregory Claeys, *Machinery, Money, and the Millennium: From Moral Economy to Socialism, 1815–1860* (Princeton, N.J., 1987), 26–32.

177. Thomas Bartlett, "An End to Moral Economy: The Irish Militia Disturbances of 1793," *Past and Present,* 99 (1983), 41–64.

178. David Dickson, "Paine and Ireland," in David Dickson, Daire Keogh, and Kevin Whelan, eds., *The United Irishmen: Republicanism, Radicalism, and Rebellion,* (Dublin 1993), 135–151. See also Kevin Whelan, "The Republic in the Village," in Whelan, *The Tree of Liberty: Radicalism, Catholicism, and the Construction of Irish Identity, 1760–1830* (Cork, 1996), 62–74.

179. Iain McCalman, *Radical Underworld: Prophets, Revolutionaries, and Pornographers in London, 1795–1840* (Cambridge, 1988), 11.

180. Ian McBride, "William Drennan and the Dissenting Tradition," in David Dickson, Daire Keogh, and Kevin Whelan, eds., *The United Irishmen: Republicanism, Radicalism, and Rebellion* (Dublin, 1993), 49–62; Whelan, "The Republic in the Village."

181. We lack a thoroughgoing analysis of O'Connor's work, but for an excellent introduction, see Patrick Kelly, "Irish Writers and the French Revolution," in *La storia della storiographia europea sulla rivoluzione francese* (Rome, 1990), 342–345; see also James Livesey, "Introduction," in Arthur O'Connor, *The State of Ireland,* ed. James Livesey (Dublin, 1998), 1–26.

182. Arthur O'Connor, *The State of Ireland, to Which Are Added His Addresses to the Electors of the County of Antrim,* 2d ed. (London, 1798). For other Irish writers, mostly conservative, who deployed political economy in their analyses of the Revolution, see Kelly, "Irish Writers and the French Revolution," 341–342, 345–349.

183. O'Connor, *The State of Ireland,* 38.

184. Ibid., 37.

185. Ibid., 33.

186. Ibid., 49.

187. Ibid., 30.

188. *The Press,* 1 (28 September 1797).

189. William Manning, *The Key of Liberty: The Life and Democratic Writings of William Manning, "A Laborer," 1747–1814,* ed. Michael Merrill and Sean Wilentz (Cambridge, Mass., 1993), 156.

190. As David Dickson has put it, "in Ireland the 'rights of man' were being transmuted into the rights of Irishmen" (Dickson, "Paine and Ireland," 149).

191. Margot Finn, *After Chartism: Class and Nation in English Radical Politics, 1848–1874* (Cambridge, 1993), 22–53; James E. Epstein, "The Constitutionalist Idiom," in

Epstein, *Radical Expression: Political Language, Ritual, and Symbol in England, 1790–1850* (Oxford, 1994), 3–28.

192. Benjamin Constant, *De la force du gouvernement actuel et de la nécessité de s'y rallier* (Paris, 1988; orig. ed. 1796), 74.

193. Benjamin Constant, "Troisième lettre à un député," *Nouvelles politiques,* 26 June 1796, reprinted in Ephraim Harpaz, ed., *Recueil d'articles, 1795–1817* (Geneva, 1978), 23.

194. Benjamin Constant, "Deuxième lettre à un député," in Ephraim Harpaz, ed., *Recueil d'articles, 1795–1817* (Geneva, 1978), 20–21.

195. Benjamin Constant, "Moition sur la nécessité de laisser au peuple l'élection libre de la totalité du prochain corps électoral, par Saladin, repésentant du peuple," *Le sentinelle,* 2 September 1795, reprinted in Ephraim Harpaz, ed., *Recueil d'articles, 1795–1817* (Geneva, 1978), 31.

196. Benjamin Constant, *De l'esprit de conquête et de l'usurpation* (Paris, 1986), 139–148.

197. Benjamin Constant, *Fragment d'un ouvrage abandonné sur la possibilité d'une constitution républicaine dans un grand pays,* ed. Henri Grange (Paris, 1991), 137–139, 223–227. See also Stephen Holmes, *Benjamin Constant and the Making of Modern Liberalism* (New Haven, Conn., 1984), 16.

198. Biancamaria Fontana, *Benjamin Constant and the Post-Revolutionary Mind* (New Haven, Conn., 1991), 23.

199. Germaine de Staël, *Des circonstances actuelles qui peuvent terminer la Révolution et des principes qui doivent fonder la république en France,* ed. Lucia Omacini (Geneva, 1979), 254–255.

200. Ibid., 255.

201. Constant, *De la force du gouvernement actuel,* 72.

202. Benjamin Constant, abandoned preface to *Adolphe,* in *Oeuvres,* (Paris, 1979), 197, cited in Tzvetan Todorov, *Benjamin Constant: La passion démocratique* (Paris, 1997), 50.

203. Holmes, *Benjamin Constant and the Making of Modern Liberalism,* 14.

204. Benjamin Constant, *Principes de politique,* ed. Etienne Hofmann (Paris, 1997).

205. Ibid., 369.

206. Ibid.

207. Ibid., 271.

208. Ibid., 373.

209. Benjamin Constant, *De la liberté des modernes comparée à celle des anciens* (Paris, 1986).

210. Ibid., 289.

211. Ibid., 290.

212. Ibid.

213. Edmund Burke, *A Philosophical Inquiry into Our Ideas of the Sublime and the Beautiful* (Cambridge, 1993), 71.

214. Constant, *Principes de politique,* 372.

215. Ibid.

216. Ibid.
217. Ibid., 411.
218. Ibid., 418.
219. Ibid., 425.
220. See Judith Shklar, "The Liberalism of Fear," in Nancy Rosenblum, ed., *Liberalism and the Moral Life* (Cambridge, Mass., 1989), 21–38, for an analysis of this logic in more formal terms.

3. The Agricultural Republic as Rhetoric and Practice

1. Quintilian, *Institutio oratoria,* ed. and trans. H. E. Butler, 4 vols. (London, 1920), 3:232, 358, quoted in Quentin Skinner, *Reason and Rhetoric in the Philosophy of Hobbes* (Cambridge, 1996), 181–182.
2. Skinner, *Reason and Rhetoric,* 182–188.
3. Bronislaw Baczko, *Comment sortir de la Terreur: Thermidor et Révolution* (Paris, 1983), 93.
4. Bronislaw Baczko, "Vandalism," in François Furet and Mona Ozouf, eds., *A Critical Dictionary of the French Revolution* (Cambridge, Mass., 1989), 861.
5. Henri-Baptiste Grégoire, "Rapport sur les moyens de rassembler les metériaux nécessaires à former les annales de civisme, et sur la forme de cet ouvrage, séance du 28 septembre 1793, Convention nationale," in *Oeuvres,* vol. 3 (Paris, 1977), 3.
6. Henri-Baptiste Grégoire, *Rapport sur les déstructions opérées par le vandalisme, et sur les moyens de le réprimer* (Paris, Year II [1794]), 7–8.
7. Henri-Baptiste Grégoire, "Rapport et décret sur les moyens d'améliorer l'agriculture en France, par l'établissment d'une maison d'économie rurale dans chaque département (13 vendémiaire an II)," in *Oeuvres,* vol. 2 (Paris, 1978), 7–8.
8. J. M. Heurtault-Lamarville, *Rapport fait par Heurtault-Lamarville, député du Cher, au nom des commissions d'instruction publique et d'institutions républicaines réunies, sur les écoles spéciales de peinture, de sculpture et d'architecture,* (Paris, Year VI), 10.
9. Grégoire, "Rapport et décret sur les moyens d'améliorer l'agriculture en France," 7, 2–3.
10. Ibid., 23.
11. Henri-Baptiste Grégoire, "Nouveaux développements sur l'amélioration de l'agriculture par l'établissement de maisons de l'économie rurale," in *Oeuvres,* 2:132.
12. "Rapport sur les destructions opérées par le vandalisme, par Grégoire," *La décade philosophique,* 3, no. 16 (10 Vendémiaire, Year III), 18.
13. Joanna Kitchen, *Un journal "philosophique": La décade (1794–1807)* (Paris, 1965), 14–15.
14. "Desséchement des étangs," *La décade philosophique,* 3, no. 18 (30 Vendémiaire, Year III), 139.
15. "Analyse du rapport fait au nom du comité d'agriculture par Eschasseriaux," *La décade philosophique,* 1, no. 4 (10 Prairial, Year III), 210–215.

16. Ibid., 218.

17. Ibid., 223.

18. Joseph Borelly, "Prospectus," *Journal d'agriculture et d'économie rurale,* 1 (Paris, Year III), 1–6.

19. Ibid., 16–17.

20. Ibid., 13.

21. Ibid., 17.

22. Jean-Baptiste Dubois, *Vues générales sur l'amélioration de l'agriculture en France, présentés à la commission d'agriculture et des arts* (Paris, Year III), 4.

23. Ibid., 29.

24. Ibid., 7.

25. Ibid., 36.

26. "Vues générales sur l'amélioration de l'agriculture en France," *La décade philosophique,* 4, no. 25 (10 Nivôse, Year III), 19.

27. Jean-Baptiste Dubois, "Observations sur l'économie rurale, considérée dans ses rapports avec l'instruction publique," *La décade philosophique,* 7, no. 50 (30 Brumaire, Year IV), 269. In fact, Young was the secretary; the president was Sir John Sinclair.

28. Ibid., 270.

29. Ibid., 273.

30. The evolution of social class in the Revolution is a theme that needs further work. For studies that bookend the period, see Robert Forster, Louis Bergeron, and Guy Chaussinand Nogaret, *"Les masses de granit": Cent mille notables du premier empire* (Paris, 1979). The stormy petrel of social revolution was Babeuf: see R. B. Rose, *Gracchus Babeuf: The First Revolutionary Communist* (Stanford, Calif., 1978).

31. See Felicity Rosslyn, "Good Humour and the Agelasts: Horace, Pope, and Gray," in Charles Martindale and David Hopkins, eds., *Horace Made New: Horatian Influences on British Writing from the Renaissance to the Twentieth Century* (Cambridge, 1993), 184–198.

32. Anthony Low, *The Georgic Revolution* (Princeton, N.J., 1985), 3–6.

33. *Georgics I,* ll. 137–142, in Virgil, *The Georgics with John Dryden's Translation* (Ashington, 1981), 31.

34. Low, *Georgic Revolution,* 221.

35. Andrew McCrae, *God Speed the Plow: The Representation of Agrarian England, 1500–1660* (Cambridge, 1996), 121–131.

36. C. A. Bayly argues that "agrarian patriotism" was the dominant discourse of the creation of the Second British Empire; see *Imperial Meridian: The British Empire and the World, 1780–1830* (London, 1989), 125.

37. Joseph Addison, "Essay on Georgics," in John Dryden, *Works,* ed. William Frost, vol. 5 (Berkeley, Calif., 1987), 145.

38. See Pierre Fulcrand de Rosset, *L'agriculture, ou, les géorgiques françaises* (Paris, 1777).

39. Lionel Rothkrug, *Opposition to Louis XIV: The Political and Social Origins of the French Enlightenment* (Princeton, N.J., 1965), 234.

40. *La feuille villageoise, adressée, chaque semaine, à tous les villages de la France pour les instruire des lois, des événements, des découvertes qui intéressent tout citoyen*. On the paper, see Melvin Edelstein, *La feuille villageoise: Communication et modernisation dans les régions rurales pendant la Révolution* (Paris, 1977), and Melvin Edelstein, "*La Feuille Villageoise* and Rural Political Modernisation," *Studies on Voltaire and the Eighteenth Century*, 287 (1991), 237–260.

41. Jeremy Popkin, "Journals: The New Face of News," in Robert Darnton and Daniel Roche, eds., *Revolution in Print* (Berkeley, Calif., 1989), 158. Cérutti's partners in the enterprise were Rabaut de Saint-Etienne and Philippe-Antoine Grouvelle.

42. "Prospectus," *La feuille villageoise*, 1 (September 1790), 5.

43. Joseph-Antoine-Joachim Cérutti, *Traduction libre ou plutôt imitation de trois odes d'Horace applicables au temps présent* (Paris, 1789), 19.

44. Ibid.

45. Ibid., 26.

46. "Suite de la géographie universelle," *La feuille villageoise*, 1, no. 4 (21 October 1790), 51.

47. "Première lettre de Félicie à Marianne," *La feuille villageoise*, 1, no. 6 (15 November 1790), 102.

48. Ibid., 103.

49. Joseph-Antoine-Joachim Cérutti, *Les jardins de Betz: Poème, accompagné des notes instructives sur les travaux champêtres, sur les arts, les lois, les révolutions, la noblesse, le clergé, etc.* (Paris, 1792), 9.

50. See John Markoff, "Violence, Emancipation, and Democracy: The Countryside in the French Revolution," *American Historical Review*, 100 (1995), 360–386, for a compelling argument for an autonomous peasant revolution. The issue is explored at greater length in Chapter 4.

51. Edelstein, *La feuille villageoise*, 21.

52. Gary Kates, *The Cercle Social, the Girondins, and the French Revolution* (Princeton, N.J., 1985), 237.

53. "Lettre sur Cérutti," *La feuille villageoise*, 3, no. 25 (15 March 1792), 580.

54. *La feuille villageoise*, 9, no. 7 (5 Brumaire, Year III), 97–101, no. 8 (10 Brumaire, Year III), 113–120, no. 9 (15 Brumaire, Year III), 129–135, no. 11 (25 Brumaire, Year III), 161–169, no. 12 (20 Brumaire, Year III), 177–182, no. 13 (5 Frimaire, Year III), 193–197.

55. Edelstein, *La feuille villageoise*, 313.

56. *La feuille villageoise* (5 Brumaire, Year III), 97.

57. Gilles Postel-Vinay, *La terre et l'argent: L'agriculture et le crédit en France du XVIIIe siècle au début du XXe siècle* (Paris, 1998), 96.

58. *La feuille villageoise*, 9, no. 9 (15 Brumaire, Year III), 135; 9, no. 11 (25 Brumaire, Year III), 165.

59. Ibid., 9, no. 12 (20 Brumaire, Year III), 178.

60. Ibid., 179.

61. Jacques Delille, *L'homme des champs, ou, les géorgiques françaises* (Strasbourg, Year VIII).

62. Ibid., xvi, 59, 60.

63. Ibid., iii.

64. Ibid., vi, vii.

65. Pierre Jean-Baptiste Chaussard, *Examen de l'homme des champs, appel aux principes, ou, observations classiques et littéraires sur les géorgiques françaises* (Paris, Year IX), 6.

66. See Chapter 6 for a discussion of cultural policy. The georgic is still used as an aesthetic ground from which to interrogate the revolutionary experience: see Claude Simon, *Les géorgiques* (Paris, 1981).

67. R. B. Rose, "The 'Red Scare' of the 1790's: The French Revolution and the 'Agrarian Law,'" *Past and Present*, 103 (May 1984), 116.

68. Ibid., 121–123; Kates, *Cercle Social*, 212–213.

69. P. M. Jones, "The 'Agrarian Law': Schemes for Land Redistribution during the French Revolution," *Past and Present*, 133 (November 1991), 106.

70. Ibid., 96. The *partage* movement is discussed extensively in Chapter 4.

71. See Chapter 4 for a full account of the political context for this measure.

72. Harold T. Parker, *The Cult of Antiquity and the French Revolutionaries* (Chicago, 1937), 112.

73. Rosalind Mitchison, *Agricultural Sir John: The Life of Sir John Sinclair of Ulbster* (London, 1962), 157.

74. Arthur Young, *The Example of France a Warning to England* (Bury St. Edmunds, 1793), 32–33, 6.

75. Mirabeau and Quesnay, *Eléments de la philosophie rurale* (The Hague, 1767), xxxviii.

76. Robert C. Allen, *Enclosure and the Yeoman: The Agricultural Development of the South Midlands, 1450–1850* (Oxford, 1992), 11; Robert C. Allen and Cormac O'Grádá, "On the Road again with Arthur Young: English, Irish, and French Agriculture during the Industrial Revolution," *Journal of Economic History*, 48 (1988); Robert C. Allen, "The Growth of Labour Productivity in Early-Modern English Agriculture before Mechanisation," *Explorations in Economic History*, 28 (1991).

77. Jean-Laurent Rosenthal, *The Fruits of Revolution: Property Rights, Litigation, and French Agriculture, 1700–1860* (Cambridge, 1992), 15. Gregory Clark disagrees with the proposition that enclosure merely increased the return to capital by driving down that to labor, without any change in productivity; see "Labor Productivity and Farm Size in English Agriculture before Mechanisation: A Note," *Explorations in Economic History*, 28, no. 2 (April 1991), 249.

78. Louis-Pierre Couret-Villeneuve, *Lettre au Citoyen Sicard, instituteur des sourds et muets, membre de l'Institut national, et de la Société libre des sciences, lettres, et arts de Paris* (Paris, Year V), 3.

79. François de Neufchâteau, *Les lectures du citoyen ou suite de mémoires sur des objets de bien public: Premier mémoire, sur l'établissement d'un grenier d'abondance, ou magazin public, dans chaque canton du royaume* (Toulouse, 1790); *Dix épis de bled au lieu d'un, ou, la pierre philosophique de la République* (Paris, Year III); *Arrête de l'administration du département des Vosges, pour parvenir à la fondation de trois nouveaux villages* (Epinal, Year V).

80. "Extrait de livres—les lectures du citoyen," *La feuille du cultivateur*, 6, no. 48 (Year VI), 191.

81. François de Neufchâteau, *Des améliorations dont la paix doit être l'époque* (Epinal, Year V).

82. Ibid., 70, 12.

83. Ibid., 56.

84. Ibid., 4.

85. Ibid., 47.

86. Ibid., 58–59.

87. Drew McCoy, *The Elusive Republic: Political Economy in Jeffersonian America* (New York, 1982); Ronald Schechter, "Translating the 'Marseillaise': Biblical Republicanism and the Emancipation of Jews in Revolutionary France," *Past and Present*, 143 (May 1994), 121.

88. Jones, *The Peasantry in the French Revolution* (Cambridge, 1988), 132.

89. Octave Festy, "La place de l'agriculture dans le gouvernement de la France sous le Directoire et le Consulat," *Revue d'histoire économique et sociale*, 31 (1951), argues on the contrary that agriculture ceased to be an important feature of government thinking in this period. His argument turns on the disbandment of the Committee on Agriculture and Arts and its subsumption in the fourth section of the Ministry of the Interior. A consideration of the work of the section, the pamphlet literature, and the correspondence of the ministry does not support this view.

90. Maurice Agulhon refers to them as "agrarians," a term which excludes their other commitments: Maurice Agulhon, "L'essor de la paysannerie, 1789–1852," in Etienne Juillard, ed., *Histoire de la France rurale*, vol. 3, *Apogée et crise de la civilisation paysanne* (Paris, 1976), 49.

91. AN, F10 302, "Rapport présenté au ministre," 23 Frimaire, Year IV. The subsidy continued when Lefebvre took over as editor. Ginguené remained editor of the *Décade philosophique* until its closure in 1807.

92. AN, F10 247, "Copie de l'organisation de chacun des trois conseils de la 4ème division, d'après la decision du ministre du 25 brumaire an 4."

93. B. Barère, *De la pensée du gouvernment* (Paris, Year V), 59.

94. George Dejoint, *La politique économique du Directoire* (Paris, 1951), 37.

95. L. M. La Révellière-Lépeaux, *Mémoires*, 3 vols. (Paris, 1895), 2:110–111.

96. Dominique-Joseph Garat, *Rapport fait par Garat, sur la résolution relative aux dépenses du ministère de l'intérieur pendant l'an 7* (Paris, Year VII), 3–4.

97. Boissy d'Anglas, *Discours préliminaire au projet de constitution pour la République française* (Paris, 1795), 25.

98. "Lettre du ministre de l'intérieur aux administrations centrales des départements et aux commissaires près des dites administrations," *La feuille du cultivateur*, 7 (Year VI), 197.

99. Ibid., 199.

100. "Aux administrations centrales," 22 Fructidor, Year V, in *Recueil*, 1:lxxiii.

101. Ibid.

102. "Economie rurale," *La décade philosophique,* 1 (Year II), 335.

103. J. B. Dubois, "Agriculture: Cours d'agriculture," *La décade philosophique,* 5 (Year III), 327; Armand Joseph Béthune Charost, *Vues générales sur l'organisation de l'instruction rurale en France* (Paris, Year III), 4.

104. Charles Pinel, "Encouragements dûs à l'agriculture," *La décade philosophique,* 6 (Year IV), 394.

105. Joseph Eschasseriaux, "Economie rurale et politique: Analyse du rapport fait au nom du comité de l'agriculture," *La décade philosophique,* 1 (Year II). For an enthusiastic endorsement of Eschasseriaux's report, see Borelly, "Prospectus," *Journal d'agriculture et d'économie rurale* (Year III), 21.

106. M. A. Giraud, "Economie rurale: Réflexion sur la nécessité et la possibilité d'améliorer les laines en France," *La décade philosophique,* 1 (Year II), 397–401; "Economie rurale: Bêtes à laine," *La décade philosophique,* 3 (Year III), 14–17.

107. Martin Chassiron, "Quelques idées sur l'état politique de la France depuis la Révolution, sur sa population, son agriculture, et son commerce," *La feuille du cultivateur,* 6 (Year V), 328.

108. Mathieu Depère, "Mémoire sur les subsistances et l'agriculture," *La feuille du cultivateur,* 6 (Year V), 117.

109. J. M. Coupé, "Sur les abus des grandes exploitations rurales, et les moyens de multiplier les subsistances," *Journal d'agriculture et d'économie rurale,* 4, no. 20 (Year VII), 374.

110. François de Neufchâteau, "Arrêté de l'administration centrale du département des Vosges, pour parvenir à la fondation de trois nouveaux villages," *La feuille du cultivateur,* 6 (Year V), 74.

111. J. B. Dubois, "Agriculture: Vues générales sur l'amélioration de l'agriculture en France," *La décade philosophique,* 4 (Year III), 19.

112. Pinel, "Encouragements dûs à l'agriculture," 393.

113. Flamen d'Assigny, *De l'agriculture, considérée dans ses rapports avec l'économie politique, d'où l'on déduit la nécessité d'établir des fermes experimentales pour fonder l'art agricole* (Paris, Year XII), 7.

114. J. B. Rougier-Labergerie, *Observations sur l'instauration des sociétés d'agriculture, et sur les moyens d'utiliser leurs travaux* (Paris, Year VIII), 17.

115. This was the argument of J. Bosc, *Essai sur les moyens d'améliorer l'agriculture, les arts, et le commerce en France* (Paris, Year VIII).

116. Jean-Baptiste Rougier-Labergerie, *Essai politique et philosophique sur le commerce et la paix, considérés sous leurs rapports avec l'agriculture* (Paris, Year V), 21.

117. Antoine Dannivère, "Économie politique: Preuves arithmétiques de la nécessité d'encourager l'agriculture et d'abandonner, dans les temps ordinaires, l'approvisionnement des grains au commerce libre," *La décade philosophique,* 6 (Year VI), 130.

118. "Le ministre de l'intérieur aux commissaires du Directoire exécutif près des administrations de département, sur les abus du renversement des terres labourées et ensemencées," *La feuille du cultivateur,* 8 (Year VII), 97.

119. Rougier-Labergerie, *Essai politique et philosophique sur le commerce et la paix,* 4.

120. Anonymous, *Principes de commerce entre les nations: Ouvrage traduit de l'anglais* (Paris, 1790), 10.

121. J. A. Roucher, "Economie politique: Recherches sur la nature et causes de la richesse des nations, traduites de l'anglais, de Smith," *La décade philosophique*, 3 (Year III), 401.

122. "Politique extérieure: Vues ambitieuses et tyranniques du ministère anglais," *La décade philosophique*, 4 (Year III), 497.

123. Norman Hampson, *The Perfidy of Albion: French Perceptions of England during the French Revolution* (New York, 1998), 120–127.

124. "Politique: Affaires étrangères," *La décade philosophique*, 4 (Year IV), 42; "Convention Nationale: Discours de Boissy d'Anglas sur la diplomatie de la France," *La décade philosophique*, 4 (Year III), 316.

125. *Rédacteur*, 475 (15 Germinal, Year V), 3.

126. "Politique raisonnée: De la maison d'Authriche et de la coalition, ou, les intérêts de l'Allemagne et l'Europe," *La décade philosophique*, 23 (Year VIII), 14.

127. Athanase Veau, *Opinion sur la nécessité de perfectionner en France l'agriculture, les arts, et les sciences par les établissements adaptés aux localités et à l'intérêt général de la République* (Paris, Year III), 11.

128. "Extrait des livres: Letters and Papers on Agriculture, Planning, etc., Selected from the Correspondence Book of the Society of Bath, etc., 5 volumes," *La feuille du cultivateur*, 5 (Year III), 34.

129. "Agriculture: Observations sur l'agriculture hollandaise," *La décade philosophique*, 5 (Year III), 461.

130. "Politique raisonnée: Sur la situation politique et financière de l'Angleterre," *La décade philosophique*, 16 (Year VI), 138; "Agriculture: Cultures étrangères-épiceries," *La décade philosophique*, 7 (Year III), 81.

131. "Economie rurale: Lettre aux auteurs de la *Décade*," *La décade philosophique*, 4 (Year III), 336.

132. "Agriculture: Cultures étrangères-épiceries," 83.

133. BN, N.Aq.Fr. 21565, f. 71, Constantin-François de Chasseboeuf de Volney to La Révellière-Lépeaux, 14 January 1797.

134. J. G. Busch, *Le droit des gens maritimes, considéré comme l'objet d'un traité de commerce à annexer à celui de pacification entre l'Allemagne et la France* (Hamburg, 1796), 34.

135. BN, N.Aq.Fr. 23654, ff. 82–85, Daucourt to Reubell, n.d.

136. BN, N.Aq.Fr. 21565, f. 68, Volney to La Révellière-Lépeaux, 12 Floréal, Year V.

137. BN, N.Aq.Fr. 21566, f. 5, "Note adressée au citoyen Directeur La Révellière-Lépeaux, par le citoyen Rozier, nommé au consulat-général de la République française près les Etats-Unis."

138. AN, AF III 309.37.

139. La Révellière-Lépeaux, *Mémoires*, 2:257–258.

140. Joseph Fauchet, *Coup d'oeil sur l'état de nos rapports actuels avec les Etats-Unis de l'Amérique Septentrionale* (Paris, Year V), 16–19.

141. Talleyrand, "Mémoire sur les rélations commerciales des Etats-Unis avec

l'Angleterre, lu 15 germinal an V," in *Mémoires de l'Institut national des sciences et arts: Sciences morales et politiques,* vol. 2 (Paris, Year VII), 89.

142. Ibid., 99.

143. Charles Theremin, *De l'incompatibilité du systême démagogique avec le systême d'économie politique des peuples modernes* (Paris, Year VIII), 5.

144. Charles Theremin, *De la situation intérieure de la République* (Paris, Year V), 8.

145. Theremin, *De l'incompatibilité du systême démagogique,* 9.

146. "Conduite administrative pendant la guerre," 27 Pluviôse, Year VII, in *Recueil,* 2:49–50.

147. AN, F12 596, "Rapport présenté au Directoire exécutif par le ministre de l'intérieur," 16 Prairial, Year VI.

148. AN, AF III 93, dossier 400, "Rapport présenté au Directoire exécutif par le ministre de l'intérieur," 19 Nivôse, Year VII.

149. AN, F12 586, "Rapport présenté au minstre de l'intérieur," 19 Thermidor, Year VII.

150. AN, F10 247, "Procès-verbal du conseil d'agriculture, 49ème séance," 18 Germinal, Year IV.

151. About 6 million myriagrams of grain were exported under this measure.

152. AN, AF III 93, dossier 392, "Rapport présenté au Directoire exécutif," 13 Vendémiaire, Year VII.

153. AN, AF III 94, dossier 400, "Rapport présenté au Directoire exécutif par le ministre de l'intérieur," 29 Frimaire, Year VII.

154. Ibid.

155. AN, F12 1559, "Rapport par le bureau consultatif du commerce," 6 Nivôse, Year VI.

156. AN, F12 1559, "Le ministre de l'intérieur au ministre des finances," 7 Frimaire, Year VII.

157. "Taxe d'entretien des routes," 25 Thermidor, Year VI, in *Recueil,* 1:58.

158. Isser Woloch, *The New Regime: Transformations of the French Civic Order, 1789–1820s* (New York, 1994), 164–66.

159. "Recherche de pièces concernant la navigation intérieure," 3 Thermidor, Year VI, in *Recueil,* 1:338.

160. AN, AF III, dossier 93, "Plan des commissions qui vont être établies pour la navigation intérieure," Year VII, 4.

161. Ibid., 10.

162. Ibid.

163. "Secours aux indigents," 15 Thermidor, Year VI, in *Recueil,* 1:39.

164. "Hospices civils-enfants abandonnés," 1 Vendémiaire, Year VII, "Liquidation de la dette des hospices," 5 Vendémiaire, Year VII, in *Recueil,* 1:183, 186.

165. AN, 27 AP 13, dossier 5, "Decrête du ministère de l'intérieur," 9 Ventôse, Year VII.

166. "Travaux à établir dans les dépôts de mendicité," 5 Fructidor, Year VI, in *Recueil,* 1:69.

167. Ibid., 72–76.

168. Ibid., 76.

169. BN, N.Aq.Fr. 23654.333, undated ms. note.

170. Jan Goldstein, *Console and Classify: The French Psychiatric Profession in the Nineteenth Century* (Cambridge, 1987), 115.

171. AN, 27 AP 8, Pinel to François de Neufchâteau, 26 Vendémiaire, Year VII.

172. AN, 27 AP 1, dossier 1, François de Neufchâteau to M. Challan, 22 Messidor, Year XII.

173. Grégoire, "Nouveaux développements sur l'amélioration de l'agriculture par l'établissement de maisons d'économie," in *Oeuvres,* 2:123–125.

174. AN, 27 AP 2, dossier 4, "Baud au citoyen ministre de l'intérieur," 8 Ventôse, Year VII.

175. François de Neufchâteau, *Voyages agronomiques dans la sénatorie de Dijon* (Paris, 1806), viii.

176. "Abus du renversement des terres labourées et ensemencées," 9 Frimaire, Year VII, in *Recueil,* 1:297–298.

177. AN, F10 336, "François de Neufchâteau aux citoyens Dupin, Mors, et autres signataires du lieu de Pontempeirat, département de la Loire," 24 Nivôse, Year VII.

178. AN, F10 245, "Le ministre de l'intérieur aux administrateurs du département de la Haute-Garonne," 29 Thermidor, Year VII; F10 245, "Rapport présenté au ministre de l'intérieur," Messidor, Year VII.

179. AN, 245, "Le ministre de l'intérieur aux administrateurs du département des Hautes-Alpes," 19 Floréal, Year VII.

180. Pierre Serna, *Antonelle, aristocrate révolutionnaire* (Paris, 1997), 319–324; Isser Woloch, *Jacobin Legacy: The Democratic Movement under the Directory* (Princeton, N.J., 1970), 13, 20.

181. AN, F10 247, "Procès-verbal du conseil d'agriculture, 34e séance," 12 Ventôse, Year VI.

182. "Etablissement d'une société d'agriculture dans le département de la Creuse," *La feuille du cultivateur,* 6, no. 21 (17 Germinal, Year VI), 127–128.

183. AN, 27 AP 6, François de Neufchâteau, "Mémoire en forme de lettre, au citoyen ministre de l'intérieur, avec un projet d'arrêt, sur le moyen de rendre les sociétés d'agriculture le plus utiles possible," Pluviôse, Year IX.

184. "Procès-verbal de l'inauguration de la société libre d'agriculture, de commerce et des arts du département de la Nièvre, 16 fructidor an VI," *La feuille du cultivateur,* 8, no. 12 (27 Brumaire, Year VII), 61.

185. *Rédacteur,* 947 (2 Thermidor, Year VI).

186. For a list of the societies, see "Fondation des sociétés libres d'agriculture," *La feuille du cultivateur,* 8, no. 37 (2 Germinal, Year VII), 211–212.

187. "Le ministre de l'intérieur aux administrations centrales du département, aux commissaires du Directoire exécutif, et aux sociétés d'agriculture," *Rédacteur,* 1192 (3 Germinal, Year VII).

188. Bibliothèque Saint Geneviève, Paris, ms. 4124, "François de Neufchâteau aux administrations centrales des départements," 9 Prairial, Year VII.

189. AN, 27 AP 1, dossier 2, François de Neufchâteau to Gilbert, 29 Vendémiaire, Year VII.

190. AN, 27 AP 3, J. B. Dubois to François de Neufchâteau, 2 Germinal, Year X.

191. François de Neufchâteau, *Analyse des annuaires statistiques du département du Bas-Rhin pour les années VII, VIII, et IX, lu à la société d'agriculture de Paris, le 14 germinal an X* (Paris, Year X).

192. Jean-Claude Perrot, "The Golden Age of Regional Statistics (Year IV–1804)," in Jean-Claude Perrot and Stuart Wolff, eds., *State and Statistics in France, 1789–1815* (London, 1984), 23–26.

193. François de Neufchâteau, *Rapport sur la perfectionnement des charrues, fait à la société d'agriculture du département de la Seine* (Paris, Year IX).

194. AN, F10 303, "Rapport présenté au ministre de l'intérieur," 9 Frimaire, Year VII.

195. François de Neufchâteau, *Des vins et des fruits, extrait des notes du hiutième lieu de la nouvelle edition du théâtre de l'agriculture et mesnages des champs, d'Olivier de Serres, publiée par la société d'agriculture du département de la Seine* (Paris, Year XIV), 2.

196. AN, 27 AP 1, dossier 1, François de Neufchâteau to Challan, 22 Messidor, Year XII.

197. AN, F10 245, "Rapport présenté au ministre de l'intérieur," 29 Floréal, Year VII.

198. *Bulletin décadaire,* 1 (10 Vendémiaire, Year VII), 1.

199. AN, F10 245, "Rabier aux citoyens composant le Directoire exécutif, Chevannes," 11 Floréal, Year VII.

200. AN, F10 245, "Nougaret au ministre de l'intérieur, Montpellier," 1 jour complémentaire, Year VII.

201. AN, F10 245, François de Neufchâteau to citoyen Signoret, 29 Fructidor, Year VII.

202. Howard Brown, "From Organic Society to Security State: The War on Brigandage in Revolutionary France," *Journal of Modern History,* 69, no. 4 (November 1997), 661–695.

203. Woloch, *The New Regime,* 390.

204. Alan Forrest, *Conscripts and Deserters: The Army and French Society during the Revolution and Empire* (Oxford, 1989), 34–39.

205. Howard G. Brown, *War, Revolution, and the Bureaucratic State: Politics and Army Administration, 1791–1799* (Oxford, 1995), 237.

206. Dejoint, *La politique économique du Directoire,* 16.

207. Guy Lemarchand, "Du féodalisme au capitalisme: A propos des conséquences de la Révolution sur l'évolution de l'économie française," *Annales historiques de la Révolution française,* 66, no. 272 (April/June 1988), 191.

208. Gilles Postel-Vinay, "A la recherche de la révolution économique dans les campagnes (1789–1815)," *Revue historique,* 40, no. 6 (November 1989), 1019.

209. See Chapter 4 for further discussion. For a negative view of the performance of the agricultural sector, see T. J. A. Le Goff and D. M. G. Sutherland, "The Revolution and the Rural Economy," in Alan Forrest and Peter Jones, eds., *Re-*

shaping France: Town, Country, and Region during the French Revolution (Manchester 1991), 52–85.

210. J. C. Toutain, *Le produit intérieur brut de la France de 1780 à 1982* (Paris, 1987); C.-E. Labrousse, *Esquisse du mouvement des prix et des revenus en France au XVIIIe siècle,* 2 vols. (Paris, 1984; orig. ed. 1933).

211. David R. Weir, "Les crises économiques et les origines de la Révolution," *Annales ESC,* 46, no. 4 (July/August 1991), 931.

212. Postel-Vinay, "La révolution économique," 1025.

213. Ibid., 1023. The rural population grew by 0.35 percent per annum, and the urban population fell by 0.31 percent per annum between 1790 and 1806.

214. French wages rates were 3 percent higher than British, on average, throughout the nineteenth century; see Patrick O'Brien and Caglar Keydar, *Economic Growth in France and Britain: 1780–1914* (London, 1978), 74.

215. Gérard Béaur, "La Révolution et la question agraire: Vieux problèmes et perspectives nouvelles," *Annales ESC,* 48, no. 1 (January/February 1993), 140.

216. Robert Duplessis, *Transitions to Capitalism in Early Modern Europe* (Cambridge, 1997), 170–171.

217. Maurice Agulhon, "L'essor de la paysannerie, 1789–1852," in Etienne Juillard, ed., *Histoire de la France rurale,* vol. 3, *Apogée et crise de la civilisation paysanne* (Paris, 1976), 14–175.

218. George W. Grantham, "The Diffusion of the New Husbandry in Northern France, 1815–1840," *Journal of Economic History,* 38, no. 2 (June 1978), 311–312.

219. On the centrality of agriculture to the early stages of French economic growth, see John Nye, "Changing French Trade Conditions, National Welfare, and the 1860 Anglo-French Treaty of Commerce," *Explorations in Economic History,* 28, no. 2 (1991), 460–477.

220. Jean-Laurent Rosenthal, *The Fruits of Revolution, Property Rights, Litigation, and French Agriculture, 1700–1860* (Cambridge, 1992), 52.

221. Judith Miller, *Mastering the Market: The State and the Grain Trade in Northern France, 1700–1860* (Cambridge, 1999).

222. Marc Bloch, *La lutte pour l'individualisme agraire au XVIIIe siècle* (Brionne, 1984; orig. ed. 1930), 511–527.

223. Postel-Vinay, "La révolution économique," 1018.

224. Philip T. Hoffman, *Growth in a Traditional Society: The French Countryside, 1450–1815* (Princeton, N.J., 1996), 72–73. This conclusion is supported by local studies: see Jonathan Dewald, *Pont Saint Pierre, 1398–1789: Lordship, Community, and Capitalism in Early Modern France* (Berkeley, Calif., 1987), 5.

225. Tessie P. Liu, *The Weaver's Knot: The Contradictions of Class Struggle and Family Solidarity in Western France, 1750–1914* (Ithaca, N.Y., 1994), 128–157.

226. Ibid., 231.

227. Roger Chartier, *The Cultural Origins of the French Revolution,* trans. Lydia Cochrane (Durham, N.C., 1991), 89.

4. Big Theories and Small Farms

1. Georges Lefebvre, *Les paysans du Nord pendant la Révolution française* (Bari, 1959), 531–550.
2. Georges Lefebvre, "The Place of the Revolution in the Agrarian History of France," in Robert Forster and Orest Ranum, eds., *Rural Society in France: Selections from the Annales, Economies, Sociétiés, Civilisations* (Baltimore, 1977), 37. For a critique of Lefebvre, see Hilton L. Root, "The Case against George Lefebvre's Peasant Revolution," *History Workshop*, 28 (1989), 88–102.
3. A. Ado, *The Peasant Movement in France during the Great Bourgeois Revolution of the End of the Eighteenth Century*, in Russian (Moscow, 1971). Albert Soboul, "A la lumière de la Révolution française: Problème paysan et révolution bourgeoise," in Soboul, *Problèmes paysans de la révolution, 1789–1848: Etudes d'histoire révolutionnaire* (Paris, 1983), 19.
4. Florence Gauthier, *La voie paysanne dans la Révolution française: L'exemple picard* (Paris, 1977).
5. Simon Schama, *Citizens: A Chronicle of the French Revolution* (New York, 1989), 322.
6. William Sewell, *Work and Revolution in France: The Language of Labour from the Old Regime to 1848* (Cambridge, 1980), 109–113; Richard M. Andrews, "The Justices of the Peace of Revolutionary Paris, September 1792–November 1794 (Frimaire Year III)," in Douglas Johnson, ed., *French Society and the Revolution* (Cambridge, 1976), 167–217. Of course, the notion that the sans-culottes had a moral economy consciousness predated revisionism; see George Rudé, *The Crowd in the French Revolution* (Oxford, 1959).
7. For Miller's account of the impediments to capitalist transformation of France, see Judith A. Miller, "Politics and Urban Provisioning Crises: Bakers, Police, and Parlements in France, 1750–1793," *Journal of Modern History*, 64, no. 2 (June 1992), 227–262.
8. François Crouzet, *Britain Ascendant: Comparative Studies in Franco-British Economic History*, trans. Martin Thom (Cambridge, 1990), specifically "England and France in the Eighteenth Century," 43.
9. René Sedillot, *Le coût de la Révolution française* (Paris, 1987), 245. Guy Lemarchand, "Du féodalisme au capitalisme: A propos des conséquences de la Révolution sur l'évolution de l'économie française," *Annales historiques de la Révolution française*, 60, 272 (1988), 196–201.
10. François Crouzet, "Wars, Blockade, and Economic Change in Europe, 1792–1815," in *Britain Ascendant*, pp. 295–317.
11. L. M. Cullen, "History, Economic Crises, and Revolution: Understanding Eighteenth-Century France," *Economic History Review*, 66, 4 (1993), 654–655. Cullen is a notable dissident from the pessimistic view of French economic history and denies the catastrophic nature of the Revolution.
12. For a good account of one such career, see Serge Chassange, *Oberkampf: Un en-*

trepreneur capitaliste au siècle des Lumières (Paris, 1980). For an argument that the military supply system was not a corrupt deformation of French economic life, see Howard G. Brown, "A Discredited Regime? The Directory and Army Contracting," *French History*, 4, 1 (1990), 48–76.

13. Florin Aftalion, *The French Revolution: An Economic Interpretation*, trans. Martin Thom (Cambridge, 1990).

14. On comparative tax rates in Britain and France, see Peter Mathias and Patrick O'Brien, "Tax in England and France, 1715–1810," *Journal of European Economic History*, 5 (1976), 601–650. On inflation and its effects, see François Crouzet, *La grande inflation: La monnaie en France de Louis XVI à Napoléon* (Paris, 1993).

15. Patrick O'Brien and Caglar Keydar, *Economic Growth in Britain and France: 1780–1914* (London, 1978), 12.

16. Eugene Nelson White, "The French Revolution and the Politics of Government Finance, 1770–1815," *Journal of Economic History*, 55, no. 2 (June 1995), 240. For a critique of an economistic approach to understanding the Revolution, see David R. Weir, "Les crises économiques et les origines de la Révolution française," *Annales ESC*, 46, no. 4 (July–August 1991), 917–947.

17. Michael Sonenscher, "The Nation's Debt and the Birth of the Modern Republic: The French Fiscal Deficit and the Politics of the Revolution of 1789," *History of Political Thought*, 18, no. 1 (Spring 1997), 64–103, 18, no. 2 (Summer 1997), 267–325. For a similar argument outlining the rationality of the debt debate, see Kathryn Norberg, "The Fiscal Crisis of 1788 and the Financial Origins of the Revolution of 1789," in Philip T. Hoffman and Kathryn Norberg, eds., *Fiscal Crises, Liberty, and Representative Government, 1450–1789* (Stanford, Calif., 1994), 253–298.

18. The model for this approach is Charles Sabel and Jonathan Zeitlin, "Historical Alternatives to Mass Production: Politics, Markets, and Technology in Nineteenth-Century Industrialisation," *Past and Present*, 108 (August 1985), 133–176. Works that explore the history of economic institutions from this perspective include Jean-Laurent Rosenthal, *The Fruits of Revolution: Property Rights, Litigation, and French Agriculture, 1700–1860* (Cambridge, 1992); William R. Reddy, *The Rise of Market Culture: The Textile Trade and French Society, 1750–1900* (Cambridge, 1984); Michael Sonenscher, *Work and Wages: Natural Law, Politics, and the Eighteenth-Century Trades* (Cambridge, 1989); Thomas L. Haskell and Richard F. Teichgraeber III, *The Culture of the Market: Historical Essays* (Cambridge 1993).

19. O'Brien and Keydar, *Economic Growth*, 23.

20. For a good example of what is gained from this approach, see Philip T. Hoffmann, "Institutions and Agriculture in Old Regime France," *Politics and Society*, 16, nos. 2–3, (September 1988), 241–264.

21. The institutional approach to an understanding of *partage* has been pioneered by Kathryn Norberg, "Dividing up the Commons: Institutional Change in Rural France, 1789–1799," *Politics and Society*, 16, no. 2 (1988) 265–286, and

Philip T. Hoffman, *Growth in a Traditional Society: The French Countryside, 1450–1815* (Princeton, N.J., 1996), 26–77.

22. For an overview, see Nadine Vivier, *Propriété collective et identité communale: Les biens communaux en France, 1750–1914* (Paris, 1998).

23. Norberg, "Dividing the Commons"; Florence Gauthier, *La voie paysanne dans la Révolution française: L'exemple picard* (Paris, 1977).

24. Peter Jones's work on *partage* has opened up the possibility of the kind of analysis presented here. See Jones, "Agrarian Radicalism during the French Revolution," in Alan Forrest and Peter Jones, eds., *Reshaping France: Town, Country, and Region during the French Revolution* (Manchester, 1991), 137–152; Jones, "The 'Agrarian Law': Schemes for Land Redistribution during the French Revolution," *Past and Present*, 133 (1991), 96–133.

25. Jones, "Agrarian Radicalism," 147.

26. The petitions analyzed in this chapter are found in AN, F10 series, boxes 228, 229, 330, 331, 332, 333a, 333b, 334a, 334b, 247, 248, 249, 270, 271.

27. For an analysis of the effect of the Revolution on rural France along these lines, see John Markoff, "Violence, Emancipation, and Democracy: The Countryside in the French Revolution," *American Historical Review*, 100 (1995).

28. Roger Chartier, "Figures of the 'Other': Peasant Reading in the Age of the Enlightenment," in Chartier, *Cultural History: Between Practices and Representations*, trans. Lydia Cochrane (Ithaca, N.Y., 1988), 153–155. For the longer-term "apprenticeship to national politics," see Roger Chartier, *The Cultural Origins of the French Revolution*, trans. Lydia Cochrane (Durham, N.C., 1991), 145–151.

29. For some insightful remarks on the generation of the idea of interest, see William Scott, "The Pursuit of 'Interests' in the French Revolution: A Preliminary Survey," *French Historical Studies*, 19, no. 3 (Spring 1996), 811–851.

30. A. J. R. Turgot, "Réflexions sur la formation et la distribution des richesses," in Turgot, *Oeuvres*, vol. 5, ed. Dupont de Nemours (Paris 1808), 71.

31. Arthur Young, *Travels in France during the Years 1787, 1788, and 1789*, ed. Constantia Maxwell (Cambridge, 1929), 279.

32. John Markoff, *The Abolition of Feudalism: Peasants, Lords, and Legislators in the French Revolution* (University Park, Pa., 1996), 53.

33. Philippe Steiner differentiates between four orders of economic rationality in this period: that of the *savants*, the administrators, the merchants, and the producers. The developmental approach was that of the *savants*. See Philippe Steiner, *Sociologie de la connaissance économique: Essai sur les rationalisations de la connaissance économique (1750–1850)* (Paris, 1998), 70–79.

34. Hilton L. Root, *The Fountain of Privilege: Political Foundations of Markets in Old Regime France and England* (Berkeley, Calif., 1994), 8.

35. Denis Diderot, "Apologie de l'Abbé Galiani," in, Diderot, *Oeuvres politiques*, ed. Paul Vernière (Paris 1963), 80.

36. For the details of the legislation on this issue, see Peter M. Jones, *The Peasantry in the French Revolution* (Cambridge, 1988), 137–166. Forty-one departmental

replies and another sixty-four responses from communal and district administrations are analyzed in this section.

37. Gauthier, *La voie paysanne*, 65.

38. Markoff, *The Abolition of Feudalism.*

39. AN, F10 330, Haut-Rhin, 28 November 1791; Seine-et-Marne, 14 December 1791; Jura, 14 December 1791; Meurthe, 19 December 1791; Seine-Inférieure, 28 December 1791; Hautes-Alpes, 31 March 1792: Var, 16 December 1791.

40. Of the forty-seven replies, twenty-six supported at least the principle, and twenty-one were against even in principle.

41. One should use the term "moral economy" with care. As its coiner, E. P. Thompson, has pointed out, the polarity of moral and political economy can often misrepresent the complexity of particular contexts: "The Moral Economy Revisited," in Thompson, *Customs in Common* (London, 1991), 269–271.

42. AN, F10 330, Ariège, 29 December 1791; Oise, 3 March 1792; Aube, 30 March 1792; Gers, 31 March 1792; Nièvre, 11 April 1792; Haute-Garonne, 27 April 1791; Haute-Saône, 24 March 1792; Loiret, 24 March 1792; Basses-Pyrénées, 27 March 1792.

43. AN, F10 330, 15 December 1790.

44. AN, F10 330, 27 March 1793. In March and April 1792 similar concerns were voiced by the departmental authorities of the Aube, Maine-et-Loire, Morbihan, Drôme, and Somme.

45. See Hilton L. Root, *Peasants and King in Burgundy: Agrarian Foundations of French Absolutism* (Berkeley, Calif., 1987), 155–204.

46. AN, F10 330, 28 November 1790.

47. AN, F10 330, 9 September 1792.

48. AN, F10 330, Ardeche, 18 December 1791; Haute-Vienne, 30 December 1792; Mayenne, 6 April 1792; Rhône-et-Loire, 25 May 1792.

49. AN, F10 330, Ariège, 29 December 1790; Cantal, 20 January 1792; Charente, 24 March 1792; Creuse, 26 June 1792; Landes, 28 July 1792.

50. AN, F10 330, 1 February 1792.

51. AN, F10 330, Jura, 14 December 1791; Ardeche, 18 December 1791; Lot, 28 December 1791; Marne, 28 March 1792.

52. AN, F10 332, Manche, 3 May 1792. This supports William Scott's argument that "classic" liberalism was discredited before the Revolution. See Scott, "The Pursuit of 'Interests' in the French Revolution: A Preliminary Survey," *French Historical Studies*, 19, no. 3 (Spring, 1996), 815.

53. For examples, see petitions concerned with the tax base in AN, F10 330, from La Morlaye (Oise), 17 February 1791; Beauregard (Tarn-et-Garonne), 24 January 1791; Saint Froget (Tarn-et-Garonne), 6 January 1790; Vassens (Aisne), 24 April 1791; Saint Omer (Pas-de-Calais), 22 March 1792; petitions using moral economy vocabulary from Saponay (Aisne), 4 January 1791; Dornas (Ardeche), 2 August 1790; Baumes (Drôme), 9 July 1790; Cherbourg (Manche), 23 April 1792; petitions using the idea of maintenance of production from Monvalent (Dordogne), 6 April 1791; Vassens (Oise), 24 April 1790;

Evreux (Eure), 12 June 1792; Beuveille (Moselle), 14 April 1790; Pontpoint (Oise), 1 January 1792; Longwy (Moselle), 3 April 1791.

54. AN, F10 332, Leaz (Ain), 27 April 1792; Guemont (Haute-Marne), 16 March 1792; Doubs, 6 March 1791.

55. AN, F10 332, Montcornet sur Serre, 15 September 1790.

56. AN, F10 332, Roquefort (Aveyron), 10 January 1791.

57. AN, F10 332, Saint Sever Cap (Landes), 25 May 1791. This commune was particularly affected by *partage*. The idea was heavily contested by large farmers (F10 333a, 1 January 1792), and even when the commune forced through the measure large landowners tried to stifle its effects by buying up the small lots and enclosing them (F10 330, Gros, undated).

58. AN, F10 332, Chopin (Ardennes), 12 October 1790.

59. AN, F10 332, Buffon (Côte d'Or), 23 August 1790; F10 330, Paris (Seine), 31 March 1792. It is interesting to note that Paris was considerably less inclined toward modernizing than most areas in its hinterland.

60. Other communities that made similar claims in this early debate were AN, F10 332, Cambronne (Oise), 9 August 1790; Anthieux and Tourville (Seine-Inférieure), 28 January 1792; Glos and Saint Martin (Calvados), 30 September 1790.

61. Northern departments with above average agricultural productivity (above 11.5 quintals to the hectare) were Nord, Pas-de-Calais, Somme, Aisne, Manche Calvados, Eure, Seine-Inférieure, Oise, Seine-et-Oise, Seine, Seine-et-Marne. Southern departments with above average surface area sown (above 26 percent of workable land) and average or worse productivity were Lot et Garonne, Landes, Gers, Basses-Pyrénées, Hautes-Pyrénées, Haute-Garonne, Ariège, Dordogne, Lot, Tarn. Figures from Gérard Béaur, Philipe Minard, and Alexandra Laclau, eds., *Atlas de la Révolution française,* vol. 10, *Economie* (Paris, 1997), 62. These are also the regions studied by Kathryn Norberg.

62. The Basses-Pyrénées, Landes, Lot, Haute-Garonne, and Gers were the departments where both these conditions were present. For the extent of sharecropping, see Béaur, Minard, and Laclau, *Economie,* 54–55. For the extent of dispute in the sharecropping zone, see Jones, *The Peasantry in the French Revolution,* 101.

63. See Hoffman, *Growth in a Traditional Society,* 60–77, for an analysis of the economic rationality of sharecropping in a rural world organized around local, imperfect markets.

64. Béaur, Minard, and Laclau, *Economie,* 33.

65. Hoffman argues that autarky demanded between five and ten hectares depending on soil quality. However, he also points out that since we do not know exactly how much land was worked by subsistence farmers, we are also ignorant of their dependence on labor markets. See *Growth in a Traditional Society,* 39.

66. AN, F10 332, Saint Porquier (Haute-Garonne), 12 December 1792.

67. AN, F10 330, Pontac (Basses-Pyrénées) 17 June 1790; F10 329, Mont de Mersan (Landes), 14 February 1793. *Partage* continued to be a live issue in

Pontac, where administrators followed up the first petition with a second, F10 332, 8 December 1792.

68. Mont de Mersan (Landes), 15 December 1790. The department repeated its request on 28 July 1792.

69. Bressel (Haute-Gironde), 19 October 1792.

70. Gondrin (Gers), 16 November 1792.

71. Saint Sever (Landes), 25 May 1791.

72. AN, F10 330, Saint Jory (Haute-Garonne), 5 January 1793.

73. Gers, 31 March 1792.

74. Pau (Basses-Pyrénées), 27 March 1792.

75. The eight edicts allowing *partage* were 1769 (Trois Evéchés), 1771 (Lorraine, Auch, and Pau), 1774 (Bourgogne, Alsace), 1777 (Flanders), 1779 (Artois), 1781 (Cambrésis).

76. Gauthier, *La voie paysanne dans la Révolution française,* 140–142.

77. Early petitions from northern departments demanding reintegration of common lands came from AN, F10 331, Cambronne (Oise), 9 July 1790; Varses (Seine-et-Marne), 10 April 1790; Ivy (Seine-et-Oise), 29 July 1790; Barou (Oise), 2 February 1790; Saint Pathus (Seine-et-Marne), 29 June 1792; Beauserre (Oise), 1 September 1792; Velaune (Seine-et-Oise), 1 October 1792; Mandeville (Calvados), 11 February 1792; Aouzy (Calvados), 20 March 1792; Lequille (Aisne), 3 April 1792; Amiens (Somme), 6 April 1792; Offoy (Somme), 15 April 1792; Hermival (Calvados), 24 August 1792.

78. AN, F10 330, Coulonbiers (Calvados), 1 January 1792.

79. AN, F10 330, Pontpoint (Oise), 6 November 1791.

80. AN, F10 330, Pontpoint (Oise), 11 November 1791.

81. Note also the disproportionate literacy of some of the departments concerned. See the charts in Dominique Julia, Serge Bonin, and Claude Langlois, eds., *Atlas de la Révolution française,* vol. 2, *L'enseignement, 1760–1815* (Paris, 1987), 12.

82. AN, F10 332, Annet sur Marne (Seine-et-Marne), 10 May 1790.

83. AN, F10 330, Beauvais (Oise), 3 March 1792.

84. AN, F10 330, Ronquerolle (Seine-et-Oise), 12 June 1792.

85. For examples see AN, F10 332, Prouche (Somme), 5 November 1791; F10 330, Neuil Aubry (Seine-et-Oise), 22 October 1790, and Beauvais (Eure), 5 February 1791.

86. AN, F10 330, Saint Omer (Pas-de-Calais), 7 January 1792.

87. AN, F10 333a, Conseil Général (Seine-Inférieure), 28 December 1791; Rouen (Seine-Inférieure), 12 January 1792; Pas-de-Calais, 22 March 1792.

88. AN, F10 332, Vassens (Aisne), 24 April 1791.

89. AN, F10 332, Marchienne (Nord), 11 December 1790.

90. AN, F10 333a, Longuet, Caen (Calvados), 1 November 1792.

91. AN, F10 333a, Avranches (Manche), 23 April 1792, 24 June 1792.

92. For a discussion of this policy, see P. M. Jones, "The 'Agrarian Law': Schemes for Land Redistribution during the French Revolution," *Past and Present,* 133 (1991), 105.

93. AN, F10 329, Montdragon (Drôme), 26 February 1793.

94. Eugene White analyzes the politics of fiscal reform in the same way in "The French Revolution and the Politics of Government Finance, 1770–1815," *Journal of Economic History,* 55, no. 2 (June 1995), 241–244.

95. For examples, see AN, F10 330, Aisne, 19 November 1792, or F10 333a, Gard, 11 December 1792. For communes, see AN, F10 330, Châteaudouble (Var), 6 January 1793; for Jacobins, F10 333a, Ners (Gard), 13 December 1792, or the collective petition of the clubs of the Basses-Alpes, F10 329, 7 March 1793. For the *société populaire,* see AN, F10 330, Connaux (Gard), 8 January 1793.

96. AN, F10 333, undated (late 1792).

97. AN, F10 330, Montigny (Seine-et-Marne), 23 December 1792.

98. AN, F10 329, Nîmes (Gard), 7 March 1793.

99. AN, F10 329, Saint Hilaire (Allier), 16 May 1793.

100. AN, F10 329, Epinal (Vosges), 12 January 1793.

101. AN, F10 329, Larrey (Côte-d'Or), 4 January 1793.

102. AN, F10 330, Legrand (Aveyron), 20 January 1793.

103. AN, F10 333a, Harcourt (Eure), 1 January 1793.

104. AN, F10 330, Andelys (Eure), 9 December 1792; F10 329, Charres (Seine-et-Oise), 16 March 1793.

105. AN, F10 329, Langry (Oise), 12 April 1793.

106. AN, F10 330, Donjon (Allier), 22 March 1793.

107. AN, F10 329, Paris (Seine), 9 April 1793.

108. AN, F10 329, Marly sous Marle (Ain), 17 December 1792; Courchaton (Haute-Saône), 14 February 1793; Quevauvilliers (Somme), 14 May 1793.

109. R. B. Rose, "The 'Red Scare' of the 1790s: The French Revolution and the 'Agrarian Law,'" *Past and Present,* 103 (May 1984), 113.

110. AN, F10 330, Valence (Drôme), 27 March 1792.

111. The campaign spilled over into the Bouches du Rhône, which was otherwise resistant to *partage.* Norberg, "Dividing Up the Commons," 271.

112. On the politicization of this department, see Anne-Marie Duport, *Journées révolutionnaires à Nîmes* (Nîmes, 1988).

113. AN, F10 333a, Uzès (Gard), 19 February 1793.

114. AN, F10 329, Louveze (Drôme), 23 February 1793; Suze la Rousse, 24 February 1793; Allan, 25 February 1793; Montdragon, 26 February 1793; Canart, 26 February 1793; Saint Cicile, 27 February 1793; Saint Paul en Chaux, 28 February 1793; Rochejude, 18 February 1793; Bouchet, 28 February 1792.

115. AN, F10 333b, Valance (Drôme), 26 January 1794.

116. AN, F10 333a, Ners (Gard), 13 December 1792; group petition (Maine-et-Loire), 20 December 1792; La Roque de l'Albère (Pyrénées-Orientales), 12 January 1793.

117. Jean-Pierre Gross, *Fair Shares for All: Jacobin Egalitarianism in Practice* (Cambridge, 1997), 96.

118. AN, F10 329, Bordeaux (Gironde), 17 March 1793; petition addressed from Friends of Liberty and the Constitution.

119. AN, F10 329, Paris (Seine), 9 April 1793. For an analysis of the conflicting imperatives that created this kind of systematic suspicion, see Patrice Higonnet, *Class, Ideology, and the Rights of Nobles in the French Revolution* (Oxford, 1987).

120. AN, F10 333a, Louhaus (Saône-et-Loire), 10 December 1792.

121. AN, F10 329, Saint George (Rhône-et-Loire), 21 March 1793.

122. Jones, "Agrarian Law," 110–113.

123. Jean-Laurent Rosenthal argues that the revolutionaries rationalized rights to water usage and transport in the same way. See Rosenthal, *The Fruits of Revolution: Property Rights, Litigation, and French Agriculture, 1700–1860* (Cambridge, 1992), 52.

124. Lefebvre, *Paysans du Nord,* 544–545.

125. Gauthier, *La voie paysanne dans la Révolution française,* 192–202; G.-R. Ikni, "Recherches sur la propriété foncière: Problèmes théoriques et méthode," *Annales historiques de la Révolution française,* 52 (1980), 390–424.

126. AN, F10 333a, Nesles le Repos (Marne), 13 December 1793; Villeneuve (Jura), 1 November 1793; Bordeaux (Gironde), 22 December 1793; Châteauroux (Indre), 10 Nivôse, Year II; Neusarverden (Bas-Rhin), 5 Pluviôse, Year II; Caen (Calvados), 6 Ventôse, Year II; Sarreguemines (Moselle), 9 Ventôse, Year II; Montaut (Basses-Pyrénées), n.d.; Nancy (Meurthe), 30 Messidor, Year II; Bucey (Aube), 24 Vendémiaire, Year II.

127. Jones, *The Peasantry in the French Revolution,* 148–149.

128. Vivier, *Propriété collective et identité communale,* 127–128.

129. AN, F10 333b, Ardèche, 19 Germinal 2.

130. Lefebvre, *Paysans du Nord,* 548–550.

131. AN, F10 333a, Chandessignes (Cantal), 17 July 1793; Tatonville (Meurthe), 18 July 1793; Charroux (Allier), 15 August 1793; Graignes (Manche), 30 August 1793; Gouraimient (Meuse), 1 September 1793.

132. AN, F10 329, Grey (Calvados), 30 August 1793.

133. AN, F10 333b, Vire (Calvados), 15 January 1794; F10 329, Bucey (Aube), 29 September 1794.

134. The evidence presented by scholars such as Higonnet and Gross that local Jacobins in some parts of France retained their ability to mediate the demands of politics on the complexity of local societies does not amount to a reversal of the general trend.

135. AN, F10 333b, undated [early 1795] (Creuse); F10 329, 17 Floréal, Year III [6 May 1795], Fontenay (Eure-et-Loire); F10 329, 21 Floréal, Year III [10 May 1795], Dorat (Haute-Vienne); F10 329, 22 Floréal, Year III [11 May 1795], Roueux (Vosges); F10 329, 25 Messidor, Year III [13 July 1795], Bayeux (Calvados).

136. AN, F10 329, 29 Pluviôse, Year IV [17 February 1796], Grais (Orne); F10 329, 6 Ventôse, Year IV [24 February 1796], Aigurande (Indre).

137. AN, F10 329, 25 Messidor, Year III [13 July 1795], Magnac (Haute-Vienne).

138. AN, F10 329, 11 Pluviôse, Year IV [30 January 1796], Saint Vincent (Dordogne).

139. For the debate on forced arbitration, see *Procès-verbal des 500,* vol. 2, p. 169, 12 Nivôse, Year IV; vol. 4, p. 581, 30 Ventôse, Year IV; vol. 7, p. 111, 6 Prairial, Year IV.

140. J. Ph. Garran-Coulon, *Conseil des cinq-cents: Rapport sur les biens communaux, fait, au nom du comité de législation, par J. Ph. Garran, député du Loiret; Imprimé par ordre de la Convention nationale, et réimprimé par ordre du Conseil des cinq-cents* (Paris, Year IV).

141. Ibid., 7.

142. Ibid., 14.

143. Ibid., 21, 26, 31.

144. The village of Bourg d'Oyzan tried to claim a portion of the common, which it argued had been alienated by the seigneur in 1265. AN, F10 334b, Bourg d'Oyzan (Isère), 25 Prairial, Year V [17 February 1797].

145. *Procès-verbal des 500,* vol. 7, p. 343, 20 Prairial, Year IV.

146. AN, F10 334a, Sauverney (Creuse), 3 Floréal, Year IV [22 April 1796].

147. AN, F10 334a, Aveline (Calvados), 3 jour complémentaire, Year IV [19 September 1796]; Aigueperse (Puy de Dome), 7 Vendémiaire, Year V [18 October 1796]; Ros-Landrieux (Indre), Year VI.

148. AN, F10 334b, Sansproux (Pas-de-Calais), 12 Ventôse, Year IV [2 March 1796]. Petitions seeking definitive title include Argennes (Calvados), 5 Messidor, Year IV [23 June 1796]; Rosières (Aisne), 14 Thermidor, Year IV [12 July 1796]; Mont Saint Vincent (Saône-et-Loire), 4 Vendémiaire, Year V [25 September 1796]; Gurie (Allier), 15 Ventôse, Year V [5 March 1797]; Chaussée (Marne), 27 Fructidor, Year V [13 September 1797]; Demandoulx (Basses-Alpes), 30 Fructidor, Year V [16 September 1797].

149. AN, F10 334a, "Question relative à l'exécution de l'article 12 de la loi du 10 juin 1793, concernant le mode de partage de biens communaux et du décret du 8 août 1793 intervenu relativement à cet article."

150. Jean-Philippe Garran-Coulon, *Nouvelle rédaction du projet de résolution rélatif aux biens communaux, proposé au nom de la commission* (Paris, Year IV), articles 2, 3, and 5.

151. Jean-François Barailon, *Opinion de Jean-François Barailon, député par le département de la Creuse, sur la loi du 10 juin 1793, relative au mode de partage des communaux, séance du 26 fructidor an IV* (Paris, Year IV), 2.

152. François Rivaud, *Observations sur le partage des biens communaux, la loi du 10 juin 1793, et le projet de résolution présenté par Garran-Coulon, par F. Rivaud, membre du Conseil des cinq-cents* (Paris, Year IV), 4.

153. Ibid., 15–22.

154. *Procès-verbal des 500,* vol. 10, pp. 500–506, 26 Fructidor, Year IV.

155. For a petition pointing this out, see AN, F10 334a, Doubs, 20 Pluviôse, Year V [8 February 1797].

156. *Procès-verbal des 500,* vol. 19, pp. 430–431, 15 Prairial, Year V.

157. Ibid., vol. 10, p. 502, 26 Fructidor, Year IV.

158. The three readings of the bill were ibid., vol. 21, p. 319, 15 Thermidor, Year V;

vol. 22, pt. 1, p. 251, 11 Fructidor, Year V; vol. 25, pp. 309–361, 19 Frimaire, Year VI.

159. Cabanis, *Opinion de Cabanis, contre le projet de partage des biens communaux* (Paris, Year VII), 6.

160. AN, F10 334b, Schlestatt (Bas-Rhin), 30 Fructidor, Year IV [16 September 1796].

161. AN, F10 334b, Souterraine (Creuse), 12 Germinal, Year V [April 1 1797]; F10 333b, Meurthe, 25 Messidor, Year VI [14 July 1798].

162. AN, F10 334a, Paris (Seine), 23 Brumaire, Year V [13 November 1796].

163. *Procès-verbaux du Conseil des cinq-cents*, vol. 24, p. 439. Antoine-François Delpierre, *Opinion de Delpierre, député par le département des Vosges, sur la demande en rapport de la loi du 10 juin 1793, qui a permis la partage des communaux, et sur le projet de lui subsister un autre mode de partage, fondé sur la différence des fortunes, séance du 19 frimaire an 6* (Paris, Year VI).

164. *Procès-verbal des 500*, vol. 25, p. 309, 19 Frimaire, Year VI.

165. *Opinion de Delpierre*, 1–2.

166. *Communaux* were the true commons from which any villager could take what resources they chose and on which they could run as many beasts as they had. *Parcours* was the seasonal right to pasture on the stubble of the tilled fields and was strictly proportional to the land held by a household.

167. *Opinion de Delpierre*, 13.

168. Ibid.

169. Ibid., 16.

170. The polarity is a dangerous one, and E. P. Thompson, who introduced it to historical debate, has warned against its overuse: see Thompson, "The Moral Economy Revisited," in his *Customs in Common* (Harmondsworth, 1991), 269–271. The term "moral economy" was coined by Richard Southey, who used it in rejecting radicalism in favor of paternalism: see Donald Winch, *Riches and Poverty: An Intellectual History of Political Economy in Britain, 1750–1834* (Cambridge, 1996), 5.

171. Thomas Paine, *Agrarian Justice Opposed to Agrarian Law and to Agrarian Monopoly; Being a Plan for Meliorating the Condition of Man by Creating in Every Nation a National Fund* (Cork, 1797); John Thelwall, *The Rights of Nature, against the Usurpation of Establishments; A Series of Letters to the People of Britain, on the State of Public Affairs and the Recent Effusions of the Right Honorable Edmund Burke*, 2 vols. (London, 1796).

172. Antoine-François Delpierre, *Conseil des cinq-cents: Analyse des motifs principaux qui ont dicté le projet de résolution sur l'emploi des biens communaux, au nom d'une commission spéciale, séance du 9 nivôse an 7* (Paris, Year VII), 2.

173. Antoine-François Delpierre, *Conseil des cinq-cents: Rapport au nom d'une commission spéciale sur les avantages qui résulteront de la conversion des biens communaux en propriétés privées, par l'amélioration du sort des indigents, la tranquillité des communes, et la moralité de leurs habitants; pour le perfectionnement de l'agriculture, la diminution de l'impôt foncier, l'extermination du vagabondage et de la mendicité, séance du 29 prairial an 6* (Paris, Year VI), 8.

174. Ibid., 13–14.

175. Conscription of soldiers and a shortage of workers provoked many landowners to demand that the Ministry of the Interior regulate wages; see AN, F10 245 [unfolioed], "Rabier aux citoyens composant le Directoire exécutif, 11 floréal an VII," for an example. In the margins of a petition entitled *Rapport analytique présenté au ministre de l'intérieur: Le Citoyen Dudevant, de la Société des arts et sciences de Bordeaux, demeurant à La Roque près Castel-Jaloux, envoyé au ministre, quelque réflexions sur les causes de la dégradation de l'agriculture de son pays,* which complained of this shortage of labor, Minister François de Neufchâteau remarked that only an end to the war and the release of labor from the army could do anything about it.

176. Delpierre, *Procès-verbal des 500,* 19 Frimaire, Year VI, 11; 29 Prairial, Year VI, 11; 9 Nivôse, Year VII, 6.

177. Perrin (de la Gironde), *Conseil des cinq-cents: Opinion de Perrin (de la Gironde) sur le partage des biens communaux, séance du 23 nivôse an 7* (Paris, Year VII), 2. For another speech in total accord with Delpierre's views, see Houssert, *Conseil des cinq-cents: Opinion de Houssert, sur l'emploi des biens communaux, séance du 22 nivôse an 7* (Paris, Year VII), and Heurtault-Lamerville, *Conseil des cinq-cents: Opinion de Heurtault-Lamerville, député du Cher, sur le partage des communaux, séance du 3 pluviôse an 7* (Paris, Year VII).

178. Mansord, *Opinion de Mansord (du Mont Blanc) sur le partage des communaux, séance du 9 nivôse an 7* (Paris, Year VII), 10. See also Perrin's opinion, cited in previous note, 12.

179. Bergier, *Conseil des cinq-cents: Opinion de Berger, sur le projet de résolution proposé par la commission concernant le partage des biens communaux, séance du 28 nivôse an 7* (Paris, Year VII), 5–10; Cunier, *Opinion de Cunier (du Bas-Rhin), contre la conversion forcée, générale et définitive des biens communaux en propriétés privées, séance du 3 pluviôse an 7* (Paris, Year VII), 8.

180. Trumeau, *Conseil des cinq-cents: Opinion de Trumeau, contre le partage forcé des communes, séance du 9 nivôse an VII* (Paris, Year VII), 6–7.

181. See Nicolas-Louis François de Neufchâteau, *Des améliorations dont la paix doit être l'époque* (Epinal, Year V) and *Arrêté de l'administration centrale du département des Vosges, pour parvenir à la fondation de trois nouveaux villages* (Epinal, Year V). For Delpierre and François de Neufchâteau's collaboration under Napoleon, see Antoine François Delpierre, *Tribunat—Discours prononcé par le Citoyen Delpierre, en présentant un ouvrage de Citoyen François (de Neufchâteau) intitulé: Tableau des vues que se propose la politique anglaise dans toutes les parties du monde* (Paris, Year XII).

182. AN, 27 AP2, dossier 2. The refusal of the parlement at Nancy to register the royal *arrêt* allowing partition, and the subsequent exercise of hunting rights on what were plowed and planted fields became a cause célèbre. For an account of the political problems the measure occasioned in Burgundy, see Hilton L. Root, *Peasants and the King in Burgundy: The Foundations of Rural Absolutism* (Berkeley, Calif., 1987), 109–150.

183. AN, F10 334b, Mandre (Meurthe), 15 Pluviôse, Year V [3 February 1797]; F10

334a, Grenade (Haute-Garonne), 15 Ventôse, Year VI [5 March 1798]; F10 334b, Genainville (Seine-et-Oise), 3 Nivôse, Year VI [23 December 1798].

184. AN, F10 334b, Saint Quentin (Pas-de-Calais), 19 Prairial, Year VI [7 June 1798].

185. AN, F10 334b, Genainville (Seine-et-Oise), 3 Nivôse, Year VI [23 December 1798].

186. AN, F10 334b, Rousillon (Isère), 18 Nivôse, Year VI [7 January 1798].

187. AN, F10 334a, Bressols (Haute-Garonne), 1 Thermidor, Year VI [19 July 1798].

188. AN, F10 334b, Ferte (Seine-Inférieure), 20 Pluviôse, Year VI [8 February 1798].

189. AN, F10 334a, Denis le fermant (Eure), 15 Nivôse, Year VI [4 January 1798]; F10 334a, Miserande (Gers), 27 Nivôse, Year VI [16 January 1798]; F10 334b, Ferte (Seine-Inférieure), 15 Ventôse, Year VI [5 March 1798]; F10 334b, Departmental Administration (Mont Terrible), 7 Floréal, Year VI [26 April 1798]; F10 334b, Celier (Loire-Inférieure), 16 Floréal, Year VI [5 May 1798]; F10 334b, Lessieux (Isère), 7 Thermidor, Year VI [25 July 1798]; F10 334a, Landricourt (Aisne), 3 Fructidor, Year VI [20 August 1798]; F10 334a, Bourges les Bains (Allier), 6 Germinal, Year VII [26 March 1799]; F10 334b, Henneveux (Pas-de-Calais), 13 Germinal, Year VII [2 April 1799].

190. AN, F10 334a, Montagne (Basses-Alpes), 3 Germinal, Year VI [23 March 1798]; F10 334a, Moutel (Gard), 14 Fructidor, Year VI [31 September 1798].

191. AN, F10 334, Gasny (Eure), 3 Nivôse, Year VI [26 December 1797].

192. AN, F10 334a, Saint Laurent Daigon (Gard), 26 Frimaire, Year VI [18 December 1797].

193. AN, 284 AP 16, dossier 5, Benjamin Constant to the Directeurs [19 Brumaire, Year VIII].

194. See Béaur, Minard, and Laclau, *Economie*, 47.

195. Seymour Martin Lipset, *Political Man: The Social Bases of Politics* (Baltimore, 1981; orig. ed. 1959), 31. See also Larry Diamond, "Economic Development and Democracy Reconsidered," in Gary Marks and Larry Jay Diamond, eds., *Re-examining Democracy: Essays in Honor of Seymour Martin Lipset* (Newbury Park, Calif., 1992), 93–139.

196. Seymour Martin Lipset, "The Social Requisites of Democracy Reconsidered," *American Sociological Review*, 59, no. 1 (February 1994), 2.

197. Dietrich Rueschmeyer, Evelyne Huber Stephens, and John D. Stephens, *Capitalist Development and Democracy* (Chicago, 1992), 271.

198. Tom Garvin, *1922: The Birth of Irish Democracy* (New York, 1996), 191.

199. Arthur O'Connor, *A Letter from General Arthur Condorcet-O'Connor to General Lafayette on the Causes Which Have Deprived France of the Advantages of the Revolution of 1830* (London, 1831), 22.

200. Hilton L. Root, *The Fountain of Privilege: Political Foundations of Markets in Old Regime France and England* (Berkeley, Calif., 1994), 8.

201. This was the structural problem of all absolutist states; see Thomas Ertman, *Birth of the Leviathan: Building States and Regimes in Medieval and Early Modern Europe* (Cambridge, 1997), 139–151.

202. On the social innovations among the French subaltern classes in the eighteenth century, see Michael Sonenscher, *Work and Wages: Natural Law, Politics, and Eighteenth-Century French Trades* (Cambridge, 1988); David Garrioch, *Neighbourhood and Community in Paris, 1760–1790* (Cambridge, 1986), esp. 116–122. For the change in the repertoire of even the subsistence rioter, see Cynthia A Bouton, *The Flour War: Gender, Class, and Community in Late Ancien Régime French Society* (University Park, Pa., 1993), esp. 251–261. For an argument that subaltern consciousness remained corporatist until much later, see William Sewell, *Work and Revolution in France: The Language of Labor from the Old Regime to 1848* (Cambridge, 1980).

203. Amartya Sen, "Moral Codes and Economic Success," Development Economics Research Programme Discussion Paper 49, London School of Economics (October 1993), 12–16.

204. For his discussion of the idea of utility as an explanatory category, see Amartya Sen, *Inequality Reexamined* (Oxford, 1992).

205. William M. Reddy, *The Rise of Market Culture: The Textile Trade and French Society, 1750–1900* (Cambridge, 1984), 22.

206. Charles Sabel and Jonathan Zeitlin, "Historical Alternatives to Mass Production: Politics, Markets, and Technology in Nineteenth-Century Industrialisation," *Past and Present,* 108 (August 1985), 134.

5. Learning to Be Free

1. AN, F17 1338, "Le ministre de l'intérieur aux professeurs et bibliothécaires des écoles centrales," 20 Fructidor, Year V.

2. For an account of Talleyrand's report, see R. R. Palmer, *The Improvement of Humanity: Education and the French Revolution* (Princeton, N.J., 1985), 94–101.

3. Jean-Antoine Nicolas de Caritat, Marquis de Condorcet, "Premier mémoire: Nature et objet de l'instruction publique," in Charles Coustel and Catherine Kintzler, eds., *Ecrits sur l'instruction publique,* 2 vols. (Paris, 1989), 1:45.

4. Ibid., 35.

5. For a discussion of one development of this paradox in Condorcet's thought, see Lucien Gillard, "Condorcet, deux autres paradoxes," *Annales HSS,* 1 (January–February 1996), 201–214. For a full discussion of the theme, see Keith Michael Baker, *Condorcet: From Natural Philosophy to Social Mathematics* (Chicago, Ill., 1975). For Condorcet's definitive statement of the problem as applied to elections, see "Sur les élections," *Journal d'instruction sociale,* 1 (1 June 1793), 25–32.

6. Condorcet, "Rapport et projet de décret sur l'organisation générale de l'instruction publique, présentés à l'Assemblée nationale sous nom du comité d'instruction publique les 20 et 21 avril 1792," in Charles Coustel and Catherine Kintzler, eds., *Ecrits sur l'instruction publique,* 2 vols. (Paris, 1989), 2:134.

7. Ibid., 97.

8. Adam Smith, *An Enquiry into the Nature and Causes of the Wealth of Nations,* eds. R. H. Campbell, A. S. Skinner, and W. B. Todd, 2 vols. (Indianapolis, 1981), 2:781–788.

9. Condorcet, "Premier mémoire," 52.

10. Ibid., 48, 53.

11. Condorcet, *Esquisse d'un tableau historique du progrès de l'esprit humain,* ed. Alain Pons (Paris, 1988), 218.

12. Condorcet, "Rapport et projet de décret sur l'organisation de l'instruction publique," 110.

13. Condorcet was using a classic strategy of Enlightenment social theory by trying to identify one feature of modern life that could innoculate against the bad effects of another. See the essays in Jean Starobinski, *Le remède dans le mal: Critique et légitimation de l'artifice dans l'âge des lumières* (Paris, 1989).

14. Lakanal, *Rapport fait au Conseil des cinq-cents, par Lakanal, un de ses membres, sur les livres élémentaires présentés au concours ouvert par la loi du 9 pluviôse an II* (Paris, Year IV), 10.

15. Condorcet, "Premier mémoire," 45–46; "Rapport et décret sur l'organisation de l'instruction publique," 87, 147.

16. Luminais, *Conseil des cinq-cents: Opinion de Luminais, sur le projet de Roger Martin, tendant à établir des écoles sécondaires, et à restraindre le nombre des écoles centrales, séance du 28 brumaire an 6* (Paris, Frimaire, Year VI), 2.

17. The laws prescribed a three-stage curriculum: (1) upon entry at twelve years, drawing, natural history, ancient and modern languages; (2) upon entry at fourteen years, mathematics, physics, and chemistry; (3) upon entry at sixteen years, general grammer, history, literature, and legislation.

18. P. C. F. Daunou, *Rapport sur l'organisation des écoles spéciales* (Paris, Messidor, Year V), 4–9. The report was never delivered.

19. *La décade philosophique,* 1, no. 5, (20 Prairial, Year II), 279–280.

20. AN, F17 1449, "Observations sur les écoles primaires," 4 Vendémiaire, Year IV.

21. Hagley Library w/2/a/3/425 f.9, Dupont de Nemours to Bernardin de Saint-Pierre, 27 Frimaire, Year III (17 December 1794).

22. Carla Hesse, "Economic Upheavals in Publishing," in Robert Darnton and Daniel Roche, eds., *Revolutions in Print* (Berkeley, Calif., 1989), 93.

23. For the figures, see the table in Carla Hesse, *Publishing and Cultural Politics in Revolutionary Paris, 1789–1810* (Berkeley, Calif., 1991), 202. In 1788, by contrast, 1,166 had been published.

24. *La décade philosphique,* 3, no. 22 (Year III) 393–394.

25. Guizot, quoted in Palmer, *The Improvement of Humanity,* 123.

26. For Guizot's laws, see Robert Gildea, *Education in Provincial France, 1800–1914: A Study of Three Departments* (Oxford, 1984), 39–40.

27. AN, AF III 93, dossier 400, "Rapport présenté au Directoire exécutif par le ministre de l'intérieur sur l'état actual de la République," 20 Pluviôse, Year IV.

28. Three of the five projected central schools for Paris petitioned the Council of

Five Hundred to be allowed to enter their premises and begin to teach in Ventôse, Year IV (February 1796): *Procès-verbal des 500*, vol. 4, p. 444, 24 Ventôse, Year IV.

29. BN, N.Aq.Fr. 9192, ff. 15–22, "Direction générale de l'instruction publique," undated ms. [Brumaire, Year V].

30. For this theme in the Revolution, see Ted Margadant, *Urban Rivalries in the French Revolution* (Princeton, N.J., 1992).

31. *Procès-verbal des 500*, vol. 4, pp. 74–75, 7 Ventôse, Year IV; vol. 7, pp. 109–110, 6 Prairial, Year IV. Villars, *Rapport et résolution, sur le placement de l'école centrale, pour le département du Nord, prononcées au Conseil des cinq-cents dans la séance du 4 prairial, an 4 de la République* (Paris, Year IV), 2. See also Mathieu Defresnoy, François Simeon Bezard, and Jacques Michel Coupé, *Quelques idées sur le placement de l'école centrale dans le département de l'Oise* (Paris, Year IV).

32. *Procès-verbal des 500*, vol. 7, p. 110, 6 Prairial, Year IV; vol. 8, p. 38, 3 Messidor, Year IV; vol. 8, p. 143, 9 Messidor, Year IV.

33. *Procès-verbal des 500*, vol. 1, p. 46, 14 Brumaire, Year IV. Lakanal, *Rapport sur les livres élémentaires.*

34. Lakanal, *Projet d'éducation du peuple français, présenté à la Convention nationale, au nom du comité d'instruction publique, par Lakanal, le 26 juin 1793* (Paris, 1793). For a discussion of the proposal, see Dominique Julia, *La Révolution: Les trois couleurs du tableau noir* (Paris, 1981).

35. As Palmer notes, the proposal had no social base of support even from the sans-culottes, who favored more technical education: *The Improvement of Humanity*, 137–139, 155–160.

36. AN, AB XIX 333, Lakanal, "Discours préliminaire."

37. Isser Woloch, "The Right to Primary Education in the French Revolution," in Renée Waldinger, Philip Dawson, and Isser Woloch, eds., *The French Revolution and the Meaning of Citizenship* (Westport, Conn., 1993), 149.

38. AN, AB XIX 333, Lakanal, "Discours sur l'éducation nationale." Lakanal continued to harass the Institut National and proposed that it be required to concern itself with the practical arts and award prizes to enterprising artisans: *Rapport sur les livres élémentaires.*

39. *Procès-verbal des 500*, vol. 3, p. 462, 28 Pluviôse, Year IV; vol. 7, p. 318, 19 Prairial, Year IV. On the neo-Jacobin support for this policy, see Isser Woloch, *Jacobin Legacy: The Democratic Movement under the Directory* (Princeton, N.J., 1970), 30–35.

40. Hagley Library w/2/a/13/423, Dupont de Nemours to Boissy d'Anglas, 7 Vendémiaire, Year III (28 September 1794).

41. *Procès-verbal des 500*, vol. 3, p. 462, 28 Pluviôse, Year IV; vol. 7, p. 22, 3 Prairial, Year IV; vol. 10, p. 205, 10 Fructidor, Year IV. The Directory finally persuaded the legislature that rather than printing the books the state should buy one thousand copies of the eight winning entries for the departmental libraries. Thus they could reward the winners without infringing on copyright.

42. *Procès-verbal des 500,* vol. 13, p. 415, 29 Frimaire, Year V.

43. Roger Martin, *Motion d'ordre sur la loi du 3 brumaire relative à l'instruction publique* (Paris, Year V), 3, 8.

44. *Procès-verbal des 500,* vol. 19, pp. 362–363, 12 Prairial, Year V.

45. Roger Martin, *Rapport fait par Roger Martin, au nom de la commission d'instruction publique, sur l'organisation des écoles primaires* (Paris, Year V), 2.

46. Ibid., 4.

47. *La décade philosophique,* 9, no. 70 (Year IV), 16. The comment was Ginguené's.

48. Martin, *Rapport sur l'organisation des écoles primaires,* 4. Ibid., 4, no. 26 (20 Nivôse, Year III), 101. For a concrete proposal to set up a girl's primary school, see AN, AF III 109.2, "Charles Coucher aux citoyens composant l'administration municipale de la commune de Saumur," 12 Frimaire, Year V.

49. AN, AF III 109.3, Léonard Bourdon, *Pétition au Conseil des cinq-cents, sur l'éducation commune* (Paris, Brumaire, Year VI).

50. Ibid.

51. BN, N.Aq.Fr. 9192, f. 145, Dambreville, *Sur les avantages que la République doit retirer de l'établissement des écoles primaires et sur le mesures qu'il convient de prendre pour lui assurer la jouissance de ces avantages,* undated ms.

52. Nicolas-Louis François de Neufchâteau, *De l'éducation de la jeunesse, avec des notes intéressantes: Epitre,* (Paris, 1771), 30.

53. BN, Fonds Allemands, ms. 199 f. 205, "Le ministre de l'intérieur au Citoyen Oberlin, professeur et bibliothécaire aux Ecoles centrales du Bas-Rhin," 12 Fructidor, Year 5.

54. Nicolas-Louis François de Neufchâteau, *Méthode pratique de lecture: Ouvrage compris dans la liste officielle des livres élémentaires consacrés au premier degré d'instruction* (Paris, Year VII), 98.

55. Ibid., 128.

56. Martin, *Rapport sur l'organisation des écoles primaires,* 10–11.

57. Audouin, *Motion d'ordre par Audouin, pour la formation d'une commission qui soit chargé de présenter un travail sur les institutions républicaines* (Paris, Year V), called for a five-man commission on such institutions. The committees on education and republican institutions merged in Messidor, Year VI. *Procès-verbal des 500,* vol. 32, p. 201, 13 Messidor, Year VI, 201. For a generally critical account of this campaign, see Isser Woloch, "Republican Institutions, 1797–1799," in Colin Lucas, ed., *The French Revolution and the Creation of Modern Political Culture,* vol. 2, *The Political Culture of the French Revolution* (Oxford, 1987), 371–387.

58. *Procès-verbal des 500,* vol. 24, p. 109, 6 Brumaire, Year VI. Roger Martin, *Rapport fait par Roger Martin, sur les écoles primaires, secondaires, et centrales au nom de la commission d'instruction publique* (Paris, Brumaire, Year VI).

59. Palmer, *Improvement of Humanity,* 152–154.

60. Martin, *Rapport sur les écoles primaires, secondaires, et centrales,* 9.

61. Ibid., 11.

62. Luminais, *Opinion sur le projet de Roger Martin,* 3.

63. *Procès-verbal des 500,* vol. 24, p. 617, 28 Brumaire, Year VI.

64. François Maugenest, *Opinion de Maugenest sur les projets de résolution relatives aux écoles primaires, secondaires, et centrales* (Paris, Year VI), 3; Jean-François Ehrmann, *Opinion de Jean-François Ehrmann, député par le département du Pas-de-Calais, sur le projet de résolution pour l'organisation des écoles primaires, présenté au nom de la commission d'instruction publique, par Roger Martin* (Paris, Year VI) 3.

65. Jean-François Barailon, *Opinion de Jean-François Barailon, député par le département de la Creuse, sur les trois projets de résolution, relatifs aux écoles primaires, sécondaires, et centrales, présentés au nom de la commission d'instruction publique* (Paris, Year VI), 10.

66. Marin, *Opinion de Marin, sur les projets de résolution présentés au nom de la commission d'instruction publique* (Paris, Year VI), 4–10.

67. Pison-Dugalland, *Opinion de Pison-Dugalland, sur le rapport de la commission d'instruction publique* (Paris, Year VI), 3.

68. *Procès-verbal des 500*, vol. 25, p. 175, 11 Frimaire, Year VI. P. Mortier-Duparc, *Opinion de P. Mortier-Duparc, député de la Sarthe, sur l'organisation des enseignements primaire et central* (Paris, Year VI), 5–7.

69. For the debate on supervision of private and religious schools, see *Procès-verbal des 500*, vol. 23, pp. 194–196, 12 Vendémiaire, Year VI; vol. 25, pp. 146–147, 9 Frimaire, Year VI; vol. 26, p. 570, 28 Nivôse, Year VI; vol. 28, pp. 660–661, 28 Ventôse, Year VI; vol. 30, p. 48, 4 Germinal, Year VI; vol. 38, pp. 507–508, 24 Nivôse, Year VII.

70. For that debate, see Isser Woloch, *The New Regime: Transformations of the French Civic Order, 1789–1820s* (New York, 1994), 203–207.

71. "Demande d'un compte détaillé sur les établissements d'instruction publique," in *Recueil,* 1:63.

72. BN, N.Aq.Fr. 9192, f. 46 "Réponses à la circulaire du 20 fructidor an 5."

73. For literacy figures, see Colin Jones, *The Longman Companion to the French Revolution* (London, 1988), 296–298.

74. AN, F1c I 12, "Résultat du dépouillement des comptes mensaires, rendus au ministre de l'intérieur, par les commissaires du Directoire exécutif près les administrations centrales," Nivôse, Year VII.

75. Anne-Marie Duport, "L'enjeu de l'école dans le Gard de la révolution à la monarchie de juillet," *Annales historiques de la Révolution française,* 297 (July–September 1994), 485.

76. AN, AF III* 131, f. 105, "Message au Conseil des cinq-cents," 3 Brumaire, Year VII.

77. J.-M. Heurtault-Lamerville, *Rapport par Heurtault-Lamerville sur les écoles primaires* (Paris, Year VII), 3.

78. Daniel Roche, *The People of Paris: An Essay in Popular Culture in the Eighteenth Century,* trans. Marie Evans (Leamington Spa, 1987), 233.

79. AN, AF III 109, f. 81, "Mémoire sur la situation de l'esprit public dans les campagnes, adressé par les citoyens du canton de Mont Gangere, département de l'Yonne, pluviôse an VI." For the political spur to reading in the countryside, see Roger Chartier, "Figures of the 'Other': Peasant Reading in the Age of

the Enlightenment," in Chartier, *Cultural History: Between Practices and Representations,* trans. Lydia Cochrane (Ithaca, N.Y., 1988), 153–156.

80. Roger Chartier, Marie-Madeline Compère, and Dominique Julia, *L'éducation en France du XVIe au XVIIIe siècle* (Paris, 1976), 44. There was particularly strong continuity between the educative efforts of reformed Christians and Jansenists and the revolutionary aspiration: see David A. Bell, "*Lingua Populi, Lingua Dei:* Language, Religion, and the Origins of French Revolutionary Nationalism," *American Historical Review,* 100, no. 5 (December 1995), 1434.

81. Maugenest, *Opinion sur les projets de résolution relatives aux écoles primaires,* 6.

82. Ehrmann, *Opinion sur le projet de résolution pour l'organisation des écoles primaires,* 7.

83. Ibid., 2. He listed German, Italian, Spanish, Flamand, Dutch, and Breton as the languages he had in mind.

84. Barailon, *Opinion sur trois projets de résolution,* 5, 16.

85. AN, AF III 93, dossier 392, f. 139, "Arrête du 27 brumaire an VI"; f. 138, "Le ministre de l'intérieur aux administrations centrales des départements," 29 Frimaire, Year VI.

86. Condorcet, "Rapport et projet de décret sur l'organisation générale de l'instruction publique," 134.

87. Catherine Marot, "Le recrutement des écoles centrales," *Revue historique,* 556 (October–December 1985), 368–369; Chartier, Compère, and Julia, *L'éducation en France du XVIe au XVIIIe siècle,* 190.

88. *Procès-verbal des 500,* vol. 31, p. 272, 17 Prairial, Year VI. For foundations of central schools, see Dominique Julia, Hugette Bertrand, Serge Bonin, and Alexandra Laclau, *Atlas de la Révolution française,* vol. 2, *L'enseignement, 1760–1815* (Paris, 1987), 40.

89. AN, F1c I 12, "Résultat du dépouillement des comptes mensaires," Messidor, Year VI; Frimaire, Year VII; Brumaire, Year VII.

90. AN, F1c I 12, "Résultat du dépouillement des comptes mensaires," Pluviôse, Year VII.

91. AN, AF III* 131, "Message au Conseil des cinq-cents," 3 Brumaire, Year VII.

92. Daunou, *Rapport sur l'organisation des écoles spéciales,* 4–9.

93. Martin, *Motion d'ordre sur la loi du 3 brumaire,* 4.

94. AN, AF III 93, dossier 392, f. 138, "Le ministre de l'intérieur aux administrations centrales des départements," 29 Frimaire, Year VI.

95. AN, F17a 1014, dossier 5, notes on the formation of the Conseil d'Instruction Publique (undated); these record the earliest discussion of this measure.

96. AN, F17 1011, "Memorandum du ministre de l'intérieur enregistré au Conseil des cinq-cents, séance du 11 brumaire an VII."

97. AN, F17 1011, "Rapport présenté au ministre de l'intérieur sur les attributions et les travaux du conseil d'instruction publique," undated.

98. AN, F17 1338, "Le ministre de l'intérieur aux membres composant le Conseil d'instruction publique," 3 Ventôse, Year VII. The identification of Ideologues

and *idéologie* in this period is difficult: see Martin Staum, *Minerva's Message: Stabilising the French Revolution* (Montreal, 1996), 39–41.

99. Palmer, *The Improvement of Humanity,* 270.

100. AN, F17 1011, François de Neufchâteau to Destrutt de Tracey, 5 Ventôse, Year VII.

101. AN, F17 1338, "Le président du conseil au ministre de l'intérieur," 4 Messidor, Year VII.

102. Martin Staum, "Idéologie dans les écoles centrales," in François Azouvi, ed., *L'institution de la raison: La révolution culturelle des idéologues* (Paris, 1992), 171.

103. Palmer, *The Improvement of Humanity,* 56

104. Staum, "Idéologie dans les écoles centrales," 180.

105. C. Désirat and T. Horde, "La fabrique des élites: Théories et pratiques de la grammaire générale dans les écoles centrales," *Annales historiques de la Révolution française,* 243 (January–March 1981), 82, 84.

106. Destrutt de Tracy, *Observations sur le système actuel d'instruction publique* (Paris, Year IX).

107. Ibid., 2–5.

108. Désirat and Horde, "La fabrique des élites," 73.

109. Chartier, Compère, and Julia, *L'éducation en France du XVIe au XVIIIe siècle,* 198.

110. BN, N. Aq. Fr. 9192, Chantreau, "Observations sur les écoles centrales du Midi," ms., n.d.

111. M. Guy, "L'enseignement de l'histoire dans les écoles centrales (an IV–an XII)," *Annales historiques de la Révolution française,* 243 (January–March 1981), 94.

112. AN, F17 1338, "Le président du conseil au ministre de l'intérieur," 17 Floréal, Year VII.

113. Staum, "Idéologie dans les écoles centrales," 176.

114. Chartier, Compère, and Julia, *L'éducation en France du XVIe au XVIIIe siècle,* 147–149.

115. See AN, F17 1338, "Le ministre de l'intérieur aux professeurs et bibliothécaires des écoles centrales," 20 Fructidor, Year V, for the circular. The replies are stored in AN, F17 13441–14.

116. The replies to the circulars have been tabulated in a relational database to allow manipulation of the data.

117. Désirat and Horde, "La fabrique des élites," 79.

118. Staum, "Idéologie dans les écoles centrales," 195.

119. Of seventy-six general grammar teachers, forty (52 percent) used Condillac, and fourteen used Locke. Harris and Domergue were cited by six and eight teachers, respectively. Harris's 1752 text came out in French translation in 1796.

120. Dominique Julia, "Le choix des professeurs en France: Vocation ou concours? 1700–1850," *Pedagogica historica,* 30, no. 1 (1994), 185–187.

121. Ibid., 191–192.

122. Ibid., 193.

302   **Notes to Pages 188–191**

123. The Revolution was damaging to other professions, such as that of barrister, which retained corporate trappings. See Michael P. Fitzsimmons, *The Parisian Order of Barristers and the French Revolution* (Cambridge, Mass., 1987), 57–59, 114.

124. Thirty-three of those in general grammar and fifty-eight of those in belles lettres had taught in the old colleges.

125. Of the 24 natural history teachers, only 5 had previously held positions in institutions of formal education, but another 11 had some scientific or medical training.

126. For another account of professionalization under the Directory, see Howard G. Brown, "Politics, Professionalism, and the Fate of Army Generals after Thermidor," *French Historical Studies*, 19, no. 1 (Spring 1995), 133–152.

127. *Procès-verbal des 500*, vol. 21, p. 21, 2 Thermidor, Year V.

128. P. J. Andouin, *Rapport fait par P. J. Andouin, sur une difficulté relative aux professeurs des écoles centrales* (Paris, Year IV), 2.

129. *Procès-verbal des 500*, vol. 29, p. 48, 4 Germinal, Year VI; AN, F17 1335, dossier 6, "Le ministre de l'intérieur aux administrations centrales des départements," 14 Fructidor, Year VI.

130. L. S. Mercier, *Second rapport par L. S. Mercier, fait au nom d'une commission spéciale, sur l'enseignement des langues vivantes* (Paris, Year IV), 10.

131. Smith, *The Wealth of Nations*, 2:700.

132. Roger Martin, *Rapport fait par Roger Martin au nom de la commission d'instruction publique, séance du 6 ventôse an 5* (Paris, Year V), 2–3.

133. L. B. Guyton, *Opinion de L. B. Guyton, sur le projet de résolution de la commission d'instruction publique, rélatif à l'incompatibilité des functions de l'enseignement public, etc.* (Paris, Year V), 5.

134. Roger Martin, *Rapport fait par Roger Martin, au nom de la commission d'instruction publique, sur l'organisation définitive des écoles centrales* (Paris, Year V), 2–3.

135. *Procès-verbal des 500*, vol. 8, p. 254, 13 Messidor, Year IV.

136. L. S. Mercier, *Rapport fait par Mercier, au nom d'une commission spéciale, sur l'enseignement des langues vivantes* (Paris, Year IV), 7.

137. Ibid., 2

138. F. Lamarque, *Opinion de F. Lamarque sur l'enseignement des langues vivantes* (Paris, Year IV), 7.

139. Ibid., 6. Lamarque thought this through and proposed that the schools teach the major world languages: Arabic, Greek, Latin, Slavic, and German.

140. Martin, *Motion d'ordre sur la loi du 3 brumaire*, 6.

141. Roger Martin, *Rapport sur l'organisation définitive des écoles centrales*, 3, 7; Martin, *Rapport sur les écoles primaires, secondaires, et centrales*, 9.

142. Martin, *Rapport sur les écoles primaires, secondaires, et centrales*, 10, 18.

143. Daunou, *Rapport sur l'organisation des écoles spéciales*, 7; *Procès-verbal des 500*, vol. 36, p. 131, 6 Brumaire, Year VII.

144. The reform was never formally approved, as the counterproposal by Pison-Dugalland had to be considered. See Pison-Dugalland, *Opinion sur le rapport de*

la commission d'instruction publique, and *Procès-verbal des 500,* vol. 42, p. 96, 4 Prairial, Year VII.

145. AN, F17 1338, "Le ministre de l'intérieur aux professeurs des écoles centrales," 24 Messidor, Year VI.

146. The complete list of suitable authors was Corneille, Despéaux, Molière, Racine, Voltaire, Fénélon, Lafontaine, Saint-Lambert, Batteux, Marmontel, and Desessarts. The last three and Fénélon were the recommended critics.

147. All told he mentioned 102 texts.

148. AN, F17 1135, "Rapport présenté au ministre de l'intérieur," Brumaire, Year VIII.

149. Bernardin de Saint-Pierre was the paradigmatic anti-Ideologue republican intellectual. See Staum, *Minerva's Message,* 53–54.

150. François de Neufchâteau, *Le conservateur, ou recueil des morceaux inédits de l'histoire, de politique, de littérature, et de philosophie,* 2 vols. (Paris, Year VIII), 1:xv.

151. History teachers cited thirty authors; twenty of those were cited on two or fewer syllabi (these included Livy, Holbach, Condorcet, and Volney).

152. This was obvious to the Council on Public Instruction also. In their final report they wrote that Montesquieu, Hobbes, Filangieri, and Beccaria were the most important authors in the legislation course. BN, N.Aq. Fr. 9193. "Conseil d'instruction publique: Extrait du procès-verbal de la séance du 16 pluviôse an VIII."

153. It was tied with Hugh Blair's *Lectures on Rhetoric and Belles Lettres* (Edinburgh, 1983).

154. Ibid., 15.

155. Ibid., 15, 18.

156. AN, F17 1335, dossier 9, f. 91, "Rapport présenté au ministre de l'intérieur," Brumaire, Year VIII.

157. William Reddy, *The Invisible Code: Honor and Sentiment in Postrevolutionary France, 1815–1848* (Berkeley, Calif., 1997), 46–60.

158. Auber, *Réflexions sur l'utilité de l'étude des belles-lettres dans les républiques* (Rouen, Year VI), 4.

159. Couret-Villeneuve, *Manuel social de morale et de politique, ou, déclaration des droits et des devoirs de l'homme et du citoyen, avec la traducation italienne, suivie d'un dictionnaire analytique des mots qu'elle contient* (Paris, Year VII), 88.

160. Nancy K. Miller, "Performances of the Gaze: Staël's *Corrine or Italy,*" in Miller, *Subject to Change: Reading Feminist Writing* (New York, 1988), 162–203.

6. Dance Like a Republican

1. Louis-Sebastien Mercier, *Le nouveau Paris,* 6 vols. (Paris, 1798), 3:157.

2. See Annik Pardailhé-Galabrun, *La naissance de l'intime* (Paris, 1988); Anthony Giddens, *Transformation of Intimacy: Love, Sexuality, and Eroticism in Modern Societies* (Cambridge, 1992); Orest Ranum, "Courtesy, Absolutism, and the Rise of the French State, 1630–1660, *Journal of Modern History,* 52, no. 3 (September

1980), 426–451. The classic account of the development of a private sphere of intimacy remains Norbert Elias's *The Civilising Process,* trans. Edmund Jepbcott, 2 vols. (Oxford, 1979). Elias's account of the genesis of the practices of rational self-mastery suffers from its underemphasis on sociable, collective experiments in self-presentation and so overindividuates the eighteenth-century subject.

3. See Keith Michael Baker, "Fixing the French Constitution," in Baker, *Inventing the French Revolution* (Cambridge, 1990), 252–305; Carol Blum, *Rousseau and the Republic of Virtue: The Language of Politics in the French Revolution* (Ithaca, N.Y., 1986); David A. Bell, "The 'Public Sphere,' the State, and the World of Law in Eighteenth-Century France," *French Historical Studies,* 17, no. 4 (Fall 1992), 912–934; Dena Goodman, "Public Sphere and Private Life: Towards a Synthesis of Current Historiographical Approaches to the Old Regime," *History and Theory,* 31 (1992), 1–20; Benjamin Nathans, "Habermas's 'Public Sphere' in the Era of the French Revolution," *French Historical Studies* (Spring 1990), 620–644; Mona Ozouf, "L'opinion publique," in Keith Michael Baker, ed., *The Political Culture of the Old Regime* (Oxford, 1987), 419–434. For a reading based on gender categories, see Joan Landes, *Women and the Public Sphere in the Age of the French Revolution* (Ithaca, N.Y., 1988). For critiques of the research paradigm, see David Bien, "François Furet, the Terror, and 1789," *French Historical Studies,* 16, no. 4 (Fall 1990), 777–783, and Ferenc Fehér, *The Frozen Revolution: An Essay on Jacobinism* (Cambridge, 1987).

4. Isaiah Berlin, "Two Forms of liberty," in Berlin, *Four Essays on Liberty* (Oxford, 1964), 118–172. The incoherences in this argument have recently been explored by John Gray, *Isaiah Berlin* (London, 1995), and Quentin Skinner, "The Republican Ideal of Political Liberty," in Gisela Bock, Quentin Skinner, and Maurizio Viroli, eds., *Machiavelli and Republicanism* (Cambridge, 1993), 293–304.

5. Mercier, *Le nouveau Paris,* 1:77.

6. For an account of these developments, see Robert M. Isherwood, *Farce and Fantasy: Popular Entertainment in Eighteenth-Century Paris* (Oxford, 1986).

7. James H. Johnson, "Revolutionary Audiences and the Impossible Imperatives of Fraternity," in Bryant T. Regan and Elizabeth Williams, eds., *Recreating Authority in Revolutionary France* (New Brunswick, N.J., 1992), 68–74.

8. Louis-Sebastien Mercier, *Tableau de Paris: Nouvelle édition corrigée et augmentée,* 8 vols. ([Amsterdam], 1782–1787), 1:xvi.

9. Ibid., 8–15.

10. Mercier, *Le nouveau Paris,* 1:35.

11. Mona Ozouf points out that the inverse of "public" was "particular" and not "private" as late as 1798, in "L'opinion publique," 419. For an analysis of the hybridity, see Bruno Latour, *We Have Never Been Modern,* trans. Catherine Porter (New York, 1991), esp. 27–29, 35–37, 70–72.

12. Rebecca L. Spang, "Rousseau in the Restaurant," *Common Knowledge* (Spring 1996), 103.

13. Michèle Root-Bernstein, *Boulevard Theater and Revolution in Eighteenth-Century Paris* (Ann Arbor, Mich., 1984), 100–128.

14. Thomas E. Crow, *Painters and Public Life in Eighteenth-Century Paris* (New Haven, Conn., 1985), 206–214.

15. See Sarah Maza, "The Rose-Girl of Salency: From Theatricality to Rhetoric," in Maza, *Private Lives and Public Affairs: The Causes Célèbres of Prerevolutionary France* (Berkeley, Calif., 1987), 68–111.

16. Jean Starobinski, *1789: The Emblems of Reason,* trans. Barbara Bray (Cambridge, Mass., 1988), 48.

17. Ibid., 117.

18. Mona Ozouf, *La fête révolutionnaire, 1789–1799* (Paris, 1989), 327.

19. De Moy, *Des fêtes, ou, quelques idées d'un citoyen français relativement aux fêtes publiques et d'un culte national* (Paris, Year VII), 1.

20. Boissy d'Anglas, "Législation, morale publique, arts: Essai sur les fêtes nationales, suivi de quelques idées sur les arts et sur la nécessité de les encourager, adressé à la Convention nationale, par Boissy d'Anglas," *La décade philosophique,* 2, no. 10 (10 Thermidor, Year II), 27.

21. Boissy d'Anglas, "Législation, morale publique, arts: Essai sur les fêtes nationales, second extrait," *La décade philosophique,* 2, no. 11 (20 Thermidor, Year II), 74–75.

22. Mona Ozouf, "Revolutionary Religion," in François Furet and Mona Ozouf, eds., *A Critical Dictionary of the French Revolution,* trans. Arthur Goldhammer (Cambridge, Mass., 1989), 565.

23. For an account of the dialogue between these two registers of religiosity, see Suzanne Desan, *Reclaiming the Sacred: Lay Religion and Popular Politics in Revolutionary France* (Ithaca, N.Y., 1990).

24. On the dechristianization campaign, see Michel Vovelle, *The Revolution against the Church: From Reason to the Supreme Being,* trans. Alan José (Cambridge, 1991); Albert Soboul, *Mouvement populaire et gouvernment révolutionnaire en l'an II, 1793–1794* (Paris, 1973), 204–230.

25. Of course, this was a complex and contested process. For an account stressing the ambiguities and tensions of the appropriation of sovereignty by such projects, see Lynn Hunt, *Politics, Culture, and Class in the French Revolution* (Berkeley, Calif., 1984), 87–119.

26. Maximilien Robespierre, *Rapport fait au nom du comité du salut public, par Maximilien Robespierre, sur les rapports des idées religieuses et morales avec les principes républicains, et sur les fêtes nationales, séance du 18 floréal, l'an second de la République française* (Paris, Year II), 11–14.

27. Patrice Higonnet, *Sister Republics: The Origins of French and American Republicanism* (Cambridge, Mass., 1988), 260–264.

28. *Rédacteur,* 571 (21 Messidor, Year V), 2.

29. See Nannerl O. Keohane, *Philosophy and the State in France: The Renaissance to the Enlightenment* (Princeton, N.J., 1980), 153–174.

30. Sarah Hanley, *The Lit de Justice of the Kings of France: Constitutional Ideology in Legend, Ritual, and Discourse* (Princeton, N.J., 1983), 319.

31. Ian M. Wilson argues that the Hobbesian view of sovereignty was more dominant in France than in England in the eighteenth century, introduced to gen-

eral readership through Barbeyrac's work: see Wilson, "The Influence of Hobbes and Locke in the Shaping of the Concept of Sovereignty in Eighteenth-Century France," *Studies on Voltaire and the Eighteenth Century,* 101 (1973), 55.

32. See Keith Michael Baker, *The French Revolution and the Making of Modern Political Culture,* vol. 1, *The Political Culture of the Old Regime* (Oxford, 1987), specifically "Representation," 476. Julian Swann's detailed account of the constitutional politics of the era fully supports this contention: see Swann, *Politics and the Parlement of Paris under Louis XV* (Cambridge, 1995).

33. Monique Cottret, "Aux origines du républicanisme Janseniste: Le mythe de l'église primitive et le primitivisme des lumières," *Revue d'histoire moderne et contemporaine,* 31 (January–March 1984), 100. Dale Van Kley, "Church, State, and the Ideological Origins of the French Revolution: The Debate over the General Assembly of the Gallican Clergy in 1765," *Journal of Modern History,* 59 (December 1979), 641.

34. Reinhart Koselleck, *Critique and Crisis: Enlightenment and the Pathogenesis of Modern Society* (Cambridge, Mass., 1988), 8.

35. Abbé Emery, *Principes de Messieurs Bossuet et Fénélon sur la souveraineté tiré du 5e avertissement sur les lettres de M. Jurieu, et d'un essai sur le gouvernment civil* (Paris, 1791), iii.

36. Lucien Jaume, "Citoyenneté et souveraineté: Le poids de l'absolutisme," in Baker, *The Political Culture of the Old Regime,* 517.

37. This reading of Sieyès and indeed of the goal of revolutionary culture is Patrice Higonnet's: see *Class Ideology and the Rights of Nobles in the French Revolution* (Oxford, 1981), and *Sister Republics,* 224–226.

38. For Sieyès's attitude toward all forms of political theology, see Murray Forsyth, *Reason and Revolution: The Political Thought of the Abbé Sieyès* (Leicester, 1987), 33.

39. Claude Lefort, "La Révolution comme religion nouvelle," in Baker, *The Political Culture of the Old Regime,* 391. Mona Ozouf, "Regeneration," in François Furet and Mona Ozouf, eds., *A Critical Dictionary of the French Revolution,* trans. Arthur Goldhammer (Cambridge, Mass., 1989), 781.

40. Pierre Rosanvallon, "L'utilitarisme français et les ambiguïtés de la culture politique prérevolutionnaire (position d'un problème)," in Baker, *The Political Culture of the Old Regime,* 438.

41. L. N. M. Carnot, *Réponse de L. M. N. Carnot, citoyen français, l'un des fondateurs de la République, et membre constitutionnel du Directoire exécutif, au rapport fait sur la conjuration du 18 fructidor, au conseil des cinq-cents par J. Ch. Bailleul au nom d'une commission spéciale* (Paris, Year VI), 47. Carnot and La Révellière-Lépeaux, though otherwise reliable in their accounts of events and personalities, cannot be trusted on each other.

42. L. M. N. Carnot, *Histoire du Directoire constitutionnel, comparée à celle du gouvernement qui lui a succédé, jusqu'à 30 prairial an 7; contenant en abrigé, celle de la République française, pendant cette mémorable époque; enrichie de notes curieuses et secrètes* (Paris, Year VIII), 18.

43. Carnot, *Réponse au rapport,* 49.

44. [L. M. La Révellière-Lépeaux], *Extrait des registres des déliberations du Directoire exécutif, du 23 fructidor, an 5e de la république, une et indivisible* (Paris, Year V), 5.

45. François de Neufchâteau, "Le ministre de l'intérieur aux administrations centrales et municipales," 15 Fructidor, Year V, in *Recueil,* 1:lviii.

46. "Le ministre de l'intérieur aux commissaires du Directoire exécutif près des administrations centrales et municipales," 24 Fructidor, Year V, in *Recueil,* 1:xcv.

47. Louis-Marie La Révellière-Lépeaux, *Réflexions sur la culte, sur les cérémonies civiles, et sur les fêtes nationales* (Paris, Year V), 4.

48. L. M. La Révellière-Lépeaux and Paul Barras, *Détails de la conspiration, liste de conjurés, leurs noms, leur demeures, et leur translation au Temple* (Paris [Year V]), 3–4; La Révellière-Lépeaux, *Extrait des registres du 23 fructidor,* 1–2.

49. *Le conservateur,* 1, no. 14 (28 Fructidor, Year V), 107.

50. *La décade philosophique,* 15, no. 8 (Year VI), "Des moyennes de rétablir sans secousses l'harmonie entre le corps législatif et le Directoire exécutif, si elle venait à être troublée," 406. For the politics of the review, see Joanna Kitchen, *Un journal "philosophique": La décade (1794–1807)* (Paris, 1965), 52; Marc Regaldo, *Un milieu intellectuel: La décade philosophique (1794–1807),* 5 vols. (Paris, 1976), 1:419–422.

51. AN, AF III* 8, dossier 24, "Discours du président du Directoire exécutif à la fête de la République," 1 Vendémiaire, Year VI. L. M. La Révellière-Lépeaux, *Discours prononcé par L. M. LaRévellière-Lépeaux, président du Directoire exécutif, à la fête de la République, le premier Vendémiaire an VI* (Paris, Year VI), 2.

52. L. M. La Révellière-Lépeaux, *Mémoires de La Révellière-Lépeaux, membre du Directoire exécutif de la République française et de l'Institut national, publiés par son fils sur le manuscript autographe de l'auteur et suivis des pièces justificatives et des correspondances inédits,* 3 vols. (Paris, 1875), 2:39.

53. Ibid., 1:284–285.

54. La Révellière-Lépeaux, *Réflexions sur la culte,* 3.

55. The best account of the theophilanthropic movement remains Albert Mathiez, *La théophilanthropie et le culte décadaire: Essai sur l'histoire religieuse de la Révolution française* (Paris, 1903).

56. Chemin-Depontès, *Année religieuse des théophilanthropes* (Paris, Year V), 5–7.

57. Chemin-Depontès, *Qu'est-ce que la théophilanthropie? ou, mémoire contenant l'origine et l'histoire de cette institution, ses rapports avec le Christianisme, et l'aperçu de l'influence qu'elle peut avoir sur tous les cultes* (Paris, Year X), 9.

58. Chemin-Depontès, *Evangile républicain, ou, la morale évangélique d'accord avec la morale républicaine* (Paris, Year VII).

59. Chemin-Depontès, *Qu'est-ce que la théophilanthropie,* 14

60. Chemin-Depontès, *Evangile républicain,* 45.

61. Chemin-Depontès, *Code de religion et de morale naturelles à l'usage des adorateurs de Dieu et amis des hommes* (Paris, Year VII), xviii–xix.

62. Chemin-Depontès, *Année religieuse des théophilanthropes,* 30–31.

63. Chemin-Depontès, *Qu'est-ce que la théophilanthropie,* 31–32.

64. Albert Mathiez, *La théophilanthropie et le culte décadaire,* 170, 244.

65. La Révellière-Lépeaux, *Réflexions sur la culte*, 34.

66. Carnot, *Réponse de L. M. N.Carnot*, 47.

67. Ozouf, *La fête révolutionnaire*, 260–261.

68. Olwen Hufton, *Women and the Limits of Citizenship in the French Revolution* (Toronto, 1992).

69. Joseph F. Byrnes, "Celebration of the Revolutionary Festivals under the Directory: A Failure of Sacrality," *Church History*, 63, no. 2 (June 1994), 202.

70. AN, F17 1135, dossier 5, "Le ministre de police générale au ministre de l'intérieur," 21 Vendémiaire, Year VI.

71. AN, AF III 109, dossier 500, f. 8, "Conseil des Anciens approuve l'acte d'urgence du 5 Messidor an VI"; F17 1135, dossier 5, f. 55, "Extrait des registres des délibérations du Directoire exécutif," 3 Nivôse, Year VI.

72. In this regard there was a pronounced continuity in the fortunes of the republic under the Directory from the earlier period; see Jean-Pierre Gross, *Fair Shares for All: Jacobin Egalitarianism in Practice* (Cambridge, 1997), 24.

73. For a full account of the disaster, see Mathiez, *La théophilanthropie et la culte décadaire*, 455–543.

74. AN, F1c I 86, "Nécessité de célébrer les fêtes décadaires dans toutes les communes," Ventôse, Year VII. This note formed the basis of the Council of Five Hundred's discussion of the means of supporting the fêtes on 14 Germinal.

75. Ibid.

76. AN, F1c I 85, "Le ministre de l'intérieur aux administrations centrales," 3 Pluviôse, Year VII; "Le ministre de l'intérieur au commissaire du Directoire exécutif près l'administration municipale du canton de Besançon," Nivôse, Year VII.

77. Colin Lucas, "The Rules of the Game in Local Politics under the Directory," *French Historical Studies*, 16, no. 2 (Fall 1989), 347.

78. The minister himself asked the minister of police to find and punish a priest in the Oise who had written a particularly effective attack on the *décade;* AN, F17 1232, dossier 4, f. 58, "Le ministre de l'intérieur au ministre de la police," Vendémiaire, Year VII.

79. AN, F1c I 86, "Le ministre de la police générale au ministre de l'intérieur," 22 Frimaire, Year VI.

80. AN, F17 1243, "Le ministre de l'intérieur au commissaire du Directoire exécutif près l'administration centrale du département de l'Allier," 30 Ventôse, Year VII; "Le ministre de l'intérieur à l'agent national de la commune de Monsigny, département de la Moselle," 15 Ventôse, Year VII.

81. AN, F17 1296, dossier 1, f. 96, "Le ministre de l'intérieur au chef de la cinquième division," 29 Floréal, Year VI.

82. AN, F1c I 12, "Résultat du dépouillement des comptes mensaires . . . ," Messidor, Year VI.

83. AN, F17 1338, dossier 8, f. 90, "Extrait des registres des délibérations du Directoire exécutif," 14 Germinal, Year VI.

84. Chemin-Depontès, *Qu'est-ce que la théophilanthropie*, 14–19.

85. Jean-René Suratteau and Alain Bischoff, *Jean-François Reubell: L'alsatien de la Révolution française* (Strasbourg, 1995), 350.

86. Louis-Marie La Révellière-Lépeaux, *Du Panthéon et du théâtre national* (Paris, Year VI), 11.

87. Louis-Marie La Révellière-Lépeaux, *Essai sur les moyens de faire participer l'universalité des spectateurs à tout ce qui se pratique dans les fêtes nationales* (Paris, Year VI), 7.

88. Ibid., 12; La Révellière-Lépeaux, *Du Panthéon,* 10–13.

89. "Lettre de Boniface Veridick à Polyscope sur son projet de théâtre pour le peuple," *La décade philosophique,* 9, no. 70 (10 Germinal, Year IV), 38.

90. L. M. La Révellière-Lépeaux, *Moyens de faire participer l'universalité des spectateurs* (Paris, Year V), 20.

91. De Moy, *Des fêtes,* 26. De Moy collaborated with François de Neufchâteau on the creation of a coherent cycle of revolutionary festivals; see *Recueil,* 2:344n.

92. De Moy, *Des fêtes,* 25.

93. Ibid., 10.

94. Jacques Delille, *L'homme des champs, ou, les géorgiques françaises* (Strasbourg, Year VIII), iii.

95. De Moy, *Des fêtes,* 33.

96. Denis Diderot, *Essai sur les règnes de Claude et Néron* (Paris, 1986), 319, "Entretiens avec Catherine II," in *Oeuvres politiques* (Paris, 1963), 289–295. For the controversy on the introduction of seating in the Paris theaters, see Jeffrey S. Ravel, "Seating the Public: Spheres and Loathing in the Paris Theatres," *French Historical Studies,* 18, no. 1 (Spring 1993), 173–210.

97. Ozouf, *La fête révolutionnaire,* 193–94.

98. AN, F17 1344.36, dossier, f. 17, "Le ministre de l'intérieur aux administrations centrales des départements, Paris," 13 Messidor, Year VI.

99. AN, F1c I 85, "Rapport présenté au ministre de l'intérieur," 13 Prairial, Year IV.

100. AN, F1c I 85, "Rapport présenté au ministre de l'intérieur," Thermidor, Year V.

101. AN, F1c I 85, "Instruction sur la célébration des fêtes nationales, adressé par le ministre de l'intérieur aux commissaires du pouvoir exécutif près des administrations départementales et municipales, Paris," 27 Thermidor, Year V.

102. La Révellière-Lépeaux, *Mémoires,* 1:382.

103. See, for example, Mongez, *Discours prononcé par le Citoyen Mongez, membre de l'Institut national et de l'administration des monnaies, dans l'hôtel des monnaies de Paris, lors de la plantation de l'arbre de la liberté* (Paris, Year VII), or Maugaret, *Discours prononcé par le commissaire du Directoire exécutif près l'administration départementale de la Gironde à la fête de l'agriculture* (Bordeaux, Year V).

104. Larévellière-Lépeaux, *Essai sur les moyens de faire participer l'universalité des spectateurs à tout ce qui se pratique dans les fêtes nationales,* 7.

105. AN, F1c I 12, "Résultat du dépouillement des comptes mensaires . . .," Nivôse, Year VII.

106. AN, AF III* 121, f. 1517, *arrêt* of 8 Vendémiaire, Year VI, granting 10,000 francs to the minister of the interior for the funeral expenses.

107. AN, AF III 8*, dossier 24, 10 Vendémiaire, Year VI.
108. *Le conservateur,* 1, no. 26 (5 Vendémiaire, Year VI), 204.
109. On 9 Floréal, Year VII, two negotiators, Roberjot and Bonnier, along with the legation secretary Rosensteil, were killed. A third negotiator, Jean Debry, managed to escape. The attack, by the Szeckler hussars, happened as the convoy of French negotiators' coaches left Rastatt for France; minister of the interior, *Déclaration individuelle sur l'assasinat des ministres français à Rastadt* (Paris, Year VII), 12.
110. "Discours prononcé par le ministre de l'intérieur, le 1er prairial, an 7 de la République, pour l'ouverature de l'Ecole clinique de médicine, établie à l'Hospice de l'Unité, rue des Pères," in *Recueil,* 2:226. The idea that war could lead to national annihilation was inspired by the fate of Poland, which had ceased to exist in 1795 after the third partition among Austria, Prussia, and Russia, and underlined by the suppression of the Venetian republic in the 1797 treaty of Campo Formio. See François Furet, *The French Revolution, 1770–1814,* trans. Antonia Nevill (Oxford, 1992), 191–192.
111. Minister of the interior, *Cérémonie funèbre en mémoire des ministres français assassinés près de Rastadt par les troupes autrichiennes* (Paris, Year VII), 5.
112. AN, AA 64, f. 257, François de Neufchâteau to Jean Debry, 14 Prairial, Year VII.
113. "Le Ministre de l'Intérerieur aux administrations centrales et municipales," 2 Prairial, Year VII, in *Recueil,* 2:227–228.
114. Marie-Joseph Chénier, *Discours prononcé par M. J. Chénier de l'Institut national, à la cérémonie funèbre, célébrée au Champs de Mars, le 20 prairial an VII de la République française en l'honneur de nos ministres assassinés par l'Autriche* (Paris, Year VII), 17–19.
115. Ibid., 12.
116. AN, F17 1232, dossier 12, f. 112, "Rapport présenté au ministre de l'intérieur," 30 Floréal, Year VII.
117. Mona Ozouf argues that the institution of the 10 Fructidor festival is evidence that the festivals were still animated by the ideal of the sacralization of the sovereign; see *La fête révolutionnaire,* 192–204. This view assumes the festivals of Years VI and VII were inspired by La Révellière-Lépeaux's ideas.
118. "Le ministre de l'intérieur aux administrations centrales et municipales: Fête de la jeunesse," 17 Ventôse, Year VII, in *Recueil,* 2:106–107.
119. "Le ministre de l'intérieur aux administrations centrales de département: Dispositions pour la Fête de l'agriculture," 21 Ventôse, Year VII, in *Recueil,* 2:121.
120. Ibid., 122–123.
121. *Rédacteur,* 613 (3 Fructidor, Year V), 1.
122. AN, F10 613, "Questions présentés par le ministre de l'intérieur au Directoire exécutif," n.d.
123. AN, F10 613, "Notes pour le ministre," n.d. [Year VII].
124. Ibid.
125. "Le ministre de l'intérieur aux administrations centrales et municipales: Fêtes commémoratives des 14 juillet, 10 août, 9 thermidor, et 18 fructidor," 30 Prairial, Year VII, in *Recueil,* 2:280.

126. "Le ministre de l'intérieur aux administrations centrales et municipales: Fête des époux," 1 Germinal, Year VII, in *Recueil,* 2:156–157.

127. "Le ministre de l'intérieur aux administrations centrales et municipales: Fête de la reconnaissance," 21 Floréal, Year VII, in *Recueil,* 2:211–216.

128. Ibid., 212.

129. Ibid.

130. Ibid., 214.

131. Ibid., 213.

132. Ibid., 215.

133. Bibliothèque Sainte Geneviève, Paris, MS 4124 (dossier 3) f. 70, "Le ministre de l'intérieur aux administrations centrales et municiples," 30 Frimaire, Year VII; François de Neufchâteau, *Anniversaire du 18 fructidor: Programme* (Paris, Year VI), 2.

134. "Le ministre de l'intérieur aux administrations centrales et municipales: Solennité du 2 pluviôse," 30 Frimaire, Year VII, in *Recueil,* 1:56.

135. AN, F17 1232, dossier 8, "Extrait des registres des déliberations du Directoire exécutif," 28 Pluviôse, Year VI; "Le ministre de l'intérieur aux administrations centrales et municipales: Fête de la souveraineté du peuple," 30 Pluviôse, Year VII, in *Recueil,* 2:58.

136. Ibid., 56, 59.

137. "Le ministre de l'intérieur aux administrations centrales et municipales: Fêtes commémoratives des 14 juillet, 10 août, 9 thermidor, et 18 fructidor," 3 Prairial, Year VII, in *Recueil,* 2:282.

138. Ibid., 285.

139. AN, F17 1344.36, dossier 3, f. 15, "Le ministre de l'intérieur aux administrations des départements," 10 Fructidor, Year VI.

140. Ibid.

141. AN, F17 1232, dossier 11, "Fête de la fondation de la République: Programme," Year VI.

142. "Le ministre de l'intérieur aux administrations centrales de département: Exposition publique des produits de l'industrie française," 9 Fructidor, Year VI, in *Recueil,* 1:103.

143. "Le ministre de l'intérieur aux administrations centrales des départements: Fête du 1er vendémiaire," 10 Fructidor, Year VI, in *Recueil,* 1:116.

144. Ibid., 121.

145. Bibliothèque Municipale de Nancy, MS 11091, f. 84, "Prière composée pendant que l'auteur étoit détenu au Luxembourg, en 1793."

146. "Le ministre de l'intérieur: Fête du 1er vendémiaire," 10 Fructidor, Year VI, 126.

147. See Thomas Crow, *Emulation: Making Artists for Revolutionary France* (New Haven, Conn., 1995), for the evolution of Géricault's aesthetic from this problem. For an attempt to illustrate the distinctive virtues of the commercial republican, see David's *Sabine Women.*

148. "Discours prononcé par le Cen Treilhard, président du Directoire exécutif, au Champs-de-Mars, le 1er vendémiaire an VII, pour l'anniversaire de la

fondation de la République," *Bulletin décadaire de la République française,* 2 (20 Vendémiaire, Year VII), 3.

149. "Le ministre de l'intérieur: Fête du 1er vendémiaire," 10 Fructidor, Year VI, 125.

150. "Discours prononcé au Champ-de-Mars par le ministre de l'intérieur, pour l'ouverature de l'exposition publique des produits de l'industrie française," 3e jour complémentaire, Year VI, in *Recueil,* 2:296.

151. Ibid., 295.

152. Thomas Bugge, *Science in France in the Revolutionary Era: Described by Thomas Bugge, Danish Astronomer Royal and Member of the International Commission of the Metric System,* trans. Maurice Crosland (Cambridge, Mass., 1969), 136.

153. "Discours prononcé au Champ-de-Mars par le ministre de l'intérieur, pour l'ouverature de l'exposition publique," 293.

154. AN, AF III 93, dossier 392, "Le ministre de l'intérieur au Directoire exécutif," 5 Vendémiaire, Year VII.

155. Bugge, *Science in France,* 133; *Rédacteur,* 1014 (5 Vendémiaire, Year VI).

156. "Plan du *Bulletin décadaire,*" *Bulletin décadaire de la République française,* 1 (Year VII), 4.

157. P. C. F. Daunou, *Conseil des 500: Discours prononcé par P. C. F. Daunou, président du Conseil des cinq-cents, pour l'anniversaire de la fondation de la République, séance du 1er vendémiaire an VII* (Paris, Year VII), 5.

158. Ibid., 6.

159. Ibid., 7.

160. What follows is heavily indebted to Edouard Pommier, *L'art de la liberté: Doctrines et débats de la Révolution française* (Paris, 1991).

161. Edouard Pommier, "La théorie des arts," in Pommier, *Aux armes et aux arts! Les arts de la Révolution, 1789–1799* (Paris, 1988), 168.

162. "Beaux-Arts: Des théâtres, anciens et modernes, et de l'art dramatique," *La décade philosophique,* 1, no. 3 (30 Floréal, Year II), 139; "Arts: Lycée des arts, séance publique du 10 prairial," *La décade philosophique,* 1, no. 5 (20 Prairial, Year II), 279–280.

163. Pommier, "La théorie des arts," 176–179. Ironically, by removing these figures to the Parc de Sceaux the assembly guaranteed their survival when other, less obviously absolutist images were to be destroyed after 1792.

164. For a statement of such total politicization, see "Administration: La commission des travaux publics aux artistes," *La décade philosophique,* 1, no. 5 (20 Prairial, Year II), 318–319.

165. Bronislaw Baczko, "Vandalism," in François Furet and Mona Ozouf, eds., *A Critical Dictionary of the French Revolution,* trans. Arthur Goldhammer (Cambridge, Mass., 1989), 860–868.

166. Henri-Baptiste Grégoire, *Rapport sur les déstructions opérées par le vandalisme, et sur les moyens de le réprimer* (Paris, Year II), 7–8.

167. See, among others, Germaine de Staël, *Considérations sur la Révolution française* (Paris, 1983), 75; Lacratelle le jeune, *Où faut-il s'arrêter?* (Paris, Year V), 14.

168. "Beaux Arts: Rapport sur les destructions opérées par le vandalisme, et sur les moyens de les réprimer, par Grégoire," *La décade philosophique,* 3, no. 16 (10 Vendémiaire, Year III), 21.

169. Quatremère de Quincy, *Considérations sur les arts de dessin en France* (Paris, 1791). As Harold T. Parker argues, French classicism was largely Roman, and the most prominent enthusiast for Athens had been Camille Desmoulins; see Parker, *The Cult of Antiquity and the French Revolution* (Chicago, Ill., 1937), 20, 72–75.

170. "Variétés: De l'art de voir dans les beaux arts, traduit de l'Italien de Milizia; suivi des institutions propres à les faire fleurir en France, par le Général Pommereuil," *Rédacteur,* 888 (3 Prairial, Year VI).

171. J. B. Leclerc, *De la poésie, considérée dans ses rapports avec l'éducation nationale* (Paris, Year VI), 18.

172. Gabriel-Raimond-Jean Olivier, *L'esprit d'Orphée, ou, de l'influence respective de la musique, de la morale, et de la législation* (Paris, Year X), 3.

173. Ibid., 1–2.

174. Cynthia Verba, *Music and the French Enlightenment* (Oxford, 1992), 81–83.

175. Pommier, *L'art de la liberté,* 258–260.

176. BN, N.Aq.Fr. 9192, ff. 102–103, "Rapport à presenter au ministre de l'intérieur, sur l'établissement du bureau d'encouragement des sciences et des lettres," n.d. [Year V].

177. Nina Rattner Gelbart, *Feminine and Opposition Journalism in Old Regime France* (Berkeley, Calif., 1987), 202–246.

178. The same tensions and new demands were being confronted by the academy painters: see Crow, *Painters and Public Life in Eighteenth-Century Paris,* 132, 179–181.

179. François de Neufchâteau, "Mémoire à consulter et consultation pour le sieur Lonvay de la Saussaye, contre le troupe des Comédiens français ordinaires du Roi," in Du Coudray, *Correspondance dramatique, ou, lettres critiques et historiques sur les spectacles,* 2 vols. (Paris, 1777), 1:55–61.

180. For the demand for administrative reorganization, see "Mémoire à consulter et consultation, par le sieur Palissot de Montenoy, contre le troupe des Comédiens français," in Du Coudray, *Correspondance dramatique* (see previous note), 1:32–34, and "Commentaire de François de Neufchâteau sur l'arrêt de conseil," in the same work, 2:146–149. For the demand for a second theater, voiced at a meeting of dramatists held by Beaumarchais, see Jean-François Ducis to M. Delayre, Versailles, 25 August 1777, in Paul Albert, ed., *Lettres de Jean-François Ducis* (Paris, 1879), 31.

181. P. C. F. Daunou, *Influence de Boileau sur la littérature françoise, discours couronné par l'Académie royale de Nîmes* (Paris, 1787), 3, 16.

182. BN, N.Aq.Fr. 21556, f. 188, Daunou to La Révellière-Lépeaux, 30 Ventôse, Year VI; f. 190, Daunou to La Révellière-Lépeaux, 6 Germinal, Year VI.

183. AN, F21 1078, "Rapport présenté au Directoire exécutif par le ministre de l'intérieur," 20 Fructidor, Year VII.

184. AN, AF III* 129, f. 51, Arrêt, 29 Germinal, Year VI; 171 AP, dossier 18, f. 3, "Le

citoyen Mirbeck, commissaire du gouvernement près de l'administration du théâtre de la république et des arts au Citoyen Barras, membre du Directoire exécutif," 29 Germinal, Year VI.

185. AN, F21 1078, "Rapport presenté au Directoire exécutif par le ministre de l'intérieur," 20 Fructidor, Year VII.

186. Ibid. Sagaret also founded an acting school to guarantee institutional continuity.

187. AN, F21 1100, "Les administrateurs du théâtre de la République et les arts au ministre de l'intérieur," 6 Germinal, Year VII.

188. AN, F21 1100, "Rapport presenté au ministre de l'intérieur," Germinal, Year VII; F17 1295, dossier 9, f. 341, "Rapport présenté au ministre de l'intérieur," 11 Vendémiaire, Year V.

189. AN, F21 1112, "Rapport présenté au ministre de l'intérieur," Nivôse, Year VII. The comic opera eventually opened in Year IX.

190. M. J. Chénier, *Motion d'ordre, par Chénier, sur les théâtres: Séance du 26 brumaire an 6* (Paris, Year VI), 2.

191. AN, F17, dossier 1, f. 7, "Le ministre de l'intérieur à l'administration centrale du département de la Dyle," 5 Brumaire, Year V.

192. AN, AF III* 119, f. 1041, "Message au bureau central du canton de Paris," 29 Frimaire, Year V; AF III* 120, f. 1068, "Message au Conseil des cinq-cents," 22 Nivôse, Year V.

193. AN, F17 1078, "Le Directoire exécutif au Conseil des cinq-cents," Fructidor, Year VII.

194. For the early history of this principle in the Revolution, see Carla Hesse, *Publishing and Cultural Politics in Revolutionary Paris, 1789–1810* (Berkeley, Calif., 1991), 83–124.

195. Bibliothèque de l'Arsenal, MS 3979, fifth division, "Bureau des théâtres, propriété des ouvrages dramatiques," 11 Frimaire, Year VII.

196. AN, F17 1056, dossier 14, "Hennequin au ministre de l'intérieur," 12 Nivôse, Year VII.

197. AN, F17 1059, dossier 3, "Le ministre de l'intérieur aux citoyens composant le Jury des arts," 30 Pluviôse, Year VII.

198. For the art schools, see Ginguené's report on the republic's artistic institutions, in BN, N.Aq.Fr. 9192, f. 164. For the refoundation of the Prix de Rome, see AN, AF III* 130, Arrêt, 23 Fructidor, Year VI. This put into effect the law of 3 Brumaire, Year VI.

199. AN, F17 1059, dossier 3, "Le ministre de l'intérieur aux citoyens composant le Jury des arts," 30 Pluviôse, Year VII.

200. Ibid.

201. "Rapport présenté au Directoire exécutif par le ministre de l'intérieur," 13 Prairial, Year VII, in *Recueil*, 2:265, 269.

202. Pommier, *L'art de la liberté*, 450–453.

203. "Discours prononce le 9 thermidor par le ministre de l'intérieur, et adressé aux citoyens Thouin, Moëtte, Barthélemy, et Tinet," in Directoire Exécutif, *Extrait*

du procès-verbal de la séance du Directoire exécutif du 10 thermidor an VI (Paris, Year VI), 11–12.

204. Ibid., 12.

205. Ibid., 11.

206. Ibid., 13.

207. "Discours prononcé au théâtre de la République et des arts, avant la distribution des prix aux élèves du conservatoire de musique," 14 Frimaire, Year VII, in *Recueil,* 2:300.

208. Ibid., 304.

209. AN, 27 AP 13, "Discours prononcé par le ministre de l'intérieur à la séance d'ouverature des cours de l'Ecole polytechnique," 10 Germinal, Year VII.

210. Ibid.

211. François de Neufchâteau, *Discours prononcé par le ministre de l'intérieur, le 1er prairial an VII, pour l'ouverature de l'Ecole clinique de médicine, établie à l'hospice de l'unité, rue des pères* (Paris, Year VII), 4.

212. Jonathan Beecher, *Charles Fourier: The Visionary and His World* (Berkeley, Calif., 1986), 36.

213. Ibid., 71.

214. Charles Fourier, *The Theory of the Four Movements,* trans. Gareth Stedman Jones and Ian Patterson (Cambridge, 1996), 199, 204.

215. Ibid., 263.

216. Jonathan Beecher and Richard Bienvenu, *The Utopian Vision of Charles Fourier: Selected Texts on Work, Love, and Passionate Attraction* (Columbia, Miss., 1983), 32.

217. Fourier, *Theory of the Four Movements,* 85.

218. Ibid., 156.

Conclusion

1. AN, 284 AP 16, dossier 5, Benjamin Constant to the Directors, [19 Brumaire, Year VIII].

2. Martyn Lyons, *Napoleon Bonaparte and the Legacy of the French Revolution* (London, 1994), 105.

3. AN, f17 1135, "Le ministre de l'intérieur au Citoyen Ginguené," Brumaire, Year VIII.

4. Carnot, *Discours prononcé par le Citoyen Carnot, sur la motion relative au gouvernement héréditaire* (Paris, Year XII), 2, 3, 7.

5. AN, 29 AP 78, f. 525, notes for a response to Carnot.

6. A. C. Thibeaudeau, *Mémoires, 1799–1815* (Paris, 1813), 123–124.

7. P. L. Roederer, *Mémoires sur la Révolution, le Consulat, et l'Empire* (Paris, 1942), 110.

8. Hagley Library, w2/a/13/2447, P. L. Roederer to Dupont de Nemours, 10 Vendémiaire, Year IX. He preferred to stay and agitate for the post of ambassador.

9. Dupont de Nemours to Madame de Staël, 19 Pluviôse, Year VIII, in James F.

Marshall, ed., *De Staël–Dupont Letters: Correspondence of Madame de Staël and Pierre Samuel Dupont de Nemours and of Other Members of the Dupont and Necker Families* (Madison, Wis., 1968), 15.

10. Madame de Staël to Dupont de Nemours, 30 Germinal, Year IX, in Marshall, *De Staël–Dupont Letters* (see previous note), 78.

11. Hagley Library, w/2/b/28/4808, "Du premier magistrat," Year IX.

12. Ibid.

13. The idea was inspired by the American vice presidency.

14. Hagley Library, w/2/a/7/1288, Dupont de Nemours to Mr. Crawford, 1 August 1815.

15. Thibeaudeau, *Mémoires, 1799–1815*, 77.

16. A. C. Thibeaudeau, *Mémoires sur le Consulat, 1799 à 1804, par un ancien conseiller d'état* (Paris, 1827), 8–9.

17. Ibid., 10.

18. Ibid., 236.

19. Henri-Baptiste Grégoire, *Les ruines de Port-Royal en mille huit cent-un* (Paris, n.d.).

20. Ibid., 27.

21. Ibid., 24.

22. L. M. La Révellière-Lépeaux, *Mémoires de La Révellière-Lépeaux, membre du Directoire exécutif de la République française et de l'Institut national, publiés par son fils,* 3 vols. (Paris, 1875), 1:297.

23. Ibid., 365–366.

24. "Sur les divisions politiques qui existent en France, et leurs résultats probables," *La décade philosophique,* 13, no. 23 (Messidor, Year V), 313–317.

25. Ibid., 314. The *Décade* singled out Dumolard, Pastoret, Portalis, Muraire, Dupont de Nemours, and Tronçon de Coudray for praise as the most intelligent members of the opposition.

26. For such an argument, see Lynn Hunt, David Lansky, and Paul Hanson, "The Failure of the Liberal Republic in France, 1795–1799: The Road to Brumaire," *Journal of Modern History,* 51 (December 1979), 734–759.

27. AN, 171 AP, dossier 10, f. 10, 13 Frimaire, Year VI.

28. Albert Sorel, *L'Europe et la Révolution française,* vol. 5, *Bonaparte et le Directoire, 1795–1799* (Paris, 1903), 32.

29. Howard Brown, "A Discredited Regime: The Directory and Army Contracting," *French History,* 4, no. 1 (March 1990), 48–52.

30. Sorel, *L'Europe et la Révolution française,* 274.

31. AN, 117 AP 1, dossier 1, "Quelques observations pour servir de base aux instructions aux plenipotentiaires de la République au congrès de Rastadt," 7.

32. AN, 117 AP 1, dossier 1, "Sur la formation du congrès," 21 Brumaire, Year VI; "Quelques observations pour servir de base aux instructions aux plenipotentiaires de la République au congrès de Rastadt," 14.

33. AN, F1c I 12, "Compte morale et politique," Thermidor, Year VI.

34. AN, 284 AP 12, dossier 3, Talleyrand to Sieyès, 19 Vendémiaire, Year VII.

35. AN, 117 AP 1, dossier 3, Talleyrand to Treilhard, 9 Ventôse, Year VI, 3 Floréal, Year VI.

36. AN, 284 AP 12, dossier 3, Talleyrand to Sieyès, 4 Brumaire, Year VII.

37. AN, 284 AP 12, dossier 3, Sieyès to Talleyrand, 20 Brumaire, Year VII; Talleyrand to Sieyès, 27 Nivôse, Year VII.

38. Germaine de Staël, *Considérations sur la Révolution française* (Paris, 1983), 327.

39. George Canning to George Ellis, 14 July 1797, in James Harris, *Diaries and Correspondence of James Harris, First Earl of Malmesbury,* 3 vols. (London, 1844), 3:397–398.

40. Georges Lefebvre, *La France sous le Directoire, 1795–1799,* ed. Jean-René Suratteau (Paris, 1983), 391.

41. L. N. M. Carnot, *Histoire du Directoire constitutionnel, comparée à celle du gouvernement qui lui a succédé, jusqu'à 30 prairial an VII* (Paris, Year VIII), 53–57, 159–161.

42. La Révellière-Lépeaux, *Mémoires,* 2:55–56.

43. Mathieu Dumas, *Des résultats de la dernière campagne* (Paris, Year V), 27.

44. BN, N.Aq.Fr. 23654, ff. 335, MS note dated 16 Brumaire, Year X.

45. Diary entry for 14 July 1797, in Harris, *Diaries and Correspondence,* 409.

46. Ellis to Canning, in Harris, *Diaries and Correspondence,* 438.

47. Sorel, *L'Europe et la Révolution française,* 215.

48. Malmesbury to Grenville, 29 August 1797, in Harris, *Diaries and Correspondence,* 508.

49. AN, AF III 93, dossier 397, "Rapport présenté au Directoire exécutif par le ministre de l'intérieur," 19 Thermidor, Year VI, 9.

50. Ibid., 4.

51. BN, N.Aq.Fr. 23654, f. 79, "Adresse aux français par un ami de l'humanité."

52. AN, AF III 310, f. 495, "Extrait des observations sur les établissements français en Afrique et en Asie, et sur leurs rapports avec la nation anglaise," 17 Frimaire, Year V.

53. L. M. N. Carnot, *Réponse de L. M. N. Carnot, citoyen français, l'un des fondateurs de la République, et membre constitutionnel du Directoire exécutif, au rapport fait sur la conjuration du 18 fructidor, au Conseil des cinq-cents par J. Ch. Bailleul au nom d'une commission spéciale* (Paris, Year VI), 67.

54. Lesage, *J'ai peur! Et je les fais peur!! Lettre d'un militaire à l'un de ses camarades de l'armée d'Italie, sur la cause des débats actuels entre les majorités du Conseil des cinq-cents et du Directoire exécutif* (Paris, n.d. [Year V]), 1.

55. Lesage, *J'ai tort et tu as tort, cède et je cèderai . . . que le plus sage commence: Seconde lettre d'un militaire à l'un de ses camarades de l'armée d'Italie sur les débats du Conseil des cinq-cents et du Directoire exécutif* (Paris, n.d. [Year V]), 2

56. Ibid., 4.

57. Louis-Sebastien Mercier, *Le nouveau Paris,* 8 vols. (Paris, 1798), 3:11.

58. Hagley Library, w/2/a/7/1296, Dupont de Nemours to Carnot, 10 August 1815.

59. Hagley Library, w/2/b/29/4838, "Plan de Dupont de Nemours pour la rétablissement de la République," late April 1814.

60. Ibid.

61. Hagley Library, w/2/b/29/4838, "Sénatus-Consulte portant rétablissement de la République."

62. Ibid.

63. Hagley Library, w/2/a/7/1224 Dupont de Nemours to E. I. Dupont, 2 April 1814.

64. George Weill, *Histoire du parti républicain en France de 1814 à 1870* (Paris, 1900), 1.

65. James Livesey, "Speaking the Nation: Radical Republicans and the Failure of Political Communication in 1848," *French Historical Studies,* 20, no. 3 (Summer 1997), 459–480.

66. The issue of peasant politicization remains controversial. For contrasting views, see Eugen Weber, *Peasants into Frenchmen: The Modernisation of Rural France, 1870–1914* (London, 1977), and Maurice Agulhon, *La République au village: La population du Var de la Révolution à la IIe République* (Paris, 1979).

67. Jacques Rancière, *The Nights of Labor: The Workers' Dream in Nineteenth-Century France,* trans. John Drury (Philadelphia, 1989). Linda Orr, *Headless History: Nineteenth-Century French Historiography of the Revolution* (Ithaca, N.Y., 1990).

Index